COMMON USAGE DICTIONARY

German-English
English-German

BY **Genevieve A. Martin** AND
Theodor Bertram

BASED ON THE METHOD DEVISED BY
RALPH WEIMAN
FORMERLY CHIEF OF LANGUAGE SECTION,
U. S. WAR DEPARTMENT

CONTAINING OVER 15,000 BASIC TERMS WITH
MEANINGS ILLUSTRATED BY SENTENCES AND
1000 ESSENTIAL WORDS ESPECIALLY INDICATED

Crown Publishers, Inc., New York

INTRODUCTION

The German Common Usage Dictionary lists the most frequently used German words, gives their most important meanings and illustrates their use.

1. The *basic* words are indicated by capitals.

2. Only the most important meanings are given.

3. These meanings are illustrated, wherever necessary, by means of everyday phrases and sentences. Where there is no close English equivalent for a German word or where the English equivalent has several different meanings, the context of the illustrative sentences helps to make the meanings clear.

4. Each important word is followed by the everyday expressions in which it most frequently occurs. The Common Usage Dictionary serves accordingly as a phrase book or conversation guide: it contains thousands of everyday sentences which are of practical importance (for traveling, correspondence, etc.) or which serve as illustrations of the grammatical features of current written and spoken German. The Common Usage Dictionary should, therefore, prove helpful both to beginners who are building up their vocabulary and to advanced students who want to perfect their command of colloquial German.

5. In translating the German phrases and sentences an attempt has been made to give not a mere translation but an equivalent — that is, what an English speaker would say in the same situation. (Literal translations have been added to help the beginner.) The user is thus furnished with numerous examples of how common German expressions (particularly the very idiomatic and the very colloquial ones) can best be translated into English. This feature makes the Common Usage Dictionary especially useful for translation work.

6. The English-German part contains the most common English words and their German equivalents. By consulting the sentences given under the German word in the German-English part the reader can observe whether it does so only in certain cases.

EXPLANATORY NOTES

Literal translations are in parentheses.

Gender is indicated by *m.* for masculine, *f.* for feminine, and *n.* for neuter.

Case is indicated by *nom.* for nominative, *gen.* for genitive, *dat.* for dative, *acc.* for accusative.

Table of Contents

A

AB 1. *adv.* off, down, away from, from.

ab heute from today.

ab und an now and then.

ab und zu to and fro, now and then.

von hier ab from here.

von nun ab henceforth.

2. *separable prefix (implies a movement down or away, imitation, appropriation, deterioration, destruction).*

Das Flugzeug stürzte ins Meer ab. The plane fell down into the sea.

Einige alte Häuser werden abgebaut. Some old houses will be demolished.

Er hat ihm tausend Mark abgeschmeichelt. He got a thousand marks from him by flattery.

Ich schreibe meine Aufgabe ab. I copy my homework.

Abart *f.* variety.

abbeissen to bite off.

sich die Nägel abbeissen to bite one's nails.

abbezahlen to pay off.

abbiegen to turn off.

Abbild *n.* copy, image.

abbinden to unbind.

Abbitte *f.* apology.

abbrechen to break up, interrupt, deduct, gather.

Blumen abbrechen to gather flowers.

die Arbeit abbrechen to cease work.

abdanken to dismiss, abdicate.

Der Fürst hat abgedankt. The prince has abdicated.

abdrehen to turn off, switch off.

Drehen sie das Radio ab! Turn off the radio!

abdrucken to print.

ABEND *n.* evening.

diesen Abend this evening.

Es wird Abend. It is getting dark.

heute Abend tonight.

Abenteuer *n.* adventure.

auf Abenteuer ausgehen to look for adventure.

abenteuerlich adventurous.

Abenteurer *m.* adventurer.

ABER but, however, anyway.

Ich wollte ausgehen aber das Wetter war zu schlecht. I wanted to go out but the weather was too bad.

Das Kind wollte spielen, die Mutter aber wollte nicht. The child wanted to play but the mother did not want to.

Der König aber . . . as for the king . . .

Nein aber! I say!

Nun aber! But now!

tausend und aber tausend thousands and thousands.

abermals again, once more.

abfahren to set off, depart.

Der Zug fährt um drei Uhr ab. The train leaves at three.

Sie fuhr übel ab. She got the worst of it.

Abfahrtsort *m.* place of departure.

abfinden to settle, come to an agreement.

abführen to lead away, carry away.

Abführung *f.* removal.

Abgabe *f.* tax, tribute, delivery.

abgabenfrei tax free.

abgabenpflichtig taxable.

Abgang *m.* departure, exit.

ABGEBEN to give, supply, deliver, pay taxes.

sich mit etwas abgeben to occupy oneself with a matter.

Wir können die Waren zu diesem Preis nicht abgeben. We cannot supply the merchandise on these terms.

abgehen to depart, go off.

Er lässt sich nichts abgehen. He denies himself nothing.

von seinem Vorhaben nicht abgehen to persist in one's plans.

abgemacht agreed.

abgewinnen to win from.

abgewöhnen to disaccustom, give up.

Ich habe mir das Rauchen abgewöhnt. I have given up smoking.

Abgrund *m.* abyss, precipice.

abhalten to hold off, restrain.

Lassen Sie sich nicht abhalten. Don't let me stop you.

abhängen to unhang, hang up (phone), disconnect.

abhängig sloping, dependent on.

abheben to lift off, uncover, become detached.

Die helle Gestalt hebt sich auf dem dunkeln Hintergrunde vorteilhaft ab. The light figure is brought into relief against the dark background.

Abhilfe *f.* relief.

abholen to get, collect.

Das Taxi wird mich abholen. The taxi will pick me up.

Abkunft *f.* descent, origin.

ablenken to divert, distract.

ablesen to pick up, read off.

abliefern to deliver.

ABMACHEN to remove, loosen, agree, settle.

Abgemacht! Agreed!

abnehmen to take off, gather, pick up (phone).

Er nimmt seinen Hut ab. He takes off his hat.

Abneigung *f.* dislike, antipathy.

Abort *m.* lavatory.

abräumen to take away, remove.

ABREISE *f.* departure.

eine unvorhergesehene Abreise an unexpected departure.

Absage *f.* refusal.

absagen to refuse, to cancel, call off.

eine Gesellschaft absagen lassen to call off a party.

Falls Sie mir nicht absagen, komme ich. Unless you call it off, I'll come.

Abscheu *m.* aversion, horror.

abscheulich horrible, abominable, nasty.

Das war abscheulich von ihm. It was very nasty of him.

ABSCHIED *m.* departure.

Abschied nehmen to take leave.

Ich werde Abschied von Ihnen nehmen. I am going to leave you.

Den Abschied bekommen to be dismissed.

Der Offizier hat seinen Abschied genommen. The officer has been placed on the retired list.

abschreiben to copy, to deduct.

abseits prep. (gen.) aside, apart, away from.

ABSICHT *f.* intention, purpose, view.

in der Absicht with the intention.

Er tat es in böser Absicht. He did it with a malicious intention.

absichtlich on purpose.

Abstand *m.* distance, interval.

Er nahm Abstand von seiner Erbschaft. He gave up his inheritance.

Absturz *m.* fall, crash.

Er wurde bei einem Flugzeugabsturz getötet. He was killed in a plane crash.

ABTEIL *n.* compartment, division, section.

Abteil erster Klasse *n.* first-class compartment.

Nichtraucherabteil *n.* non-smoking compartment.

Abteilung *f.* department (in a store).

Schuhabteilung *f.* shoe department.

abtrocknen to dry off, wipe.

das Geschirr abtrocknen to dry the dishes.

abwärts downward.

abwechseln to vary, change, alternate.

abwesend absent.

Abwesenheit *f.* absence.

abzahlen to pay off.

abziehen to retain, take off, subtract.

Der Arbeitgeber zieht die Steuer vom Einkommen ab. The employer retains taxes from the salary.

Abzugskanal *m.* sewer.

ach! Ah! Oh!

ACHT eight.

heute in acht Tagen A week from today.

achtmal eight times.

ACHTE eighth.

achten to esteem, regard, respect.

ACHTUNG *f.* esteem.

Achtung! Beware! Attention!

achtungsvoll respectful.

ACHTZEHN eighteen.

ACHTZEHNTE eighteenth.

ACHTZIG eighty.

ACHTZIGSTE eightieth.

ACKER *m.* field, soil.

Ackerbau *m,* agriculture.

ackern to plough.

Ackersmann *m.* ploughman.

addieren to add up.

Adel *m.* nobility, aristocracy.

Ader *f.* vein.

Adjektiv *n.* adjective.

adlig noble.

ADRESSE *f.* address.

Hier ist meine Adresse. Here is my address.

adressieren to address.

Adverb *n.* adverb.

Affe *m.* monkey.

Affekt *m.* excitement.

affektiert affected.

Agent *m.* agent.

ahnen to have a presentiment.

Es ahnt mir Unglück. I have a presentiment of evil.

Ich habe keine Ahnung. I don't have the slightest idea.

ähnlich similar, like.

ähnlich sehen to look alike

Ähnlichkeit *f.* similarity, resemblance.

Akademie *f.* academy, university.

Akten *pl.* deeds, documents.

Aktie *f.* share, stock.

aktiv active.

Akzent *m.* accent, stress.

Alarm *m.* alarm.

Alkohol *m.* alcohol, liquor.

ALL (aller, alle, alles) entire, whole, every, each, any.

all die Leute	everybody.
all und jeder	each and every.
alle Tage	every day.
auf alle Fälle	in any case.
ohne allen Grund	for no reason at all.

ALLEIN alone, single, solitary, apart, lonesome.

Ich bin allein.	I am lonesome.
Sie lebt allein.	She lives alone.

allerart diverse.

allgemein universal.

Alphabet *n.* alphabet.

ALS when, than, as, like.

Als Bismarck starb. When Bismarck died.

Sie ist grösser als ihr Bruder. She is taller than her brother.

als ob as if, as though

Er tut als ob er die Antwort kenne. He acts as if he knew the answer.

so bald als as soon as

ALSO so, thus, in this way.

"Also sprach Zarathustra.." "Thus spoke Zarathustra..."

ALT old, aged, ancient.

alte Sprachen ancient languages (classics)

altehrwürdig venerable.

altgläubig orthodox.

altmodisch old-fashioned.

eine alte Junger an old maid.

ALTER *n.* age, old age, antiquity.

Mittelalter *n.* Middle Ages.

älter older, elder, senior.

Altertum *n.* antiquity.

Altertumshändler *m.* antique dealer.

älteste oldest.

am (an dem) on, at.

Amerikaner *m.* —in *f.* American.

amerikanisch American.

AMT *n.* office, charge, board.

In compound words, the suffix *amt* designates
a government office:

das Auswärtige Amt the Foreign Office.

Polizeiamt *n.* police station

Zollamt *n.* customs.

in Amt und Würden stehen to be a person of
position.

amüsant amusing.

AMÜSIEREN to amuse.

sich amüsieren to enjoy oneself.

Ich habe mich in der Gesellschaft sehr
amüsiert. I enjoyed myself at the party.

AN 1. *prep.* (*dat. when answering question, Wo?;
acc. when answering question, Wohin?, and
depending on the idiom*).

an die Arbeit gehen to go to work.

an der Arbeit sein to be at work.

an der Donau on the Danube.

an und für sich in itself.

Er starb an seinen Wunden. He died of his
wounds

Es ist an mir. It is my turn.

Ich gehe an die Tür. I go to the door.

Ich weiss, was an der Geschichte dran ist. I
know what the story is.

soviel an mir liegt as far as I am concerned.

2. *separable prefix.* (*implies movement
closer to the speaker, proximity, contact,
attraction, climbing, beginning*).

Der Hund ist angebunden. The dog is tied.

Der Tag bricht an. The day begins.

Er behielt seine Schuhe an. He kept his
shoes on.

Er zieht seine Jacke an. He puts his coat on.

Ich steige langsam den Berg hinan. I climb the
mountain slowly.

anbehalten to keep on.

Ich will meinen Mantel anbehalten. I'll keep
my coat on.

anbieten to offer, volunteer.

Anblick *m.* sight, view.

Andenken *n.* memory, souvenir.

zum Andenken an meine Eltern. In memory of
my parents.

ANDER other, another, different, next.

am anderen Morgen the next morning.

anderer Meinung sein to be of a different
opinion.

ein andermal another time.

einen Tag um den andern every other day.

etwas anderes another thing, something
different.

nichts anderes als nothing but.

unter anderem among other things.

anderenfalls otherwise.

anderseits on the other side.

andeuten to indicate.

Anerbieten *n.* offer, proposal.

Anfall *m.* attack, fit.

Herzanfall *m.* heart attack.

Anfang *m.* beginning, start.

anfangen (to) begin, start.

von Anfang, bis zu Ende from beginning to end.

Anfrage *f.* inquiry.

anfragen to inquire.

anfreunden (sich) to become friends.

angemessen suitable, accurate.

Angesicht *n.* face, countenance.

von Angesicht zu Angesicht face to face.

angesichts considering, in view of.

Angewohnheit *f.* habit, custom.

angrenzen to border.

Angriff *m.* attack.

in Angriff nehmen to set about.

Angst *f.* anxiety.

ängstigen to frighten.

sich ängstigen vor to be afraid of.

sich ängstigen um to feel anxious about.

anhaben to wear, have on.

Ich kann ihm nichts anhaben. I cannot find any
weak spot in him.

anhalten to stop, pull up.

anhören to listen to.

Anker *m.* anchor.

anklagen to accuse.

ankleiden to dress.

anklopfen to knock at.

ANKOMMEN to arrive, approach, reach.

Es kommt darauf an, ob Sie Zeit haben. It
depends on whether you have time.

Wir müssen es darauf ankommen lassen. We have
to take a chance on it.

ANKUNFT *f.* arrival.

anmelden to announce, notify, report.

Anmut *f.* grace, charm.

anmutig graceful, charming.

Annahme *f.* acceptance, assumption.

annehmen to accept, receive, assume, take care
of.

anpassen to fit, suit, adapt.

anprobieren to try on.

anrechnen to charge.

zu viel anrechnen to overcharge.

Ich rechne Ihnen Ihre Hilfe hoch an. I
appreciate your help very much.

Anrede *f.* address.

anreden to address, accost.

Der Schutzmann redete mich an. The policeman
called me.

anregen to incite, stimulate, excite.

Ansage *f.* announcement, notification.

ansagen to announce, notify.

anschauen to look at, contemplate.

anschaulich evident, clear.

Anschrift *f.* address (letter).

anschuldigen to accuse.

ANSEHEN to look at, consider, regard.

dem Ansehen nach to all appearances.

im Ansehen stehen to be esteemed.

vom Ansehen kennen to know by sight.

Ansicht *f.* view, sight, opinion.
   nach meiner Ansicht   according to my opinion.
Ansichtskarte *f.* picture postcard.
Ansprache *f.* speech, address.
Anspruch *m.* claim, pretension.
   Anspruch haben auf   to be entitled to.
Anstand *m.* manners, decency, etiquette.
   ohne Anstand   without hesitation.
anständig decent, respectable.
ANSTATT (statt)
   1. *prep.* *(gen.)* instead of; also *conj.*
   Statt eines Regenschirmes nahm er einen Stock. Instead of an umbrella, he took a stick.
   Anstatt seine Arbeit zu tun, geht er spazieren. Instead of doing his work, he takes a walk.
anstrengen (sich) to strain, exert.
anstrengend tiring, trying, exacting.
ANTWORT *f.* answer.
ANTWORTEN to answer.
anvertrauen to entrust, confide.
Anwalt *m.* lawyer, attorney.
anwesend present.
Anwesenheit *f.* presence.
Anzahl *f.* quantity, amount.
anzahlen to pay on account.
Anzeige *f.* notice, advertisement.
anzeigen to notify, report, announce.
   Ich halte es für angezeigt. I consider it advisable.
ANZUG *m.* suit, dress.
anzüglich suggestive, personal.
Anzüglichkeit *f.* suggestive remark.
anzünden to light the fire, set fire to.
APFEL *m.* apple.
   in den sauren Apfel beissen   to swallow a bitter pill.
APFELSINE *f.* orange.
Apotheke *f.* pharmacy.
Apotheker *m.* pharmacist.
Apparat *m.* apparatus, appliance, telephone.
   Bleiben Sie am Apparat! Hold the wire!
Appetit *m.* appetite.
applaudieren to applaud.
APRIL *m.* April.
Äquator *m.* equator.
ARBEIT *f.* work, job.
ARBEITEN to work, manufacture.
   arbeitsfähig able-bodied
   arbeits unfähig unfit for work
Arbeiter *m.* (**-in**, *f.*) worker, laborer.
   Arbeiterstand *m.* working class.
Arbeitgeber *m.* employer.
Arbeitnehmer *m.* employee.
arbeitsam industrious, diligent.
Architekt *m.* architect.
Architektur *f.* architecture.
arg bad, mischievous.

   Sie dachte an nichts Arges. She meant no harm.
Ärger *m.* Annoyance, anger, worry.
ärgerlich annoying, angry.
ärgern to annoy, irritate, bother.
Argument *n.* argument.
Aristokrat *m.* aristocrat.
Aristokratie *f.* aristocracy.
aristokratisch aristocratic.
ARM *m.* arm.
ARM poor
Armband *n.* bracelet.
Armbanduhr *f.* wrist watch.
Ärmel *m.* sleeve.
Armlehne *f.* arm of chair.
Armut *f.* poverty.
Arrest *m.* arrest.
ART *f.* kind, manner, way, type.
artig good, well-behaved.
Artikel *m.* article.
Arznei *f.* medicine (drug).
Arzneikunde *f.* pharmacy (profession of).
Ast *m.* branch (tree).
Atem *m.* breath, suspense.
   Dieser Kriminalroman halt uns in Atem. This detective story keeps us in suspense.
atemholen to take breadth.
atemlos breathless.
atemraubend breath-taking.
   Der Film war atemraubend. The movie was breath-taking.
Athlet *m.* athlete.
atmen to breathe.
AUCH also, too even.
   was auch whatever.
   wer auch whoever.
   wo auch wherever.
   Was auch geschieht, Sie sind verantwortlich. Whatever happens, you are responsible.
   Wer auch kommen mag, ich bin nicht zu Hause. Whoever comes, I am not home.
   Wo auch immer er auftauchen mag, man wird ihn erkennen. Wherever he appears, he will be recognized.
AUF 1. *prep.* *(dat. when answering question, Wo?; acc. when answering question, Wohin?, and depending on the idiom)* on, upon, at, in. to, for, during.
   Er kommt auf die Strasse hinab. He comes down to the street.
   Ich kaufe Gemüse auf dem Markt. I buy vegetables at the market.
   Ich traf sie auf dem Ball. I met her at the ball.
   Ich fahre auf das Land. I drive to the country.
   Sie wohnen auf oliesem Schloss. They live in that castle.
   Die Jäger gehen auf die Jagd. The hunters go hunting.
   Der Tag folgt auf die Nacht. The day follows the night.
   alle bis auf einen   all except one.

auf der Rückfahrt von Wien during the return from Vienna.
auf Deutsch in German.
auf einmal suddenly.
auf keinen Fall in no case.
auf Wiedersehen! Good-bye!
Liebe auf den ersten Blick love at first sight.
2. *adv.* up, upwards.
auf und ab up and down.
3. *Conj.* auf dass in order to.
auf dass nicht for fear that.
4. *Separable prefix (implies motion upward or outward, opening, completion).*
Ich setze meinen Hut auf. I put my hat on.
Die Sonne geht auf. The sun is rising.
Bitte, machen Sie das Fenster auf. Please open the window.

aufbewahren to keep, preserve, stock.
Aufbewahrung *f.* preservation, storage.
aufbrauchen to use up.
aufeinander one on top of the other.
Aufenthalt *m.* stay, residence.
aufessen to eat up.
Auffassung *f.* conception, interpretation.
Aufgabe *f.* task, duty, problem.
aufgeben to commission, order, lose, give up, resign, check, send.
die Hoffnung aufgeben to lose hope.
ein Telegramm aufgeben to send a telegram.
aufhängen to hang up.
aufheben to pick up, rise, abolish.
aufheitern to cheer up.
aufklären to clear, explain.
Aufklärung *f.* explanation.
aufmachen to open, unlock, undo.
Aufmachung *f.* make up.
aufmerken to pay attention, attend.
aufmerksam attentive.
Aufmerksamkeit *f.* attention.
Aufnahme *f.* taking up, admission, enrollment, snapshot.
aufnahmefähig receptive.
Aufnahmeprüfung *f.* entrance examination.
aufnehmen to lift, take up, admit, photograph, record (a voice).
aufpassen to adapt, fix, pay attention.
Aufgepasst! Attention!
Aufpasser *m.* watcher, spy.
aufräumen to arrange, put in order, clean.
aufrecht upright, straight.
aufregen to stir up, excite.
aufregend exciting, seditious.
Aufregung *f.* excitement, agitation.
Aufsatz *m.* main piece, top, ornament, article (newspaper).
aufschliessen to unlock.
Aufschluss *m.* opening up, explanation, information.
Aufschluss über eine Sache geben to give some information about something.
aufschreiben to write down.
Aufsehen *n.* sensation, attention.

Er erregt Aufsehen. He attracts attention.
Aufstand *m.* tumult, revolt.
AUFSTEHEN stand up, rise, get up.
aufstehen gegen to rebel against.
Stehen Sie auf! Get up!
aufstellen to set up, erect, draw up, nominate.
Eine Behauptung aufstellen to make a statement.
Auftrag *m.* commission, instruction.
im Auftrage von by order of.
einen Auftrag ausführen to execute a commission.
auftragen to carry up, serve up, draw, charge.
Er hat mir viele Grüsse an Sie aufgetragen. He sends you his regards. ("He charged me with many greetings for you.")
aufwachen to awake.
aufwachsen to grow up.
Aufwand *m.* expenditure, expense.
aufwärts upwards.
Er schwimmt den Fluss aufwärts. He swims upstream.
aufwecken to awaken.
aufziehen to bring up, raise, wind a watch, pull up, tease.
Einen aufziehen to make fun of somebody.
Aufzug *m.* procession, parade, attire, outfit, act (play), elevator.
AUGE *n.* eye.
Er versuchte mir Sand in die Augen zu streuen. He tried to deceive me ("throw dust into my eyes").
gute Augen haben to have good eyesight.
grosse Augen machen to look very surprised.
Ich habe kein Auge zugemacht. I did not sleep a wink.
unter vier Augen privately ("between four eyes").
Wir haben ihn aus den Augen verloren. We lost sight of him.
Augenarzt *m.* oculist.
Augenblick *m.* moment.
im Augenblick for the moment.
augenblicklich immediately.
Augenbraue *f.* eyebrow.
Augenlid *n.* eyelid.
Augenwimper *f.* eyelash.
AUGUST *m.* August.
Auktion *f.* auction sale.
AUS 1. *prep. (dat.)* out, out of, for, from, in, upon.
Aus den Augen, aus dem Sinn. Out of sight, out of mind.
Er kommt aus dem Theater. He comes out of the theater.
Er hat es aus Liebe getan. He did it for love.
Meine Uhr ist aus Gold. My watch is made of gold.
Sie stammt aus Paris. She is a native of Paris.
2. *adv.* out, over, up.
von hier aus from here.
von mir aus for my part.
3. *separable prefix.* *Implies the idea of*

motion out (in this case also combines with hin or her), achievement .
Die Vorstellung ist aus. The performance is over.
Ich gehe aus dem Speisezimmer hinaus. I go out of the dinning room.
ausbessern to repair.
ausbilden to form, develop, cultivate, educate, train.
ausbleiben to stay away, fail to appear, escape.
Ihre Strafe wird nicht ausbleiben. You will not escape punishment.
Ausblick *m.* outlook, prospect.
ausbrechen to break out, vomit.
in Tränen ausbrechen to burst into tears.
Ausbruch *m.* outbreak, eruption, escape.
Ausdauer *f.* perseverance, assiduity.
ausdauern to hold out, outlast, endure.
ausdehnen to expand, prolong.
ausdenken to invent, conceive, imagine.
Ausdruck *m.* expression, phrase.
ausdrücken to squeeze, express.
sich kurz und klar ausdrücken to express oneself briefly and to the point.
auseinander apart, separately.
ausführen to take out, export, realize.
ausführlich *adj.* detailed, full; in detail, fully.
Erzählen Sie mir alles ausführlich. Tell me everything in detail.
ausfüllen to fill out, stuff.
Ausgabe *f.* delivery, edition, issue, publication.
Ausgang *m.* way out, exit, end.
ausgeben to give out, deliver, issue, deal (cards).
ausgehen to go out, come out, run out, proceed, start from, end.
frei ausgehen to go free.
ihm geht die Geduld aus. He is losing his patience.
Wie wird diese Sache ausgehen? How will this matter end?
AUSGEZEICHNET excellent, distinguished.
ausgleichen to make even, equalize, settle, arrange, compensate.
aushalten to bear, suffer, support, hold out, last.
Aushang *m.* notice (posted); poster.
aushängen to hang out, post a notice.
Aushilfe *f.* aid (temporary); assistant.
auskleiden to undress.
auskommen to manage, get along.
Es ist schwer mit ihm auszukommen. It is difficult to get along with him.
Ich komme nicht mit dem Papier aus. I can't manage with the paper. (I don't have enough of it.)
Auskunft *f.* information, intelligence.
Auskunftei *f.* information bureau.
auslassen to leave out, omit, let out.
Auslese *f.* choice, selection.
auslesen to select, choose, read through.
ausmachen to put out, constitute, come to, settle, amount.
Das macht nichts aus. It does not matter.

Ausmass *n.* measurement, scale, proportion.
mit solchem Ausmass to such an extent.
ausmessen to measure, survey.
Ausnahme *f.* exception.
ohne Ausnahme without exception.
auspacken to unpack.
Ausrede *f.* excuse, pretense.
ausreden to finish speaking, excuse.
einem etwas ausreden to dissuade somebody from something.
ausrichten to execute, deliver, obtain.
Haben Sie es ihm ausgerichtet? Did you give him the message?
Ausruf *m.* cry, exclamation.
ausrufen to cry out, admonish, proclaim.
ausruhen to rest.
Aussage *f.* statement, assertion, declaration, evidence.
aussagen to affirm, declare, give evidence.
ausschalten to cut out, switch off.
Schalten Sie den Motor aus! Switch off the motor!
ausscheiden to separate, withdraw.
ausschiffen to disembark, land.
ausschliessen to exclude.
ausschliesslich exclusive.
ausschmücken to decorate, adorn.
ausschneiden to cut out, snipe.
AUSSEHEN to look out, appear.
Aussehen *n.* look, air.
aussen on the outside, abroad, without.
von aussen from the outside.
aussenden to send out.
AUSSER 1. *prep. (dat.)* out of, out, besides.
ausser der Jahreszeit out of season
ausser sich beside oneself.
2. *with gen.* out of.
ausser Landes out of the country.
3. *conj.* except, unless, but.
Ausser Sonntags, gehe ich jeden Tag in die Schule. I go to school every day except Sunday.
ausserdem besides, moreover.
aussetzen to set out, put out, offer, bequeath.
auszusetzen haben to find fault with.
Aussicht *f.* view, prospect.
aussinnen to plan, plot, scheme.
aussöhnen to reconcile.
aussondern to separate, select.
Aussprache *f.* pronunciation, accent.
aussprechen to pronounce, express.
aussuchen to seek out, search.
Austausch *m.* exchange.
austauschen to exchange.
Auster *f.* oyster.
austragen to deliver, distribute.
austreten to tread under, trample, retire.
Ausverkauf *m.* clearance sale.
ausverkaufen to sell out, clear off (a shop).
Auswahl *f.* choice, assortment, selection.
auswählen to choose, select.
Auswanderer *m.* emigrant.

auswandern to emigrate.
Auswanderung *f.* emigration.
auswärtig foreign, abroad.
Ausweg *m.* way out.
ausweichen to avoid, evade, shun.
Ausweis *m.* certificate, document, identity card.
ausziehen to undress, pull out, extract, move, remove.
Auszug *m.* departure, extract, removal.
Auto *n.* automobile, car.
Autobahn *n.* parkway.
Autobus *m.* bus.
Axt *f.* axe.

B

Bach *m.* brook.
BACKEN to bake, fry.
Bäcker *m.* baker.
Backobst *n.* dried fruit.
Backofen *m.* oven.
Backpulver *n.* baking powder.
BAD *n.* bath, spa.
Badeanstalt *f.* baths, swimming pool.
Badeanzug *m.* bathing suit.
Badehose *f.* bathing shorts.
Bademantel *m.* bathrobe.
Badeort *m.* spa.
Badetuch *n.* bath towel.
Badewanne *f.* bathtub.
Badezimmer *n.* bathroom.
BAHN *f.* track, road, way, railway.
Bahnarbeiter *m.* railway man.
Bahnbeamte *m.* railroad official.
Bahngleis *n.* track.
BAHNHOF *m.* station.
Bahnsteig *m.* platform.
Bahnübergang *m.* railroad crossing.
Balance *f.* balance, equilibrium.
balancieren to balance.
BALD soon, shortly.
  bald. . ., bald. . . sometimes. . ., sometimes. . .
  bald darauf soon after.
Balkon *m.* balcony.
Ball *m.* ball, dance.
Ballett *n.* ballet.
Ballon *m.* balloon.
Band *n.* ribbon.
Bande *f.* band, gang.
bändigen to tame, to break.
Bandmass *n.* tape measure.
BANK *f.* 1. bench, seat.
  durch die Bank all, without exception.
  auf die lange Bank schieben to postpone, delay.
  2. bank.
  Geld auf der Bank haben to have money in the bank.
Bankanweisung *f.* check.
Bankbeamte *m.* bank clerk.
BAR bare, naked, devoid of.
  barfuss barefoot.

Bär *m.* bear.
Bargeld *n.* cash.
  bar zahlen to pay cash.
barmherzig merciful.
Barmherzigkeit *f.* mercy.
Baron *m.* (**-in,** *f.*) Baron (ess).
Bart *m.* beard, whiskers.
BAU *m.* building, construction, edifice, frame.
Bauch *m.* belly, stomach.
BAUEN to build, construct, cultivate.
  Luftschlösser bauen to build castles in the air.
Bauer *m.* peasant.
Bauernhof *m.* farm.
Bauernvolk *n.* countryfolk.
baufällig dilapidated.
BAUM *m.* tree, pole.
Baumschule *f.* nursery (trees).
Baumwolle *f.* cotton.
Baustein *n.* brick.
beabsichtigen to intend.
beachten to observe, notice.
Beachtung *f.* consideration, attention.
beachtenswert noteworthy.
Beamte *m.* official, civil servant.
  Zollbeamte *m.* customs officer.
beängstigen to alarm.
beanspruchen to claim, demand.
beanstanden to object, reject.
beantworten to answer, reply.
beaufsichtigen to supervise.
beben to tremble.
  vor Angst beben to tremble with fear.
Becher *m.* cup, goblet, dice box.
bedacht thoughful, considerate.
bedanken to thank.
Bedarf *m.* need, requirement.
bedauerlich deplorable, regrettable.
bedecken to cover.
  Der Himmel ist bedeckt the sky is overcast.
bedenken to think, think over, reflect, ponder.
  sich eines andern bedenken to change one's mind.
bedenklich doubtful.
Bedenkzeit *f.* time for reflection.
Bedienung *f.* service.
  einschliesslich der Bedienung service included.
bedürfen to need, require.
Bedürfnis *n.* need, want necessity.
beeindrucken to impress.
beerdigen to bury.
Beerdigung *f.* funeral.
befassen to occupy.
  Er befasst sich mit Politik. He is in politics.
Befehl *m.* order, command.
befehlen to order, command.
befestigen to fasten, fortify.
befolgen to obey.
befreien to free, liberate.

Befreier m. liberator.

Befreiung f. liberation.

befreunden to befriend.

    sich befreunden mit to become friends with.

befriedigen to satisfy, content.

befriedigend satisfying.

Befriedigung f. satisfaction, gratification.

Befund m. state, condition, report.

befürchten to apprehend, fear.

Befürchtung f. apprehension, fear.

befürworten to recommend.

begabt gifted.

begeben (sich) to set about.

begegnen to meet, encounter.

begeistern to inspire, fill with enthusiasm.

begeistert inspired, enthusiastic.

Begeisterung f. inspiration, enthusiasm.

Beginn m. beginning.

BEGINNEN to begin, start.

beglaubigen to attest, certify.

begleiten to accompany.

    nach Hause begleiten to see (someone) home.

begründen to found, to prove.

Behaglichkeit f. comfort.

behalten to keep, retain, remember.

    Behalten Sie das Kleingeld! Keep the change!

behandeln to handle, deal with.

beharren to persist, remain firm.

    beharren auf to insist on.

behaupten to maintain, assert, affirm.

Behelf m. help, expedient.

behelfen (sich) to manage, do without.

BEI 1. prep. (dat.) at, by, near, with, because of, in case of.

    bei der Hand by Hand.

    Bei Feuer, müssen wir die Feuerwehr rufen. In case of a fire, we must call the fire department.

    Bei ihrem Charakter wird sie unglücklich werden. With (because of) her character, she will be unhappy.

    bei Tage by day.

    bei weitem by far.

    beim Metzger at the butcher's.

    Er arbeitet bei Licht. He works by light.

    Hast du Geld bei dir? Do you have any money on you?

    Ich kaufe meine Kleider bei Engels. I buy my clothes at Engels.

    Meine Schwester wohnt bei mir. My sister lives with me.

Beichte f. confession.

beichten to confess.

BEIDE both.

    wir beide both of us.

    einer von beiden one of the two.

    keiner von beiden neither of them.

    beiderseits on both sides, mutually.

BEIFALL m. approval, approbation, applause.

beifolgend herewith, enclosed.

beiläufig accidental, casual; incidentally.

beilegen to add, enclose.

Beileid n. sympathy.

    Beileid bezeigen to console somebody.

beim (bei dem) at, by.

BEIN n. leg, bone.

    sich kein Bein ausreissen to take it easy.

    Er ist immer auf den Beinen. He's always on his feet.

beinahe nearly, almost.

beipflichten to agree with, assent to.

beisammen together.

beiseite aside, apart.

BEISPIEL n. example.

    zum Beispiel for example.

    Das ist ein schlechtes Beispiel. This is a bad example.

beispiellos unheard of.

beissen to bite.

    Der Hund beisst nicht. The dog does not bite.

beistehen to help, stand by.

beistimmen to agree with.

Beitrag m. contribution, subscription.

bejahen to answer in the affirmative, assent, accept.

bejammern to lament.

bejammernswert deplorable, lamentable.

bekämpfen to combat, fight, struggle.

BEKANNT well-known, acquainted.

    bekannt machen mit to introduce to.

Bekannte m. acquaintance, friend.

Bekanntmachung f. publication, announcement, notice.

bekennen to confess, admit, profess.

    sich schuldig bekennen to plead guilty.

beklagen to complain, lament.

BEKOMMEN to get, receive, catch, agree with.

    Das ist nicht mehr zu bekommen. You can't get that any more.

    Es bekommt mir nicht. It does not agree with me.

bekräftigen to confirm, corroborate.

belächeln to smile at.

belachen to laugh at.

belästigen to molest, trouble.

beleben to animate, revive.

Beleg m. proof, evidence, illustration.

BELEGEN to cover, reserve.

    Ich möchte einen Platz belegen. I want to reserve a seat.

    belegte Brötchen sandwiches.

    eine Vorlesung belegen to enroll for a course.

belehren to enlighten, instruct.

    eines Besseren belehren to correct.

beleidigen to offend, insult.

beliefern to supply.

belohnen to reward.

Belohnung f. reward.

belügen to lie (falsify).

belustigen to amuse, entertain.

Belustigung f. amusement.

bemerkbar noticeable, perceptible.

bemerken to notice, observe, remark.
bemerkenswert noticeable, noteworthy.
Bemerkung *f.* remark, observation.
bemitleiden to pity, be sorry for.
bemitleidenswert deplorable.
benachrichtigen to inform, advise.
Benachrichtigung *f.* information, advice.
benachteiligen to prejudice.
Benachteiligung *f.* prejudice, injury.
benehmen to behave.
   Benimm dich nicht wie ein kleines Kind!
   Don't behave like a child!
beneiden to envy.
benommen confused, dizzy.
benötigen to require.
benutzen to use, employ, utilize.
beobachten to observe, watch.
   heimlich beobachten to shadow.
BEQUEM suitable, convenient, lazy.
   Sei nicht so bequem! Don't be so lazy!
bequemen to condescend, comply, submit.
Bequemlichkeit *f.* convenience.
beraten to advise.
Berater *m.* adviser.
beratschlagen to deliberate.
berechnen to calculate, estimate.
bereden to talk over, persuade.
Beredsamkeit *f.* eloquence.
Bereich *m. & n.* reach, range, area, zone.
BEREIT ready, prepared.
   bereit halten to keep ready.
   bereitwillig willing, ready.
Bereitwilligkeit *f.* willingness.
bereuen to repent, regret.
BERG *m.* mountain, hill.
   über alle Berge sein to be out of the woods.
   Mir standen die Haare zu Berge. My hair stood on end.
Bergmann *m.* miner.
berichten to report.
berichtigen to correct, amend, settle (a bill).
Berichtigung *f.* correction, amendment.
berücksichtigen to consider.
Berücksichtigung *f.* consideration, regard.
BERUF *m.* profession, occupation.
beruflich professional.
berufstätig working.
beruhigen to quiet, calm.
Beruhigung *f.* reassurance, comfort.
BERÜHMT famous, celebrated.
Berühmtheit *f.* fame, celebrity.
besänftigen to soften, appease, soothe.
beschädigen to damage, injure, harm.
beschäftigen to occupy, engage, employ.
Beschäftigung *f.* occupation.
beschäftigungslos unemployed, out of work.
Bescheid *m.* answer, information.
   Bescheid geben to inform.
   Ich habe ihm gehörig Bescheid gesagt. I told

him off.
bescheiden modest, moderate.
Bescheidenheit *f.* modesty.
bescheinen to shine upon.
bescheinigen to certify, attest.
Bescheinigung *f.* certificate, receipt.
beschleunigen to hasten, accelerate.
beschränken to limit, confine, restrict.
Beschränkung *f.* limitation, restriction.
beschreiben to write upon, describe.
Beschreibung *f.* description.
beschuldigen to accuse.
Beschuldigung *f.* accusation.
Beschwerde *f.* hardship, trouble, complaint.
beschweren (sich) to complain.
   Beschwerdebüro *n.* complaint department.
beschwichtigen to calm, pacify, appease.
Besen *m.* broom.
besetzen to trim, occupy, set.
   Es ist alles besetzt! All seats are occupied.
   Besetzt! Occupied! Busy!
Besetzung *f.* occupation, cast.
   Die Besetzung ist aussergewöhnlich gut.
   The cast is outstanding.
besichtigen to view, inspect, visit.
Besichtigung *f.* view, inspection.
besiegen to conquer, beat, defeat.
besinnen to consider, reflect.
   sich eines Besseren besinnen to think better of.
besinnlich contemplative, thoughtful.
Besitz *m.* possession, property, estate.
besorgen to take care of, fetch, procure, provide.
Besorgnis *f.* fear, alarm.
Besorgung *f.* care, management.
   Besorgungen machen to go shopping.
besprechen to discuss, talk over, criticize, review.
BESSER better.
   umso besser so much the better.
bessern to improve, recover.
   sich bessern to improve oneself.
Besserung *f.* recovery, improvement.
   Gute Besserung! I hope you will get well soon!
best(er-es) best.
beständig constant, permanent, steady;
   constantly, all the time.
Beständigkeit *f.* constancy, stability.
bestätigen to confirm, ratify.
bestechen to bribe, corrupt.
bestechlich corruptible.
Bestechung *f.* corruption.
Besteck *n.* one setting of silver.
bestellen to arrange, order, tell, cultivate.
   Waren bestellen to order goods.
   zu sich bestellen to send for.
BESTIMMEN to decide, fix, intend, define, induce.
   bestimmen über to dispose of.
   bestimmt! agreed!
Bestimmtheit *f.* certainty, precision.

bestrafen to punish.

Bestrafung *f.* punishment.

BESUCH *m.* visit, company, attendance.

BESUCHEN to visit, attend.

Besucher *m.* visitor, spectator, audience.

beteiligen to give a share, take part, take an interest.

beteiligt sein to participate.

Beteiligung *f.* share, participation.

betonen to stress, accent, emphasize.

Betonung *f.* stress, emphasis.

beträchtlich considerable.

betreffen to concern.

was mich betrifft so far as I am concerned.

betreten to tread on.

Betreten des Rasens verboten! Keep off the grass!

Betrieb *m.* management, plant, factory.

in Betrieb sein to be working.

ausser Betrieb not working, closed

in Betrieb setzen to set in motion.

betrinken to get drunk.

betrüben to grieve, distress.

Betrug *m.* deception, fraud, swindle.

betrügen to deceive, defraud, trick.

BETT *n.* bed.

das Bett hüten to be confined in bed.

früh zu Bett gehen to go to bed early.

Bettdecke *f.* blanket, bedspread.

betteln to beg.

Bettlaken *n.* sheet.

Bettler *m.* beggar.

Bettwäsche *f.* bed linen.

beugen to bend, bow.

beunruhigen to disturb, alarm, upset.

beurlauben to grant leave, take leave.

beurlaubt absent on leave.

Beutel *m.* bag, purse.

bevollmächtigen to empower, authorize.

BEVOR before.

bewachen to watch over.

bewältigen to master.

bewegen to move, stir.

Beweggrund *m.* motive.

Was war der Beweggrund des Verbrechens? What was the motive of the crime?

beweglich movable, mobile, quick, lively.

BEWEGUNG *f.* movement, agitation, motion.

Einer politischen Bewegung angehören to belong to a political party.

Beweis *m.* proof, evidence.

beweisen to prove, demonstrate.

Beweisführung *f.* demonstration.

bewerben to apply for, compete.

Bewerber *m.* applicant, candidate.

Bewerbung *f.* application, courtship.

bewilligen to consent, concede.

bewusst conscious.

sich einer Sache bewusst sein to be conscious or aware of something.

bewusstlos unconscious.

BEZAHLEN to pay.

sich bezahlt machen to pay for itself (be lucrative).

bezaubernd charming.

bezichtigen to charge with.

Bezug *m.* covering, cover, case.

in Bezug auf in regard to.

Bezug nehmen auf to refer to.

unter Bezugnahme auf with reference to.

Bibel *f.* Bible.

Bibliothek *f.* library.

Bibliothekar *m.* librarian.

Biene *f.* bee.

Bier *n.* beer.

BIETEN to offer.

sich alles bieten lassen to put up with everything.

BILD *n.* image, picture, illustration, portrait, likeness.

BILDEN to form, shape, educate.

Der Präsident hat ein neues Kabinett gebildet. The president has formed a new cabinet.

die bildenden Künste fine arts.

Bildseite *f.* face, head (coin).

Bildung *f.* formation, constitution.

billig just, reasonable, fair, moderate.

binden to bind, tie.

BIS until, as far as, about.

zwei bis drei Pfund. About two or three pounds.

bis an *(acc.)* up to.

bis in alle Ewigkeit till the end of time.

bis auf *(acc.)* except for.

Mir gefällt der Film bis auf das Ende. I like the film except for the ending.

alle bis auf einen all except one.

bis auf weiteres until further notice.

bis zu *(dat.)* (down) to.

von dem Kopf bis zu den Füssen from head to foot.

bis jetzt so far.

bisher till now.

bisweilen sometimes.

Bischof *m.* bishop.

bisschen a bit, a little, a while.

Das ist ein bisschen stark. That's going a bit too far.

Er kam ein bisschen spät. He came a little late.

Bissen *m.* bite, mouthful.

Bitte *f.* request, prayer.

BITTE please. bitte, bitte schön, bitte sehr. (In response to a request: Here you are. In response to thanks: You are welcome; don't mention it.)

Wie, bitte? I beg your pardon?

BITTEN to ask, beg, implore.

Ich bitte um Entschuldigung. I beg your

pardon, I am sorry.

bitter bitter.

blamieren to expose to ridicule.

sich blamieren to make a fool of oneself.

BLATT *n.* leaf, petal, blade, sheet.

sich kein Blatt vor den Mund nehmen to speak plainly.

Blattern *f.* smallpox.

blättern to leaf through the pages of a book.

Blatternimpfung *f.* smallpox vaccination.

BLAU blue.

Blech *n.* tin.

Blei *n.* lead.

BLEIBEN to stay, remain, keep, last.

bleiben lassen to leave alone.

Das bleibt unter uns. That's between you and me.

Es bleibt dabei Agreed.

sich gleich bleiben to remain the same.

stehen bleiben to stop, stand still.

bleibend permanent, lasting.

bleich pale, faded, faint.

bleichen to bleach.

Bleistift *m.* pencil.

blenden to blind, dazzle.

BLICK *m.* glance, look, gaze.

auf den ersten Blick at first sight.

Er warf ihm einen bösen Blick zu. He gave him a dirty look.

blind blind, false.

ein blinder Alarm a false alarm.

Blindheit *f.* blindness.

blinken to glitter, glimpse, twinkle, signal.

Blitz *m.* lightening, flash.

blitzen to lighten, flash, sparkle.

Block *m.* block, log, pad, stocks.

blond blond, fair.

BLOSS bare, naked, uncovered; merely, only.

Ich tue es bloss Ihnen zu gefallen. I am only doing it to please you.

blühen to bloom.

BLUME *f.* flower.

Lasst Blumen sprechen! Say it with flowers!

Blumenkohl *m.* cauliflower.

Bluse *f.* blouse.

BLUT *n.* blood, race, parentage.

blutarm anemic.

Blutdruck *m.* blood pressure.

bluten to bleed.

Blutprobe *f.* blood-test.

Blutvergiftung *f.* blood-poisoning.

Boden *m.* floor, ground, soil, attic.

Bogen *m.* bow, curve, arch.

BOHNE *f.* bean.

grüne Bohnen string beans.

weisse Bohnen dried beans.

Bombardement *n.* bombardment.

bombardieren to bomb.

Bombe *f.* bomb.

Atombombe *f.* atomic bomb.

Bonbon *m.* & *n.* candy.

BOOT *n.* boat.

Bootsfahrt *f.* boatride.

Börse *f.* purse, stock exchange.

Börsenmakler *m.* stockbroker.

bösartig ill-natured, wicked, malicious.

BÖSE bad, angry, evil.

boshaft malicious, mischievous.

Bote *m.* messenger.

Botschaft *f.* news.

Botschafter *m.* ambassador.

boxen to box.

Brand *m.* burning, fire, conflagration.

in Brand geraten to catch fire.

Brandschaden *m.* damage by fire.

BRATEN *m.* roast.

Brathuhn *n.* roast chicken.

Bratkartoffeln *pl.* fried potatoes.

Bratapfel *m.* baked apple.

BRATEN to roast, grill, fry.

Brauch *m.* usage, use, custom.

brauchbar useful, practicable.

BRAUCHEN to use, employ, need.

Wie lange werden Sie noch brauchen? How much more time will it take you?

Brauhaus *n.* brewery, tavern.

BRAUN brown.

Brause *f.* shower, douche, spray.

brausen to storm, rage, roar, rush.

sich abbrausen to take a shower.

Braut *f.* fiancee.

Brautführer *m.* best man.

Brautjungfer, *f.* bridesmaid.

Brautkleid *n.* wedding dress.

Brautpaar *n.* engaged couple.

Bräutigam *m.* bridegroom.

brav good, honest, excellent.

BRECHEN to break, pick.

Er spricht ein gebrochenes Deutsch. He speaks broken German.

BREIT broad, wide, flat.

weit und breit high and low.

Breite *f.* breadth, width, latitude.

Bremse *f.* brake.

bremsen to put the brakes on.

BRENNEN to burn, brand, bake, roast.

darauf brennen to be anxious.

Es brennt in der Stadt. There is a fire in town.

Brett *n.* board, plank, shelf, stage.

am schwarzen Brett on the board.

BRIEF *m.* letter.

Briefkasten *m.* letter-box.

Briefmappe *f.* attaché case.

Briefmarke *f.* stamp.

Briefpapier *n.* stationery.

Brieftasche *f.* wallet, pocket-book.

Briefträger *m.* mailman.

Briefumschlag *m.* envelope.

Brille *f.* glasses.
BRINGEN to bring, fetch, carry, put, take.
    dazu bringen to induce to.
    Er hat sich ums Leben gebracht. He's
    committed sucide.
    es zu etwas bringen to achieve something.
    Ich werde das in Ordnung bringen. I'll
    straighten that out.
    um etwas bringen to deprive of.
britisch British.
BROT *n.* bread.
    Brötchen   roll.
    sein Brot verdienen to earn one's living.
Brötchen *n.* roll.
Bruch *m.* break, fracture, fraction.
Bruchteil *m.* fraction.
BRÜCKE *f.* bridge (also dental).
    Er hat alle Brücken hinter sich abgebrochen.
    He has burnt his bridges behing him.
BRUDER *m.* brother.
    Bruderschaft *f.* fraternity.
Brunnen *m.* spring, well, fountain.
Brust *f.* breast, chest, bosom.
Bube *m.* boy, jack of cards.
BUCH *n.* book.
Buchdeckel *m.* cover, binding.
Buchführung *f.* bookkeeping.
Buchhaltung *f.* bookkeeping.
Buchhändler *m.* bookseller.
Buchhandlung *f.* bookshop.
Büchse *f.* can.
Büchsenöffner *m.* can opener.
Buchstabe *m.* letter, character.
Buchumschlag *m.* jacket (book).
Bügelbrett *n.* ironing board.
Bügeleisen *n.* iron (for pressing).
bügeln to press
Bühne *f.* stage, platform.
Bund *m.* league, confederation.
Bündel *m.* bundle.
bunt colored, lively, gay.
    Das ist mir zu bunt. I'm fed up with it.
Burg *f.* castle, citadel.
Bürge *f.* bail.
bürgen to guarantee, vouch for.
Bürger *m.* citizen, townsman.
Bürgerkrieg *m.* civil war.
Bürgermeister *m.* mayor.
Bürgersteig *m.* pavement.
BÜRO *n.* office.
Bürobote *m.* office boy.
bürokratisch bureaucratic.
Bursch *m.* youth, lad, fellow.
Burschenschaft *f.* students' association.
Bürste *f.* brush.
bürsten to brush.
Busch *m.* bush.
Busse *f.* penitence, repentance.
    Busse tun to do penance.

büssen to suffer for, expiate.
Büste *f.* bust.
Büstenhalter *m.* brassiere.
BUTTER *f.* butter.
Butterbrot *n.* slice of bread and butter.

C

Café *n.* café.
Cello *n.* cello.
Cellist *m.* cellist.
Champagner *m.* champagne.
Charakter *m.* character, disposition.
charakteristisch characteristic.
Chauffeur *m.* chauffeur.
Chef *m.* head, boss, chief.
Chemie *f.* chemistry.
chemisch chemical.
Chinese *m.* Chinese (person).
chinesisch Chinese.
Chirurg *m.* surgeon.
Chor *m.* choir, chorus.
Choral *m.* chorale.
Chorgesang *m.* choir singing.
Choristin *f.* chorus-girl.
Chorknabe *m.* choir-boy.
Christ *m.* Christian.
Christenheit *f.* Christendom.
Christentum *f.* Christianity.
Chronik *f.* chronicle.
Cousin *m.* (Vetter *m.*) cousin (man).
Cousine *f.* (Kusine) cousin (woman).
Creme *m.* cream (cosmetic).

D

DA 1. *adv.* there, here.
    2. *conj.* when, because, as, since.
    da sein to be present.
    da stehen to stand near, stand by.
DABEI near, near by, close to, moreover.
    dabei bleibt es there the matter ends.
dableiben to stay, remain.
Dach *n.* roof.
    unter Dach und Fach safe.
Dachkammer *f.* attic.
DADURCH through it, by it, thereby.
    dadurch dass through the fact that.
    Er ist dadurch berühmt geworden. That made
    him famous.
DAFÜR for that, for it, instead of it.
    dafür sein to be in favor of.
    Ich kann nichts dafür. It is not my fault.
DAGEGEN 1. *adv.* against it.
    nichts dagegen haben to have no objection.
    2. *conj.* on the other hand.
DAHEIM at home.
DAHER from there.
    Ich komme gerade daher. I am just coming
    from there.
DAHIN to there.

bis dahin by then.
Ich gehe sofort dahin. I am going there
right now.
dahinten behind.
damalig then, of that time.
Dame *f.* lady, queen (cards), checkers.
eine Partie Dame spielen to play a game of
checkers.
DAMIT 1. *adv.* with it, by it.
Was wollte er damit sagen? What does he mean
by that?
2. *conj.* so that, in order to.
Ich sage es noch einmal damit Sie es nicht
vergessen. I say it once more so that you won't
forget it.
damit nicht for fear that.
Dämmerlicht *n.* dusk.
Dämmerung *f.* twilight, dawn.
Dampf *m.* vapor, steam.
Dampfbad *n.* steam bath.
dämpfen to damp, tone down, extinguish, steam
(cooking).
Dämpfer *m.* steamer.
DANACH afterwards, after that, thereafter.
Es sieht danach aus. It looks like it.
daneben 1. *adv.* near it, next to it, close by.
2. *conj.* besides, moreover, at the same time,
also.
DANK *m.* thanks, gratitude, reward.
Gott sei Dank! Thank God!
zum Dank as a reward.
DANKBAR grateful, thankful.
DANKE! thank you!
Danke schön! Thank you very much!
DANKEN to thank.
Nichts zu danken. Not at all, don't mention it.
DANN then, thereupon.
dann und wann now and then.
DARAN (dran) at it, of that, in it, in that.
Ich glaube daran. I believe in it.
nahe daran sein to be near, on the point of.
Wer ist dran? Whose turn is it?
DARAUF (drauf) on, upon it, after that, thereupon.
darauf aus sein to be out to, aim at.
Es kommt darauf an. It all depends.
Ich lege keinen Wert darauf. I'm not interested
in it.
DARAUS (draus) of it, of that, from this, from that.
Daraus ist nichts geworden. Nothing came of it.
darbieten to offer, present.
Darbietung *f.* entertainment, performance.
DAREIN (drein) into it, therein.
DARIN (drin) in it, in that.
Es ist nichts darin. There is nothing to it.
darlegen to explain.
Darlegung *f.* explanation, exposition.
Darlehen *n.* loan.
DARÜBER (drüber) 1. *adv.* over it, above it,
about it.

Darüber besteht kein Zweifel. There is no doubt
about that.
darüber hinaus beyond that.
2. *conj.* meanwhile.
DARUM (drum) round it, for it, about it.
Ich kann mich nicht darum kümmern. I can't
take care of that.
DARUNTER (drunter) under it, underneath, among
them, by that.
Was verstehen Sie darunter? What do you mean
by that?
DAS 1. *neuter article (nom. and acc.).* the.
2. *demons. pron.* that.
3. *rel. pron.* which, that.
das jenige das the one which.
dasselbe the same.
dasein to exist, be present.
Dasein *n.* existence, life.
Kämpf für das Dasein struggle for life.
DASS *conj.* that.
dass doch if only.
Datum *n.* date.
Dauer *f.* length, duration.
auf die Dauer for long.
DAUERN to last, continue
lange dauern to take a long time.
Dauerwelle *f.* permanent wave.
Daumen *m.* thumb.
DAVON for it, from this, from that, of it, of that.
Was halten Sie davon? What do you think of it?
Geben Sie mir ein Paar davon. Give me a pair
of them.
Das hängt davon ab. It depends.
DAVOR in front of it, of it, of that.
Sie stehen direkt davor. They stand right in
front of it.
DAZU to it, for it, for that purpose.
Es ist schon zu spät dazu. It is already too late
for that.
dazu gehören to belong to it.
dazu tun to add to.
dazwischen in between.
Decke *f.* cover, blanket.
Deckel *m.* cover, lid.
DECKEN to protect, cover, guard, secure.
Deckung *f.* cover, shelter, protection.
in Deckung gehen to take cover.
Defekt *m.* defect, deficiency.
Degen *m.* sword.
DEIN *(poss. adj. fam. form.)* your.
DEIN(er, e, es) *(poss. pron. fam. form.)* yours.
DEM *dat. sing of der and das* to the, to this, to
whom, to which.
demnach then.
demnächst soon, shortly.
demzufolge accordingly.
Wie dem auch sei be that as it may.
Demokrat *m.* democrat.
Demokratie *f.* democracy.

Demut *f.* humility.

demütig humble.

demütigen to humiliate.

Demütigung *f.* humiliation.

DEN *acc. sing. of* der; *dat. pl. of* die. the, this, to them, whom, that.

DENEN *dat. pl. of* die *(rel. pron.)* to whom, to which.

DENKEN to think, intend, mean.
Was denken Sie zu tun? What do you intend to do?
denken an to remember, think of.
sich denken to imagine.
Das kann ich mir schon denken. I can well imagine.

Denker *m.* thinker.

DENN for, because, then.
es sei denn, dass unless.

dennoch nevertheless.

deponieren to deposit.

DER 1. *masc. article (nom.)* the; *fem. (gen. & dat.)* of the, to the; *pl. (gen.)* of the.
2. *demons. pron.* this.
3. *rel. pron.* which, who, that.
derjenige der the one who, he who.
derselbe the same.

DEREN *gen. fem. and pl. of* die, *(rel. pron.)* whose.

DES *gen. sing. of* der *and* das of the.

DESHALB therefore, for that reason.

DESSEN *gen. sing. of* der *and* das *pron.* whose.

Detektiv *m.* detective.

deuten to point out, explain, interpret.

deutlich distinct, clear; distinctly, clearly.

Deutlichkeit *f.* distinctness, clearness.

DEUTSCH German.

DEUTSCHE *m. & f.* German (person)

DEUTSCHLAND *n.* Germany.

Deutung *f.* interpretation, explanation.

Devise *f.* foreign bill, motto.

DEZEMBER *m.* December.

Dialekt *m.* dialect.

Diamant *m.* diamond.

Diät *f.* diet.
Diät leben to diet.

DICH *acc. of* du. (fam. form) you.

DICHT thick, dense, tight, close.

dichten to compose, write poetry, invent.

Dichter *m.* poet.

Dichtung *f.* poetry, fiction.

DICK thick, stout, fat.
Er ist dick geworden. He got fat.

Dickkopf *m.* blockhead.

DIE 1. *fem. article (nom. and acc.),* the.
pl. article (nom. and acc.). the.
2. *demons. pron.* this.
3. *rel. pron.* who, which, that.
diejenige die she who, the one which.
dieselbe the same.

DIEB *m.* thief, burglar.
Halten Sie den Dieb! Stop the thief!

DIENEN to serve.
Womit kann ich dienen? Can I help you?

Diener *m.* servant.

Dienerin *f.* maid.

dienlich serviceable.

Dienst *m.* service, duty, situation, employment.
ausser Dienst off duty.
zu Diensten stehen to be at a person's disposal.

DIENSTAG *m.* Tuesday.

Dienstbutenzimmer *n.* servant's room.

diensteifrig zealous.

Dienstmädchen *n.* maid.

Dienstselle *f.* headquarters.

DIES(er,-e,-es) this, that.

DIESMAL this time.

DIESSEITS *(gen.)* on this side.

Diktat *n.* dictation, treaty.

DING *n.* thing, object.
guter Dinge sein to be in high spirits.
vor allen Dingen first of all.

Diplom *n.* diploma, certificate.

Diplomatie *f.* diplomacy.

diplomatisch diplomatic.

DIR *dat. of* du *(fam. form)* you, to you.

direkt direct

Direktor *m.* director.

Dirigent *m.* conductor.

dirigieren to conduct, direct.

diskret discreet, tactful.

Diskretion *f.* discretion.

diskutieren to discuss.

Distanz *f.* distance.

DOCH however, anyway, nevertheless, but, still, yet; surely, of course, yes(in answer to a negative question); indicates a well-known fact.
Willst du nicht kommen? Doch. Won't you come? Of course.
Habe ich doch gewusst, dass er schwer krank war. I knew (very well) he was very ill.
Ich werde doch gehen. I will go anyhow.
Ja doch! of course.
Sie werden doch zugeben, dass er recht hatte. But you will admit he was right.
Und doch ist es nicht so traurig, wie Sie denken. And still it is not so sad as you think.

DOKTOR *m.* doctor.
den Doktor machen to take the degree of doctor.

Doktorarbeit *f.* thesis for doctorate.

Dokument *n.* document.

dokumentieren to prove.

Dolch *m.* dagger.

dolmetschen to interpret.

Dolmetscher *m.* interpreter.

Dom *m.* cathedral.

Donner *m.* thunder.
vom Donner gerührt thunderstruck.

donnern to thunder.

Donnerschlag *m.* thunderbolt.

DONNERSTAG *m.* Thursday.

Donnerwetter *n.* thunderstorm.

    Donnerwetter! Good heavens!

doppeldeutig ambiguous.

Doppelpunkt *m.* colon.

doppelt double.

    Doppelbett, *n.* double bed.

    Doppelzimmer, *n.* room with twin beds.

DORF *n.* village.

Dorn *m.* thorn.

DORT there, yonder.

    dorther from there.

    dorthin there, that way, over there.

Dose *f.* box, can, dose, amount.

DRAHT *m.* wire, cable, line.

drängen to push, press, hurry, urge.

    Nicht drängen! Do not push!

draussen outside, outdoors, abroad.

drehen to turn, rotate, revolve.

DREI three.

Dreieck *n.* triangle.

DREISSIG thirty.

DREISSIGSTE thirtieth.

DREIZEHN thirteen.

DREIZEHNTE thirteenth.

dringen to enter, get in, penetrate.

    dringen auf to insist on.

dringend urgent.

DRITTE third.

Droge *f.* drug.

Drogerie *f.* chemist's shop.

drüben over there, yonder.

Druck *m.* pressure, compression.

    in Druck gehen to go to press.

drucken to print.

Druckknopf *m.* push button.

Drukfehler *m.* misprint.

Dschungel *f.* jungle.

DU *pers. pron. fam. form.* you.

    auf du und du stehen to be on intimate terms.

Duft *m.* scent, smell, fragrance.

DUFTEN to smell sweet, be fragrant.

duftig sweet-smelling, fragrant.

dulden to endure, bear, suffer.

dumm stupid, dull, ignorant.

    Sei nicht so dumm! Don't be so stupid!

    Es wurde mir zu dumm. I got sick and
    tired of it.

Dummheit *f.* stupidity, blunder.

Dummkopf *m.* stupid fellow, dunce.

düngen to fertilize.

Dünger *m.* fertilizer, manure.

dunkel dark, gloomy, vaguely.

    Ich erinnere mich dunkel... I vaguely
    remember...

Dunkelheit *f.* darkness, obscurity.

dunkeln to get dark.

DÜNN thin, weak, rare.

DURCH 1. *prep. (acc.)* through, across, by, by

means of, because of.

    Durch den Krieg wurden viele Städte
    zerstört. Many cities were destroyed because
    of the war.

    Er bestand die Prüfung durch viel Arbeit.
    He passed the examination by working hard.
    (through much work.)

    Er schickt es durch die Post. He sends it
    by post.

    Ich ging durch den Wald. I walked through
    the forest.

    die ganze Zeit durch all the time.

    durch und durch through and through.

2. *prefix.*

    a) *inseparable.* through, across, around.

    Die Milchstrasse durchzieht den Himmel. The
    milky way goes across the sky.

    b) *separable.* implies the idea of accomplishment.

    Ich lese das Buch durch. I read the book to
    the end.

durcharbeiten to work through, study thoroughly.

durchaus thoroughly, absolutely.

    durchaus nicht not at all, not in the least.

durcheinander confusedly, in disorder.

durchfahren to drive through.

Durchfahrt *f.* thoroughfare, passage.

    Keine Durchfahrt! No thoroughfare!

durchfechten to fight out.

durchfinden to find one's way through.

durchführbar to carry out, accomplish, execute.

Durchfuhrung *f.* accomplishment, execution,

Durchführung *f.* accomplishment, execution,
    performance.

Durchgang *m.* passageway.

    Kein Durchgang! No trespassing!

durchgehen to go through, pass through, run away.

durchhalten to hold out, carry through.

durchmachen to go through, suffer.

    Sie haben viel durchgemacht. They have gone
    through a lot.

Durchmesser *m.* diameter.

durchnehmen to work through, go over.

Durchreise *f.* journey through, passing through,
    transit.

durchreisen to travel through, cross.

Durchreisevisum *n.* transit visa.

durchschauen to look through.

Durchschlag *m.* collander, strainer, carbon copy.

durchschlagend powerful.

Durchschlagpapier *n.* carbon paper.

durchschneiden to cut through.

durchsetzen to achieve.

durchsuchen to search through.

Durchsuchung *f.* search, police raid.

durchtrieben cunning, sly, artful.

Durchzug *m.* march through, passage through.

DÜRFEN to be allowed to, be permitted.

    Darf ich, bitte? May I, please?

    Darf ich um den nächsten Tanz bitten? May I
    have the next dance?

Darf man hier rauchen? Is smoking allowed here?

dürftig poor, needy, indigent.

DÜRR dry, parched, dried, lean, skinny.

dürres Holz dry wood.

DÜRRE *f.* dryness, drought.

Durst *m.* thirst.

Das macht Durst. That makes (one) thirsty.

dürsten to be thirsty, long for, crave.

durstig thirsty.

Dusche *f.* shower-bath.

duschen (sich) to take a shower.

Dutzend *n.* dozen.

dutzendmal dozens of times.

E

Ebbe *f.* ebb, low tide.

die Ebbe und die Flut the ebb and flow.

EBEN even, flat, smooth.

eben erst just now.

eben deshalb for that very reason.

ebenfalls likewise, too, also.

ebenmässig symmetrical, proportional.

ebenso just as, just so, quite as.

zu ebener Erde on the ground floor.

Ebene *f.* plain.

ebnen to level, smooth.

Echo *n.* echo.

ECHT genuine, true, real, legitimate.

Echtheit *f.* legitimacy.

Ecke *f.* corner, angle.

eckig triangular, cornered.

edel noble, well-born, generous.

Efeu *n.* ivy.

Effekt *m.* effect, stocks.

Effekthascherei *f.* showing off.

effektvoll effective.

Egoismus *m.* egoism.

Egoist *m.* egoist.

egoistisch egoistic.

egozentrisch egocentric.

EHE before, until.

ehemals formerly.

eher sooner, rather.

Ehe *f.* matrimony, marriage.

Ehefrau *f.* wife, spouse.

Ehegatte *m.* husband.

Ehepaar *n.* married couple.

ehelich matrimonial, conjugal.

Ehescheidung *f.* divorce.

Ehescheidungsklage *f.* divorce suit.

Eheschliessung *f.* marriage.

EHRE *f.* honor, reputation, respect.

Meine Ehre steht auf dem Spiel. My honor is at stake.

ehren to honor.

ehrenamtlich honorary.

Ehrenbezeigung *f.* mark of respect.

Ehrenwort *n.* word of honor.

ehrerbietig respectful.

Ehrerbietung *f.* deference, respect.

Ehrfurcht *f.* respect, awe, reverence.

Ehrgefühl *n.* sense of honor, self-respect.

Ehrgeiz *m.* ambition.

ehrgeizig ambitious.

Ehrlichkeit *f.* honesty.

Ehrlosigkeit *f.* dishonesty, infamy.

EI *n.* (*pl.* Eier) egg.

Eigelb *n.* egg yolk.

Eiweiss *n.* egg white.

Rühreier scrambled eggs.

Spiegeleier fried eggs.

Weiche Eier soft-boiled eggs.

Eiche *f.* oak.

Eichhörnchen *n.* squirrel.

Eifer *m.* zeal, ardor.

Eifersucht *f.* jealousy.

eifersüchtig jealous.

eifrig eager, keen, zealous.

EIGEN own, proper, particular, special, choosy.

Er ist sehr eigen im Essen. He is very fussy about his food.

eigenartig odd, peculiar, strange, queer.

eigensinnig stubborn, obstinate.

eigentlich real, actual; actually, really, exactly, just, as a matter of fact, indeed.

Was heisst das eigentlich? What does it actually mean?

Eigentum *n.* property.

eigentümlich queer, odd, peculiar.

eignen (sich) to be suited, qualified.

EILE *f.* hurry, haste, speed.

Es hat keine Eile. There's no hurry about it.

Eile mit Weile. Haste makes waste.

EILEN (sich) to hurry.

Das eilt sehr. This is very urgent.

Das eilt nicht. There's no hurry.

eilig fast, hasty.

es eilig haben to be in a hurry.

Eilzug *m.* fast train, express.

EIN, eine, ein 1. *indefinite article.* a, an.

2. *number.* one.

3. *pron.* one.

Eines Tages some day.

ein für allemal once for all.

4. *separable prefix* (implies the idea of entrance or reduction in volume).

Die Lehrerin trat in das Schulzimmer ein. The teacher (*fem.*) entered the classroom.

Läuft dieser Stoff ein? Does this material shrink?

EINANDER each other, one another.

Wir haben einander jahrelang nicht gesehen. We have not seen each other for years.

einarbeiten to get used to, familiarize with.

einatmen to inhale.

Einbahnstrasse *f.* one-way street.

einbiegen to turn into.

Biegen Sie in diese Strasse ein. Turn into

this street.

einbilden to imagine, fancy, think, believe.

Einbildung *f.* imagination, conceit, presumption.

einbrechen to break open, through.
　Heute Nacht ist ein Deibe bei ihm eingebrochen.
　Last night a thief broke into his house.

Einbrecher *m.* burglar.

Einbruch *m.* house-breaking, burglary.

EINDRUCK *m.* impression.
　Er tut es bloss, um Eindruck zu machen. He does it only to show off.

EINFACH simple, plain, single; simply, plainly, elementary.
　einfache (Fahrt) one-way (ticket).

Einfall *m.* falling down, collapse, idea, whim.
　Wie kommen Sie auf den Einfall? What gave you the idea?

einfältig simple.

Einfluss *m.* influence.

einflussreich influential.

Einfuhr *f.* importation, import.

einführen to introduce, import, inaugurate.

Einführung *f.* importation.

Einfuhrzoll *m.* import duty.

Eingabe *f.* petition, memorial.

EINGANG *m.* entrance.
　Kein Eingang. No entrance.
　Verbotener Eingang! Keep out!

eingeben to give, administer, inspire.

eingebildet imaginary.

Eingebung *f.* inspiration.

Eingemachte *n.* preserves, jam.

eingestehen to admit, confess.

eingewöhnen to accustom.

Einhalt *m.* stop.
　Einhalt gebieten to put a stop to.

einhalten to observe, follow, keep to, meet.
　Wird er den Termin einhalten? Will he meet the deadline?

Einhaltung *f.* observance.

Einheit *f.* unity, union, unit.

einheitlich uniform.

einholen to bring in, collect, gather, make up.
　einholen gehen to go shopping.

einig in agreement, united, unanimous.

einigemal several times.

einigen to come to terms, unite, unify.

Einig (-er, -e, -es) some, any, a few.

einigermassen to some extent, somewhat.

Einigkeit *f.* harmony.

Einigung *f.* agreement.

einjagen to alarm, frighten.

EINKAUF *m.* purchase, buying.

EINKAUFEN to buy, purchase, shop.
　Einkaufspreis, *m.* cost price.

Einkommen *n.* income.

Einkommensteuer *f.* income tax.

einladen to invite.

EINLADUNG *f.* invitation.

Einlass *m.* entrance, admission.

einlassen to admit, let in.

einleben to settle down, familiarize oneself.

einleiten to begin, initiate, introduce, institute.

Einleitung *f.* introduction.

einmachen to preserve.

Einmachglas *n.* preserves jar.

EINMAL once, formerly.
　auf einmal all at once.
　Es war einmal...Once upon a time there was...
　noch einmal once more.

einmengen to meddle with, interfere.

einmütig unanimous.

Einnahme *f.* occupation, capture, conquest.

einnehmen to engage, occupy, receive, collect, captivate.

einnehmend captivating.

einordnen to arrange, classify, file.

einpacken to wrap up.

einpflanzen to plant, inculcate.

einrahmen to frame.

einreden to persuade, talk someone into.

einreichen to hand in, deliver, present.

einreihen to insert, include, arrange.

Einreise *f.* entry into a country.

Einreiseerlaubnis *f.* permit to enter a country.

einrichten to arrange, prepare, manage, furnish.
　sich einrichten to plan.

Einrichtung *f.* furniture.

EINS one, the same.
　Es kommt auf eins hinaus. It comes to the same thing.

EINSAM lonely, solitary, lonesome.

Einsamkeit *f.* loneliness, solitude.

einschläfern to lull to sleep.

einschalten to insert, put in.

einschenken to pour in.

einschlafen to fall asleep.

einschlagen to drive in (nail), break, wrap up.
　Schlagen Sie mir das, bitte, ein. Will you please wrap that for me?

einschliessen to lock up, enclose.

einschliesslich inclusive.

Einschreibebrief *m.* registered letter.

einschreiben to enter, note down, register.

einschreiten to intervene, proceed.

einschüchtern to intimidate.

EINSEITIG one-sided, partial.

einsetzen to put it, insert.
　sich einsetzen für to speak on behalf of.

Einspruch *m.* protest, objection.
　Einspruch erheben to object to, protest against.

EINST once, one day.
　einstmals once, formerly.
　einstweilen meanwhile, for the present.
　einstweilig temporary.

einsteigen to get in.

Nach Düsseldorf einsteigen! (Passengers) to Düsseldorf, all aboard!

einstellen to put on, adjust, stop, cease.
Arbeit einstellen to strike.
Betrieb einstellen to close down.
sich einstellen auf to be prepared.

Einstellung *f.* adjustment, enlistment, attitude.
Ich verstehe Ihre Einstellung nicht. I don't understand your attitude.

einstimmen to join in.

einstimmig unanimous.

einstudieren to study, rehearse.

einteilen to divide, plan, distribute.

Einteilung *f.* division, distribution, arrangement.

eintönig monotonous.

Eintönigkeit *f.* monotony.

Eintracht *f.* harmony, union, concord.

eintreffen to arrive, happen.
Was ich befürchtete, ist eingetroffen. What I was afraid of has happened.

EINTRETEN to go in, enter.
Bitte, treten Sie ein! Won't you come in, please!
eintreten für to stand up for.
eintreten in to join.

EINTRITT entrance, entry.
Eintritt verboten! No admission!
Eintritt frei! Admission free!

Eintrittsgeld *n.* admission fee.

Eintrittskarte *f.* ticket.

EINVERSTANDEN agreed.
einverstanden sein to agree.

Einverständnis *n.* agreement, consent.

Einwand *m.* objection, protest.

einwandfrei faultless, perfect.

Einwanderer *m.* immigrant.

einwandern to immigrate.

Einwanderung *f.* immigration.

einwechseln to change money.

einwenden to object.

einwilligen to consent.

Einwilligung *f.* consent.

Einwurf *m.* slit, slot.

Einzahl *f.* singular.

einzahlen to pay in.

Einzahlung *f.* payment.

EINZELN individual, particular, separate, single.
Kann man jeden Band einzeln kaufen? Can I buy each volume separately?
jeder einzelne each and every one.

einziehen to pull in, draw, move in.
Sie sind schon in ihre neue Wohnung eingezogen. They have already moved into their new apartment.

EINZIG only, sole, unique.
einzig und allein solely, entirely.
Er ist das einzige Kind. He is the only child.

Einzug *m.* entry, entrance, moving in.

EIS *n.* ice, ice cream.
Eisbahn, *f.* rink.
Eisschrank, *m.* refrigerator.
eisig icy.

EISEN *n.* iron.
zum alten Eisen werfen to junk.

Eisenbahn *f.* railway.
Eisenbahnwagen, *m.* railway car.

Eisenwaren *pl.* hardware.

eisern(er-e,-es) of iron, inflexible.
der eiserne Vorhang the iron curtain.
Er hat einen eisernen Willen. He has an iron will.

eitel vain, conceited, idle.

Eitelkeit *f.* vanity, conceit.

Elefant *m.* elephant.

elegant elegant.

Eleganz *f.* elegance.

Elektriker *m.* electrician.

elektrisch electric.

elektrisieren to electrify.

Elektrizität *f.* electricity.

Element *n.* element.

elementar elementary.

Elend *n.* misery, misfortune, distress.

elend miserable, ill; miserably.

Elfenbein *n.* ivory.

ELFTE eleventh.

Ellenbogen *m.* elbow.

elterlich parental.

ELTERN *pl.* parents.

elternlos orphan.

Emigrant *m.* emigrant.

Empfang *m.* receipt, reception.

EMPFANGEN to receive, welcome.

Empfänger *m.* receiver, addressee.

empfänglich susceptible.

Empfangsnahme *f.* receipt (paper).

empfehlen to recommend.

empfinden to experience, feel, perceive.

empfindlich sensitive.

Empfindlichkeit *f.* sensitiveness.

empören to rouse, excite, shock.

Empörung *f.* rebellion.

ENDE *n.* end, result, conclusion, extremity.
am Ende in the end, after all.
Ende gut, alles gut. All is well that ends well.
letzten Endes finally.
zu Ende führen to finish.
zu Ende gehen to come to an end.

ENDEN to end, finish, stop, die.

Endergebnis *n.* final result.

endgültig final, definite.

endlos endless.

Endstation *f.* terminus.

Energie *f.* energy.

energisch energetic, vigorous.

ENG narrow, tight, close, intimate.
    engherzig narrow-minded.
engagieren to engage.
Engel m. angel.
Engländer m. Englishman.
Engländerin f. Englishwoman.
Englisch n. English.
    auf Englisch in English.
Enkel m. 1. ankle.
    2. grandson.
Enkelkind n. grandchild.
Enkeltochter f. (Enkelin) grandaughter.
entbehren to be without, lack, miss.
entbehrlich superfluous, spare.
Entbehrung f. privation, want.
entdecken to discover, find out, detect.
Entdecker m. discoverer.
Entdeckung f. discovery.
Ente f. duck.
entehren to dishonor.
enteignen to expropriate, dispossess.
Enteignung f. expropriation.
enterben to disinherit.
entfalten to unfold, develop, display.
entfernen to remove, take away, depart.
    sich entfernen to leave.
entfernt far off, far away, distant.
    nicht im entferntesten not in the least.
Entfernung f. distance.
entfliehen to run away, escape.
entfremden to estrange, alienate.
Entfremdung f. estrangement, alienation.
entführen to carry off, elope.
Entführung f. abduction, elopement, kidnapping.
entgegen toward, opposed to, contrary to.
entgegen arbeiten to work against, counteract.
entgegengehen to go to meet, face.
entgegengesetzt opposite.
entgegenhalten to object, contrast.
entgegenkommen to come to meet.
    auf halbem Weg entgegenkommen to meet halfway.
entgegenkommend obliging, kind, helpful.
entgegennehmen to accept, receive.
entgegensehen to look forward to, expect.
entgegensetzen (entgegenstellen) to oppose, contrast.
entgegentreten to advance toward, oppose.
entgegnen to reply, answer.
Entgegnung f. reply.
entgehen to escape, elude.
enthalten to contain, hold, include.
    enthalten sein to be included.
entkommen to escape.
entladen to unload, discharge.
Entladung f. discharge.
entlassen to dismiss.
Entlassung f. dismissal.

entledigen to get rid of, perform, execute.
entmutigen to discourage, dishearten.
entnehmen to take from, gather, understand.
enträtseln to solve, decipher.
entrüsten to provoke, irritate, make angry.
Entrüstung f. anger, indignation.
entsagen to renounce, abandon.
    dem Thron entsagen to abdicate.
entschädigen to compensate.
Entschädigung f. compensation.
Entscheid m. answer.
entscheiden to decide, make up one's mind.
    Entscheiden Sie das. You decide that.
entscheidend decisive, critical.
Entscheidung f. decision, judgment, sentence. award.
entschieden decided, firm, resolute.
Entschiedenheit f. determination, certainty.
entschliessen to decide, make up one's mind.
    Ich habe mich anders entschlossen.
    I've changed my mind.
Entschlossenheit f. determination.
Entschluss m. resolution, decision.
entschuldbar excusable.
ENTSCHULDIGEN to excuse.
    Entschuldigen Sie, bitte! Please excuse me!
    Ich bitte vielmals um Entschuldigung.
    I am awfully sorry.
    sich entschuldigen to apologize.

entschwinden to vanish, disappear.
entsetzen to dismiss from, relieve, frighten.
entsetzlich terrible, dreadful.
entsinnen to remember, recollect, recall.
entspannen to relax.
Entspannung f. relaxation, rest, recreation.
entstehen to arise, originate.
Entstehung f. rise, origin, formation.
entstellen to distort, misrepresent.
enttäuschen to disappoint.
Enttäuschung f. disappointment.
ENTWEDER...ODER either...or.
entwerfen to draw up, design.
entwerten to depreciate, cancel.
ENTWICKELN to develop, explain.
    einen Film entwickeln to develop a film (photographic).
Entwicklung f. development.
Entwicklungsjahre pl. adolescence.
entwürdigen to degrade, disgrace.
Entwurf m. sketch, draft.
entziehen to deprive of, take away from, withdraw.

entzücken to delight, charm, enchant.
entzückend charming, delightful.
entzwei in two, torn, broken.
entzweien to estrange, alienate.
Episode f. episode.
Epoche f. epoch, era.

ER he.

er selbst himself.

erarbeiten (sich) to get through hard work.

erbarmen to feel pity, have mercy.

erbärmlich pitiful, miserable.

erbarmungslos merciless, pitiless.

Erbe *m.* heir.

Erbe *n.* heritage, inheritance.

erben to inherit.

Erbfolge *f.* succession.

erblassen to turn pale.

erblicken to catch sight of, perceive.

erbrechen to break open, vomit.

Erbschaft *f.* inheritance, legacy.

Erbse *f.* pea.

Erbstück *n.* heirloom.

Erbteil *n.* portion of inheritance.

Erdbeben *n.* earthquake.

Erdbeere *f.* strawberry.

Erdboden *m.* ground, soil, earth.

ERDE *f.* earth, ground, soil.

auf der Erde on earth.

Erdgeschoss *n.* ground floor.

zu ebener Erde on the ground floor.

Erdkunde *f.* geography.

erdolchen to stab.

Erdteil *m.* continent.

ereignen to happen, occur, pass.

Wann hat sich das ereignet? When did that
happen?

Ereignis *n.* event, occurrence, incident.

erfahren to learn, experience.

Erfahrung *f.* experience, information.

Wo kann ich das erfahren? Where can I get this
information?

aus Erfahrung by experience.

erfahrungsgemäss from experience.

erfinden to find out, discover, invent.

Erfinder *m.* inventor .

Erfindung *f.* invention.

Erfolg *m.* success, result, outcome.

erfolgen to result, follow.

erfolglos unsuccessful, fruitless.

erfolgreich successful.

erforderlich necessary, requisite.

erforschen to explore, investigate.

Erforschung *f.* exploration, investigation.

ERFREUEN to give pleasure, gladden, be
pleased, rejoice.

erfreulich delightful, gratifying, satisfactory.

erfreulicherweise fortunately.

ERFREUT glad, pleased, delighted.

Sehr erfreut (in social introductions). How do
you do? (Delighted.)

erfrieren to die of cold, freeze to death.

erfrischen to refresh.

Erfrischung *f.* refreshment.

ergänzen to complete, restore.

Ergänzung *f.* completion, restoration.

ergeben to produce, yield, result in.

ergeben devoted.

Ihr ergebener yours faithfully.

ergiebig productive.

ergreifen to seize, take hold of.

ergreifend moving, touching.

ergriffen moved, touched.

Ergriffenheit *f.* emotion.

erhalten to receive, obtain, preserve.

Erhalter *m.* supporter.

erhältlich obtainable.

Erhaltungszustand *m.* condition, state of
preservation.

erheben to raise, lift up, collect.

erhebend elevating, impressive.

erheblich considerable.

Erhebung *f.* raising, elevation, revolt.

erhitzen to heat, warm.

erholen to recover, get better.

Erholung *f.* recovery, rest, recreation.

ERINNERN to remind.

Erinneren Sie mich später daran. Remind me
about it later.

sich erinnern an to remember, recall.

Ich kann mich nicht mehr daran erinnern. I
can't remember it any more.

Erinnerung *f.* rememberance, recollection, memory.

Erinnerung wachrufen to evoke memories.

zur Erinnerung in memory of.

erkälten to chill.

sich erkälten to catch a cold.

erkämpfen to win by fighting.

erkennbar recognizable.

ERKENNEN to recognize, perceive, realize.

zu erkennen geben to show, indicate.

sich zu erkennen geben to make oneself known.

erkenntlich recognizable, grateful.

Erkenntnis *f.* knowledge, perception, understanding.

ERKLÄREN to explain, account for, declare.

ERKLÄRUNG *f.* explanation, interpretation,
declaration.

erkranken to fall ill, be taken ill.

Erkrankung *f.* illness.

erkundigen to inquire, make inquiries.

Erkundigung *f.* inquiry.

ERLAUBEN to allow, permit, presume.

Erlauben Sie, bitte! Allow me, please!

Erlaubnis *f.* permission, leave, license.

erleben to experience.

Erlebnis *n.* event.

erledigen to carry through, wind up, dispatch.

erledigt sein to be dead tired.

erleichtern to facilitate, ease, relieve.

Erleichterung *f.* facilitation, relief.

erlogen false, untrue, fabricated.

erlösen to save, redeem, deliver.

Erlösung *f.* redemption, release, deliverance.

ermächtigen to empower, authorize.

Ermahnung *f.* exhortation, admonition.

ermässigen to reduce, abate.

Emässigte Preise reduced prices.

ermöglichen to make possible, enable.

ermorden to murder, assassinate.

Ermordung *f.* murder, assassination.

emüden to tire out, weary.

Ermüdung *f.* fatigue, weariness.
ermutigen to encourage.
ernähren to nourish, feed, support.
Ernährung *f.* nourishment, food, support, maintenance.
ernennen to nominate, appoint.
Ernennung *f.* nomination, appointment.
erneuern to renew, renovate, replace.
Erneuerung *f.* renewal, renovation.
erniedrigen to humiliate, depress.
Erniedrigung *f.* humiliation, degradation.
ERNST serious, severe, grave; seriously.
    Sie nimmt die Sache ernst. She takes the matter seriously.
    ernst meinen to be serious about something.
Ernst *m.* seriousness, earnestness, gravity.
    Ernst machen mit to put into practice.
    Ernstfall, *m.* emergency.
Ernte *f.* harvest, crop.
Erntearbeit *f.* harvesting.
ernten to harvest.
erobern to conquer, capture.
eröffnen to open, start, disclose.
erörtern to discuss.
Erörterung *f.* discussion.
erpressen to extort, blackmail.
Erpressung *f.* extortion, blackmail.
erraten to guess.
erregbar excitable, irritable.
erregen to excite, stir up.
Erregung *f.* excitement, agitation.
erreichbar attainable, within reach.
erreichen to reach, attain, get.
ERSATZ *m.* substitute, equivalent, spare.
    Ersatzreifen *m.* spare tire.
    Ersatzteil *m.* spare part.
erschaffen to create, produce.
Erschaffung *f.* creation.
erscheinen to appear, come out.
Erscheinung *f.* appearance, figure, apparition.
erschiessen to shoot; to kill by shooting.
Erschiessung *f.* execution by gunfire.
erschöpfen to exhaust.
    erschöpfend exhaustive.
Erschöpfung *f.* exhaustion.
erschrecken to frighten.
erschrocken frightened.
erschüttern to shake, upset, shock.
    Die Nachricht hat uns erschüttert. We were shocked by the news.
erschweren to make more difficult, aggravate.
ersetzen to replace, compensate, restore.
ersparen to save, economize.
ERST first, at first, only.
    der erste beste the first that comes.
    eben erst just now.
    erst als not till.
    erst recht nicht certainly not.
    Zum ersten, zum zweiten, zum dritten! Going, going, gone!
Erstaufführung *f.* opening night.
erstaunen to astonish.

erstaunlich astonishing.
erstenmal (zum) for the first time.
erstens firstly.
erstgeboren first-born.
ersticken to suffocate.
erstmalig first, for the first time.
Ertrag *m.* produce, yield, profit, returns.
erträglich bearable, endurable.
ertränken to drown.
ertrinken to be drowned.
erübrigen to save, spare.
erwachen to awake.
erwachsen to grow up.
    die Erwachsenen the grown-ups, adults.
erwägen to consider, weigh.
erwähnen to mention.
ERWARTEN to wait for, await, expect.
Erwartung *f.* expectation, hope.
    in Erwartung Ihrer Antwort looking forward to your reply.
erwartungsvoll expectant, full of hope.
erweitern to widen, expand.
Erweiterung *f.* widening, expansion.
Erwerb *m.* acquisition, gain, profit.
erwerben to acquire, gain.
erwerbslos unemployed, out of work.
Erwerbslosenunterstützung *f.* unemployment relief.
ERZÄHLEN to tell, relate, narrate.
Erzählung *f.* story, tale, narrative.
erzeugen to breed, produce, procreate.
Erzeugnis *n.* product.
    Deutsches Erzeugnis. Made in Germany.
Erzeugung *f.* procreation, production.
erziehen to raise, educate, train.
erzieherisch educational.
Erziehung *f.* education, upbringing.
Erziehungswesen *n.* educational system.
erzürnen to get angry.
erzwingen to force, extort.
ES it.
essbar edible.
ESSEN to eat, dine.
Essen *n.* food, dinner, meal.
Essenszeit *f.* mealtime.
Essig *m.* vinegar.
Esslöffel *m.* tablespoon.
Esswaren *pl.* provisions, victuals.
Esszimmer *n.* dining room.
Etage *f.* floor.
Etagenwohnung *f.* flat.
ETWA nearly, about, by chance.
ETWAS some, something, any, anything, a bit, somewhat.
EUCH *acc. and dat.* of ihr (fam. form pl.) you, to you.
EUER *poss. adj.* (fam. pl. form) your.
EUER(ER, -E, -ES) *poss. pron.* (pl. fam. form) yours.
euerseits on your part.
euresgleichen like you, of your kind.
euretwegen for your sake, on account of you.
Europa *n.* Europe.

evakuieren to evacuate.
evangelisch Protestant.
Evangelium *n.* Gospel.
EWIG eternal, forever, all the time.
Ewigkeit *f.* eternity.
exakt exact.
Examen *n.* examination.
Examensarbeit *f.* thesis, paper.
examinieren to examine.
Excellenz *f.* Excellency.
Exemplar *n.* sample.
exemplarisch exemplary.
exerzieren to drill.
Existenz *f.* existence.
existieren to exist, live.
Experiment *n.* experiment.
experimentieren to experiment.
Export *m.* export.
Exporteur *m.* exporter.
exportieren to export.
Extrablatt *n.* special edition.
Extrakt *m.* extract.
exzentrisch eccentric.

F

Fabel *f.* fable, story, plot.
fabelhaft fabulous.
Fabrik *f.* factory, mill, plant.
Fabrikanlage *f.* plant.
Fabrikant *m.* manufacturer.
Fabrikarbeiter *m.* factory worker.
Fabrikat *n.* product (manufactured).
Fabrikation *f.* making.
fabrizieren to manufacture.
Fach *n.* compartment, shelf, drawer.
    Was ist Ihr Fach? What's your line?
Fächer *m.* fan.
Fachkenntnis *f.* technical knowledge.
Fachmann *m.* expert, specialist.
Fackel *f.* torch.
Faden *m,* thread.
    an einem Faden hängen to hang by a thread.
FÄHIG able.
    fähig sein to be able, capable.
Fähigkeit *f.* capability.
Fahne *f.* flag, banner.
Fahnenflucht *f.* desertion.
Fahnenflüchtige *m.* deserter.
Fahrbahn *f.* road, track.
fahrbar passable, navigable.
Fähre *f.* ferry.
FAHREN to drive, ride, go, travel.
    Fahren Sie rechts! Keep to the right!
    Fahrendes Volk *n.* tramps.
    mit dem Schiff fahren to sail.
    spazieren fahren to go for a ride.
Fahrer *m.* driver.
Fahrgast *m.* passenger.
Fahrgeld *n.* fare.
Fahrkarte *f.* ticket (transportation).
Fahrkartenschalter *m.* ticket window.

fahrlässig careless, negligent.
Fahrlässigkeit *f.* carelessness, negligence.
Fahrplan *m.* timetable.
    fahrplanmässig on schedule.
Fahrrad *n.* bicycle.
Fahrschein *m.* transportation ticket (bus).
Fahrstrasse *f.* highway.
Fahrstuhl *m.* lift, elevator.
    Fahrstuhlführer, *m.* elevator boy, attendant.
FAHRT *f.* ride, journey, trip.
    Hin-und Rückfahrt round trip.
    in voller Fahrt at full speed.
    Was kostet die Fahrt, bitte? How much is the fare, please?
Fahrzeug *n.* vehicle, vessel.
Fakultät *f.* faculty.
FALL *m.* fall, drop, case, accident.
    auf jeden Fall, auf alle Fälle in any case.
    auf keinen Fall! On no account!
    Gesetzt den Fall dass... Supposing that...
Falle *f.* trap.
FALLEN to fall.
    fallen lassen to let fall, drop.
    im Felde fallen to be killed in action.
    in den Rücken fallen to attack from behind.
    in Ohnmacht fallen to faint.
    Das Fest fällt auf einen Sonntag. The holiday falls on a Sunday.
    Das fällt nicht weiter ins Gewicht. That is of no further consequence.
falls in case, in the event.
Fallschirm *m.* parachute.
FALSCH wrong, incorrect, false.
    Sie hat falsche Zähne. She has false teeth.
    Das Geld ist falsch. The money is counterfeit.
    falsch verstehen to misunderstand.
fälschen to falsify, forge.
Fälscher *m.* forger.
Falschheit *f.* falseness, falsehood.
Falschspieler *m.* cheat (at cards).
Fälschung *f.* forgery.
Falte *f.* pleat, fold, wrinkle.
falten to fold.
familiär familiar, intimate.
FAMILIE *f.* family.
Familienname *m.* last name.
Fanatiker *m.* fanatic.
Fang *m.* catch, capture, prey.
fangen to catch, capture.
FARBE *f.* color, paint.
    farbenblind color blind.
färben to color, dye.
    sich die Haare färben to dye one's hair.
farbig colored.
farblos colorless, pale.
Fasching *m.* carnival.
Fass *n.* barrel, cask.
    Das schlägt dem Fass den Boden aus. That's the last straw.
Fassade *f.* front (of a building).
FASSEN to catch, seize, hold, apprehend, grasp,

comprehend.
Fassen Sie sich kurz! Make it short!
ins Auge fassen to consider.
Fassung *f.* setting, composure.
aus der Fassung bringen to upset, disconcert.
fast almost, nearly.
faul lazy, rotten, lazy.
Das ist eine faule Sache. This is a shady business.
faulen to rot, be lazy.
Faulheit laziness.
Faulpelz *m.* idler, lazybones.
Faust *f.* fist.
auf eigene Faust on one own's responsibility.
faustdick hinter den Ohren haben to be sly.
Fausthandschuh *m.* mitten; boxing glove.
FEBRUAR *m.* February.
FEDER *f.* pen, feather.
Federhalter *m.* penholder.
federleicht light as a feather.
Federvieh *n.* poultry.
Fee *f.* fairy.
feenhaft fairylike.
fegen to sweep.
Fehl *m.* blame.
fehl wrong.
fehl am Platze sein to be out of place.
Fehlbetrag *m.* deficit.
FEHLEN to miss, make a mistake, lack, be absent.
es an nichts fehlen lassen to spare no pains.
Sie werden mir sehr fehlen. I'll miss you very much.
Was fehlt Ihnen? What's the matter with you?
FEHLER *m.* fault, defect, mistake, blunder.
Das ist mein Fehler. That is my fault.
Fehlgriff *m.* mistake.
Fehlschlag failure.
Feier *f.* festival, celebration, ceremony, party.
feierlich solemn, festive, ceremonious.
Feierlichkeit *f.* solemnity, ceremony.
feiern to celebrate.
Sie feiern ihre goldene Hochzeit. They are celebrating their golden anniversary.
Feierstunde *f.* leisure hour, festive hour.
Feiertag *m.* holiday.
feige cowardly.
Feigheit *f.* cowardice.
feil for sale, mercenary.
feil bieten to offer for sale.
feil halten to have for sale.
FEIN fine, thin, delicate, refined, distinguished, elegant.
Feind *m.* enemy.
feindlich hostile.
feinfühlig sensitive.
Feingefühl *n.* tact.
Feinheit *f.* fineness, grace, elegance, refinement, subtlety.
Feinschmecker *m.* gourmet.
FELD *n.* field, plain, ground, square.

Schlachtfeld, *n.* battlefield.
Feldstecher *m.* binoculars.
Feldzug *m.* campaign.
Fell *n.* skin, hide, coat, fur (animals).
Diese Katze hat ein schönes Fell. This cat has a beautiful fur.
Fels *m.* rock, cliff.
felsenfest firm as a rock.
felsig rocky, craggy.
FENSTER *n.* window.
Fensterbank *f.* window-sill.
Fensterflügel *m.* window-sash.
Fensterrahmen *m.* window-frame.
Fensterscheibe *f.* window pane.
Ferien *pl.* holidays, vacation.
FERN far, distant, remote.
von fern from afar, from a distance.
Ferne *f.* distance.
ferner further, furthermore, besides.
Ferngespräch *n.* long-distance phone call.
Fernglas *n.* binoculars, field glass.
fernmündlich by telephone, over the telephone.
Das Telegramm wurde mir fernmündlich durchgegeben. The telegram was given to me over the phone.
Fernsehen *n.* television.
Fernsprechbuch *n.* telephone directory.
Fernsprecher *m.* telephone.
Fernsprechstelle *f.* telephone booth.
FERTIG ready, ready-made, finished, done.
fertigbringen to bring about, accomplish.
sich fertig machen to get ready.
Werden Sie damit fertig werden? Will you be able to manage this by yourself?
FEST *n.* festival, feast.
FEST firm, hard, rigid, steady, solid, stiff, stable, firmly, stiffly, fully.
eine feste Stellung a permanent post.
fester Schlaf sound sleep.
festbinden to tie, bind, fasten.
Festessen *n.* banquet.
festfahren to get stuck.
Festhalle *f.* banqueting hall.
festhalten to hold tight.
festigen to make firm.
Festigkeit *f.* solidity, firmness.
festlegen to fix, lay down, invest.
festlich festive, solemn.
Festlichkeit *f.* festivity.
festmachen to fasten, attach, fix, settle.
Festnahme *f.* arrest, seizure.
festsetzen to fix, set, settle.
Der Preis wird auf hundert Mark festgesetzt. The price has been fixed at one hundred marks.
festsitzen to be stuck, fit tightly.
Festspiel *n.* festival performance.
Feststellung *f.* statement, determination, identification.
Festtag *m.* holiday, feast.
Festung *f.* fortress, stronghold.

FETT fat, plump, fertile, rich, greasy.
Fett *n.* grease, fat.
fettig fatty, greasy.
Fetzen *m.* rag, scrap.
FEUCHT damp, humid, muggy.
FEUER *n.* fire, firing, bombardment.
   Feuer! Fire!
   Feuer fangen to catch fire.
   Feuer geben to give a light.
feuerfest fireproof.
Feuergefahr *f.* danger of fire.
feuergefährlich inflammable.
Feuerlöscher *m.* fire-extinguisher.
Feuerung *f.* fuel.
Feuerversicherung *f.* fire insurance.
Feuerwache *f.* fire station.
Feuerwerk *n.* firework.
Feuerzeug *n.* lighter.
Fieber *n.* fever, temperature.
   Fieber messen to take the temperature.
fieberhaft feverish.
Fiebermesser *n.* thermometer.
fiebern to be feverish, have a temperature.
Fieberthermometer *n.* clinical thermometer.
Fieberwahn *m.* delirium.
Figur *f.* figure, form, shape.
Filiale *f.* branch.
FILM *m.* film, picture, movie.
Filmaufnahme *f.* shooting of film.
filmen to film.
Filmstreifen *m.* filmstrip.
Filter *m.* filter.
filtern to filter, strain.
Filz *m.* felt.
filzig stingy.
Finanz *f.* finance.
Finanzamt *n.* revenue office.
finanziell financial.
finanzieren to finance, support.
FINDEN to find, discover, meet with, think, consider.
Finder *m.* finder.
findig clever, ingenious.
Findigkeit *f.* cleverness.
FINGER *m.* finger.
Fingerabdruck *m.* fingerprint.
Fingerfertigkeit *f.* dexterity, skill.
Fingerhut *m.* thimble.
Fingerspitze *f.* tip of the finger.
Fingerspitzengefühl *n.* flair.
Fingerzeig *m.* hint, tip.
finster dark, gloomy, obscure.
Finte *f.* feint, trick.
Firma *f.* firm, business.
FISCH *m.* fish.
FISCHEN to fish.
Fischer *m.* fisherman
Fischerei *f.* fishing, fishery.
Fischgräte *f.* fish-bone.
Fischhändler *m.* fishmonger.
FLACH flat, plain, level.

Fläche *f.* surface, plain, area.
Flachland *n.* flat country, plain.
Flagge *f.* flag.
flaggen to deck with flags.
Flamme *f.* flame.
FLASCHE *f.* bottle.
Flaschenbier *n.* bottled bier.
Flaschenhals *m.* neck of a bottle.
Flaschenöffner *m.* bottle opener.
flatterhaft fickle, inconsistent.
Flatterhaftigkeit *f.* fickleness.
flattern to flutter, wave.
FLECK *m.* place, spot, stain.
   vom Fleck kommen to get on, make headway.
Flecken *m.* spot, stain.
fleckenlos spotless.
fleckig spotted, stained.
Flegel *m.* boor, impertinent person.
flegelhaft rude, insolent.
Flegeljahre *pl.* teens.
flehen to implore, beseech.
flehentlich fervent.
FLEISCH *n.* flesh, meat, pulp.
Fleischbrühe *f.* meat broth.
Fleischer *m.* butcher.
fleischig fleshy, plump.
fleischlos meatless.
FLEISS *m.* diligence, industry.
   mit Fleiss on purpose.
fleissig diligent, industrious.
flicken to patch, mend, repair.
Flieder *m.* lilac.
Fliege *f.* fly.
FLIEGEN to fly, rush.
   in die Luft fliegen to blow up.
Flieger *m.* airman, aviator, pilot.
Fliegeralarm *m.* air raid alarm.
fliehen to run away, flee.
fliessen to flow, run.
   fliessendes Wasser running water.
   fliessend sprechen to speak fluently.
flink quick, agile, nimble.
Flinte *f.* shotgun, rifle.
   die Flinte in das Korn werfen to give up.
Flirt *m.* flirtation.
flirten to flirt.
Flitter *m.* tinsel.
Flitterwochen *pl.* honeymoon.
Floh *m.* flea.
Flöte *f.* flute.
flöten to play the flute.
flott afloat, floating.
Flotte *f.* fleet, navy.
Fluch *m.* curse, imprecation.
fluchen to curse, swear.
Flucht *f.* flight, escape.
flüchten to flee, escape.
flüchtig careless, passing, superficial.
   Er ist nur ein flüchtiger Bekannter. He is only a passing acquaintance.
Flüchtling *m.* fugitive.

FLUG *m.* flight (aerial).
Flugblatt *n.* pamphlet.
Fluggast *m.* air passenger.
Flughafen *m.* airport.
Flugplatz *m.* airfield.
Flugwesen *n.* aviation, aeronautics.
Flugzeug *n.* airplane.
Flugzeugführer *m.* pilot.
Flugzeugträger *m.* aircraft carrier.
Flur *f.* field, meadow.
Flur *m.* hall, corridor.
FLUSS *m.* river.
flüssig liquid, fluid.
Flüssigkeit *f.* fluidity.
Flusslauf *m.* course of a river.
flüstern to whisper.
Flut *f.* tide, flood.
fluten to stream, flow.
FOLGE *f.* sequence, succession.
    Folge leisten to comply with.
Folgeerscheinung *f.* consequence, effect.
FOLGEN to follow, succeed, obey, mind.
    daraus folgt hence follows.
folgendermassen as follows.
folgern to infer, conclude, deduce.
Folgerung *f.* inference, conclusion, deduction.
folglich consequently.
folgsam obedient, docile.
Folgsamkeit *f.* obedience, docility.
Folter *f.* torture.
foltern to torture.
fordern to demand, ask, claim, require.
Forderung *f.* demand, claim, challenge.
Form *f.* form, shape.
Formalität *f.* formality.
Format *n.* size, weight, importance.
Formel *f.* formula.
formell formal.
formen to form, shape.
förmlich formal, ceremonious, regular.
Formlosigkeit *f.* formlessness, shapelessness.
Formular *n.* form.
formulieren to formulate, define.
formvollendet perfect in form.
forschen to investigate, search.
Forschung *f.* inquiry, investigation.
Förster *m.* forester, gamekeeper.
FORT *adv. and separable prefix* (implies movement away from speaker, or continuation). away, off, gone, on (going on).
    in einem fort on and on.
    und so fort and so forth.
fortan henceforth, from this time.
Fortbildung *f.* further study.
fortfahren to drive away, remove, continue.
    Bitte, fahren Sie fort! Please go on!
fortführen to lead away, go on, continue.
fortgehen to go away.
fortgesetzt continuous, incessant.
fortschreiten to advance, proceed, make progress.
Fortschritt *m.* progress.

fortschrittlich progressive.
fortsetzen to continue, carry on, pursue.
Fortsetzung *f.* continuation, pursuit.
    Fortsetzung folgt to be continued.
Fracht *f.* freight.
Frachtdampfer *m.* freighter.
FRAGE *f.* question, inquiry, problem.
    das ist noch die Frage that remains to be seen.
    eine Frage stellen to ask a question.
    ohne Frage undoubtedly.
FRAGEN to ask, inquire.
    fragen nach to ask for.
    nichts danach fragen not to care about something.
    sich fragen to wonder.
    Es fragt sich, ob es der Mühe wert ist. It is a question whether it is worth the trouble.
Fragezeichen *n.* question mark.
fraglich in question, questionable, doubtful.
fraglos unquestionable.
FRAU *f.* woman, wife, Mrs.
    gnädige Frau Madam.
    Ihre Frau Gemahlin your wife.
Frauenarzt *m.* gynecologist.
FRÄULEIN *n.* young lady, girl, Miss.
fraulich womanly.
frech impudent, insolent.
Frechheit *f.* impudence, insolence.
FREI free, vacant, open, liberal, spontaneous, frank; freely, frankly, at ease.
    die freie Zeit leisure, spare time.
    Es ist mein freier Tag. This is my day off.
    Ist dieser Platz frei? Is this seat taken?
    unter freiem Himmel, im Freien outside, in the open air.
Freibillet *n.* complimentary ticket.
Freidenker *m.* freethinker.
freien to court, woo.
Freier *m.* suitor.
freigeben to set free, release, open (to the public).
freigebig liberal, generous.
Freigebigkeit *f.* liberality, generosity.
Freigeist *m.* freethinker.
freihalten to hold, treat.
Freiheit *f.* freedom.
freilassen to release, set free.
Freilassung *f.* release.
Freimut *m.* frankness, candor.
freimütig frank, candid.
freisprechen to acquit, absolve.
Freispruch *m.* acquittal.
Freistelle *f.* scholarship, free place.
FREITAG *m.* Friday.
freiwillig voluntary, spontaneous.
Freiwillige *m.* volunteer.
FREMD strange, foreign, unknown, exotic.
    fremdes Gut other people's property.
fremdartig strange, odd.
FREMDE *m.* foreigner, tourist, foreign country.
    in der Fremde abroad.
Fremdenführer *m.* tourist guide.

Fremdenverkehr m. tourist traffic.
Fremdsprache f. foreign language.
Fremdwort n. foreign word.
Fressen n. animal food, feed.
fressen to eat (animals), feed.
FREUDE f. joy, delight, pleasure, cheer.
    Freude haben an to enjoy, delight in.
    freudestrahlend beaming with joy.
freudelos joyless, cheerless.
freudig joyful, cheerful.
freuen to please, delight.
    sich freuen to be pleased, rejoice.
    Es freut mich sehr, Sie kennenzulernen. I am
    very glad to meet you.
    sich freuen auf to look forward to.
FREUND m. **–in** f. friend.
FREUNDLICH friendly, kind, obliging, pleasant.
Freundlichkeit f. friendliness.
Freundschaft f. friendship.
freundschaftlich friendly, serviceable.
FRIEDE m. peace.
Friedensbruch m. breach of peace.
Friedensvertrag m. peace treaty.
Friedhof m. churchyard, cemetery.
friedlich peaceful.
friedliebend peace-loving.
frieren to freeze, be cold, get cold.
    Mich friert (es). I am cold.
FRISCH fresh, bright, lively, new.
    auf frischer Tat in the very act of.
    frisch gestrichen wet paint.
    frische Eier fresh eggs.
    frische Wäsche clean linen.
FRISÖR m. barber, hairdresser.
frisieren to fix one's hair.
    sich frisieren lassen to have one's hair done.
Frisur f. hairdressing, hairdo.
froh glad, happy.
frohgemut cheerful.
FROHLICH merry, happy.
    Fröhliche Weihnachten! Merry Christmas!
Fröhlichkeit f. cheerfulness.
Frohsinn m. cheerfulness.
fromm pious, religious, godly.
Front f. front (military).
Frosch m. frog.
Frost m. frost, cold, chill.
frösteln to shiver, feel chilly.
FRUCHT f. fruit, crop, produce.
fruchtbar fruitful, fertile.
Fruchtbarkeit f. fruitfulness, fertility.
fruchtbringend fruit-bearing, productive, fertile.
fruchten to bear fruit, to have effect.
Fruchtsaft m. fruit juice.
FRÜH early in the morning.
    heute früh this morning.
    morgen früh tomorrow morning.
Frühe f. morning, dawn.
    in aller Frühe very early.
früher earlier, sooner, former.
    früher oder später sooner or later.
frühestens at the earliest.

FRÜHLING m. Spring.
FRÜHSTÜCK n. breakfast.
frühstücken to breakfast.
Fuchs m. fox.
fügen to join, put together, add, submit.
fügsam yielding, submissive.
Fügung f. dispensation, coincidence.
fühlbar tangible, perceptible.
FÜHLEN to feel, sense, be sensitive to.
    sich gut fühlen to feel well.
FÜHREN to lead, conduct, direct, handle, carry.
    Wer führt?. Who is ahead?
    Er führt immer das grosse Wort. He is always
    bragging.
    Er führt etwas im Schilde. He is up to
    something.
Führer m. leader, driver, pilot, guidebook.
Führerschein m. driving license.
Führung f. leadership, command, direction,
    management, behavior, conduct.
Führungszeugnis n. reference, certificate.
FÜLLEN to fill, stuff.
    sich füllen to fill up.
    Das Stadion füllt sich langsam. The stadium
    is slowly filling up.
Fund m. finding.
Fundament n. foundation.
fundieren to lay a foundation.
FÜNF five.
FÜNFTE fifth.
FÜNFZEHN fifteen.
FÜNFZEHNTE fifteenth.
FÜNFZIG fifty.
FÜNFZIGSTE fiftieth.
Funk m. wireless, radio (communications medium).
Funke m. spark.
funkeln to sparkle.
Funker m. telegraphist.
Funkspruch m. radiogram.
FÜR prep. (acc.) for, by, to.
    ein für allemal once for all.
    Er Schritt für Schritt vorwärts. He
    walks forward step by step.
    Ich arbeite für mich. I work for myself.
    Ich habe Karten für das Theater. I have
    tickets for the theater.
    Stück für Stück piece by piece.
    Tag für Tag day by day.
    was für ein? what kind of?
FURCHT f. fear, fright, dread, anxiety.
furchtbar awful, horrible, terrible; awfully, terribly.
fürchten to fear.
fürchterlich terrible, horrible, frightful.
furchtlos fearless, intrepid.
Furchtlosigkeit f. fearlessness, intrepidity.
furchtsam timid, nervous.
Furchtsamkeit f. timidity.
Fürst m. (–in f.) prince(ss).
Fürwort n. pronoun.
FUSS m. foot, base, bottom.
    auf eigenen Füssen stehen to be independent.
    auf freien Fuss setzen to set at liberty.

Er lebt auf grossem Fuss. He is living in grand style.
Ich stehe mit ihm auf gutem Fuss. I am on good terms with him.
zu Fuss on foot.
Fussball *m.* soccer.
Fussbank *f.* footstool.
Fussgänger *m.* pedestrian.
nur für Fussgänger for pedestrians only.
Fussspur *f.* footprint.
Fusstapfe *f.* footstep.
Fusstritt *m.* kick.
Futter *n.* 1. food, feed (animals). 2. sheath, lining.
Futterseide *f.* silk for lining.

G

Gabe *f.* present, gift, talent.
Gabel *f.* fork.
gähnen to yawn, gape.
GANG *m.* walk, stroll, walk, aisle, course, gear, hall, errand.
in Gang setzen to start, set.
in vollem Gang in full swing.
Gans *f.* goose.
Gänseblümchen *n.* daisy.
GANZ all, whole, entire, complete; in full, wholly, entirely, thoroughly, altogether.
die ganze Stadt the whole town.
ganz anders quite different.
ganz besonders more especially.
ganz gleich all the same, no matter.
ganz und gar wholly.
ganz und gar nicht not at all.
im ganzen on the whole.
im grossen und ganzen on the whole.
von ganzem Herzen with all my heart.
GAR done, cooked through; fully, very, quite, even.
gar kein...no...whatsoever.
gar nicht not at all.
gar nichts nothing at all.
Garage *f.* garage.
Garderobe *f.* wardrobe, cloakroom.
Garderobenmarke *f.* check (cloakroom).
Garderobennummer *f.* check (cloakroom).
Gardine *f.* curtain.
Garn *n.* yarn, thread.
garnieren to trim, garnish.
Garnitur *f.* trimming, outfit.
garstig nasty, ugly.
GARTEN *m.* garden.
Gartenhaus *n.* summer house.
Gartenlaube *f.* garden house (pavilion).
Gärtner *m.* gardener.
Gas *n.* gas.
Gashahn *m.* gas tap.
Gasleitung *f.* gas pipes, gas supply.
Gasse *f.* narrow street, alley.
GAST *m.* visitor, guest.
gastfreundlich hospitable.
Gastfreundschaft *f.* hospitality.
Gastgeber *m.* host.
Gasthaus *n.* inn, hotel.

Gasthof *m.* inn, hotel.
gastlich hospitable.
Gastspiel *n.* guest performance.
Gastwirt *m.* innkeeper.
Gasuhr *f.* gas meter.
Gatte *m.* husband.
Gattin *f.* wife.
Gaumen *m.* palate.
Geächtete *m.* outlaw.
Gebäck *n.* pastry, cookie.
Gebärde *f.* gesture, movement.
gebärden (sich) to behave, conduct oneself.
Gebäude *n.* building, structure, edifice.
GEBEN to give, present, produce, yield.
Das gibt mir zu denken. That makes me wonder.
es gibt there is, there are.
gegeben werden to play (in theater).
Was wird heute im Theater gegeben? What's playing tonight at the theater?
Gebet *n.* prayer.
Gebiet *n.* district, territory, area, field.
gebieten to order, command.
Gebirge *n.* mountain chain.
gebirgig mountainous.
Gebiss *n.* set of teeth, denture.
Gebot *n.* order, command, law.
Gebrauch *m.* use, customs, rites.
gebrauchen to use, make use of.
gebräuchlich usual, in use.
Gebühr *f.* duty, tax, fee, rate.
gebühren to be due, proper.
gebührenfrei tax-free.
gebührenpflichtig taxable.
gebührlich suitable, proper.
GEBURT *f.* birth, origin, extraction.
Geburtshelferin *f.* midwife.
Geburtsjahr *n.* year of birth.
Geburtsschein *m.* birth certificate.
Geburtstag *m.* birthday.
Gedächtnis *n.* memory, remembrance.
aus dem Gedächtnis from memory.
GEDANKE *m.* thought, idea.
sich Gedanken machen to worry.
Wie kommen Sie auf den Gedanken? What gives you that idea?

gedankenlos thoughtless.
Gedankenlosigkeit *f.* thoughtlessness.
Gedeck *n.* cover (at table), set of table linens.
gedeihen to grow, develop, succeed.
gedenken to intend, think of.
Gedenkfeier *f.* commemoration.
Gedicht *n.* poem.
gediegen pure, solid.
Gedränge *n.* crowd, throng.
gedruckt printed.
Geduld *f.* patience, endurance.
gedulden (sich) to have patience.
geduldig patient.
Gefahr *f.* danger, risk.
gefährden to endanger, expose to danger.
gefährlich dangerous, perilous.
gefahrlos safe, secure, without danger.

gefahrvoll dangerous, perilous.
GEFALLEN to please, suit.
    Das gefällt mir. I like that.
    sich gefallen lassen to submit, put up with.
gefällig pleasant, agreeable.
Gefangene *m.* prisoner, captive.
    Kriegsgefangene *m.* prisoner of war.
Gefangenschaft *f.* captivity, confinement.
Gefangensetzung *f.* capture, arrest.
Gefängnis *n.* prison, jail.
Gefäss *n.* container, receptacle.
gefasst composed, collected, calm.
    sich gefasstmachen auf to be prepared for.
Geflügel *n.* birds, poultry, fowl.
Geflüster *n.* whispering.
Gefolge *n.* suite, entourage.
GEFÜHL *n.* feeling, sentiment, sense, emotion, sensation.
gefühllos numb, heartless.
Gefühllosigkeit *f.* numbness, heartlessness.
gefühlvoll tender, sentimental.
gegebenenfalls eventually, possibly.
GEGEN *prep. (acc.)* against, about, around, toward, for, to, compared with.
    Die Soldaten kämpfen gegen den Feind. The soldiers fight against the enemy.
    Er schwamm gegen den Strom. He swam against the current.
    Es ist gegen neun Uhr. It is about nine o'clock.
    gegen voriges Jahr compared with last year.
    gegeneinander against each other.
    Waren gegen Geld tauschen to exchange goods for money.
GEGEND *f.* country, region, district.
Gegenseite *f.* opposite side.
gegenseitig reciprocal, mutual.
Gegenstand *m.* subject.
gegenstandlos pointless.
Gegenteil *n.* contrary, opposite.
    im Gegenteil on the contrary.
gegenüber opposite.
Gegenwart *f.* present, presence.
gegenwärtig present.
Gegenwert *m.* equivalent.
Gegner *m.* opponent, adversary, enemy.
Gehalt *m.* content.
Gehalt *n.* salary.
gehaltlos worthless.
gehaltvoll valuable, substantial.
gehässig spiteful, malicious.
Gehässigkeit *f.* spite, malice.
geheim concealed, hidden, clandestine.
GEHEIMNIS *n.* secret, mystery.
geheimnisvoll mysterious.
Geheimpolizei *f.* secret police.
GEHEN to go, walk, pass, move, leave; run, work (machinery).
    an die Arbeit gehen to go to work.
    Das geht nicht. That won't do.
    Es geht mir gut, danke. I am fine, thank you.
    Es geht nichts über gutes Bier. There is nothing like good beer.
    Es geht um Tod und Leben. It is a matter of life and death.
    gehen auf (nach) to face on, look out on.
    gehen lassen to let go, give up.
    sich gehen lassen to let oneself go.
    Wie geht es Ihnen? How are you?
Gehilfe *m.* assistant, clerk, helper.
Gehirn *n.* brain.
GEHÖR *n.* hearing; ear (mus.).
gehorchen to obey.
GEHÖREN to belong to, be owned by.
    Das gehört nicht zur Sache. That's beside the point.
    Dazu gehört Zeit. That takes time.
gehorsam obedient.
Geige *f.* violin.
geigen to play the violin.
GEIST *m.* spirit, genius, mind.
geistesabwesend absent-minded.
Geistesgegenwart *f.* presence of mind.
geisteskrank of unsound mind, insane.
geistesschwach feeble-minded.
geistig spiritual, intellectual, mental.
geistlich religious, spiritual.
geistlos spiritless, lifeless, dull.
geistreich ingenious, spiritual, witty.
Geiz *m.* stinginess, avarice.
geizig avaricious, stingy.
Geizkragen *m.* miser.
Gelände *n.* country, countryside.
Geländer *n.* railing, banister.
gelangen to reach, arrive, attain to.
gelassen calm, collected.
Gelassenheit *f.* calmness, composure.
geläufig fluent, familiar, current.
gelaunt disposed.
    gut gelaunt in good humour.
    schlecht gelaunt cross, bad-tempered.
Geläute *n.* chime, ringing of bells.
GELB yellow.
gelblich yellowish.
Gelbsucht *f.* jaundice.
GELD *n.* money.
    Bargeld, *n.* cash.
    Kleingeld, *n.* change.
Geldentwertung *f.* inflation.
Geldschein *m.* paper money.
Geldschrank *m.* safe.
Geldstück *n.* coin.
Geldtasche *f.* purse.
Gelee *m.* jelly.
gelegen 1. situated.
    2. convenient.
    Er kam gerade zu gelegener Zeit. He came just at the right time.
Gelegenheit *f.* opportunity, occasion, chance.
Gelegenheitskauf *m.* bargain.
gelegentlich occasional, accidental.
gelehrig docile, teachable.
Gelehrigkeit *f.* docility.

Gelehrsamkeit *f.* learning, erudition.
gelehrt learned, scholarly, erudite.
Gelehrte *m.* scholar, savant.
Geleise *n.* track.
Geleit *n.* escort, convoy.
geleiten to accompany, escort, convoy.
Geleitwort *n.* motto.
Gelenk *n.* joint, articulation.
Geliebte *m. & f.* lover, mistress, beloved.
gelingen to succeed, manage.
gelten to matter, mean, be worth, have
  influence, be valid.
  Das gilt nicht. That does not count.
  gelten als to be considered as.
Geltungstrieb *m.* desire to dominate.
gemächlich comfortable.
Gemahl *m.* husband.
Gemahlin *f.* wife.
gemäss suitable.
GEMEIN ordinary, general, low, vulgar, common.
  der Gemeine the private soldier.
  Es war gemein von ihm. It was mean of him.
  gemeinhaben mit to have in common with.
Gemeinde *f.* community, congregation, parish,
  municipality.
Gemeinheit *f.* vulgarity, basness, bad trick.
gemeinnützig beneficial to the community.
Gemeinschaft *f.* community.
  in Gemeinschaft mit together with.
GEMÜSE *n.* vegetables.
Gemüsehändler *m.* greengrocer.
Gemüt *n.* soul, mind, heart, feelings.
gemütlich good-natured, cozy.
Gemütlichkeit *f.* comfort, coziness.
GENAU close, tight, exact, accurate.
  Er nimmt es sehr genau. He is very
  particular.
  Nehmen Sie es nicht zu genau! Don't
  take it too literally!
Genauigkeit *f.* exactness, accuracy, precision.
General *m.* general.
genesen to recover, get better.
Genesung *f.* recovery, convalescence.
genial full of genius.
Genialität *f.* originality.
Genick *n.* nape (of neck).
Genie *n.* genius.
genieren to trouble, inconvenience, bother.
geniessbar eatable, drinkable.
geniessen to eat, enjoy, have the benefit of.
Genosse *m.* companion.
GENUG sufficient, enough.
Genugtuung *f.* satisfaction, compensation.
Geographie *f.* geography.
GEPÄCK *n.* luggage, baggage.
Gepäckabfertigung *f.* luggage office, cloakroom.
Gepäckannahme *m.* luggage counter.
Gepäckaufbewahrung *f.* luggage counter.
Gepäckausgabe *f.* luggage office.
Gepäckschein *m.* receipt for registered baggage.

Gepäckstück *n.* bag, parcel.
Gepäckträger *m.* porter.
GERADE direct, upright, straight, honest; just,
  exactly, directly.
  nun gerade now more than ever.
  geradeaus straight on.
Gerät *n.* tool, implement, utensil.
geraten to succeed, turn out well.
  aneinander geraten to come to blows.
  Ihm gerät nichts. He never succeeds in anything.
  in Brand geraten to catch fire.
geräumig roomy, spacious.
Geräusch *n.* noise.
geräuschlos noiseless.
geräuschvoll noisy.
GERECHT just, fair, equitable.
Gerechtigkeit *f.* justice, righteousness,
  fairness.
Gerede *n.* talk, humor.
Gereiztheit *f.* irritation.
Gericht *n.* dish, course, judgment.
  Jüngstes Gericht. Last Judgment.
  vor Gericht in court.
Gerichtshof *m.* court of law.
gering small, little, unimportant.
  nicht im geringsten not in the least.
  geringfügig unimportant.
Gerippe *n.* skeleton.
GERN gladly, with pleasure, readily, easily.
  gern essen to like (to eat something).
  Gern geschehen! Don't mention it!
  gern haben to like (a person or object).
  gern tun (or any verb of action) to like (to do
  something).
  Ich esse gern Eisbein mit Sauerkraut. I like
  pig's knuckles with sauerkraut.
  Sie hat ihn gern. She likes him.
  Tanzen Sie gern? Do you like to dance?
Geruch *m.* smell, scent, odor.
geruchlos odorless.
Gerücht *n.* rumor, report.
Gerüst *n.* scaffold, stage.
GESANG *m.* song, singing.
Gesanglehrer *m.* singing teacher.
GESCHÄFT *n.* business, transaction,
  commerce, commercial firm, store.
geschäftlich commercial.
Geschäftsführer *m.* manager.
Geschäftsmann *m.* business man.
geschäftsmässig commercial.
Geschäftsviertel *n.* shopping district.
Geschäftszeit *f.* office hours.
GESCHEHEN to happen, occur, be done.
  Es geschieht ihm recht. It serves him right.
  Es ist um mich geschehen. I am done for.
  geschehen lassen to allow, permit.
Geschenk *n.* present, gift.
GESCHICHTE *f.* story, history.
Geschichtsbuch *n.* history book.

Geschick n. fate, destiny.

geschickt clever, capable.

Geschirr n. crockery, dishes, china.

GESCHLECHT n. sex, gender, kind, species, race, family, stock.

geschlechtlich sexual.

GESCHMACK m. taste, flavor.

    Geschmack finden an to like.

geschmacklos insipid, in bad taste.

Geschmacklosigkeit f. bad taste.

geschmackvoll tasteful.

Geschrei n. shouting, screaming, clamor.

Geschwätz n. idle talk.

geschwätzig talkative.

geschwind quick, fast, swift, prompt, speedy.

Geschwindigkeit f. quickness, rapidity.

    Geschwindigkeitsgrenze 60 km. Speed limit 60 kilometers.

Geschwister pl. brother(s) and sister(s).

Geselle m. fellow, companion, journeyman.

Geselligkeit f. sociability, social life.

GESELLSCHAFT f. society, association, company.

    (jemanden) Gesellschaft leisten to keep (someone) company.

    in Gesellschaft socially.

Gesellschafter m. partner.

Gesellschaftsanzug m. evening clothes.

Gesellschaftskleidung f. evening clothes.

    Gesellschaftskleidung erwünscht. Evening dress requested.

Gesellschaftsspiel n. party game.

Gesetz n. law, statute.

Gesetzbuch n. code.

gesetzlich legal, lawful.

gesetzwidrig unlawful, illegal.

GESICHT n. vision, sight, hallucination. appearance, face.

    Das steht Ihnen gut (zu Gesicht). It is very becoming to you.

    Gesichter schneiden to make faces.

    Sie lachte übers ganze Gesicht. She was all smiles.

Gesichtszug m. feature.

Gesinnung f. mind, way of thinking.

gesinnungslos unprincipled.

gesinnungstreu loyal.

Gesinnugswechsel m. change of opinion.

gesittet well-mannered.

gespannt stretched, strained.

Gespenst n. ghost.

gespenstig ghostly.

Gespött n. mockery, derision.

GESPRÄCH n. talk, conversation, discourse.

gesprächig talkative.

Gesprächsstoff m. topic of conversation.

Gestalt f. form, figure, shape, build, frame, manner, fashion.

gestalten to form.

Geständnis n. confession.

gestehen to confess, admit.

Gesträuch n. shrubs, bushes, shrubbery.

Gesuch n. application, petition, request.

GESUND healthy, well, sound, natural.

    gesunder Menschenverstand common sense.

Gesundheit f. health.

    Gesundheit! God bless you!

gesundheitlich hygienic, sanitary.

gesundheitshalber for the sake of health.

Getränk n. drink, beverage.

Getreide n. grain.

Getreidehalm m. corn stalk.

Getreidespeicher m. granary.

Getümmel n. bustle, tumult.

Gewächs n. plant.

gewachsen equal to.

    Er ist der Arbeit gewachsen. He is equal to the task.

    Er ist seinem Gegner gewachsen. He is a match for his opponent.

Gewächshaus n. conservatory (greenhouse).

gewagt risky.

Gewähr f. security, surety.

gewähren to grant.

    jemanden gewähren lassen to let a person do as he pleases.

GEWALT f. power, authority, force, violence.

    in der Gewalt haben to have command of, master.

    mit aller Gewalt with all one's might.

    sich in der Gewalt haben to have self-control.

Gewaltherrschaft f. despotism.

gewaltsam violent.

gewalttätig brutal, violent.

gewandt agile, skillful, clever.

gewärtig expecting, expectant.

Gewebe n. weaving, web, tissue, fabric.

Gewehr n. rifle, weapon.

Gewerbe n. trade, business, profession.

Gewerbeschein m. trade license.

Gewerbeschule f. trade, technical school.

gewerbsmässig professional.

Gewicht n. weight.

    ins Gewicht fallen to weigh with.

gewichtig weighty, important.

Gewinn m. winning.

Gewinnanteil m. dividend.

gewinnbringend profitable, lucrative.

GEWINNEN to gain, earn, win, produce, extract.

    es über sich gewinnen to bring oneself to.

Gewinner m. winner.

gewinnsüchtig greedy (for victory).

Gewirr n. confusion, mess.

GEWISS certain, sure, fixed; certainly, indeed, of course, no doubt.

    Gewiss! Surely!

    In gewissem Sinne hat er recht. In a sense he is right.

gewissenlos unscrupulous.

gewissermassen to some extent, so to speak, as it were.

Gewissheit f. certainty.

Gewitter n. thunderstorm.

gewittern to thunder.

Gewitterregen *m.* deluge.
GEWÖHNEN to accustom.
   sich an etwas gewöhnen to get used to something.
Gewohnheit *f.* habit.
gewöhnlich usual, ordinary, common.
gewöhnt accustomed.
Gewölbe *n.* vault.
Gewühl *n.* turmoil, crowd.
Gewürz *n.* spice, seasoning, condiment.
gewürzig spiced.
geziert affected.
giessen to pour, water, spill.
Gift *n.* poison.
giftig poisonous, venomous.
Gipfel *m.* summit, peak, top.
Gipfelpunkt *m.* limit.
Giraffe *f.* giraffe.
Gitter *n.* railing, fence, grating.
Glanz *m.* brightness, glamour.
glänzen to shine, glitter, gleam.
glänzend shining, lustrous.
Glanzleistung *f.* (top) record.
glanzvoll brilliant, splendid, glorious.
GLAS *n.* glass, jar, pitcher. ,
gläsern of glass, vitreous.
GLATT even, smooth, slippery, flat; smoothly, slippery.
Glatteis *n.* slippery ice.
Glauben *m.* faith, confidence, trust, belief.
GLAUBEN to believe, trust, think, suppose.
   Sie können ihm aufs Wort glauben. You can take his word for it.
glaubhaft credible, likely, probable.
gläubig believing, faithful.
gläublich credible, likely.
glaubwürdig credible, reliable, authentic.
Glaubwürdigkeit *f.* credibility, authenticity.
GLEICH same, similar, alike, even, level, direct, equal, like, equivalent; equally, just, at once, immediately.
   es einem gleich tun to rival a person.
   Es ist mir gleich. It is all the same to me.
   gleich darauf immediately afterwards.
   Gleich und gleich gesellt sich gern. Birds of a feather flock together.
gleichberechtigt entitled to the same rights.
GLEICHEN to be equal, resemble.
gleichfalls likewise.
gleichförmig uniform.
gleichgesinnt congenial.
Gleichgewicht *n.* equilibrium, balance, poise.
gleichgültig indifferent, unconcerned.
Gleichgültigkeit *f.* indifference.
Gleichheit *f.* equality, identity, similarity.
gleichmässig proportional.
Gleichstrom *m.* direct current.
gleichviel no matter, just the same.
gleichwertig equivalent.
gleichzeitig simultaneous.
Gletscher *m.* glacier.

Glied *n.* limb, member.
gliedern to articulate, arrange, classify.
glitzern to glitter, glisten, twinkle.
Globus *m.* globe.
Glocke *f.* bell, clock.
Glockenspiel *n.* chime.
Glockenturm *m.* steeple.
GLÜCK *n.* fortune, good luck, prosperity.
   etwas auf gut Glück tun to take a chance on something.
   Glück haben to be lucky.
   Glück im Spiel, Unglück in der Liebe. Lucky at cards, unlucky in love.
   Glück wünschen to congratulate.
   Viel Glück! Good luck! Many happy returns!
glucken to succeed, be lucky.
GLÜCKLICH fortunate.
   Glückliche Reise! Have a pleasant trip!
glücklicherweise fortunately.
Glücksfall *m.* chance.
Glücksspiel *n.* game of chance.
Glückwunsch *m.* congratulations, good wishes.
Glühbirne *f.* electric bulb.
glühen to glow.
glühend glowing, fervent.
Glühwurm *m.* glowworm.
Glut *f.* glow, heat.
Gnade *f.* favor, mercy.
   auf Gnade und Ungnade at discretion.
Gnadengesuch *n.* petition for clemency.
GNÄDIG merciful, gracious.
   gnädige Frau Madam.
GOLD *n.* gold.
golden gold, of gold, golden.
Goldgrube *f.* gold mine.
goldig shining like gold.
   jedes Wort auf die Goldwaage legen to weigh one's words carefully.
Golf *m.* golf.
gönnen to wish well, allow, permit; not to begrudge.
Gönner *m.* patron.
Gotik *f.* Gothic.
GOTT *m.* God.
   Gott sei Dank! Thank God!
   leider Gottes unfortunately.
   Um Gottes willen! For Heaven's sake!
Götterdämmerung *f.* twilight of the Gods.
Gottesdienst *m.* public worship, service (church).
göttlich divine, godlike.
Grab *n.* tomb, grave.
Grabstein *m.* tombstone.
Grad *m.* degree.
Graf *m.* count.
Gräfin *f.* countess.
Gram *m.* sorrow, grief.
grämen to grieve, worry.
Gramm *n.* gram. (1,000 grams equal 1 kilogram.)
Grammatik *f.* grammar.
GRAS *n.* grass.

grässlich terrible, horrible.
Gräte *f.* fish-bone.
Gratulant *m.* congratulator, well-wisher.
gratulieren to congratulate.
GRAU gray.
grauen to be afraid, shudder, dread.
 Es graut mir vor. I am afraid.
grauenhaft horrible, ghastly.
grauenvoll awful, dreadful.
Grauhaar *n.* gray hair.
grausam cruel.
Grausamkeit *f.* cruelty.
grausig gruesome, ghastly.
Grazie *f.* grace, charm.
graziös gracious.
greifbar tangible, palpable.
greifen to seize, grasp, catch, touch, strike.
 ineinander greifen to interlock.
Greis *m.* old man.
Greisenalter *n.* old age.
Greisin *f.* old woman.
Grenze *f.* frontier, boundary, limit.
grenzenlos boundless, infinite.
Grenzverkehr *m.* traffic at or across the frontier,
 frontier trading.
Griff *m.* grip, grasp, hold, catch.
Grimm *m.* anger, rage.
grimmig furious, grim.
Grippe *f.* grippe.
grob clumsy, thick, rough, coarse.
Grobheit *f.* coarseness, rudeness.
Groll *m.* resentment, anger.
grollen to be resentful, angry.
GROSS big, tall, large, great, huge, grand.
 die grossen Ferien the summer vacation.
 gross tun to boast.
 gross ziehen to bring up.
 grosse Kinder grown-up children.
 grosser Buchstabe capital letter.
 im grossen und ganzen on the whole.
grossartig great, grand.
GRÖSSE *f.* size, dimension, largeness, tallness,
 celebrity, star.
Grosseltern *pl.* grandparents.
Grosshandel *m.* wholesale trade.
grossjährig of age.
Grossmacht *f.* great power.
grossmütig generous, magnanimous.
Grossmutter *f.* grandmother.
grosspurig arrogant.
Grossstadt *f.* big town.
Grossstädter *m.* inhabitant of a large town.
grösstenteils for the most part, largely.
Grossvater *m.* grandfather.
grosszügig generous, on a large scale.
Grün *n.* green, verdure.
GRÜN green (adj.).
 im Grünen in country surroundings.
 vom grünen Tisch aus only in theory.
GRUND *m.* ground, bottom, cause, reason.
 im Grunde after all.
 auf den Grund gehen to investigate.

Aus welchem Grunde? For what reason?
Grundbesitz *m.* real estate.
gründen to found, establish, promote.
Grundgedanke *m.* fundamental idea.
Grundlage *f.* foundation.
grundlegend fundamental.
gründlich thorough, solid, profound.
Gründlichkeit *f.* thoroughness, solidity.
Grundsatz *m.* principle.
grundsätzlich fundamental.
Grundstück *n.* piece of land, lot.
Gründung *f.* foundation, establishment.
grünen to grow green, sprout.
Gruppe *f.* group, section.
GRUSS *m.* greeting; salute (military).
GRÜSSEN to greet, salute.
 grüssen lassen to send one's regards.
gültig valid, available, good, current.
Gültigkeit *f.* validity; currency (monetary).
Gummi *m.* rubber, eraser.
Gummiabsatz *m.* rubber heel.
Gummiband *n.* rubber band.
Gummimantel *m.* raincoat.
Gummischuh *m.* galosh.
Gunst *f.* kindness, favor.
 zu Gunsten von in favor of.
günstig kind, favorable.
Gurke *f.* cucumber.
Gürtel *m.* belt, girdle.
Gusstein *m.* sink.
Gut *n.* property, good, estate, farm.
GUT good, pleasant, kind, full; well,
 pleasantly, kindly.
 es gut haben to be well off.
 Gute Besserung! I hope you get well soon!
 Guten Morgen! Good morning!
 kurz und gut in short.
 Schon gut! All right!
Gutachten *n.* expert opinion, estimate.
Gutachter *m.* assessor, surveyor.
gutartig good-natured.
Güte *f.* kindness.
Güterzug *m.* freight train.
gutgelaunt in a good temper, in good spirits.
gutgläubig credulous.
Guthaben *n.* balance, credit.
gutheissen to approve, sanction.
gutherzig kind-hearted.
gütig kind, good.
gutmachen to make amends for.
gutmütig good-natured.
Gutmütigkeit *f.* good nature.
Gutsbesitzer *m.* landowner, gentleman farmer.
Gutschein *m.* token, voucher.
gutwillig willing, voluntary.
Gymnasialbildung *f.* classical education.
Gymnasiast *m.* high-school boy.
Gymnasium *n.* high-school.
Gymnastik *f.* gymnastics.

H

HAAR *n.* **(Haare** *pl.)* hair.

sich die Haare machen to do one's hair.

Haare auf den Zähnen haben to stand up (to opponents).

um ein Haar nearly, narrowly.

kein gutes Haar an einem lassen to pull a person to pieces.

sich in die Haare geraten to come to blows.

Lassen Sie sich darüber keine grauen Haare wachsen! Don't let that give you gray hair!

haaren to shed hair (animals).

Haarnadel *f.* hairpin.

Haarspalterei *f.* hair-splitting.

Haarwasser *n.* hair tonic.

Habe *f.* property, belongings.

Hab und Gut good and chattel.

habhaft werden to obtain possession.

HABEN to have, own, possess, get.

Den wievielten haben wir heute? What is the date today?

nichts auf sich haben to be of no consequence.

Recht haben to be right.

unter sich haben to be in charge of.

Was hast du? What is the matter with you?

zu haben sein to be obtainable.

Habgier *f.* greed, avarice.

habgierig greedy, avaricious.

Habseligkeiten *pl.* belongings.

hacken to chop, mince.

Hafen *m.* port, harbor.

Hafenstadt *f.* seaport.

Haft *f.* custody, arrest, detention.

haftbar responsible, liable.

haften to stick to, cling to.

haften für to answer for (bear the responsibility).

Häftling *m.* prisoner.

haftpflichtig liable, responsible.

mit beschränkter Haftung with limited liability.

Haftung *f.* liability, responsibility.

Hagel *m.* hail.

Hagelschlag *m.* hailstorm.

HAHN *m.* rooster, cock.

Hai *m.* shark.

Haken *m.* hook, mark.

HALB half.

auf halbem Wege midway, halfway.

ein halbes Pfund half a pound.

halb durchgebraten medium done (meat).

halb so viel half as much.

halb zwei half past one.

halbieren to halve, bisect.

Halbinsel *f.* peninsula.

Halbmond *m.* crescent moon, half-moon.

Halbwelt *f.* demi-monde.

Hälfte *f.* half.

Kinder zahlen die Hälfte. Children pay half price.

Halle *f.* hall, hangar.

HALS *m.* neck, throat.

Es hängt mir schon zum Hals heraus. I am sick and tired of it already.

Hals über Kopf headlong.

um den Hals fallen to embrace.

Halsband *n.* necklace.

halsbrecherisch dangerous.

Halsschmerzen *pl.* sore throat.

Halstuch *n.* scarf.

Halt *m.* stop, halt, hold, footing.

Halt! Stop!

haltbar lasting, durable.

Haltbarkeit *f.* durability.

HALTEN to hold, support, observe, keep, celebrate, last, stop, endure, continue, follow.

an sich halten to restrain oneself.

Er hält sich für sehr klug. He thinks he is very clever.

halt machen to stop.

halten für to consider, think.

es halten mit to side with.

Halten Sie sich rechts! Keep to the right!

halten von to think of.

schwer halten to be difficult.

sein Wort halten to keep one's word. ·

viel halten auf to think highly of.

Was halten Sie von ihr? What do you think of her?

Haltestelle *f.* stop, station.

haltlos without support, unsteady, unprincipled.

Haltung *f.* behavior, attitude, self-control.

Hammer *m.* hammer.

HAND *f.* hand, palm.

auf Händen tragen to spoil.

bei der Hand sein to be ready.

die Hand im Spiel haben to have a finger in the pie.

einem die Hand geben to shake hands with someone.

Hand und Fuss haben to be to the purpose.

mit Händen und Füssen with might and main (tooth and nail).

unter der Hand secretly.

von der Hand gehen to work well.

von der Hand weisen to decline.

zur Hand handy.

Handarbeit *f.* manual work, labor.

HANDEL *m.* trade, business, affair.

Handel treiben to trade.

handelseinig werden to come to terms.

handeln to act, do.

handeln mit to trade with.

handeln von to deal with.

sich handeln um to be about, be a matter of.

Handelskammer *f.* chamber of commerce.

Handfertigkeit *f.* manual skill.

Handfesseln *f.* handcuffs.

Handgelenk *n.* wrist.

Handgemenge *f.* hand-to-hand fighting.

Handgepäck *n.* hand luggage.

handgreiflich obvious, manifest.

handgreiflich werden to use one's fists.

handhaben to handle, manage.

Handkoffer *m.* suitcase.

Händler *m.* trader, dealer.

handlich handy.

Handlung *f.* act, action, deed, business.

Handlungsweise *f.* way of acting, method of dealing.

Handschrift *f.* handwriting.

Handschuh *m.* glove.

Handstreich *m.* surprise attack.

Handtasche *f.* handbag.

Handtuch *n.* towel.

Handwerk *n.* handicraft, trade.
  einem das Handwerk legen to stop a person's activities.

hängen to hang, suspend, fix, attach.
  hängen bleiben to be caught.

hänseln to tease.

Harm *m.* grief, sorrow, insult, injury.

harmlos harmless.

Harmlosigkeit *f.* harmlessness, innocence.

Harmonie *f.* harmony.

harmonieren to harmonize, agree.

HART hard, firm, solid.
  hartherzig hard-hearted.
  harthörig hard of hearing.

Härte *f.* hardness, roughness, cruelty, severity.

hartnäckig obstinate, stubborn.

Hase *m.* hare.

Hasenbraten *m.* roast hare.

Hass *m.* hate, hatred.

hassen to hate.

hässlich ugly, nasty.

Hässlichkeit *f.* ugliness.

Hast *f.* hurry, haste.

hastig hurried, hasty.

Haube *f.* hood, cap.
  unter die Haube bringen to marry off.

Hauch *m.* breath, slight breeze.

hauchen to breathe.

Haufen *m.* heap, pile.

häufen to heap, pile, accumulate.

häufig frequent, abundant.

HAUPT *n.* chief, head.

Hauptbahnhof *m.* main station.

Hauptmann *m.* captain.

Hauptperson *f.* principal person, leading character (theater).

Hauptpostamt *n.* general post office.

Hauptquartier *n.* headquarters.

Hauptsache *f.* main thing.

hauptsächlich principal.

Hauptstadt *f.* capital.

Hauptverkehrszeit *f.* rush hours.

Hauptwort *n.* substantive, noun.

HAUS *n.* house, home, building.
  das Haus bestellen to put one's affairs in order.
  das Haus hüten to be confined to the house.
  nach Hause gehen to go home.
  von Haus aus originally.
  zu Hause at home.

Hausangestellte *m. & f.* servant.

Hausarbeit *f.* housework.

Hausaufgabe *f.* homework.

Häuschen *n.* small house.

Hausflur *m.* hall, corridor.

Hausfrau *f.* housewife.

Haushalt *m.* household.

haushalten to keep house, to economize.

Haushälterin *f.* housekeeper.

Hausherr *m.* master.

Hauslehrer *m.* private tutor.

häuslich domestic.

Häuslichkeit *f.* family life, domesticity.

Hausmeister *m.* janitor.

Hausschuh *m.* slipper.

Haussuchung *f.* police raid.

Haustier *n.* domestic animal.

Haustüre *f.* front door.

Hauswirt *m.* landlord.

HAUT *f.* skin, hide, coat.
  aus der Haut fahren to lose one's patience.
  sich seiner Haut wehren to defend oneself.

Hautfarbe *f.* complexion.

heben to lift, raise.

Heer *n.* army.

Hefe *f.* yeast.

Heft *n.* handle, notebook, pamphlet, number.

heften to pin, fasten, stitch, fix.

heftig violent, strong.

Heftigkeit *f.* violence, vehemence, intensity.

heikel delicate, ticklish, difficult.

HEIL unhurt, intact, safe, cured.

heilbar curable.

heilen to cure.

heilig holy, godly, sacred.
  Heiligabend Christmas Eve.

heilkräftig curative.

Heilmittel *n.* remedy.

heilsam curative.

Heilsarmee *f.* Salvation Army.

Heilung *f.* healing, cure.

Heilverfahren *n.* medical treatment.

HEIM *n.* home.

heim homeward.

Heimat *f.* native country, homeland.

heimatlos homeless.

Heimatstadt *f.* home town.

Heimkehr (– kunft) *f.* homecoming.

heimlich secret, private, comfortable; secretly, privately.

Heimsuchung *f.* trial, misfortune.

Heimtücke *f.* malice.

heimtückisch malicious, insidious.

Heimweg *m.* way home, return.

Heimweh *n.* homesickness.
  Heimweh haben to be homesick.

HEIRAT *f.* marriage.

heiraten to marry, get married.

Heiratsantrag *m.* proposal.

heiser hoarse.
  heiser sein to be hoarse, have a sore throat.

Heiserkeit *f.* hoarseness, sore throat.

HEISS hot.

HEISSEN to call, name, be called.
  das heisst that is.
  es heisst they say.

Ich heisse Anna. My name is Ann.
Wie heisst das auf Englisch? What is that
called in English?
heiter gay, cheerful.
Heiterkeit *f.* brightness, clearness, serenity,
cheerfulness.
heizbar with heating.
heizen to heat.
Heizkissen *n.* electric pad.
Heizkörper *m.* radiator.
Heizung *f.* heating, firing, radiator.
Held *m.* hero.
HELFEN to support, help, assist.
Ich kann mir nicht helfen. I can't help it.
Helfer *m.* helper, assistant.
Helfershelfer *m.* accomplice ("helper's helper").
HELL bright, shining, clear, light, fair, pale,
sheer.
Helle *f.* clearness, brightness.
hellhörig keen of hearing.
Helm *m.* helmet.
HEMD *n.* shirt.
Hemdbrust *f.* shirt front, dicky.
hemmen to check, stop, hinder, restrain.
Hemmung *f.* inhibition, check, stoppage, restraint.
hemmungslos free, unrestrained.
HER 1. *adv.* here, from, since, ago.
von Alters her of old, long ago.
2. *separable prefix* (implies the idea of a
movement toward the speaker)
Kommen Sie her! Come here!
herab down, downward.
herablassen to lower, let down, condescend.
Herablassung *f.* condescension.
herabsehen to look down upon.
herabsetzen to lower, degrade, reduce (price).
Herabsetzung *f.* lowering, degradation;
reduction (price).
heran on, up, near, along.
heranbilden to train, educate.
herankommen to come near.
die Dinge an sich herankommen lassen to
bide one's time.
heranwachsen to grow up.
HERAUF up, upwards.
heraufgehen to go up.
Kommen Sie herauf! Come up!
HERAUS out, from within.
Sie kommen heraus. They are coming out.
herausbekommen to get back (money); find out.
auf eins herauskommen to be all one.
herausnehmen to take out, extract.
herausstellen to turn out, appear.
herbei here, near, hither.
herbeischaffen to bring near, procure, produce.
HERBST *m.* autumn.
herbstlich autumnal.
Herd *m.* hearth, fireplace.
Herdplatte *f.* hot plate.
HEREIN in.
Kommen Sie herein! (Herein!) Come in!

Hier herein, bitte! This way, please!
hereinfallen to be taken in, disappointed.
herkommen to come near, approach, originate.
Herkunft *f.* origin, descent.
HERR *m.* master, gentleman, lord, sir, Mr.
Meine Damen und Herren Ladies and gentlemen.
Ist der Herr Doktor zu sprechen? Can I see the
doctor?
eigener Herr sein to stand on one's own feet.
Herr werden to master, overcome.
Herr im Hause sein to be the master of the
house.
herrichten to arrange.
herrisch imperious, dictatorial.
Herrschaft *f.* power, rule, command, master and
mistress (of an estate).
herrschen to rule, govern, prevail, exist.
Herrscher *m.* ruler, tyrant, dictator.
herrschsüchtig fond of power, tyrannical.
herüber across, to this side.
herüberkommen to come over.
HERUM around, round, near, about.
rundherum all around.
herumdrehen to turn round.
herumführen to lead.
herumreichen to hand around.
herumtreiben (sich) to run around.
HERUNTER down, off.
herunterkommen to come down.
Komm gleich herunter! Come down right away!
heruntersetzen to lower.
hervor out, forth.
hervorbringen to produce, yield.
hervorheben to make prominent.
hervorragen to stand out, project.
hervorragend prominent, excellent.
hervortun (sich) to distinguish oneself.
HERZ *n.* heart, feeling, mind, courage.
ans Herz legen to recommend to someone's care.
ins Herz schliessen to become fond of.
sich ein Herz fassen to take courage.
sich zu Herzen nehmen to take to heart.
unter dem Herzen tragen to be expecting a
child.
von Herzen gern with the greatest pleasure.
Was haben Sie auf dem Herzen? What's on your
mind?
herzleidend suffering from heart trouble.
herzlich hearty, cordial.
mit herzlichen Grüssen with kindest regards.
herzlos heartless.
Herzschlag *m.* heart beat, heart failure.
Heu *n.* hay.
Heufieber *n.* hay fever.
Heuchelei *f.* hypocrisy.
heucheln to feign, pretend.
Heuchler *m.* hypocrite.
HEUTE today.
heute abend tonight.
heute früh; heute morgen this morning.
heute vor acht Tagen a week ago.
heutzutage nowadays.

Hexe *f.* witch.
HIER here.
    hier und da here and there.
hierauf hereupon.
hierdurch through this, this way, thereby.
hierher here, hither.
hierherum hereabout.
hiermit herewith, with this.
hiernach after this, thereupon.
hierüber over here, about this.
hiervon hereof, from this.
hierzu to this, moreover.
hierzulande in this country.
HILFE *f.* help, assistance, support, relief.
    Hilfe leisten to help, assist.
    erste Hilfe first aid.
hilflos helpless.
hilfreich helpful, charitable.
hilfsbedürftig indigent, needing help.
HIMMEL *m.* sky, heaven.
    aus allen Himmeln fallen to be bitterly
    disappointed.
Himmelsrichtung *f.* quarter, direction, point of
    compass.
himmlisch heavenly, celestial.
HIN 1. *adv.* there, thither.
    hin und her to and fro.
    hin und her überlegen to turn over in one's
    mind.
    hin und wieder now and then.
    2. *separable prefix (implies the idea of a*
    movement away from the speaker).
    Gehen Sie hinaus. Go out.
hinab down, downward.
HINAUF up, upward.
    hinaufarbeiten to work one's way up.
    Er geht die Treppe hinauf. He goes up the
    stairs.
HINAUS out, outside, past.
    darüber hinaus beyond that.
    Ich schicke die Kinder hinaus. I am sending the
    children outside.
hinausgehen to go out.
hinauskommen to come out.
    auf eins hinauskommen to come to the same
    thing.
hinausschieben to defer, postpone, put off.
hinauswerfen to throw out, expel.
    hoch hinauswollen to aim high.
hinausziehen to draw out, put off.
Hinblick *m.* look at or toward.
    im Hinblick auf with regard to.
hinbringen to take, bring, carry.
hinderlich in the way, hindering, obstructive.
hindern to prevent, hinder, hamper.
hindurch through, throughout, across.
HINEIN in, into.
    Ich gehe in das Zimmer hinein. I go into the
    room.
hineingehen to go into.
hinfahren to convey, carry, drive to.
Hinfahrt *f.* trip there.

hinfallen to fall down.
hinfällig frail, weak.
    hinfällig werden to fail, come to nothing.
hinfort henceforth, in the future.
Hingabe *f.* surrender, devotion.
hinhalten to put off.
hinlänglich sufficient, adequate.
hinnehmen to take, accept.
hinsehen to look at.
hinsetzen to set down, sit down.
hinsichtlich with regard to.
hinstellen to place, put down, lie down.
hinten behind, in the rear, at the back.
HINTER 1. *prep. (dat. when answering question,*
    Wo?; acc. when answering question, Wohin? and
    depending on the idiom) behind, back, after.
    Hinter dem Haus ist eine Garage. There is a
    garage behind the house.
    Sie hat schon viel hinter sich. She has been
    through a lot.
    hinter sich bringen to get over, cover.
Hinterbliebene *m. & f.* survivor.
hintereinander one after the other.
    zwei Tage hintereinander two days running.
Hintergedanke *m.* underlying thought, unacknowledged
    motive.
Hintergrund *m.* background.
Hinterhalt *m.* ambush.
hinterhältig malicious, devious.
hinterher behind, afterwards.
hinterlassen to leave, leave behind.
    Hat er keine Nachricht für mich hinterlassen?
    Hasn't he left a message for me?
hinterlegen to deposit.
Hinterlist *f.* artifice, fraud, trick.
hinterlistig artful, cunning.
Hinterrad *n.* backwheel.
hinters hinter das.
    ins Hintertreffen geraten to be handicapped.
Hinüber over, across, over there, to the other side.
HINUNTER down, downward, downstairs.
    Sie geht die Treppe hinunter. She walks down
    the stairs.
Hinweg *m.* way there.
hinweg away, off.
hinwegkommen (über) to get over.
hinwegsetzen (über) to disregard.
Hinweis *m.* indication, hint, reference,
    direction.
hinweisen to show, indicate, refer.
hinwerfen to throw down.
hinzu to, near, there.
hinzufügen to add.
hinzuziehen to include, consult.
Hirn *n.* brain.
Hitze *f.* heat.
hitzig hot, hot-headed.
HOCH high, tall, lofty, great, noble.
    Es geht hoch her. Things are getting pretty
    lively.
    Hände hoch! Hands up!
    hoch anrechnen to value greatly.

Hoch lebe ...! Long live ...!
hochleben lassen to toast.
hochachten to esteem, respect.
Hochachtung *f.* esteem, respect.
hochachtungsvoll yours faithfully.
Hochbetrieb *m.* intense activity.
Hochdeutsch *n.* high German, standard German.
hochhalten to cherish, raise.
Hochhaus *n.* skyscraper.
hochherzig high-minded, magnanimous.
Hochmut *m.* pride, arrogance.
hochmütig arrogant, proud.
Hochschule *f.* university, college.
Hochsommer *m.* midsummer.
Hochspannung *f.* high tension.
Vorsicht! Hochspannung! Caution! High tension wires!
HÖCHST highest, utmost, extreme, maximum; very, extremely.
Hochstapelei *f.* swindling.
Hochstapler *m.* swindler.
höchstens at best, at most.
Höchstgeschwindigkeit *f.* top speed, speed limit.
Höchstgrenze *f.* limit.
Höchstleistung *f.* maximum output, record performance.
höchstwahrscheinlich most likely.
hochtrabend high-sounding.
Hochverrat *m.* high treason.
Hochzeit *f.* wedding, marriage.
Hochzeitreise *f.* honeymoon trip.
HOF *m.* yard, court, farm.
den Hof machen to pay court to.
HOFFEN to hope.
hoffentlich it is to be hoped.
Hoffnung *f.* hope.
sich falsche Hoffnungen machen to have illusions.
hoffnungslos hopeless.
hoffnungsvoll hopeful.
HÖHE *f.* height, altitude, latitude, top, summit, amount.
auf der Höhe sein to be up to date, to be in top form.
auf der Höhe von at the altitude of.
aus der Höhe from on high.
Das ist die Höhe. That is the limit.
in (der) Höhe von in the amount of.
Höhensonne *f.* ultraviolet light.
höher higher, superior.
HOHL hollow, concave, dull.
Höhle *f.* hole, cave.
Hohlraum *m.* empty space, cavity.
Hohn *m.* scorn, sneer, mockery, insult.
höhnen to mock, defy.
höhnisch scornful, sneering.
HOLEN to get, take, fetch.
sich Rat holen to consult.
HÖLLE *f.* hell.
höllisch hellish, infernal.
HOLZ *n* wood, timber, lumber.
hölzern wooden.

Honig *m.* honey.
horchen to listen, lend an ear, listen in, spy.
Es horcht jemand. Somebody is listening in.
HÖREN to hear, listen, attend, obey, understand.
schwer hören to be hard of hearing.
Horizont *m.* horizon.
Horn *n.* horn, bugle.
Horoskop *n.* horoscope.
ein Horoskop stellen to cast horoscope.
Hörspiel *n.* radio play.
Hose *f.* trousers, pants.
Sie hat die Hosen an. She wears the pants.
Hosenträger *pl.* suspenders.
Hotel *n.* hotel, inn.
hübsch pretty, charming, nice.
Huf *m.* hoof.
Hügel *m.* hill.
HUHN *n.* hen.
gebratenes Hühnchen roast chicken.
junges Huhn young chicken.
Huld *f.* grace, favor, charm.
huldigen to pay homage.
Humor *m.* sense of humor.
humoristisch humorous.
HUND *m.* dog.
Hundert *n.* hundred.
zu Hunderten by hundreds.
HUNDERT one hundred *(adj.)*
HUNGER *m.* hunger.
Hunger haben to be hungry.
Hungerkur *f.* reducing diet.
hungern to be hungry, starve.
Hungersnot *f.* famine.
hungrig hungry.
husten to cough.
Hustensirup, *m.* cough syrup.
HUT *m.* hat.
unter einen Hut bringen to reconcile.
hüten to guard, keep, beware.
das Zimmer hüten to be confined to one's room.
Hütte *f.* hut.

ICH I, self, ego.
Ideal *n.* ideal.
Idealist *m.* idealist.
Idee *f.* idea, notion.
identifizieren to identify.
identisch identical.
IHM *dat.* of er, es *(pers. pron., masc. and neut.)* to him, to it.
IHN *acc.* of er *(pers. pron., masc.)* him, it.
IHNEN (ihnen) *dat.* of sie *(pers. pron. pl.)* to them.
IHNEN (Ihnen) *dat.* of Sie *(pers. pron. sing. polite form)* to you.
IHR *dat.* of sie *(pers. pron. fem.)* to her, to it.
IHR (ihr) *poss. adj. (fem. and pl.)* her, its, their.
IHR (Ihr) *poss. adj. (sing. polite form)* your.
IHR(ER, -E, -ES) *poss. pron. (fem. and pl.)* hers, its, theirs.

poss. pron. (sing. polite form) your.

ihretwegen on her (its, their) account, for her sake.

Ihretwegen on your account, for your sake.

illustrieren to illustrate.

imitieren to imitate.

IMMER always, ever.

    auf immer forever.

    immer mehr more and more.

    immer wieder again and again.

    immerfort continually, constantly.

    wer auch immer whoever.

immerhin for all that, still, nevertheless.

immerzu all the time, continually.

impertinent impertinent, insolent.

imponieren to impress.

Import m. imports, importation.

Impuls m. impulse.

impulsiv impulsive.

IN prep. (dat. answering question, Wo?; acc. answering question, Wohin?) in, into, to, at.

    Die Besucher gehen in die Oper. The spectators go to the opera.

    Der Lehrer sitzt in dem Zimmer. The teacher is sitting in the room.

    Der Lehrer tritt in das Zimmer ein. The teacher goes into the room.

    Der Sänger singt in der Oper. The singer sings at the opera.

    Goethe wurde in Frankfurt geboren. Goethe was born in Frankfort.

    im Februar in February.

    im Kreise in a circle.

Inbegriff m. embodiment, essence.

inbegriffen including inclusive, included.

INDEM while, by, on, since.

indirekt indirect.

indiskret indiscreet, tactless.

Indiskretion f. indiscretion.

Industrie f. industry.

Industrielle m. manufacturer, producer.

Infektionskrankheit f. infectious disease.

infolge in consequence of, as a result of.

    infolgedessen because of that, consequently, hence.

Ingenieur m. engineer.

Inhaber m. holder, proprietor, occupant.

Inhalt m. contents, area, extent, volume, capacity.

inhaltlich with regard to the contents.

Inhaltsangabe f. summary, table of contents.

inhaltsleer empty, meaningless.

inhaltsreich full of meaning, significant.

Inhaltsverzeichnis n. contents, table of contents, index.

inmitten in the midst of.

innen within, inside, in.

INNER interior, internal, inner.

innerhalb within, inside.

innerlich inward, internal, interior.

innig hearty, intimate.

Innigkeit f. cordiality, intimacy.

ins in das.

insbesondere particularly.

Inschrift f. inscription, legend.

Insekt n. insect.

INSEL f. island.

Inserat n. advertisement.

inserieren to advertise.

insgesamt all together, collectively.

insofern in so far, as far as that goes.

insoweit in so far.

Instandhaltung f. upkeep.

inständig instant, urgent.

Instinkt m. instinct.

instruieren to instruct, brief.

Instrument n. instrument.

intelligent intelligent.

Intelligenz f. intelligence, understanding, intellect.

interessant interesting.

Interesse n. interest, advantage.

interessieren to interest.

international international.

interviewen to interview.

Inventar n. inventory, stock.

investieren to invest.

inzwischen in between, in the meantime.

IRGEND any, some.

    wenn irgend möglich if at all possible.

irgendetwas something.

irgendjemand somebody.

irgendwann sometime.

irgendwie somehow.

irgendwo somewhere.

irgendwoher from some place or other.

irgendwohin to somewhere or other.

ironisch ironical.

irre astray, wrong, confused, insane.

    irre werden an to lose confidence in.

IRRE f. wandering, mistaken course.

    in die Irre gehen to lose one's way, go astray.

    Irre machen to confuse.

irren to err, wander, lose one's way, be mistaken, be wrong.

    sich irren to be mistaken.

    Irren ist menschlich. To err is human.

Irrenanstalt f. lunatic asylum.

irritieren to irritate.

Irrsinn m. madness, insanity.

irrsinnig mad, insane.

Irrtum m. error, mistake.

    Sie sind im Irrtum. You are mistaken.

irrtümlich erroneous, wrong.

Italiener m. Italian (person).

Italienisch n. Italian (language).

italienisch Italian.

J

JA yes, really, indeed, certainly.

    Da sind Sie ja! So there you are!

    Sie wissen ja, dass ich nicht gehen kann. But you know that I can't go.

    ja sogar even.

Jacke *f.* jacket.
Jackenkleid *n.* lady's suit.
JAGD *f.* hunt, pursuit, hunting, shooting.
    auf die Jagd gehen to go hunting.
Jagdschein *m.* hunting license.
jagen to chase, pursue.
Jäger *m.* hunter, huntsman, sportsman.
jäh sudden, quick, steep.
JAHR *n.* year.
    ein halbes Jahr six months.
Jahrestag *m.* anniversary.
Jahreswende *f.* New Year, turn of the year.
JAHRESZEIT *f.* season.
jahrhundert *n.* century.
jährlich yearly, annual.
Jahrmarkt *m.* fair.
Jahrtausend *n.* thousand years, millennium.
Jahrzehnt *n.* decade.
Jähzorn *m.* sudden anger, violent temper.
jähzornig hot-tempered, irascible.
Jammer *m.* misery, wailing.
    Was für ein Jammer! What a pity!
jammern to lament, wail, moan.
JANUAR *m.* January.
Japaner *m.* Japanese (person).
japanisch Japanese (language).
jauchzen to exult, shout, rejoice.
JAWOHL of course, indeed.
JE each, ever, at all times.
    je zwei two at a time.
    Sie erhielten je ein Pfund. They received a
    pound each.
    je nach according to.
    je nachdem according as.
    Je eher umso (desto) besser. The sooner, the
    better.
jedenfalls at all events, in any case.
JEDER (jede, jedes) every, each, either, any.
jedermann everyone, everybody.
jederzeit at any time, always.
jedesmal every time.
    jedesmal wenn whenever, as often as.
jedoch however, nevertheless.
jeher von jeher at all times, from times
    immemorial.
jemals at any time.
jemand somebody, someone.
JENER (jene, jenes) that, that one, the former,
    the other.
    jenseitig opposite, on the opposite side.
JENSEITS 1. *adv.* beyond, on the other side,
    yonder.
    2. *prep. (gen.).* that side, on the other side.
jetzig present, actual.
JETZT now, at present.
Joch *n.* yoke.
Jod *n.* iodine.
Journalist *m.* journalist.
Jubel *m.* rejoicing, jubilation.
Jude *m.* Jew.
jüdisch Jewish.

JUGEND *f.* youth, young people.
Jugendfreund *m.* friend of youth.
jugendlich youthful.
Jugendliche *m. & f.* young boy or girl.
Jugendliebe *f.* first love.
Jugendzeit *f.* youth, young days.
JULI *m.* July.
JUNG young, youthful.
Junge *m.* boy, lad.
jungenhaft boyish.
jünger younger.
Jungfrau *f.* virgin, maid, maiden.
    alte Jungfer old maid.
Junggeselle *m.* bachelor.
Jüngling *m.* young man.
JUNI *m.* June.
Jura *pl.* law.
    Jura studieren to study law.
Jurist *m.* law-student, lawyer.
Justiz *f.* administration of the law.
Juwel *n.* jewel.
Juwelier *m.* jeweler.

K

Kabarett *n.* cabaret.
Kabine *f.* cabin.
Kachel *f.* glazed tile.
KAFFEE *m.* coffee.
Kaffeekanne *f.* coffee-pot.
Käfig *m.* cage.
kahl bald, bare, naked.
kahlköpfig bald-headed.
Kai *m.* wharf.
Kaiser *m.* emperor.
Kalb *n.* calf.
Kalbfleisch *n.* veal.
    Kalbsbraten *m.* roast veal.
Kalender *m.* calendar.
kalkulieren to calculate.
KALT cold, indifferent.
kaltblütig cold-blooded.
Kälte *f.* coldness, indifference.
Kamel *n.* camel.
Kamera *f.* camera.
Kamerad *m.* friend, comrade, fellow.
Kameradschaft *f.* fellowship, comradeship.
Kamin *m.* chimney, fireplace.
Kamm *m.* comb.
kämmen to comb.
Kammer *f.* small room, chamber (government).
Kammermusik *f.* chamber music.
KAMPF *m.* fight, combat, conflict, struggle.
    Kampf ums Dasein struggle for a living.
KÄMPFEN to fight.
Kanal *m.* canal, sewer.
Kanarienvogel *m.* canary bird.
Kandidat *m.* candidate.
kandidieren to be a candidate.
Kaninchen *n.* rabbit.
Kanne *f.* jug, pot, pitcher.

Kanone f. cannon.
Kante f. edge, corner.
kantig edged, angular.
Kantine f. canteen, mess.
Kanzel f. pulpit.
Kapelle f. chapel, band.
Kapital n. capital.
Kapitalsanlage f. investment.
Kapitalismus m. capitalism.
Kapitalist m. capitalist.
kapitalkräftig wealthy.
Kapitän m. captain.
Kapitel n. chapter.
kapitulieren to capitulate.
Kaplan m. chaplain.
kaputt broken, ruined, out of order.
Karfreitag m. Good Friday.
Karikatur f. caricature.
Karneval m. carnival.
Karotte f. carrot.
Karriere f. career, gallop.
KARTE f. card, ticket, map, menu.
    Karten legen to tell one's fortune.
Kartenspiel n. card game, pack of cards.
KARTOFFEL f. potato.
    Kartoffelpüree n. mashed potatoes.
    Bratkartoffeln pl. fried potatoes.
    Kartoffelsalat, m. potato salad.
Karton m. cardboard, box.
Karwoche f. Passion Week.
KÄSE m. cheese.
Kaserne f. barracks.
Kasse f. cash-box.
    Zahlen Sie, bitte, an der Kasse. Please pay
    the cashier.
Kassenschein m. receipt.
kassieren to receive money.
Kassierer m. cashier.
Kastanie f. chestnut.
Kasten m. box, chest, mailbox.
Katalog m. catalog.
Katastrophe f. catastrophe.
katastrophal catastrophic.
Katholik m. Roman Catholic.
katholisch Roman Catholic. (adj.).
Katze f. cat.
kauen to masticate, chew.
    Kaugummi, n. chewing-gum.
KAUF m. buy, purchase.
    mit in Kauf nehmen to put up with.
KAUFEN to buy, purchase.
    sich etwas kaufen to buy oneself something.
Käufer m. buyer.
Kaufhaus n. store, warehouse, department store.
Kaufladen m. store, shop.
Kaufmann m. shopkeeper, merchant.
KAUM hardly, scarcely, barely.
Kavalier m. cavalier, gentleman.
keck bold, daring, impudent.
Keckheit f. boldness.
Kegel m. ninepin.
kegeln to bowl.

Kehle f. throat.
Kehlkopf m. larynx.
KEHREN turn, to sweep.
    sich kehren an to pay attention to; to mind.
    kehrtmachen to face about, turn back.
KEIN adj. no, not one, not any.
KEIN (ER,-E,-ES) pron. none, neither.
    keiner von beiden neither of them.
keinerlei of no sort.
KEINESWEGS on no account, not at all.
Kelch m. cup, goblet, chalice.
Keller m. cellar.
KELLNER m. (−in f.) waiter, (waitress).
KENNENto know, be acquainted with.
    kennenlernen to meet, become acquainted
    with.
Kenner m. connoisseur.
Kennkarte f. identity-card.
kenntlich recognizable, distinguishable.
KENNTNIS f. knowledge, information.
    in Kenntnis setzen to inform.
    zur Kenntnis nehmen to take note of.
Kennzeichen n. identification.
Kern m. kernel, corn, seed, stone (fruit).
Kerze f. candle, sparking plug.
Kessel m. boiler, kettle.
Kette f. chain, necklace.
Kettenhund m. watch dog.
keuchen to pant, puff.
Keuchhusten m. whooping cough.
Keule f. club, leg (of lamb, etc.)
keusch pure, modest, chaste.
Keuschheit f. modesty, purity, chastity.
Kiefer m. jaw.
Kilogramm n. kilogram (2.204 pounds).
Kilometer m. kilometer (.621 miles).
Kilometerzähler m. mileage recorder.
KIND n. child.
    kleines Kind baby (infant).
    von Kind auf from childhood on.
Kindergarten m. kindergarten, nursery school.
Kinderlähmung f. infantile paralysis.
kinderlos childless.
Kindermädchen n. nursemaid.
Kinderstube f. nursery.
Kinderwagen m. baby carriage.
Kindheit f. childhood.
kindisch childish.
kindlich childlike, filial.
Kinn n. chin.
Kino n. cinema, picture show, movies.
Kirche f. church, service.
Kirchhof m. cemetery.
Kirchturm m. church steeple.
Kirsche f. cherry.
Kissen n. cushion, pillow.
Kissenbezug m. cover, pillow-case.
Kiste f. box, chest, case.
kitzeln to tickle.
kitzlig ticklish.
Klage f. lament, complaint.
klagen to lament, complain, sue.

Kläger *m.* plaintiff.

kläglich lamentable, deplorable.

klamm numb, stiff, tight.

klammern to fasten, clasp, cling to.

Klang *m.* sound, tone, ringing of bell.

Klangfarbe *f.* timbre.

klanglos soundless.

klangvoll sonorous.

Klappstuhl *m.* camp stool or chair.

Klapptisch *m.* folding table.

Klaps *m.* slap.

KLAR clear, limpid, pure, plain, evident.
    klar und deutlich distinctly, plainly.
    klar zum Gefecht ready for action.
    klar legen (stellen) to clear up, explain.
    sich klar darüber sein to realize.

Klarinette *f.* clarinet.

Klarinettist *m.* clarinetist.

KLASSE *f.* class, form, order.

Klassenlehrer *m.* class-teacher.

Klassenzimmer *n.* classroom.

Klassik *f.* classical art, classical period.

Klatsch *m.* smack, crack, gossip.

klatschen to clap, lash, applaud.
    Beifall klatschen to applaud.

Klavier *n.* piano.

Klavierspieler *m.* pianist.

kleben to stick, glue.

Klee *m.* clover, shamrock.

KLEID *n.* dress, frock, gown.
    die Kleider, *pl.* garments.

kleiden to dress, clothe, suit, become.
    Er ist immer gut gekleidet. He is always well-dressed.

Kleiderbügel *m.* coathanger.

Kleiderbürste *f.* clothes brush.

Kleiderschrank *m.* wardrobe.

Kleidung *f.* dress, clothes, clothing.

KLEIN little, small, tiny, minor.
    klein schneiden to cut in pieces.
    klein schreiben to write with small letters.
    von klein auf from infancy on.

KLEINGELD *n.* change (monetary).

kleingläubig of little faith.

Kleinholz *n.* sticks, firewood.

Kleinkram *m.* trifle.

Kleinstadt *f.* small provincial town.

kleinstädtisch provincial.

klettern to climb.

Klima *n.* climate.

klimatisch climatic.

klimmen to climb.

Klingel *f.* bell.

klingeln to ring.

Klinke *f.* doorknob; handle.

klipp snapping sound, snap of the fingers.
    klipp und klar quite clear.

klirren to clink, jingle.

klopfen to beat, knock, tap.

Kloster *n.* monastery, convent.

Klub *m.* club.

Klubsessel *m.* lounge chair, easy chair.

KLUG intelligent, sensible, clever.
    Ich werde nicht klug daraus. I can't figure it out.

Klugheit *f.* intelligence.

Klumpen *m.* lump.

KNABE *m.* boy, lad.

Knall *m.* bang, detonation, crack.

knapp narrow, tight, close, poor.
    knapp werde to run short of.

Knappheit *f.* narrowness, conciseness.

Knecht *m.* servant, farmhand, slave.

Knechtheit *f.* servitude, slavery.

kneifen to pinch, nip.

Kneipe *f.* tavern, public house.

Knie *n.* knee.

Kniehosen *pl.* breeches, shorts.

knistern to rustle, crackle.

KNOCHEN *m.* bone.

knöchern of bone, bony.

Knopf *m.* button, knob, head.

knöpfen to button.

Knopfloch *n.* buttonhole.

Knospe *f.* bud.

knospig full of buds.

Knoten *m.* knot.

knurren to growl, rumble.

knusprig crisp.

Koch *m.* cook.

Kochbuch *n.* cookbook.

KOCHEN to cook, boil.

Kochgeschirr *n.* pots and pans.

Köchin *f.* cook.

Kochlöffel *m.* ladle.

Kochtopf *m.* saucepan, pot, casserole.

Koffer *m.* trunk, bag, suitcase.

Kognak *m.* cognac, brandy.

Kohl *m.* cabbage.

Kohle *f.* coal, carbon.
    auf Kohlen sitzen to be on tenterhooks.

Kohleneimer *m.* coal bucket.

Koje *f.* cabin, berth.

Kollege *m.* colleague.

Kolonialwaren *pl.* groceries.

Kolonialwarenhandlung *f.* grocery store.

Komiker *m.* comedian.

komisch comical.

Komma *n.* comma.

kommandieren to command, order.

KOMMEN to come, arrive, get, result, happen, occur.
    Das kommt davon. That's the result.
    Das kommt nicht in Frage. This is out of the question.
    Es kommt darauf an. It depends.
    kommen lassen to send for.
    kommen sehen to foresee.
    nicht dazu kommen to have no time to.
    Wann komme ich an die Reihe? When will it be my turn?
    Wie kommt es, dass how is it that.
    zu sich kommen to recover.

kommend next.
    kommende Woche next week.

Kommentar *m.* commentary.
Kommode *f.* commode.
Komödiant *m.* comedian, actor, hypocrite.
Komödie *f.* comedy.
Kompass *m.* compass.
komplett complete; completely.
Kompliment *n.* compliment.
komponieren to compose.
Komponist *m.* composer.
Konditor *m.* pastry cook.
Konditorei *f.* pastry-shop, cafe.
Konfekt *n.* candy, chocolates, sweets.
Konfektion *f.* ready-made clothes.
Konferenz *f.* conference.
Konfession *f.* confession.
Konflikt *m.* conflict.
KÖNIG *m.* king.
königlich royal.
Konkurrent *m.* rival.
Konkurrenz *f.* competition.
konkurrieren to be in competition with, compete.
Konkurs *m.* bankruptcy.
KÖNNEN to be able to, be possible, understand.
    Das kann sein. It may be.
    Das kann nicht sein. It is impossible.
    Ich kann nicht mehr. I am exhausted.
    Er kann nichts dafür. It is not his fault.
konsequent consistent.
Konsequenz *f.* consistency.
konservativ conservative.
Konservatorium *n.* academy of music.
Konserve *f.* canned goods.
konstruieren to construct.
Konstrukteur *m.* constructor.
Konsul *m.* consul.
Konsulat *n.* consulat.
Kontinent *m.* continent.
Konto *n.* account (financial).
Kontoauszug *m.* statement (account).
Kontrakt *m.* contract.
Kontrast *m.* contrast.
Kontrolle *f.* control.
Kontrolleur *m.* controller.
kontrollieren to control.
Konversationslexikon *n.* encyclopedia.
Konzert *n.* concert.
KOPF *m.* head, brains, intellect, heading.
    auf den Kopf stellen to turn upside down.
    aus dem Kopf by heart.
    einem den Kopf waschen to give a person a dressing-down.
    Es ist mir über den Kopf gewachsen. It was too much for me.
    im Kopf behalten to remember.
    Kopf oder Schrift heads or tails.
    nicht auf den Kopf gefallen sein to be no fool.
    sich den Kopf zerbrechen to rack one's brains.
    sich etwas aus dem Kopf schlagen to dismiss something from one's mind.
    sich in den Kopf setzen to take into one's head.
    über den Kopf waschen to be too much for.

    vor den Kopf stossen to hurt, offend.
Kopfarbeit *f.* brain work.
Kopfkissen *n.* pillow.
Kopfsalat *m.* lettuce.
kopfscheu timid.
Kopfschmerzen *pl.* headache.
    Ich habe Kopfschmerzen. I have a headache.
Kopfweh *n.* headache.
Korb *m.* basket.
    Hahn im Korbe sein to be cock of the walk.
Kork *m.* cork, stopper.
    Korkzieher *m.* corkscrew.
Korn *n.* grain.
    aufs Korn nehmen to aim at.
KÖRPER *m.* body.
körperlich bodily, physical.
Körperpflege *f.* physical culture, care of the body.
Körperwärme *f.* body heat.
korrekt correct.
Korrespondenz *f.* correspondence.
Korridor *m.* corridor.
korrigieren to correct.
Kosmetik *f.* cosmetics.
Kost *f.* food, board.
kostbar precious, costly, valuable.
Kostbarkeit *f.* preciousness, object of valor.
Kosten *f.* costs, expenses.
    auf seine Kosten kommen to recover expenses, be satisfied with the deal.
KOSTEN to cost, require, taste.
Kostenanschlag *m.* estimate.
kostenlos free.
kostenpflichtig liable for the cost.
Kostenpunkt *f.* expenses.
köstlich precious, valuable, delicious.
kostspielig expensive.
Kostüm *n.* costume, tailored suit.
Kostümfest *n.* fancy dress ball.
Kotelett *n.* cutlet, chop.
Krabbe *f.* shrimp, crab.
Krach *m.* crash, noise, quarrel.
    mit Ach und Krach with difficulty, just barely.
KRAFT *f.* strength, energy, power.
    ausser Kraft setzen to annul, abolish.
    Das geht über meine Kräfte. That's too much for me.
    in Kraft treten to come into force, effect.
    nach besten Kräften to the best of one's ability.
    zu Kräften kommen to regain one's strength.
kräftig robust, strong.
kraftlos weak, feeble.
Kragen *m.* collar.
KRANK ill, sick.
    sich krank lachen to split one's sides (with laughter).
    krank werden to be taken ill.
Kranke *m.* patient.
Krankenauto *n.* ambulance.
Krankenhaus *n.* hospital.
Krankenschwester *f.* nurse.

Krankheit *f.* illness, disease.
Kranz *m.* wreath, garland.
kraus crisp, curly.
  die Stirne krausziehen to knit one's brow.
Kraut *n.* cabbage.
Krawatte *f.* necktie.
Krebs *m.* crawfish, cancer.
Kredit *f.* credit.
KREIS *m.* circle, social group.
  einen Kreis ziehen to describe a circle.
  sich im Kreise drehen to turn around, rotate.
kreisen to circle, revolve, circulate.
Kreislauf *m.* circulation, course, revolution.
KREUZ *n.* cross; clubs (cards)
  das Kreuz schlagen to cross oneself.
  das Rote Kreuz the Red Cross.
  kreuz und quer in all directions.
Kreuzung *f.* crossing.
  Eisenbahnkreuzung. Railroad crossing.
Kreuzverhör *n.* cross-examination.
Kreuzworträtsel *n.* crossword puzzle.
kriechen to creep, crawl.
KRIEG *m.* war.
  im Krieg in wartime.
  Krieg führen to make war.
Kriegsgefangene *m.* prisoner of war.
Kriegsschauplatz *m.* theater of war.
Kriminalpolizei *f.* criminal investigation department.
Kriminalroman *m.* detective-story.
Kritik *f.* criticism.
Kritiker *m.* critic.
kritiklos uncritical, undiscriminating.
kritisch critical.
kritisieren to criticize.
Krone *f.* crown.
Kronleuchter *m.* chandelier.
Krug *m.* pitcher, jar.
Krümel *n.* crumb.
krümeln to crumble.
krumm crooked, curved, bent.
krümmen to bend.
Krümmung *f.* curve.
Krüppel *m.* cripple.
Krystall *n.* crystal.
KÜCHE *f.* kitchen, cooking.
Kuchen *m.* cake, pastry.
Kuchenbäcker *m.* pastry-cook.
Küchenherd *m.* stove.
Kugel *f.* bullet, ball, globe, sphere.
Kuh *f.* cow.
  Er ist bekannt wie eine bunte Kuh. He is well-known everywhere ("like a colorful cow").
KÜHL cool, fresh, chilly.
Kühlanlage cold storage plant.
Kühle *f.* coolness, freshness.
kühlen to cool.
Kühler *m.* radiator (car).
Kühlschrank *m.* refrigerator.
Kühlung *f.* cooling, freshness.
kühn bold, daring, audacious.
Kühnheit *f.* boldness, audacity.
Kulisse *f.* wing.

kultivieren to cultivate.
Kultur *f.* culture.
Kummer *m.* grief, sorrow.
kummervoll sad, sorrowful.
Kunde *f.* customer, client, news.
Kundgebung *f.* demonstration.
kundig well-informed, experienced.
kündigen to give notice.
Kundschaft *f.* intelligence.
künftig in the future.
KUNST *f.* art.
Kunstausstellung *f.* art exhibition.
Kunstgalerie *f.* art gallery.
kunstgerecht correct.
Kunsthandel *m.* fine art trade.
Kunsthändler *m.* art dealer.
Künstler *m.* artist.
künstlich artificial, false.
Kunstmaler *m.* painter.
Kunstseide *f.* artificial silk.
Kunststoff *m.* plastics.
Kunststück *n.* feat, trick.
KUR *f.* treatment, cure.
Kurgast *m.* visitor, patient.
Kurhaus *n.* casino.
kurios odd, strange.
Kurort *m.* health resort.
Kurs *m.* course, rate of exchange.
Kurve *f.* curve, bend, turn.
  Gefährliche Kurve! Dangerous curve!
KURZ short, brief, abrupt; in short, briefly.
  den Kürzern ziehen to be the loser.
  in kurzem soon, shortly.
  kurz darauf shortly after.
  kurz oder lang sooner or later.
  kurz und bündig concisely, briefly.
  kurz und gut in short.
  vor kurzem recently.
  zu kurz kommen to come off badly.
Kürze *f.* shortness, brevity.
kürzen to shorten, abridge.
kurzgefasst concise.
Kurzgeschichte *f.* short story.
kürzlich lately, recently.
Kurzschrift *f.* shorthand.
kurzsichtig shortsighted.
Kürzung *f.* shortening, abbreviation.
Kuss *m.* kiss.
  Mit Grüssen und Küssen With love and kisses.
küssen to kiss.
Küste *f.* coast, shore.
Kuvert *n.* envelope, cover, wrapping.

L

Laborant *m.* laboratory assistant.
Laboratorium *n.* laboratory.
lächeln to smile.
  höhnisch lächeln to sneer.
Lachen *n.* laugh, laughter.
LACHEN to laugh.

lächerlich laughable, ridiculous.
    lächerlich machen to ridicule.
lachhaft ridiculous.
Laden *m.* shop, store, shutter.
Ladeninhaber *m.* shopkeeper.
Ladenschluss *m.* closing time.
Ladentisch *m.* counter.
Lage *f.* situation, position, site, condition, storage.
Lager *n.* bed, couch, layer, support.
Lageraufnahme *f.* inventory.
Lagergeld *n* storage fee.
Lagerhaus *n.* warehouse.
lagern to lie down, camp.
lahm lame, paralyzed.
Laie *m.* layman.
Laken *n.* sheet.
LAMPE *f.* lamp, light.
Lampenfieber *n.* stagefright.
Lampenschirm *m.* lamp-shade.
LAND *n.* land, mainland, ground.
    an Land gehen to land, go ashore.
    aufs Land gehen to go to the country.
    ausser Landes gehen to go abroad.
landen to land, put ashore.
Landesbrauch *m.* national custom.
Landesfarben *pl.* national colors.
Landessprache *f.* national language.
Landestracht *f.* national costume.
Landesverrat *m.* high treason.
Landesverweisung *f.* expulsion, banishment, exile.
Landhaus *n.* country house.
Landkarte *f.* map.
Landschaft *f.* landscape, scenery.
landschaftlich provincial.
Landstrasse *f.* highway, highroad.
Landung *f.* landing, disembarkation.
Landwirtschaft *f.* farming, agriculture.
landwirtschaftlich agricultural.
LANG long, tall.
    auf lange Sicht long-dated.
    auf die lange Bank schieben to put off.
    den lieben langen Tag the livelong day.
    einen Tag lang for a day.
    Es dauert lange. It takes long.
    über kurz oder lang sooner or later.
langatmig long-winded, lengthy.
Länge *f.* length, duration.
    der Länge nach lengthwise.
    in die Länge ziehen to drag on, spin out.
langen to suffice, last, be enough.
    langen nach to reach for.
Längengrad degree of longitude.
länger longer.
    Je länger, je lieber. The longer, the better.
    schon länger for some time.
Langeweile *f.* boredom.
langfristig long-dated.
LÄNGS *prep. (gen.)* along.
    Der Weg läuft längs des Stromes. The road runs along the river.
langsam slow, tardy.
    Langsam fahren! Slow down!

Langsamkeit *f.* slowness.
längst long ago, long since.
    schon längst for a very long time.
    am längsten the longest.
    längstens at the latest, at the most.
langweilen to bore.
    sich zu Tode langweilen to be bored to death.
langwierig lengthy.
Lärm *m.* noise, din, row.
LASSEN to let, allow, permit, suffer, omit, abandon.
    aus dem Spiel lassen to leave out of the question.
    Das muss man ihm lassen. One must credit him with that.
    es beim alten lassen to let things remain as they are.
    holen lassen to send for.
    Lass das! Don't!
    Lass nur! Never mind!
    Ich habe den Wagen waschen lassen. I had the car washed.
    machen (waschen, reinigen, richten, usw.) lassen to have made (washed, cleaned, fixed, etc.),
    mit sich reden lassen to be reasonable.
    sein Leben lassen to lose one's life.
    sich sagen lassen to be told, take advice.
    sich Zeit lassen to take time.
    warten lassen to keep waiting.
lässig lazy, idle, indolent.
Last *f.* load, weight, burden, charge.
lästig troublesome, annoying, irksome.
Lastwagen *m.* cart, truck, van.
Laterne *f.* lantern, lamp.
Laub *f* foliage, leaves.
Laubwald *n.* forest.
Laubwerk *n.* foliage.
Lauer *f.* ambush.
lauern to wait for.
Lauf *m.* race, course, run, current.
    in vollem Lauf at full gallop.
    freien Lauf lassen to give vent to.
Laufbahn *f.* career.
LAUFEN to run, flow, go on.
    laufen lassen to let things go.
    auf dem laufenden sein to be up to date, abreast.
laufend running.
Laufjunge *m.* errand-boy.
Laune *f.* mood, whim.
    guter Laune sein to be in good mood.
launisch moody.
Laut *m.* sound, tone.
LAUT 1. *adj.* loud, noisy, audible.
    laut werden to become known, get about.
    2. *prep. (gen.)* according to, in accordance with
    laut Befehls by order.
    laut Rechnung as per account.
lauten to sound.
läuten to ring, toll.
lautlos silent.

Lautlosigkeit *f.* silence.
Lautsprecher *m.* loudspeaker.
lauwarm lukewarm.
LEBEN *n.* life, lifetime, living.
  am Leben bleiben to survive.
  am Leben sein to be alive.
  auf Leben und Tod a matter of life and death.
  einem Kind das Leben schenken to give
  birth to a child.
  ins Leben rufen to originate, start.
LEBEN to live, be alive, dwell, stay.
lebendig living, lively.
Lebendigkeit *f.* liveliness, animation.
Lebensgefahr *f.* danger, risk of one's life.
lebensgefährlich highly dangerous.
Lebenslage *f.* position.
lebenslänglich for life, perpetual.
Lebenslauf *m.* curriculum vitae, background.
Lebensmittel *n.* food, provisions.
lebensmüde tired of life.
Lebensraum *m.* living space.
Lebensunterhalt *m.* livelihood, living.
Lebenswandel *m.* life, conduct.
Lebensweise *f.* mode of life.
Leber *f.* liver.
lebhaft lively, vivacious.
Leck *n.* leak.
lecken to lick.
LEDER *n.* leather.
LEER empty, vacant, blank, idle.
  mit leeren Händen with empty hands.
Leere *f.* emptiness, void, vacuum.
  leerlauf *m.* neutral (gear).
leeren to empty.
LEGEN to put, lay, place, lie down, calm down.
Lehne *f.* back of chair.
lehnen to lean against, rest upon.
  sich lehnen to lean back.
Lehnstuhl *m.* armchair.
Lehramt *n.* teacher's post.
Lehrberuf *m.* teaching profession.
Lehrbuch *n.* text book.
Lehre *f.* instruction, precept, advice, warning.
LEHREN to teach, instruct.
LEHRER *m.* (– in, *f.*) teacher.
Lehrfach *n.* teaching profession.
lehrhaft didactic.
Lehrjahre *pl.* years of apprenticeship.
lehrreich instructive.
Leib *m.* body, belly, womb.
Leibgericht *n.* favorite dish.
Leibschmerzen *m. pl.* stomach-ache, colic.
Leiche *f.* corpse.
LEICHT easy, light, slight, mild, careless,
  frivolous; easily.
  etwas leicht nehmen to take it easy.
  leicht möglich very probable.
leichtfertig thoughtless, frivolous.
Leichtfertigkeit *f.* thoughtlessness, frivolity.
leichtgläubig credulous.
Leichtsinn *m.* carelessness, thoughtlessness.

leichtsinnig careless, thoughtless.
LEID *n.* grief, sorrow, pain, harm.
  Er tut mir leid. I am sorry for him.
  Es tut mir leid. I am sorry about it.
  sich ein Leid antun to commit suicide.
  zu meinem Leidwesen to my regret.
leiden to suffer, bear, endure, stand.
  leiden können, leiden mögen to like.
  Sie leidet schwer darunter. It's making her
  very miserable.
Leidenschaft *f.* passion.
leidenschaftlich passionately.
leidenschaftslos dispassionate.
leider unfortunately.
  leider nicht unfortunately not.
Leihbibliothek *f.* lending library.
leihen to lend.
Leine *f.* leash.
Leinwand *f.* linen, screen.
leise soft, gentle, dim.
  mit leiser Stimme in a low voice.
Leiste *f.* strip.
leisten to perform, carry out, accomplish.
  es sich leisten können to be able to afford
  something.
leistungsfähig capable, fit, efficient.
Leistungsfähigkeit *f.* capacity for work,
  efficiency, power.
leiten to lead, conduct, manage, direct.
Leiter *m.* leader, manager, principal, head.
Leitung *f.* direction, management, guidance, line,
  pipe.
Leitungswasser tap water.
Lektion *f.* lesson (in a book).
lenkbar docile, tractable.
lenken to direct, conduct, drive, steer.
lernbegierig anxious to learn.
LERNEN to learn, study.
Lesebuch reader (book).
LESEN to read, lecture.
lesenswert worth reading.
Leser *m.* reader (person).
leserlich legible.
LETZT last, latest, final, extreme.
  in letzter Zeit lately, recently.
  letzte Neuheit latest novelty.
  letzten Endes after all.
  letzten Sonntag last Sunday.
  letztes hergeben to do one's utmost.
  zu guter Letzt finally, in the end.
letztens lately, of late.
Leuchte *f.* lamp, light.
leuchten to light, shine, beam, glow.
Leuchter *m.* candlestick.
Leuchtturm *m.* lighthouse.
Leuchtuhr *f.* luminous clock or watch.
Leuchtzifferblatt *m.* luminous dial.
leugnen to deny, disavow.
LEUTE *pl.* people, persons, folk.
Leutnant *m.* second lieutenant.

leutselig affable.

Lexikon n. dictionary.

LICHT n. light, candle, illumination.
Bitte, machen Sie das Licht an. Please turn on the light.
Licht anzünden to turn on the light.
Licht auszünden to turn off the light.
in ein falsches Licht setzen to misrepresent.
Mir ging ein Licht auf. It dawned on me.

licht
am lichten Tage in broad daylight.
lichte Augenblicke sane moments.

lichtempfindlich sensitive to light.

lichten to thin out, clear (forest).

Lichterglanz m. brightness.

Lichtpause f. photostatic copy.

Lichtreklame f. luminous sign, illuminated advertisement.

LIEB dear, nice, beloved, agreeable.
Es ist mir lieb. I am glad.
es wäre mir lieb I should like.

Liebchen n. darling, love, sweetheart.

LIEBE f. love, affection, charity.
aus Liebe for love.
mir zu Liebe for my sake.

LIEBEN to love, like, be in love.

liebenswürdig amiable, kind.

Liebenswürdigkeit f. amiability, kindness.

lieber dearer, rather.

Liebeserklärung f. declaration of love.

Liebesgeschichte f. love story.

Liebespaar n. lovers, couple.

liebgewinnen to grow fond of.

liebhaben to love.

Liebhaber m. (—in f.) lover; amateur.

Liebhaberei f. fancy, liking; hobby.

liebkosen to caress, fondle.

Liebkosung f. caress, petting.

lieblich lovely, charming.

Liebling m. darling, favorite.

Liebreiz m. charm, attraction.

Liebschaft f. love affair.

Liebste m. & f. dearest, beloved, lover, sweetheart.

LIED n. song, air.

Liederbuch n. song-book, hymn-book.

liederlich slovenly, immoral, dissolute.

lieferbar available.

Lieferfrist f. term of delivery.

liefern to deliver, yield, produce.

Lieferung f. delivery, supply.

Lieferzeit f. time (or term) of delivery.

LIEGEN to lie, rest, be situated, stand.
Das liegt an mir. It is my fault.
Mir liegt daran. I am interested in the matter.
Mir liegt nichts daran. I don't care for it.

liegenlassen to leave.

Likör m. liqueur, cordial.

Limonade f. lemonade.

lindern to soften, ease, soothe.

Linderung f. relief.

Linie f. line, descent, branch (of a family).
in erster Linie first of all.

LINK left, wrong side of a cloth, reverse of a coin.

linkisch award, clumsy.

LINKS to the left, on the left.
Gehen Sie nach links! Go to the left!
Sie liess ihn ganz links liegen. She gave him the cold shoulder.

linkshändig left-handed.

Linnen n. linen

Linse f. lentil.

Lippe f. lip.

Lippenstift m. lipstick.

List f. cunning, craft.

Liste f. list, roll, catalogue.

listig cunning, crafty, sly, astute.

Liter m. liter (1.056 quarts).

literarisch literary.

Literatur f. literature, letters.

Litfasssäule f. billboard.

Lizenz f. license, permit.

Lob n. praise.

loben to praise.

lobenswert praiseworthy.

lobpreisen to praise.

Loch n. hole, gap.

Locke f. lock, curl.

locken to entice, allure.

Löffel m. spoon.
Esslöffel, m. tablespoon.

Loge f. box (theater).

Logik f. logic.

logisch logical.

Lohn m. compensation, reward, wages.

Lohnempfänger m. wage-earner.

lohnen to reward.
Es lohnt sich. It is worth while.

Löhnung f. pay.

lokal local, suburban.

Lokomotive f. engine (of a train).

Los n. lot, chance.

LOS
1. adv. loose, slack, free.
Hier ist viel los. There's plenty going on here.
Mit ihm ist nicht viel los. He is not up to much.
Was ist los? What's up?
2. separable prefix (implies the idea of separation or quick movement).
Du kannst die Hunde loskoppeln. You can untie the dogs.
Eins, zwei, drei, los! One, two, three, go!

losbinden to untie, unloosen.

löschen to put out, extinguish.

losgehen to set out, become loose, go off.

loskommen to get away.

loswerden to get rid of.

Löwe m. lion.

LUFT f. air, breath, breeze.
aus der Luft greifen to invent.

frische Luft schöpfen to take the air.
in die Luft sprengen to blow up.
keine Luft bekommen not to be able to breathe.
luftdicht air-tight.
lüften to air.
luftig airy, breezy.
Luftkrankheit *f.* airsickness.
luftkrank sein to be airsick.
Luftkurort *m.* health resort.
luftleer airless.
luftleerer Raum vacuum
Luftpost *f.* air mail.
Luftraum *m.* atmosphere.
Lüge *f.* lie, untruth, falsehood.
lügen to lie (falsify).
Lunge *f.* lung.
Lungenentzündung *f.* pneumonia.
Lupe *f.* magnifying glass.
Lust *f.* pleasure, joy, delight, inclination, lust.
Lust haben to be inclined to.
lustig gay, funny, jolly.
sich lustig machen to make fun of.
Lustspiel *n.* comedy.
Luxus *m.* luxury.
Lyrik *f.* lyrics.

M

Machart *f.* style, description, kind, sort.
MACHEN to make, do, manufacture, cause, amount to.
Das lässt sich machen. That is feasible.
Das macht nichts. That does not matter.
Was macht Ihre Erkältung? How is your cold?
MACHT *f.* strength, might, power, authority.
mächtig strong, mighty, powerful.
machtlos powerless.
MÄDCHEN *n.* girl, servant.
Mädchen für alles general servant.
mädchenhaft girlish, maidenly.
Mädchenname *m.* maiden name.
Magen *m.* stomach.
Ich habe einen verdorbenen Magen. I have an upset stomach.
Magenverstimmung *f.* stomach upset.
mager thin, scanty.
Magerkeit *f.* leanness, skimpiness.
mähen to mow, cut, reap.
MAHL *n.* meal.
mahlen to grind, mill.
Mahnbrief *m.* request to pay.
mahnen to remind, admonish, exort.
Mahnung *f.* reminder, warning.
MAI *m.* May.
Maiglöckchen *n.* lily of the valley.
Mais *m.* corn, maize.
Major *m.* major.
MAL *n.* 1. landmark, monument, mark.
2. time, turn.
dieses Mal for once.
ein für alle Mal once and for all.
mit einem Mal suddenly.
zum ersten Mal for the first time.

mal times, once, just.
Danke vielmals thank you very much.
Viermal drei ist zwölf. Three times four is twelve.
malen to paint, portray, represent.
sich malen lassen to have one's portrait made.
Maler *m.* painter.
malerisch pictorial, picturesque.
MAN one, they, people, you.
man hat mir gesagt, dass.... I was told that....
Man sagt so. So they say.
MANCHE many, some.
manch(er,-e,-es) many a.
mancherlei various, diverse.
manchmal sometimes.
Mangel *m.* need, want, absence, lack.
aus Mangel an for want of.
mangelhaft faulty, defective.
mangeln to want, be wanting.
es mangelt mir an I am short of.
Manier *f.* manner, style.
manierlich polite, civil, mannerly.
MANN *m.* man; husband.
mit Mann und Maus with every soul.
wenn Not am Mann ist if the worst comes to the worst.
Mannesalter *n.* manhood.
mannhaft manly.
männlich male, manly.
Manschette *f.* cuff.
Manschettenknopf *m.* sleeve link.
MANTEL *m.* coat.
Mappe *f.* document case, writing case.
Märchen *n.* fairy tale.
märchenhaft fabulous, legendary.
Marine *f.* navy.
Mark *f.* mark (coin).
markant characteristic, striking.
Marke *f.* mark, sign, postage stamp, token.
MARKT *m.* market, market place.
Markthalle *f.* market-hall.
Marktplatz *m.* market place.
Marmelade *f.* jam.
Marmor *m.* marble.
Marmorplatte *f.* marble slab.
Marsch *m.* march.
marschieren to march.
MÄRZ *m.* March.
Marzipan *m. & n.* marzipan.
MASCHINE *f.* machine, engine, typewriter.
auf der Maschine schreiben to typewrite.
Maske *f.* mask, disguise.
Maskenball *m.* fancy dress ball.
Maskerade *f.* masquerade.
MASS *n.* measure, dimension, size, degree, proportion, moderation.
in hohem Mass in a high degree.
Mass nehmen to measure.
Masse und Gewichte *pl.* weights and measurements.
nach Mass gemacht made to measure.

Massarbeit *f.* made to measure (to order).
MASSE *f.* crowd, mass, quantity.
massenhaft in large quantities, wholesale.
massgebend standard.
massgeblich standard.
masshalten to observe moderation, keep within limits.
mässig reasonable, moderate, poor, mediocre.
mässigen to observe moderation, restrain.
Mässigkeit *f.* moderation, frugality.
masslos boundless, without limit.
Massregel *f.* measure, step.
Massstab *m.* yard, measure, scale.
Material *n.* material, substance.
materialisieren to materialize.
materialistisch materialistic.
Mathematik *f.* mathematics.
Matratze *f.* mattress.
Matrose *m.* sailor.
matt weak, soft, dull; mate (chess).
mattsetzen to mate (chess).
Mauer *f.* wall.
mauern to build with stones.
Maultier *n.* mule.
Maurer *m.* mason, bricklayer.
Maus *f.* mouse.
Mechanik *f.* mechanics.
Mechaniker *m.* mechanic.
mechanisch mechanical.
Medikament *n.* medicament.
Medizin *f.* medicine, remedy.
Mediziner *m.* medical student.
MEER *n.* sea, seashore.
Meerenge *f.* channel.
Meeresspiegel *m.* sea-level.
Mehl *n.* flour.
Mehlspeise *f.* pudding.
MEHR more.
desto mehr all the more.
immer mehr more and more.
je mehr...desto the more...the more.
mehr als more than.
nicht mehr no more, any more, any longer.
nie mehr never again.
nur mehr only, nothing but.
um so mehr als... all the more as.
Mehrbetrag *m.* surplus.
mehrere several.
mehreres several things.
mehrfach manifold, numerous.
Mehrheit *f.* majority.
mehrmals several times, again and again.
Mehrzahl *f.* majority, plural.
Meile *f.* mile (1.609 kilometers).
MEIN *poss. adj.* my.
MEINEN to mean, think, believe, suppose.
Was meinen Sie damit? What do you mean by that?
Was meinen Sie dazu? What do you think about it?
Wie meinen Sie? I beg your pardon?
MEIN(er,-e-es) *poss. pron.* mine.
meinerseits for my part, as far as I am concerned.

meihesgleichen my equals, people like me.
meinethalben for my sake, for all I care.
meinetwegen for my sake, for me, on my account, as far as I am concerned.
meinetwillen (um-) for my sake.
MEINUNG *f.* meaning, opinion, view.
einem die Meinung sagen to give someone a piece of one's mind.
meiner Meinung nach to my mind, in my opinion.
meist most, mostly.
die meisten most people.
MEISTENS mostly.
MEISTER *m.* master.
Meisterschaft *f.* championship.
Meistersinger *m.* mastersinger.
Meisterstück *n.* masterpiece.
Meisterwerk *n.* masterpiece.
Meldeamt *n.* registration office.
melden to report, announce, inform, apply.
Meldezettel *m.* registration form.
Meldung *f.* news, announcement, advice, notification.
melken to milk.
Melodie *f.* melody, tune.
Menge *f.* quantity, amount, lots, multitude.
in Mengen in abundance, plenty of.
mengen to mix, meddle, interfere.
MENSCH *m.* man, human being, person.
Es kam kein Mensch. Not a soul came.
seit Menschengedenken within the memory of man; immemorial.
Was für ein Mensch ist er? What sort of a person is he?
Menschenalter *n.* generation.
menschenmöglich humanly possible.
Menschheit *f.* human race.
menschlich human.
Menschlichkeit *f.* human nature.
merkbar noticeable.
merken to perceive, notice, observe, note.
sich nichts merken lassen to appear to know nothing.
merklich noticeable.
Merkmal *n.* characteristic, sign, mark.
merkwürdig characteristic, strange, peculiar, remarkable.
merkwürdigerweise strangely enough, strange to say.
Merkwürdigkeit *f.* strangeness, peculiarity.
Messe *f.* mass; fair; mess (officers').
MESSEN to measure, survey, take the temperature (of a patient).
mit Blicken messen to eye.
sich messen mit to compete with.
sich nicht messen können mit to be no match for.
MESSER *n.* knife.
Messergriff *m.* knife handle.
Messerstich *m.* stab (with a knife).
Messing *n.* brass.
Metall *n.* metal.

Meter *m. & n.* meter (39.37 inches).
Metermass *n.* tape-measure.
Methode *f.* method.
Metzger *m.* butcher.
Metzgerei *f.* butcher's shop.
Meuterei *f.* mutiny.
MICH *acc. of ich (pers. pron)* me, myself.
Miene *f.* expression (facial), air, countenance.
 gute Miene zum bösen Spiel machen to put
 up a brave show.
MIETE *f.* rent, lease.
 Die Miete ist fällig. The rent is due.
 zur Miete wohnen to be a tenant.
mieten to rent.
Mieter *m.* tenant.
mietfrei rent free.
Mietshaus *n.* apartment house.
Mietvertrag *m.* lease.
Mikrofon *n.* microphone.
Mikroskop *n.* microscope.
mikroskopisch microscopic.
MILCH *f.* milk.
Milchgeschäft *n.* dairy.
Milchgesicht *n.* baby face.
Milchglas *n.* opalescent glass.
Milchladen *m.* dairy.
Milchstrasse *f.* Milky Way.
Milchzahn *m.* milk tooth.
MILD mild, soft, gentle, mellow, kind, charitable.
Milde *f.* gentleness, kindness.
mildern to soften, extenuate.
 Mildernde Umstände extenuating circumstances.
mildtätig kind, generous.
Militär *n.* army, service.
Militärdienst *m.* active service.
militärisch military.
Militarismus *m.* militarism.
MILLIARDE *f.* billion.
MILLION *f.* million.
Millionär *m.* millionaire.
MINDER less, minor, inferior.
minderbemittelt of moderate means.
Minderheit *f.* minority.
minderjährig minor (age).
 minderjährig sein to be a minor.
Minderjährigkeit *f.* minority (age).
minderwertig inferior.
Minderwertigkeitsgefühl *n.* inferiority complex.
MINDEST least.
 nicht im mindesten not in the least, by no
 means.
mindestens at least.
Mindestlohn *m.* minimum wage.
Mine *f.* mine.
Mineral *n.* mineral.
Minister *m.* minister.
Ministerium *n.* ministry.
Ministerpräsident *m.* prime minister.
MINUTE *f.* minute.
 minutenlang for several minutes.
MIR *dat. of ich (pers. pron.)* to me, me, myself.
mischen to blend, mix, meddle, shuffle (cards).

 sich mischen to interfere.
Mischung *f.* blend, mix.
missachten to disregard, disdain.
Missachtung *f.* disregard, disdain.
missbilligen to disapprove.
Missbilligung *f.* disapproval.
missbrauchen to misuse, abuse.
missen to do without.
Misserfolg *m.* failure.
Missetat *f.* misdeed, crime.
Missetäter *m.* criminal.
missfallen to displease.
Missgeschick *n.* bad luck, misfortune.
missglücken to fail.
missgönnen to grudge.
missgünstig envious, jealous.
Misstrauen *n.* distrust, mistrust.
misstrauen to distrust, mistrust.
misstrauisch suspicious.
missvergnügt displeased.
missverstehen to misunderstand.
MIT *prep. (dat.)* with, at, by.
 Der Patient hat mit gutem Appetit gegessen.
 The patient has eaten with a good appetite.
 mit anderen Worten in other words.
 mit der Post by post.
 mit der Zeit gradually.
 Mit fünf Jahren spielte er schon Klavier. At
 the age of five, he already played the piano.
 Wir sind mit der Eisenbahn gereist. We
 traveled by train.
 2. *separable prefix (implies accompaniment or
 participation).*
 Kommen Sie mit? Are you coming along?
mitarbeiten to collaborate, cooperate, contribute.
Mitarbeiter *m.* collaborator.
Mitbesitzer *m.* joint proprietor.
mitbringen to bring along.
Mitbürger *m.* fellow citizen.
miteinander with each other, together, jointly.
mitempfinden to sympathize with.
Mitgefühl *n.* sympathy.
Mitgift *f.* dowry.
Mitglied *n.* member.
mitkommen to accompany, come along, keep up.
Mitleid *n.* sympathy, pity, mercy.
Mitleidenschaft *f.* compassion.
 in Mitleidenschaft ziehen to affect.
mitleidig compassionate.
mitleidlos pitiless.
mitmachen to take part in, go through.
 Sie hat sehr viel mitgemacht. She went
 through a lot.
mitnehmen to take along, affect.
 Ihr Tod hat ihn sehr mitgenommen. Her death
 affected him deeply.
mitschuldig implicated (in a crime).
Mitschuldige *m. & f.* accomplice.
mitspielen to join in a game; to accompany
 (music).
MITTAG *m.* noon, midday; south.
 zu Mittag essen to have lunch.

Mittagessen n. lunch.

mittags at noon.

Mittagspause f. lunch hour.

MITTE f. middle, centre, mean, medium.

Er ist Mitte Dreissig. He is in his middle thirties.

goldene Mitte golden mean.

mitteilen to impart, communicate.

Mitteilung f. information, communication, intelligence.

Mittel n. means; remedy, cure, medicine.

Er ist ohne irgendwelche Mittel. He is penniless.

Mittelalter n. Middle Ages.

Mitteleuropa n. Central Europe.

mittellos without means.

mittelmässig average, mediocre.

Mittelmeer n. Mediterranean.

Mittelstand m. middle class.

MITTEN midway, in the middle of.

mitten auf (in) in the midst of.

mittendrin right in the middle of.

mittendurch right across, right through.

MITTERNACHT f. midnight.

mitternachts at midnight.

mittlerweile meanwhile, in the meantime.

MITTWOCH m. Wednesday.

mitunter sometimes, now and then.

Mitwelt f. our age, our generation.

Mitwisser m. confidant, one in on the secret.

MÖBEL n. piece of furniture.

Möbel pl. furniture.

Möbelhändler m. furniture dealer.

Möbelstück n. piece of furniture.

möblieren to furnish.

Mode f. fashion.

Modell n. model, pattern, mold.

modern modern.

Modeschau f. fashion show.

modisch fashionable.

MÖGEN to want, wish, be able, be allowed; to like, care for.

Das mag ich nicht. I don't like that.

Das mag sein that may be so.

Er ist faul, er mag nicht lernen. He is lazy, he does not want to learn.

Ich möchte nicht. I don't want to.

Ich möchte wissen. I'd like to know.

wie dem auch sein mag be that as it may.

lieber mögen to prefer.

Ich möchte lieber auf dem Land leben. I'd rather live in the country.

möglich possible, practicable, feasible, likely.

alles mögliche all sorts of things, everything possible.

möglichst wenig as little as possible.

möglichst schnell as quickly as possible.

Nicht möglich! It can't be!

sein möglichstes tun to do one's utmost.

möglicherweise possibly, perhaps.

Möglichkeit f. possibility, chance.

Mole f. pier.

Moment m. moment.

Einen Moment! One moment!

Momentaufnahme f. snapshot.

Monarchie f. monarchy.

MONAT m. month.

monatelang for months.

monatlich monthly.

Mönch m. monk.

MOND m. moon.

Mondschein m. moonlight.

Monolog m. monologue.

MONTAG m. Monday.

Moor n. swamp.

Moos n. moss.

Mop m. mop.

moppen to mop.

Moral f. morality, morals, moral.

moralisch moral.

moralisieren to moralize.

Mord m. murder.

Selbstmord, m. suicide.

Mordanschlag m. murderous attack.

Mörder m. murderer.

MORGEN m. morning, dawn, daybreak; the following day.

früh morgens early in the morning.

Guten Morgen. Good morning.

heute morgen this morning.

morgens in the morning.

morgen tomorrow.

morgen früh tomorrow morning.

morgen in acht Tagen a week from tomorrow.

Morgen ist auch ein Tag. Tomorrow is another day.

Morgengrauen n. dawn of the day, break of the day.

morgenländisch from the Middle East.

Morgenrock m. robe.

Motor m. motor, engine.

Motorboot n. motor boat.

Motorpanne f. engine trouble.

Motorrad n. motorcycle.

Motte f. moth.

Mücke f. mosquito (gnat).

Mückenstich m. mosquito bite.

MÜDE tired, weary.

müde werden to get tired.

Müdigkeit f. weariness, fatigue.

MÜHE f. labor, toil, effort.

sich Mühe geben to take pains.

der Mühe wert worth while.

mit Müh und Not only just, barely.

Mühe machen to give troubles.

mühelos easy, effortless.

mühevoll laborious, difficult.

Mühle f. mill.

Müller m. miller.

MUND m. mouth.

den Mund halten to keep one's mouth shut.

den Mund vollnehmen to brag.

Er ist nicht auf den Mund gefallen. He has a ready tongue.

nach dem Mund reden to flatter.

Sie leben von der Hand in den Mund. They live from hand to mouth.

Mundwinkel *m.* corner of the mouth.

Munition *f.* ammunition.

munter wide-awake, alive, gay.

Münze *f.* coin, medal.
Sie nimmt alles für bare Münze. She takes everything at its face value.

mürrisch morose, sullen.

Museum *n.* museum.

Musik *f.* music.

musikalisch musical.

Muskel *m.* muscle.

Muskelkater *m.* stiffness and soreness.

MÜSSEN to have to, be obliged to, must, ought to.
Alle Menschen müssen sterben. All human beings must die.
Man müsste es ihr eigentlich sagen. Somebody really ought to tell her.
Sie müssen nicht, wenn Sie nicht wollen. You don't have to if you don't want to.

Muster *n.* sample, model, design, pattern.

mustergültig exemplary, perfect.

musterhaft exemplary, standard.

mustern to examine.

Musterung *f.* examination.

MUT *m.* courage, fortitude, state of mind.
jemandem den Mut nehmen to discourage someone.
Mut fassen to summon up courage.
Mut machen to encourage.

mutig brave.

mutlos despondent.

MUTTER *f.* mother.

Muttermal *n.* birthmark.

Muttersprache *f.* mother tongue.

Mütze *f.* cap.

N

NACH 1. *prep. (with dat.)* after, toward, according to, like, past, by, in.
dem Namen nach kennen to know by name.
der Sage nach according to the legend.
Der Vater schickt die Kinder nach Hause. The father sends the children home.
einer nach dem andren one after another, one at a time.
Es ist zehn nach fünf. It is ten after five.
Es sieht nach Schnee aus. It looks like snow.
Gehen Sie nach links. Turn left.
meiner Meinung nach in my opinion.
Nach dem Essen ruht er sich aus. He rests after meals.
nach und nach little by little.
2. *adv.* after, toward, according to.
3. *separable prefix (implies coming after, following, imitation).*
Der Schutzmann lief dem Dieb nach. The policeman ran after the thief.
Kannst du diese Arbeit nachmachen? Can you copy this work?

nachahmen to imitate.

nachahmenswert worthy of imitation.

Nachahmung *f.* imitation.

Nachbar *m.* neighbor.

Nachbarschaft *f.* neighborhood.

nachdem *conj.* after.
Nachdem er sie verlassen hatte, weinte sie. After he left, she cried.

nachdenken to reflect, think.
nachdenken über to think over.

nachdenklich thoughtful.

Nachdruck *m.* stress, emphasis, reprint, reproduction.
Nachdruck verboten. Reproduction forbidden.

nachdrücklich strong, emphatic.

nacheifern to emulate.

nachforschen to inquire into, investigate.

Nachfrage *f.* inquiry, demand.

nachgeben to yield, give way.

nachgehen to follow, investigate, inquire.

Nachgeschmack *m.* after-taste.

nachher afterwards, later.

Nachhilfe *f.* aid, help, coaching.

Nachkomme *m.* descendant.

nachkommen to come later, follow on.

Nachkriegszeit *f.* postwar period.

nachlässig negligent, careless.

Nachlässigkeit *f.* negligence, carelessness.

nachlaufen to run after.

nachlesen to look up (in a book).

nachmachen to imitate, copy, counterfeit, duplicate.

NACHMITTAG *m.* afternoon.

nachmittags afternoons, in the afternoon.

Nachnahme *f.* cash on delivery.

Nachname *m.* surname.

nachprüfen to test, check, verify.

Nachricht *f.* news, information, account, report, message.
Ist eine Nachricht für mich da? Is there a message for me?

nachsagen to repeat after.

nachsehen to revise, check, examine.

nachsenden to send after.

Nachsicht *f.* indulgence.

nachsichtig (**-sichtsvoll**) indulgent, lenient.

nächst nearest, next, closest, following.
prep. (dat.) next to, next after.

Nächstenliebe *f.* love for one's fellow men; charity.

NACHT *f.* night.
bei Nacht, des Nachts at night.
über Nacht during the night.
über Nacht bleiben to stay overnight.
zu Nacht essen to eat supper.

Nachteil *m.* disadvantage, loss, damage, injury.
im Nachteil sein to be at a disadvantage.

Nachthemd *n.* nightgown.

Nachtigall *f.* nightingale.

Nachtisch *m.* dessert.

Nachtrag *m.* supplement.

nachtragen to add.

nachträglich additional, further.

Nachweis *m.* proof, evidence.

nachweisen to prove.
Nachwirkung *f.* after-effect.
Nachwuchs *m.* after-crop, rising generation.
Nacken *m.* nape of the neck.
nackt naked, nude, bare, plain.
Nadel *f.* needle, pin.
NAGEL *m.* nail.
    an den Nagel hängen to give up.
    den Nagel auf den Kopf treffen to hit the nail
    on the head.
Nagelfeile *f.* nail file.
Nähe *f.* nearness, proximity, vicinity.
    in der Nähe near to, close at hand.
NAHE near, close to, imminent, approaching.
    nahe daran sein to be about.
    zu nahe treten to hurt one's feelings, offend.
nahen to draw near, approach.
nähen to sew, stitch.
näher nearer, closer, more intimate, further.
Nähere *n.* details, particulars.
Näherin *f.* seamstress.
nähern to bring near, place near.
nahestehen to be closely connected, be friends
    with.
Nähgarn *n.* sewing thread.
Nähmaschine *f.* sewing machine.
Nähnadel *f.* sewing needle.
Nährboden *m.* fertile soil.
nähren to feed, nurse, nourish.
    sich nähren von to live on.
Nahrung *f.* nourishment, food.
Nahrungsmittel *pl.* food, foodstuffs.
NAME *m.* name, appellation, character.
    dem Namen nach by name.
    im Namen (with gen.) on behalf of.
namenlos nameless.
Namenstag *m.* saint's day, name day.
nämlich namely, same, very.
Narbe *f.* scar.
Narkose *f.* anesthetic.
Narr *m.* fool, jester.
    zum Narren halten to make a fool of.
narren to fool.
NASE *f.* nose.
    Der Zug fuhr mir vor der Nase weg. I missed
    the train by a hair.
    Sie schlug ihm die Tür vor der Nase zu. She
    slammed the door in his face.
NASS wet, damp.
    Die Strasse ist nass. The street is wet.
    Bei Nässe glatt. Slippery when wet.
    nass werden to get wet.
Nation *f.* nation.
national national.
Nationalhymne *f.* national anthem.
NATUR *f.* nature, disposition, constitution.
Naturalismus *m.* naturalism.
naturalistisch naturalistic.
Naturgeschichte *f.* natural science.
natürlich natural, unaffected.
    Natürlich! Of course!
Natürlichkeit *f.* naturalness, simplicity.

Naturschutzgebiet *n.* national park.
naturtreu lifelike.
Nebel *m.* fog, mist, haze.
nebelhaft nebulous.
nebelig (neblig) misty, foggy.
Nebelregen *m.* drizzle.
Nebelwetter *n.* foggy weather.
NEBEN 1. *prep.* (*dat. when answering question,*
    Wo?, acc. when answering question,
    Wohin?). next, next to, beside, among,
    besides.
    2. *adv.* next to, beside, among.
    Setzen Sie sich neben mich! Sit down next
    to me!
    Er sass neben dem Mädchen. He was
    seated next to the girl.
    neben anderen Dingen among other things.
nebenan next door.
Nebenanschluss *m.* extension (telephone).
nebenbei on the side, by the way, adjoining.
    nebenbei bemerkt (gesagt) by the way,
    incidentally.
Nebenberuf *m.* additional occupation, side-line.
Nebenbuhler *m.* rival.
Nebenbuhlerschaft *f.* rivalry.
nebeneinander next to each other, side by side.
Nebeneingang *m.* side entrance.
Nebeneinnahme *f.* additional income.
Nebenerzeugnis *n.* by-product.
Nebenfluss *m.* tributary.
Nebengebäude *n.* additional building, annex.
Nebengeräusch *n.* static (radio).
nebenher (nebenhin) by the side of.
Nebenkosten *f.* incidentals, extra.
Nebenlinie *f.* branch, secondary railroad line.
Nebenmensch *m.* fellow-creature.
Nebenperson *f.* secondary character (theater).
Nebenrolle *f.* secondary part (theater).
Nebensache *f.* matter of secondary importance.
nebensächlich unimportant, immaterial.
Nebensatz *m.* subordinate clause (grammar).
Nebenstrasse *f.* side-street.
Nebenzimmer *n.* next room.
necken to tease.
Neffe *m.* nephew.
Negative *n.* negative.
Neger *m.* (**-in,** *f.*) Negro.
negieren to deny.
NEHMEN to take, accept, receive.
    Abschied nehmen to say good-bye.
    Anstoss nehmen to object.
    es sich nicht nehmen lassen to insist on
    something.
    es genau nehmen to be pedantic.
    etwas zu sich nehmen to eat something.
    genau genommen strictly speaking.
    Nehmen Sie Platz! Sit down!
    sich in Acht nehmen to be careful.
Neid *m.* envy, jealousy.
neidisch jealous, envious.
Neige *f.* slope, decline.
    auf die Neige gehen to be on the decline,

come to an end.

neigen to incline, bow.

  geneigt sein to be inclined.

Neigung *f.* slope, declivity, inclination, taste.

NEIN no.

Nektar *m.* nectar.

Nelke *f.* carnation.

NENNEN to name, call, mention.

  ein Ding beim rechten Namen nennen to call a spade a spade.

nennenswert worth mentioning.

Nennwort *n.* noun.

Nerv *m.* nerve.

  auf die Nerven fallen to drive mad.

Nervenheilanstalt *f.* mental hospital.

nervenkrank neurotic, neurasthenic.

Nervenschwäche *f.* nervous debility, neurasthenia.

nervös nervous.

Nervosität *f.* nervousness.

Nerz *m.* mink.

Nest *n.* nest.

NETT nice, neat, pretty.

Netz *n.* net, network.

NEU new, fresh, recent, modern, latest.

  Was gibt's Neues? What's new?

Neubau *m.* new building, reconstruction.

neuerdings recently, lately.

Neuerung *f.* innovation.

Neugier *f.* curiosity.

neugierig curious.

Neuheit *f.* novelty.

Neuhochdeutsch *n.* modern high German.

Neuigkeit *f.* news.

NEUJAHR *n.* New Year.

  Glückliches Neujahr! Happy New Year!

neulich recently, the other day.

NEUN nine.

NEUNTE ninth.

NEUNZEHN nineteen.

NEUNZEHNTE nineteenth.

NEUNZIG ninety.

NEUNZIGSTE ninetieth.

neutral neutral.

Neuzeit *f.* modern times.

neuzeitlich modern.

NICHT not.

  auch nicht not even.

  ganz und gar nicht not in the least.

  gar nicht not at all.

  nicht einmal not even.

  nicht mehr no longer, no more.

  Nicht wahr? Isn't it?

  noch nicht not yet.

Nichtachtung *f.* disregard.

Nichte *f.* niece.

NICHTS nothing, not anything.

  gar nichts nothing at all.

  Es macht nichts. It doesn't matter.

  Ich will nichts mehr davon hören. I don't want to hear another word about that.

  mir nichts, dir nichts quite coolly.

  nichts als nothing but.

  nichts anderes nothing else.

nichtsdestoweniger nevertheless.

nichtssagend meaningless, insignificant.

Nichtstuer *m.* idler.

Nichtstun *n.* idling.

nie never,

  fast nie hardly ever.

NIEDER down, low, mean.

  auf und nieder up and down.

niedergeschlagen downhearted, depressed.

Niedergeschlagenheit *f.* depression.

Niederlage *f.* defeat, warehouse.

niedertreten to trample.

niedrig low, inferior, humble.

NIEMALS never.

NIEMAND nobody.

Niere *f.* kidney.

nimmer never.

nimmermehr nevermore, by no means.

nirgends nowhere.

nirgendwo nowhere.

NOCH still, yet, besides.

  noch dazu in addition.

  noch ein another.

  noch einmal once more.

  noch einmal so twice as.

  noch etwas something else.

  noch immer still.

  noch nicht not yet.

  noch nie never before.

  weder....noch neither...nor.

nochmals once again.

Norden *m.* North.

  nach Norden in the direction of the North.

nordisch northern, nordic.

nördlich northern.

nordöstlich northeastern.

Nordpol *m.* North Pole.

Nordsee *f.* North Sea.

Norm *f.* standard, rule.

normal normal.

NOT *f.* distress, want.

  mit Not only just, narrowly.

  ohne Not without real cause.

  seine liebe Not haben mit to have a hard time with.

  zur Not if need be.

Notar *m.* notary.

notariell attested by a notary.

Notausgang *m.* emergency exit.

Notbehelf *m.* expedient.

Notbremse *f.* emergency brake.

Note *f.* note (music, bank, dipl.); mark (school); (*−n, pl.,* music).

Notfall *m.* emergency.

notgedrungen compulsory, forced.

nötig necessary, needful.

  nötig haben to need.

nötigenfalls if need be.

notleidend poor, distressed.

Notlüge *f.* white lie.

notwendig necessary.
Notwendigkeit *f.* necessity.
Novelle *f.* short story, short novel.
NOVEMBER *m.* November.
nüchtern empty, sober, insipid.
Nüchternheit *f.* emptiness, sobriety, insipidity.
null null.
    null und nichtig null and void.
Null *f.* zero.
numerieren to number.
    numerierte Platz *m.* reserved seat.
NUMMER *f.* number, part, ticket, size, issue.
    Seine Nummer ist besetzt. His line is busy.
    Welche Nummer tragen Sie? What size do you wear?
    die letzte Nummer the last issue (magazine).
NUN now, well, then.
    von nun an henceforth, from now on.
NUR only, sole, merely, just, possibly.
    nur mehr still more.
    Nur zu! Go on!
    wenn nur if only.
    wer nur immer whoever.
Nuss *f.* nut.
Nussbaum *m.* walnut tree.
Nussknacker *m.* nutcracker.
nutzbar useful, necessary.
nutzbringend profitable.
Nutzen *m.* profit, benefit.
nützen to be of use, be profitable, serve.
    Es nützt nicht! It's no use!
nützlich useful.
Nützlichkeit *f.* usefulness, utility.
nutzlos useless.
Nutzlosigkeit *f.* uselessness, futility.
Nylon *n.* nylon.

O

OB whether, if.
    Wir möchten wissen ob sie kommen. We want to know whether they are coming.
    als ob as if, as though.
OBEN above, up, upstairs, on top.
    auf....oben at the top of.
    dort oben up there.
    nach oben upwards.
    oben auf on top of.
    von oben bis unten from top to bottom.
    von oben herab behandeln to treat in a condescending manner.
obendrein into the bargain, in addition.
ober upper, supreme, above.
    das obere Bett the upper berth.
Ober *m.* waiter.
    Herr Ober! Waiter!
Oberbefehlshaber *m.* commander-in-chief.
Oberfläche *f.* surface, area.
oberflächlich superficial, superficially.
oberhalb upstairs, above.
Oberhemd *n.* shirt.
Oberkellner *m.* headwaiter.
Oberkörper *m.* upper part of the body.

Oberlippe *f.* upper lip.
Oberst *m.* colonel.
oberst highest, top.
Oberstleutnant *m.* lieutenant colonel.
obgleich although.
Oboe *f.* oboe.
Obrigkeit *f.* authority.
obschon although.
Obst *n.* fruit.
Obstgarten *m.* orchard.
Ochs *m.* ox.
öde dull, empty.
ODER or.
    oder aber instead.
    entweder oder either or.
Ofen *m.* stove, furnace.
offen open, free, vacant, frank, sincere.
    auf offener Strecke on the road.
    offen gestanden frankly.
offenbar obvious, evident.
Offenbarung *f.* disclosure, revelation.
Offenheit *f.* frankness, sincerity.
offenherzig frank, sincere.
offensichtlich obvious, apparent.
öffentlich public.
Öffentlichkeit *f.* publicity.
offiziell official.
Offizier *m.* officer.
öffnen to open, dissect.
Öffnung *f.* opening, gap, dissection.
OFT often, frequently.
öfter more often
    je öfter... desto the more...the more.
    des öfteren frequently.
öfters quite often.
oftmals often, frequently.
OHNE *prep.* *(acc.)* without, but, for, except.
    Er ging ohne ein Wort zu sagen. He left without saying a word.
    ohne dass without (conj.)
    ohne dass er mich angeredet hatte without his having spoken to me.
    ohne weiteres right off.
    ohne zu without (before verb).
    ohne zu antworten without answering.
    ohnehin besides, apart.
Ohnmacht *f.* faintness, unconsciousness, faint.
ohnmächtig powerless, unconscious, helpless.
    ohnmächtig werden to faint.
OHR *n.* ear, hearing.
    die Ohren steif halten to keep one's courage.
    ganz Ohr sein to be all ears.
Ohrring *m.* earring.
OKTOBER *m.* October.
ÖL *n.* oil.
Ölbaum *m.* olive tree.
Ölbild *n.* oil painting.
ölen to oil, lubricate.
Ölfarbe *f.* paint.
ölig oily.
Olive *f.* olive.

Omelette n. omelet.
ONKEL m. uncle.
OPER f. opera, opera house.
Operation f. operation.
Operette f. operetta.
Opfer n. sacrifice, martyr, victim.
opfern to sacrifice.
Opferung f. sacrifice.
Optiker m. optician.
Optimismus m. optimism.
optimistisch optimistic.
Orange f. orange.
Orchester n. orchestra.
Orden m. order, decoration.
ordentlich in order, neat, tidy.
ordnen to put in order, arrange.
ORDNUNG f. order, arrangement.
    Das finde ich ganz in Ordnung. I think it is
    quite all right.
    In Ordnung bringen to settle, straighten out.
    Ist alles in Ordnung? Is everything all right?
    nicht in Ordnung out of order.
Organ n. organ (body).
organisieren to organize.
organisch organic.
Organist m. organist.
Orgel f. organ (music).
original original.
ORT m. place, spot, locality.
    Wir fanden alles wieder an Ort und Stelle. We
    found everything back in place.
örtlich local.
Osten m. East, Orient.
    nach Osten in the direction of the
    East.
Osterfest n. Easter.
Ostern n. East.
Österreicher m. Austrian.
österreichisch Austrian.
östlich eastern.
Ostsee f. Baltic sea.
ostwärts eastward.
Ozean m. ocean.

P

Paar n. pair, couple.
paar few, some, even, matching.
    ein paar a few, several.
    ein paarmal several times.
paaren to pair, couple.
Pächter m. farmer, tenant, householder.
Päckchen n. small parcel.
packen to seize, grasp, pack.
packend thrilling, absorbing.
Paddelboot n. canoe.
paddeln to paddle.
Paket n. parcel.
Paketannahme f. parcel-receiving office.
Pakt m. pact, agreement.
Palast m. palace.
Palme f. palm.
panieren to bread.

Panik f. panic.
Panne f. breakdown, trouble (motor).
Pantoffel m. slipper, mule.
    unter dem Pantoffel stehen to be henpecked.
Pantoffelheld m. henpecked husband.
Panzer m. armor, tank.
panzern to armor, plate.
Papagei m. parrot.
PAPIER n. paper, identification paper, document.
    zu Papier bringen to write down, put on paper.
Papierbogen m. sheet of paper.
Papiergeld n. paper money.
Papierhandlung f. stationery store.
Papierkorb m. wastepaper basket.
Pappe f. cardboard.
Papst m. Pope.
Parade f. parade, review.
Paradies n. paradise.
paradiesisch paradisiacal.
parallel parallel.
Parfum n. perfume.
PARK m. park, grounds.
parken to park.
    Parkverbot! No parking!
Parkplatz m. parking place.
Parlament n. parliament.
Parodie f. parody.
Partei f. party, faction, tenant, side.
    Partei nehmen für to take the side of.
Parterre n. ground floor.
Partie f. part, section.
Partner m. partner.
Partnerschaft f. partnership.
Pass m. pass, passage, passport.
Passagier m. passenger.
Passamt n. passport division.
Passant m. passer-by.
PASSEN to fit, suit, be convenient, be suitable.
    zu einander passen to match, harmonize.
PASSEND suitable, convenient.
passieren to go through, pass, cross, happen.
    Was ist passiert? What happened? (What's
    the trouble?)
passiv passive.
Passkontrolle f. examination of passport.
Pastete f. pie, pastry.
Pastor m. pastor, minister, clergyman.
Pate m. godfather.
Patenkind n. godchild.
Patent n. letters patent.
Patentamt n. patent office.
patentieren to patent.
pathetisch pathetic.
Patient m. patient.
Patin f. godmother.
Patriot m. patriot.
patriotisch patriotic.
Pauke f. kettledrum.
Pause f. pause, interval, break, rest (music).
pausieren to pause.
Pech n. pitch, bad luck.
pechschwarz pitch-black.

Pechsträhne *f.* run of ill luck.
Pechvogel *m.* unlucky person.
Pedal *n.* pedal.
Pedant *m.* pedant.
pedantisch pedantic.
Pein *f.* pain, agony, torture.
peinigen to torment, harass.
Peiniger *m.* tormentor.
Peinigung *f.* torment, torture.
peinlich painful, embarrassing.
Peinlichkeit *f.* painfulness; carefulness, embarrassment.
Peitsche *f.* whip, lash.
Pellkartoffeln *pl.* potatoes in their jackets.
PELZ *m.* fur, pelt, skin, hide, fur coat.
Pelzhändler *m.* furrier.
Pelzmantel *m.* fur coat.
Pension *f.* pension; boarding-house.
    Er erhält eine Pension. He receives a pension.
    in Pension sein to board.
Pensionat *n.* boarding-school.
pensionieren to pension off.
per a, per.
    per Post by post.
    per Adresse care of.
Periode *f.* period.
Perle *f.* pearl, bead.
perlen to sparkle.
Perlenkette *f.* pearl necklace, string of pearls.
PERSON *f.* person, personage, character (theater).
    in Person in person.
Personal *n.* staff, employees, personnel.
Personalbeschreibung *f.* personal description of a person.
Personalien *pl.* particulars about a person.
Personenaufzug *m.* passenger elevator.
Personenkraftwagen *m.* motor-car.
Personenzug *m.* passenger train.
persönlich personal; personally.
Persönlichkeit *f.* personality.
Perücke *f.* wig.
pessimistisch pessimistic.
Pest *f.* plague, pestilence, epidemic.
Petersilie *f.* parsley.
Pfad *m.* path.
Pfadfinder *m.* (**-in**, *f.*) boy (girl) scout.
Pfahl *m.* pole, stake, pile, post.
Pfand *m.* pledge, security, forfeit.
pfänden to seize, take in pledge.
Pfandhaus *n.* pawnshop.
Pfandleiher *m.* pawnbroker.
Pfandschein *m.* pawn ticket.
Pfanne *f.* pan.
Pfannkuchen *m.* pancake.
Pfarrer *m.* priest, pastor, minister.
Pfarrgemeinde *f.* parish.
Pfau *m.* peacock.
PFEFFER *m.* pepper.
Pfefferkuchen *m.* spiced cakes, gingerbread.
Pfefferminz *n. & f.* peppermint.

pfeffern to season with pepper.
Pfeife *f.* whistle, pipe.
pfeifen to whistle, pipe.
Pfeil *m.* arrow.
Pfeiler *m.* pillar, post.
PFERD *n.* horse.
Pfiff *m.* whistle, whistling, trick.
Pfingsten *n. & f.* Pentecost, Whitsuntide.
Pfirsich *m.* peach.
PFLANZE *f.* plant.
pflanzen to plant.
Pflanzenkunde *f.* botany.
Pflaster *n.* plaster, pavement.
Pflasterstein *m.* paving-stone.
PFLAUME *f.* plum.
    gedörrte Pflaume *f.* prune.
Pflaumenmus *n.* plum jam.
PFLEGE *f.* care, attention, nursing.
Pflegeeltern *pl.* foster parents.
Pflegekind *n.* foster child.
pflegen to care for, cherish, nurse, cultivate.
PFLICHT *f.* duty, obligation.
Pflichteifer *m.* zeal.
Pflichtgefühl *n.* sense of duty.
pflichtgemäss conformable to one's duty.
pflücken to pick, gather, pluck.
Pflug *m.* plough.
pflügen to plough.
Pförtner *m.* gatekeeper.
Pfote *f.* paw.
Pfui! Shame!
Pfund *n.* pound.
Pfütze *f.* puddle.
Phänomen *n.* phenomenon.
Phantasie *f.* imagination, fancy.
phantasieren to daydream, imagine.
Phantast *m.* dreamer, visionary.
phantastisch fantastic, fanciful.
Philosoph *m.* philosopher.
Philosophie *f.* philosophy.
philosophieren to philosophize.
Photoapparat *m.* camera.
Photograph *m.* photographer.
Photographie *f.* photography.
photographieren to photograph.
Physik *f.* physics.
Pianist *m.* pianist.
Piano *n.* piano.
Picknick *n.* picnic.
Pietät *f.* reverence, piety.
pietätlos irreverent.
Pikkoloflöte *f.* piccolo.
Pilger *m.* pilgrim.
pilgern to go on a pilgrimage.
Pille *f.* pill.
Pilot *m.* pilot.
Pilz *m.* mushroom.
    Giftpilz, *m.* poisonous mushroom.
Pinsel *m.* brush, paintbrush.
pinseln to paint.
Pirat *m.* pirate.
Pistole *f.* pistol.

Plage *f.* plague.
plagen to plague, torment.
   sich plagen to struggle, overwork oneself.
Plakat *n.* placard, poster.
   Keine Plakate. Post no bills.
Plakatsäule *f.* sign post.
Plan *m.* plan, map, design; intention.
planen to plan, scheme.
Planet *m.* planet.
planlos without any fixed plan.
planmässig according to plan; methodical.
Planung *f.* planning, plan.
Planwirtschaft *f.* economic planning.
Plastik *f.* plastic art, sculpture.
plastisch plastic.
Platin *n.* platinum.
plätschern to splash.
PLATT flat, level, insipid, dull.
Plattdeutsch *n.* Low German.
Platte *f.* plate, tray; record (phonograph)
   kalte Platte cold meats.
PLATZ *m.* place, spot, room, seat; square (street).
   Platz machen to make room.
   Bitte, nehmen Sie Platz. Please have a seat.
   am Platz sein to be opportune.
Platzanweiser *m.* (**in,–***f.*) usher.
Plätzchen *n.* little place; cookie.
platzen to burst, explode, crack.
Platzmangel *m.* lack of space.
Plauderei *f.* chat, small talk, conversation.
PLAUDERN to chat, talk, gossip.
PLÖTZLICH sudden; suddenly.
plump heavy, shapeless, tactless, clumsy.
Plumpheit *f.* shapelessness, heaviness,
   clumsiness.
plumpsen to plump down.
Plunder *m.* trash.
plündern to plunder, pillage.
Plünderung *f.* plundering, sack.
Plural *m.* plural.
Pöbel *m.* mob, populace.
pöbelhaft vulgar, low.
pochen to knock, beat, throb.
Pocken *f. pl.* smallpox.
Pockenimpfung *f.* smallpox vaccination.
Podium *n.* platform, rostrum.
Poesie *f.* poetry.
Poet *m.* poet.
poetisch poetical.
Pol *m.* pole.
polar polar, arctic.
Polarforscher *m.* polar explorer.
Pole *m.* Pole (native of Poland).
polieren to polish.
Politik *f.* politics, policy.
Politiker *m.* politician.
politisch political.
politisieren to talk politics.
Politur *f.* polish.
POLIZEI *f.* police.
   Rufen Sie die Polizei! Call the police!
Polizeiamt *n.* police-station.

Polizeiaufsicht *f.* police control.
polizeilich *m.* police officer.
polizeilich of the police.
Polizeistreife *f.* police raid.
Polizeistunde *f.* curfew.
polizeiwidrig contrary to police regulations.
Polizist *m.* policeman, constable.
polnisch Polish.
Polster *n.* cushion, pillow, bolster, pad.
Polstermöbel *pl.* upholstered furniture.
Polstersessel *m.* easy chair.
Polsterung *f.* upholstery, padding, stuffing.
Pomade *f.* pomade.
Pomp *m.* pomp.
pomphaft pompous, magnificent.
pompös pompous, magnificent.
populär popular (political).
Pore *f.* pore.
porös porous.
Portemonnaie *n.* purse.
Portion *f.* portion, helping, ration, order.
Porto *n.* postage.
portofrei postfree, prepaid.
portopflichtig liable to postage fee.
Porträt *n.* portrait, likeness.
porträtieren to portray, paint a portrait.
Porträtmaler *m.* portrait painter.
Porzellan porcelain, china.
Porzellanservice *n.* set of china.
positiv positive.
Posse *f.* farce, trick
POST *f.* post, mail, post office.
Postamt *n.* post office.
Postanweisung *f.* money order.
Postbeamte *m.* post-office clerk.
Postbote *m.* postman.
Posten *m.* post, situation.
   auf dem Posten sein to feel well.
Postkarte *f.* postcard.
postlagernd general delivery.
postlich postal.
Postschliessfach *n.* post-office box.
postwendend by return mail.
Pracht *f.* splendor.
Prachtausgabe *f.* deluxe edition.
prächtig magnificent, splendid, lovely.
prachtvoll splendid, gorgeous, magnificent.
prahlen to brag, boast.
Prahlerei *f.* boasting, bragging.
prahlerisch boastful, ostentatious.
praktisch clever, handy, useful.
   Praktischer Arzt general practitioner.
praktizieren to practice (a profession).
prall blazing, tight, tense.
   in der prallen Sonne in the full glare of the sun.
Prämie *f.* premium.
prämieren to award a prize to.
Präposition *f.* preposition.
präsentieren to present.
Präsident *m.* president.
Präsidium *n.* chair, presidency
prassen to feast, revel.

präzis precise, exact, punctual.
Präzision f. precision.
predigen to preach.
Prediger m. preacher, minister.
Predigt f. sermon, lecture.
PREIS m. price, cost, rate, praise.
   um jeden Preis at any cost.
   um keinen Preis not at any price.
   zum festem Preis at fixed price.
Preisangabe f. quotation of prices.
Preisausschreiben n. prize competition.
Preisbewerber m. competitor.
Preiselbeere f. cranberry.
preisen to praise, extol, glorify.
Preiserhöhung f. rise in prices.
Preisgabe f. surrender, abandonment.
preisgeben to surrender, give up, abandon,
   sacrifice.
Preislage f. price range.
Preisrichter m. arbiter, judge.
Preissturz m. fall in prices.
Preisträger m. prize-winner.
Preistreiberei f. forcing up of prices.
preiswert reasonable, cheap.
Premiere f. first night.
Presse f. press.
Pressestimme f. press comment, review.
Priester m. priest.
Prima f. highest class of secondary school.
prima prime, first-rate.
primitiv primitive.
Prinz m. (**-essin,** f.) prince(ss).
Prinzip n. principle.
   aus Prinzip as a matter of principle.
prinzipiell on principle.
PRIVAT private, privately.
Privatrecht n. civil law.
Probe f. trial, experiment, test, probation;
   rehearsal (theater).
   auf die Probe stellen to put to the test.
   Probe ablegen to give proof of.
Probeabzug m. proof.
proben to rehearse.
probeweise on approval, on trial.
Probezeit f. time of probation.
probieren to try, taste.
   Darf ich das anprobieren? May I try this on?
Problem n. problem.
problematisch problematic.
Produkt n. product.
Produktion f. production.
Produzent m. producer, manufacturer.
produzieren to produce, show off, exhibit.
Professor m. professor.
Professur f. professorship.
Prognose f. forecast.
Programm n. program.
Projekt n. project.
Projektionsapparat m. projector.
Proklamation f. proclamation.
Prokura f. procuration, power of attorney.
prolongieren to prolong.

Promenade f. promenade.
Propaganda f. propaganda.
Prophet m. prophet.
prophetisch prophetic.
prophezeien to prophesy.
Prophezeiung f. prophecy.
Proportion f. proportion.
Prosa f. prose.
Prosit! To your health!
Prospekt m. prospect.
Protest m. protest.
   Protest erheben to protest.
Protestant m. Protestant.
protestantisch Protestant.
Protestantismus m. Protestantism.
protestieren to protest.
Protokoll n. ticket (police); protocol.
Proviant m. provision.
Provinz f. province.
provinziell provincial.
Provision f. provision, brokerage.
Prozent n. per cent.
Prozentsatz m. percentage.
prozentual expressed as percentage.
PROZESS m. lawsuit, process, proceedings, trial.
   im Prozess liegen to be involved in a law suit.
   kurzen Prozess machen mit to dispose of
   quickly.
prozessieren to be involved in a lawsuit.
Prozession f. procession.
PRÜFEN to test, investigate, inspect, examine.
Prüfer m. examiner.
Prüfling m. examinee.
PRÜFUNG f. investigation, examination.
   eine Prüfung ablegen to take an examination.
Prunk m. splendor, ostentation.
prunkvoll gorgeous, splendid.
Psychiater m. psychiatrist.
Psychiatrie f. psychiatry.
psychisch psychic.
Psychologe m. psychologist.
Psychologie f. psychology.
psychologisch psychological.
Psychopath m. psychopath.
Publikum n. public.
Pudel m. poodle.
pudelnass drenched, soaked.
Puder m. toilet powder.
pudern to powder.
Puls m. pulse.
Pulsschlag m. pulse-beat.
Pult n. desk.
Pulver n. powder, gunpowder.
Pulverfass n. powder barrel.
   auf dem Pulverfass sitzen to sit on top of a
   volcano.
PUNKT m. point, dot, spot.
   der springende Punkt the salient point.
   Punkt ein Uhr at one o'clock sharp.
pünktlich on time, punctual, prompt.
Pünktlichkeit f. punctuality.
Puppe f. doll, puppet.

Putz *m.* trimming, ornament, dress.
putzen to clean, polish.
Putzfrau *f.* charwoman.
Putzlappen *m.* duster, flannel, polishing cloth.
Pyjama *n. & m.* pajamas.

Q

Quadrat *n.* square.
Quäker *m.* Quaker.
Qual *f.* torment, torture, pain.
quälen to torment, worry, torture, bother.
Quäler *m.* tormentor.
Quälerei *f.* tormenting, torture.
Quälgeist *m.* nuisance (person).
qualifizieren to qualify.
Qualität *f.* quality.
qualitativ qualitative.
Qualitätsware *f.* high-class article.
Qualm *m.* dense smoke.
qualmen to smoke (chimney).
qualmig smoky.
qualvoll very painful, agonizing.
Quarantäne *f.* quarantine.
  unter Quarantäne stellen to quarantine.
Quecksilber *n.* mercury.
Quelle *f.* spring, fountain.
quellen to gush, well, flow.
Quellwasser *n.* spring water.
quer cross, lateral, oblique; across, obliquely.
  kreuz under quer all over.
querfeldein across country.
Querschnitt *m.* cross-section.
Querstrasse *f.* crossroad.
Quertreiberei *f.* intrigue.
quetschen to squeeze, smash.
Quetschung *f.* contusion.
Quetschwunde *f.* bruise.
quietschen to scream, squeal.
quittieren to receipt.
Quittung *f.* receipt.
Quote *f.* quota, share.

R

Rabatt *m.* discount.
Rabbiner *m.* rabbi.
Rache *f.* revenge.
rächen to revenge, avenge.
  sich rächen take revenge, get revenge.
  Deine Faulheit wird sich an dir rächen.
  You will have to suffer for your laziness.
Rachsucht *f.* thirst for revenge.
rachsüchtig revengeful.
RAD *n.* wheel, bicycle.
radfahren to cycle.
Radfahrer *m.* cyclist.
Radfahrweg *m.* cycle track.
Radiergummi *m.* eraser.
Radierung *f.* etching.
Radio *n.* radio.
Radreifen *m.* bicycle tire.
raffiniert refined.
Rahm *m.* cream.

Rahmen *m.* frame.
Rakete *f.* rocket.
Rampe *f.* ramp, platform; limelight.
ramponieren to damage.
RAND *m.* edge, brim, border, margin.
  ausser Rand und Band sein to be out of hand.
  Schreiben Sie es an den Rand! Write it in the margin!
Randbemerkung *f.* marginal note.
Rang *m.* rank, order, quality, class.
  den Rang ablaufen to get the better of.
  ersten Ranges first class, first rate.
  erster Rang first balcony, dress circle.
  zweiter Rang second balcony, upper circle.
Rangabzeichen *n.* badge of rank.
Rangordnung *f.* order of precedence.
Rangstufe *f.* degree.
rar rare, scarce.
Rarität *f.* rarity, curiosity.
rasch quick, swift, speedy.
rascheln to rustle.
rasen to rave, rage, speed.
rasend raving, raging.
  rasend machen to make mad.
Raserei *f.* raving, fury, rage.
Rasierapparat *m.* safety razor.
  elektrischer Rasierapparat electric razor.
rasieren to shave.
  sich rasieren to shave (oneself).
  sich rasieren lassen to get shaved.
Rasierklinge *f.* razor blade.
Rasiermesser *n.* razor.
Rasierpinsel *m.* shaving brush.
Rasierzeug *n.* shaving things.
Rasse *f.* race, breed.
rassig thoroughbred.
rassisch racial.
Rast *f.* resting, recreation, rest, repose.
rasten to rest.
rastlos restless, indefatigable.
Rastlosigkeit *f.* restlessness.
RAT *m.* counsel, advice, consultation, remedy.
  Rat schaffen to devise means.
  um Rat fragen to ask advice.
  zu Rat ziehen to consult.
Rate *f.* installment.
raten to advise, guess, solve.
ratenweise by installments.
Ratgeber *m.* adviser.
Ration *f.* ration.
rationell rational; economical.
ratlos at a loss, helpless.
Ratlosigkeit *f.* helplessness, perplexity.
Ratschlag *m.* counsel, advice.
ratschlagen to deliberate.
Rätsel *n.* riddle, enigma, puzzle.
  Es ist mir ein Rätsel. It puzzles me.
rätselhaft mysterious, enigmatic.
Ratte *f.* rat.
Raub *m.* robbery, plundering.
  auf Raub ausgehen to go on the prowl.
rauben to rob, plunder.

Räuber *m.* robber, thief.
Raubmord *m.* murder and robbery.
Raubtier *n.* beast of prey.
Raubvogel *m.* bird of prey.
Rauch *m.* smoke.
RAUCHEN to smoke.
    Rauchen Verboten! No Smoking!
Raucher *m.* smoker.
räuchern to smoke, cure, fumigate.
Räucherwaren *pl.* smoked meats and fish.
Rauchtabak *m.* tobacco.
Rauchzimmer *n.* smoking room.
RAUH uneven, rough, raw, hoarse, harsh.
Rauheit *f.* roughness, harshness.
RAUM *m.* place, room, space.
    Raum geben to give way, indulge.
räumen to clear away, remove, clean, evacuate.
Rauminhalt *m.* volume, capacity.
räumlich relating to space, spatial.
Räumlichkeit *f.* room, premises, space.
Raummangel *m.* lack of room.
Räumung *f.* removal, evacuation.
Raupe *f.* caterpillar.
Raupenschlepper *m.* caterpillar tractor.
Rausch *m.* drunkenness, intoxication, frenzy.
rauschen to rustle, rush, roar.
Rauschgift *n.* narcotic.
Reaktion *f.* reaction.
Rebe *f.* grape, vine.
Rebell *m.* rebel.
rebellieren to rebel.
Rechen *m.* rake.
Rechenmaschine *f.* calculating machine.
Rechenschaft *f.* account.
Rechenschieber *m.* slide rule.
RECHNEN to count, reckon,
    calculate.
RECHNUNG *f.* sum, account, bill, calculation.
    auf eigene Rechnung at one's own risk.
    auf Rechnung setzen to charge, put to one's
    account.
    in Rechnung ziehen to take into account.
    laut Rechnung as per invoice.
    Meine Rechnung, bitte. Please bring me the
    check.
    Sind Sie auf Ihre Rechnung gekommen? Did
    you get your money's worth? (Was it worth
    while?)
Rechnungsprüfer *m.* auditor.
RECHT *n.* right, privilege, title, claim, law.
    alle Rechte vorbehalten all rights reserved.
    an den Rechten kommen to meet one's match.
    mit vollem Recht for good reasons.
    nach dem Rechten sehen to see to things.
    Recht behalten to be right in the end.
    Recht geben to agree with.
    Recht haben to be right.
    Recht sprechen to administer justice.
    von Rechts wegen by rights, according to the
    law.
    zu Recht bestehen to be valid.
RECHT right, all right, right-hand, correct,

proper, genuine, lawful.
    Das ist mir recht. That's all right with me.
    Das ist nur recht und billig. That's only fair.
    die rechte Hand the right hand.
    erst recht all the more now, now more than
    ever.
    Es geschieht ihm recht. It serves him right.
    es recht machen to suit, please.
    Man kann es nicht allen recht machen. You
    cannot please everybody.
    schlecht und recht not bad.
    zur rechten Zeit in time.
Rechte *f.* right hand.
Rechteck *n.* rectangle.
rechteckig rectangular.
rechterhand on the right hand.
rechtfertigen to justify.
    sich rechtfertigen to justify oneself.
Rechtfertigung *f.* justification.
rechthaberisch dogmatic.
rechtlich just, lawful, legitimate.
Rechtlichkeit *f.* integrity, honesty.
rechtmässig lawful, legitimate.
RECHTS to the right, on the right.
    Biegen sie rechts ab! Turn to the right!
    nach rechts to the right.
    Nehmen Sie die erste Strasse rechts. Take the
    first turn to your right.
    Rechts Halten! Keep to the right!
    Rechts um! Right turn!
Rechtsanspruch *m.* legal claim.
Rechtsanwalt *m.* lawyer, counsel.
Rechtsbeistand *m.* legal adviser.
rechtschaffen honest, upright; very, extremely.
Rechtschreibung *f.* spelling.
Rechtsfall *m.* lawsuit.
Rechtsgelehrte *m.* jurist.
rechtsgültig legal, valid.
Rechtspruch *m.* verdict.
rechtsungültig illegal, invalid.
rechtsverbindlich legally, binding.
Rechtsweg *m.* legal proceedings, law.
rechtswidrig illegal.
Rechtswissenschaft *f.* jurisprudence.
rechtzeitig in good time.
recken to stretch, extend.
Redakteur *m.* editor.
Redaktion *f.* editors, editorial staff.
redaktionell editorial.
REDE *f.* talk, discourse, speech, conversation,
    rumor.
    Davon ist keine Rede! That's out of the
    question!
    Davon ist nicht dir Rede! That's not the point!
    eine Rede halten to make a speech.
    in die Rede fallen to interrupt.
    nicht der Rede wert not worth mentioning.
    Rede stehen to answer for.
    Wovon ist die Rede? What is it all about?
    zur Rede stellen to call to account.
Redefluss *m.* flow of words.
Redefreiheit *f.* freedom of speech.

redegewandt fluent, eloquent.
REDEN to talk, speak, converse, make a speech.
   begeistert reden to rave, enthuse.
   mit sich reden lassen to listen to reason.
   nicht zu reden von to say nothing of.
   von sich reden machen to cause a stir.
Redensart *f.* phrase, idiom, nonsense.
Redner *m.* orator, speaker.
redselig talkative.
reduzieren to reduce.
Reederei *f.* steamship company.
Referenz *f.* reference.
reformieren to reform.
Regal *n.* shelf.
rege active, brisk.
Regel *f.* rule, regulation, principle.
   in der Regel as a rule.
regelmässig regular, proportional.
regeln to arrange, regulate.
   geregelt regular, well ordered.
regelrecht regular, correct, proper.
REGEN *m.* rain, shower.
   Auf Regen folgt Sonnenschein. The calm follows the storm. ("After rain follows sunshine.")
Regenbogen *m.* rainbow.
regendicht waterproof.
Regenmantel *m.* raincoat.
Regenschirm *m.* umbrella.
Regenzeit *f.* rainy season.
Regie *f.* production (theater); administration, management.
regieren to rule, govern, reign.
Regierung *f.* government, reign, rule.
Regierungsbeamte *m.* government official.
Regiment *n.* regiment, government.
Regisseur *m.* stage manager.
Register *n.* register, index, table of contents.
registrieren to register.
REGNEN to rain.
   Es regnet in Strömen. It's raining cats and dogs.
regnerisch rainy.
regsam active, agile, quick.
Regsamkeit *f.* agility, activity, quickness.
Regung *f.* movement.
Reh *n.* deer.
Rehbraten *m.* roast venison.
Reibeisen *n.* grater.
reiben to rub, grate, grind.
   wundreiben (sich) to chafe.
REICH rich, wealthy, well off, plentiful, abundant.
Reich *n.* empire, kingdom.
   Deutsche Reich *n.* Germany.
   Österreich *n.* Austria.
reichen to give, present, hand.
reichhaltig full, rich, abundant.
Reichhaltigkeit *f.* fullness, richness.
reichlich plentiful, abundant, copious.
Reichsautobahn *f.* state road.
Reichtum *m.* wealth, abundance.
Reichweite *f.* range, reach.
Reif *m.* frost.
REIF ripe, mature, mellow.

Reifen *m.* tire.
reifen to ripen, mature.
Reifenpanne *f.* flat tire, blowout.
Reifenschaden *m.* flat tire, blowout.
Reifeprüfung *f.* final comprehensive examination.
Reifezeugnis *n.* final certificate, diploma.
reiflich maturely, carefully.
REIHE *f.* row, range, series, sequence.
   ausser der Reihe out of one's mind.
   der Reihe nach successively, in rotation.
   Er ist an der Reihe. It is his turn.
Reihenfolge *f.* succession, sequence.
reihenweise in rows.
reihum in turns, by turns.
Reim *m.* rhyme.
reimen to rhyme.
REIN clean, plain, sheer, pure, genuine, tidy.
   aus reinem Trotz out of sheer obstinacy.
Reinfall *m.* failure, let down.
Reingewinn *m.* net profit.
Reinheit *f.* purity, pureness.
REINIGEN to clean, cleanse, purify.
Reinigung *f.* cleaning, cleansing.
Reinigungsanstalt *f.* cleaner's.
reinlich clean, neat, tidy.
Reinlichkeit *f.* cleanliness, neatness, tidiness.
Reis *m.* rice.
REISE *f.* trip, journey, voyage.
   Glückliche Reise! Have a nice trip!
Reisebüro *n.* tourist office.
Reiseführer *m.* guidebook.
REISEN to travel.
REISENDE *m.* passenger, traveler.
Reisescheck *m.* traveler's check.
reissen to tear, pull, drag.
   an sich reissen to seize, hold up, snatch up.
   in Stücke reissen to tear to pieces.
   sich reissen um to fight for.
reissend ravenous, rapid, torrential.
   reissende Strom *m.* torrent.
Reissverschluss *m.* zipper.
reiten to ride a horse.
Reiter *m.* horseman, cavalryman.
Reithose *f.* riding pants.
Reitschule *f.* riding school.
REIZ *m.* charm, attraction; irritation; incentive.
reizbar sensitive, irritable.
reizen to irritate, excite, provoke, tempt.
reizend charming.
reizlos unattractive.
reizvoll charming, attractive.
REKLAME *f.* publicity, advertisement.
   Reklame machen to advertise.
rekonstruieren to reconstruct.
Rekord *m.* record, competition.
Rekrut *m.* recruit.
Rektor *m.* university president.
relativ relative, relating to.
Religion *f.* religion.
religiös religious.
Rennbahn *f.* racecourse.
RENNEN to run, race.

Rennfahrer m. racing cyclist.
Rennstall m. racing stable.
renovieren to renovate, redecorate.
Rentamt n. revenue office.
Rente f. revenue, pension.
Reparation f. reparation.
Reparatur f. repair.
    Wegen Reparatur geschlossen. Closed for
    repairs.
Reparaturwerkstätte f. repair shop.
Reportage f. commentary, eye-witness account.
repräsentieren to represent.
Republik f. republic.
Republikaner m. Republican.
republikanisch republican.
Reserve f. reserve.
Reserverad n. spare wheel.
reservieren to reserve.
Respekt m. respect.
respektabel respectable.
respektieren to respect.
respektlos without respect, irreverent.
respektvoll respectful.
Rest m. rest, remains, remnant.
restaurieren to repair, restore (work of art).
Restbestand m. remainder, residue.
restlos complete, without anything left over.
Resultat n. result, answer.
retten to save, preserve, rescue, deliver.
Rettung f. rescue, saving, escape.
Rettungsboot n. lifeboat.
Rettungsring m. lifebelt.
Reue f. repentance.
reuen to repent, regret.
    Es reut mich. I regret.
reumütig repentant, penitent.
Revier n. hunting ground, district.
    Polizeirevier n. district police station.
Revolte f. revolt, insurrection.
Revolution f. revolution.
revolutionär revolutionary.
Revolver m. revolver.
Rezept n. recipe, prescription.
rezitieren to recite.
Rheumatismus m. rheumatism.
rhythmisch rhythmical.
Richter m. judge.
RICHTIG right, correct, true, real, straight.
    Das ist nicht sein richtiger Name. That's not
    his real name.
    Meine Uhr geht richtig. My watch is right.
    Richtig! Quite right!
Richtigstellung f. rectification.
Richtung f. direction, line, course, tendency.
riechen to smell.
Riemen m. strap.
Riese m. giant.
riesenhaft gigantic, colossal.
Rind n. ox, cow, cattle.
Rinde f. bark, rind of cheese, crust.
Rinderbraten m. roast beef.
Rindfleisch n. beef.

Ring m. ring, circle.
ringen to struggle, wrestle.
Ringkampf m. wrestling match.
Ringkämpfer m. wrestler, athlete.
Ringrichter m. umpire.
rings round, around.
ringsum (–her) all around.
Rinne f. gutter, channel.
rinnen to flow, run.
Rinnstein m. gutter.
Rippe f. rib.
riskant risky.
riskieren to risk.
Riss m. tear, hole, gap, crack.
Ritter m. knight, cavalier.
Rittergut n. estate, manor.
ritterlich chivalrous, gallant.
Rivale m. rival.
Rock m. coat(man's); skirt.
rodeln to sled.
Rodelschlitten m. sled.
roden to root out, clear (forest, garden).
ROH raw, crude, coarse, rare (steak).
Rohmaterial n. raw material.
Rohr n. pipe, oven.
Röhre f. tube, valve.
Rolle f. roll, cylinder; part (theater).
    aus der Rolle fallen to misbehave.
    die Rollen verteilen to cast (a play).
Rollenbesetzung f. cast.
Roller m. rolling sea.
Rollmops m. herring.
Rollschuh m. rollerskate.
    Rollschuh laufen to rollerskate.
Rollstuhl m. wheelchair.
Rolltreppe f. escalator.
Roman m. novel, fiction.
Romanschriftsteller m. novelist.
Romantik f. romanticism.
Romantiker m. romanticist.
romantisch romantic.
röntgen to X-ray.
Röntgenaufnahme f. X-ray photograph.
Röntgenbild n. X-ray photograph.
Röntgenstrahlen pl. X-rays.
rosa pink, rose-colored.
Rose f. rose.
Rosenkohl m. Brussels sprouts.
Rosine f. raisin.
Rost m. 1. rust.
    2. grate.
Rostbraten m. roast beef.
rösten to roast, grill, toast.
Rostfleck m. ironmold.
rostfrei stainless.
    rostfreier Stahl stainless steel.
rostig rusty.
ROT red, ruddy.
    rot werden to blush.
rotblond auburn.
Röte f. red, redness, blush.
Rotkohl m. red cabbage.

Rotstift *m.* red pencil.
Rotwein *m.* red wine.
Rübe *f.* sugar beet.
   die rote Rübe the red beet.
Rubin m. ruby.
Rückantwort *f.* reply.
Rückblick *m.* glance back, retrospect.
RÜCKEN *m.* back, rear.
   den Rücken kehren to turn one's back.
   in den Rücken fallen to attack from the rear.
   Rücken gegen Rücken back to back.
rücken to move, push, move away.
Rückendeckung *f.* rear, cover, protection.
rückerstatten to refund.
Rückfahrkarte *f.* return ticket.
Rückfahrt *f.* return trip.
Rückfall *m.* relapse.
rückfällig relapsing.
Rückflug *m.* return flight.
Rückfrage *f.* query, search back.
Rückgabe *f.* return.
Rückgang *m.* decline, falling off.
rückgängig retrogressive.
   rückgängig machen to cancel
Rückgrat *n.* spine, backbone.
Rückhalt *m.* reserve, support.
rückhaltlos unreserved, without reserve.
Rückkehr *f.* return.
Rückkunft *f.* return.
Rücklehne *f.* back (of chair).
Rückmarsch *m.* retreat.
Rückporto *n.* return postage.
Rückreise *f.* return trip.
Rückschlag *m.* reverse, setback, reaction.
Rückschritt *m.* step back, relapse.
Rückseite *f.* back, reverse side.
Rücksicht *f.* regard, consideration.
rücksichtslos inconsiderate, reckless.
rücksichtsvoll considerate.
Rücksitz *m.* back seat.
Rücksprache *f.* discussion, consultation.
   Rücksprache nehmen to discuss, talk over.
Rückstand *m.* arrears, residue.
rückständig backward, old-fashioned.
Rückstrahler *m.* rear reflector.
Rücktritt *m.* retirement, resignation.
Rückwand *f.* back wall.
rückwärts backwards; back.
Rückwärtsgang *m.* reverse gear.
Rückweg *m.* way back, return.
rückwirkend retroactive, retrospective.
Rückwirkung *f.* reaction, retroaction.
Rückzahlung *f.* repayment.
Rückzug *m.* withdrawal, retreat.
Ruder *n.* oar, rudder, helm.
   ans Ruder kommen to come into power.
Ruderboot *n.* rowboat.
rudern to row.
Ruf *m.* reputation, cry, call.
   im Rufe stehen to be reputed, generally
   considered as.
RUFEN to call, shout.

Soll ich sie rufen lassen? Shall I send for her?
   wie gerufen kommen to come at the right
   moment.
Rufname *m.* Christian name.
Rüge *f.* censure, reprimand.
rügen to censure, reprimand.
RUHE *f.* rest, repose, calm.
   Angenehme Ruhe! Sleep well!
   in aller Ruhe very calmly.
   Lassen Sie mich in Ruhe! Leave me alone!
   Nichts bringt ihn aus der Ruhe. Nothing upsets
   him.
   Ruhe! Silence! Quiet!
   sich zur Ruhe setzen to retire.
   zur Ruhe gehen to go to bed.
ruhelos restless.
RUHEN to rest, sleep, stand still.
   ruhen auf to rest on, be based on.
Ruhestätte *f.* resting-place.
Ruhestellung *f.* at-ease position (standing).
Ruhestörer *m.* brawler, rioter.
RUHIG still, quiet, silent, calm, composed.
   Bleiben Sie ruhig sitzen! Don't get up!
   Sei ruhig! Be quiet!
Ruhm *m.* fame, glory.
rühmen to praise.
   sich rühmen to boast, brag.
rühmlich glorious, praiseworthy.
ruhmlos inglorious, obscure.
Rührei *n.* scrambled egg.
rühren to move, touch, stir.
rührend touching, moving, pathetic.
rührig active, quick.
rührselig sentimental, emotional.
Rührung *f.* emotion, feeling.
Ruine *f.* ruin.
ruinieren to ruin.
RUND round, circular, plump.
   rund heraus flatly.
   rund (her)um all around.
Rundblick *m.* panorama.
RUNDE *f.* circle, lap, beat.
   die Runde machen to make a round.
runden to make round, round.
Rundfahrt *f.* circular tour.
Rundfrage *f.* inquiry, questionnaire.
RUNDFUNK *m.* radio, wireless, broadcasting.
   im Rundfunk gehört heard over the radio.
Rundfunkgerät *n.* wireless set.
Rundfunkhörer *m.* listener (radio).
Rundgang *m.* round (military), stroll.
rundlich round, rounded.
Rundschreiben *n.* circular letter.
Rundung *f.* rounding, curve.
Russ *m.* soot.
Russe *m.* (Russin *f.*) Russian (person).
russig sooty.
russisch Russian.
Russische *n.* Russian (language).
rüsten to arm, prepare for war.
rüstig strong, robust, vigorous.
Rüstung *f.* preparation, equipment, armor.

Rutsch *m.* slide, glide, landslip.
rutschen to slide, slip, skid.
rutschig slippery.

S

Saal *m.* large room, hall.
Saat *f.* seed.
Säbel *m.* saber.
sabotieren to sabotage.
Sachbearbeiter *m.* expert.
sachdienlich relevant, pertinent.
SACHE *f.* thing, subject, business, case, cause,
    point, subject.
    bei der Sache sein to pay attention.
    gemeinsame Sache machen to make common
    cause with.
    zur Sache to the point.
Sachen *pl.* things, clothes.
    seine sieben Sachen all one's belongings.
sachgemäss appropriate, suitable.
Sachkunde *f.* expert knowledge.
sachkundig expert, competent.
Sachlage *f.* state of affairs.
sachlich factual, essential, objective.
Sachlichkeit *f.* reality, objectivity.
Sachschaden *m.* damage to property.
sachte soft, gentle, slow.
Sachverhalt *m.* facts of the case.
Sack *m.* sack, bag, pocket, purse.
Sackgasse *f.* blind alley, dead end.
säen to sow.
Saft *m.* juice, liquid, sap.
    Apfelsinensaft *m.* orange juice.
saftig juicy, succulent.
saftlos dry.
Sage *f.* legend, tale.
Säge *f.* saw.
SAGEN to say, tell, mean.
    Das hat nichts zu sagen. That does not
    matter.
    Das ist leichter gesagt als getan. That's
    easier said than done.
    Er hat es mir ins Ohr gesagt. He whispered it
    in my ear.
    Gesagt, getan. No sooner said than done.
    man sagt they say.
    sagen lassen to send word.
    sage und schreibe precisely.
    sich etwas gesagt sein lassen to be warned.
    unter uns gesagt between you and me.
    Was sagen Sie dazu? What do you say to that?
    Was wollen Sie damit sagen? What do you
    mean by that?
sagenhaft legendary, fabulous, mythical.
Sägewerk *n.* sawmill.
Sahne *f.* cream.
Saison *f.* season (social).
Saisonausverkauf *m* clearance sale.
Saite *f.* string, chord.
Saiteninstrument *n.* stringed instrument.
Salat *m.* salad.
    grüner Salat lettuce.
Salbe *f.* salve, ointment.

salben to anoint.
Salmiakgeist *m.* ammonia.
Salon *m.* drawing room.
salutieren to salute.
SALZ *m.* salt.
salzen to salt, season.
Salzgurke *f.* pickled cucumber.
salzhaltig containing salt.
salzig salted, salty.
Same m. seed.
SAMMELN to collect, gather, accumulate.
Sammelplatz *m.* assembly.
Sammelstelle *f.* assembly.
Sammler *m.* collector.
Sammlung *f.* collection.
SAMSTAG *m.* Saturday.
Samt *m.* velvet.
samt together with.
    samt und sonders one and all.
sämtlich altogether, all of them.
Sanatorium *n.* sanatorium.
SAND *m.* sand.
Sandale *f.* sandal.
Sandboden *m.* sandy soil.
sandig sandy.
SANFT soft, tender, delicate, gentle, smooth.
Sanftheit *f.* softness.
sänftigen to soften, appease.
Sanftmut *f.* gentleness.
sanftmütig gentle, meek.
Sänger *m.* (–in, *f.*) singer.
Sanitäter *m.* medical aid (person).
Sardelle *f.* anchovy.
Sardine *f.* sardine.
Sarg *m.* coffin.
sarkastisch sarcastic.
Satiriker *m.* satirist.
satirisch satirical.
SATT full, satisfied, saturated.
    Ich habe es satt. I've enough of it, I'm fed up
    with it.
    nicht satt werden never to be tired of.
Sattel *m.* saddle.
    in allen Sätteln gerecht sein to be good at
    everything.
satteln to saddle.
sättigen to satisfy, saturate.
Satz *m.* set, clause, sentence (grammar);
    proposition (philo.); phrase (music);
    sediment.
Satzbau *m.* sentence structure.
Satzzeichen *n.* punctuation mark.
sauber clean, neat, tidy.
Sauberkeit *f.* tidiness, cleanliness.
säuberlich clean, neat.
säubern to clean, clear.
Säuberung *f.* cleaning.
Sauce *f.* sauce, gravy.
SAUER sour, acid, pickled.
Sauerbraten *m.* sauerbraten.
Sauerkraut *n.* sauerkraut.
säuerlich acid, acidulous.

säuern to acidify.
Sauerstoff *m.* oxygen.
Sauerstoffgerät *n.* oxygen apparatus.
saugen to suck, absorb.
säugen to suckle, nurse.
Säugling *m.* infant, baby.
Säule *f.* pillar, column.
Saum *m.* edge, border, hem.
Säure *f.* acid, sourness, tartness, acidity.
säurehaltig containing acid.
Saxophon *n.* saxophone.
schäbig shabby, worn out.
Schäbigkeit *f.* shabbiness.
Schach *n.* chess.
    Schach bieten to defy.
Schachbrett *n.* chessboard.
Schachfeld *n.* square of a chessboard.
schachmatt checkmate.
Schachpartie *f.* chess game.
Schachtel *f.* box.
SCHADE too bad.
    Es ist schade! It is a pity!
    Wie schade! What a pity!
    zu schade für too good to.
Schaden *m.* damage, harm, injury, bias.
    Durch Schaden wird man klug. You learn by
    your mistakes.
    zu Schaden kommen to suffer damage.
SCHADEN to hurt, damage, injure, prejudice.
    Es schadet nichts. It doesn't matter.
Schadenersatz *m.* compensation.
Schadenfreude *f.* malicious joy.
schadenfroh rejoicing over another's misfortune.
schadhaft damaged, defective, dilapidated.
    sich schadlos halten to get even with.
schädlich harmful, bad.
Schaf *n.* sheep.
Schäfchen *n.* lamb.
    sein Schäfchen ins Trockene bringen
    to feather one's nest
Schäfer *m.* shepherd.
Schäferhund *m.* sheep-dog.
schaffen to create, produce, accomplish, make,
    do.
    einem zu schaffen machen to give trouble.
    sich zu schaffen machen to be busy.
    wie geschaffen für as though cut out for.
schaffend creative, working.
Schaffner *m.* conductor, (train) guard.
Schal *m.* shawl, scarf.
Schale *f.* skin, peel, rind, shell.
schälen to peel, shell, bark, skin.
Schalk *m.* rogue.
schalkhaft roguish.
Schall *m.* sound.
schalldicht soundproof.
Schalleffekt *m.* sound effect.
schallen to sound, resound.
Schalllehre *f.* acoustics.
Schallplatte *f.* record (phonograph).
Schaltanlage *f.* switch, gear.

schalten to deal with, use, direct, change gears.
Schalter *m.* switch, ticket-window.
Schaltjahr *n.* leap year.
Schaltung *f.* gear change, connection.
Scham *f.* shame, modesty.
schämen (sich) to be ashamed.
Schamgefühl *n.* sense of shame.
schamhaft modest, bashful.
schamlos shameless, impudent.
Schamlosigkeit *f.* shamelessness, impudence.
schamrot blushing red.
Schamröte *f.* blush.
schandbar infamous.
Schande *f.* shame, disgrace.
schänden to spoil, disfigure, dishonor, rape.
schändlich shameful, disgraceful.
Schändlichkeit *f.* infamy.
Schandtat *f.* crime, misdeed.
SCHARF sharp, keen, harsh, pointed, piercing,
    acute, strong, quick.
    Behalten Sie ihn scharf im Auge! Keep a sharp
    eye on him!
    Ich bin nicht so scharf darauf. I am not so
    keen on that.
Scharfblick *m.* penetrating glance.
Schärfe *f.* sharpness, rigor, acuteness.
schärfen to sharpen.
scharfkantig sharp-edged.
Scharfsicht *f.* keenness of sight, perspicacity.
scharfsichtig keen-sighted, penetrating.
Scharlach *m.* scarlet fever.
SCHATTEN *m.* shadow, shade, spirit, phantom.
    in den Schatten stellen to overshadow.
    Sie folgt mir wie ein Schatten. She follows
    me like a shadow.
Schattenseite *f.* shady side.
schattieren to shade.
schattig shady.
Schatz *m.* treasure.
Schatzamt *n.* treasury.
Schatzanweisung *f.* treasury bond.
schätzen to value, estimate, judge.
schätzenswert estimable.
Schatzmeister *m.* treasurer.
Schätzung *f.* estimate, taxation.
schätzungsweise approximately.
SCHAU *f.* sight, view, show, exhibition.
    zur Schau stellen to exhibit, display.
Schauder *m.* shudder, shivering, horror, terror,
    fright.
schauen to see, behold, gaze, view.
Schauer *m.* horror, terror, awe, thrill.
schauerlich awful.
schauern to shudder, shiver.
    mich schaudert bei I shudder at.
Schauerroman *m.* thriller.
Schaufel *f.* shovel, scoop.
schaufeln to shovel.
Schaufenster *n.* show-window.
Schaukasten *m.* show case.
Schaukel *f.* swing.

schaukeln to swing, rock.
Schaukelstuhl *m.* rocking chair.
schaulustig curious.
SCHAUSPIEL *n.* spectacle, scene, play, drama.
Schauspieler *m.* (-in, *f.*) actor (actress).
Schauspielkunst *f.* dramatic art.
Schaustellung *f.* exhibition.
Schaustück *n.* specimen.
Schaum *m.* foam.
    zu Schaum schlagen to beat up.
schäumen to foam.
schaumig foamy, frothy.
Scheck *m.* check.
Scheckbuch *n.* check book.
Scheckformular *n.* blank check.
Scheckinhaber *m.* bearer.
Scheibe *f.* (window) pane, disk, slice, target.
Scheibenwischer *m.* window-wiper.
Scheide *f.* boundary, limits, frontier.
scheiden to separate, divide, part, divorce.
    sich scheiden lassen to get a divorce.
Scheidewand *f.* partition.
Scheidung *f.* separation, divorce.
Scheidungsklage *f.* divorce suit.
SCHEIN *m.* appearance, air, look; shine; ticket, receipt.
    Der Schein trügt. Appearances are deceiving.
scheinbar apparent.
Scheinbild *n.* phantom, illusion.
SCHEINEN to shine; seem; look.
scheinheilig hypocritical.
Scheintod *m.* suspended animation.
Scheinwerfer *m.* reflector, search light, headlight (car).
Scheitel *m.* top, crown, summit.
scheitern to fail.
Schelle *f.* door bell, little bell.
Schema *n.* order, arrangement, model.
schematisch systematic, mechanical.
Schenkel *m.* thigh.
schenken to give, present with, grant.
    geschenkt bekommen to get as a present.
Schenker *m.* donor.
Schenkung *f.* donation, gift.
Schere *f.* scissors.
Scherz *m.* joke, jest, pleasantry.
scherzen to joke, make fun of.
scherzhaft joking.
Scherzwort *n.* joke.
SCHEU shy, timid.
    scheu werden to shy.
scheuen to avoid, shun.
    sich scheuen to shy away.
scheuern to scrub, rub, clean, chafe.
Schicht *f.* layer, bed, coat, shift.
Schichtwechsel *m.* change of shift.
Schick *m.* elegance, smartness, chic.
SCHICKEN to send, dispatch.
    schicken nach to send for.
    sich schicken in to put up with.
schicklich proper, decent.
Schicksal *n.* fate, destiny, lot.

Schiebefenster *n.* sash-window.
SCHIEBEN to move, push, shove.
    schieben auf to lay the blame on.
Schiebetür *f.* sliding door.
Schiebung *f.* profiteering.
Schiedsrichter *m.* umpire.
schief oblique, crooked, askance.
Schiefer *m.* slate, splinter.
Schieferdach *n.* slate roof.
Schiene *f.* rail, track, splint.
schiessen to shoot, flash, fire.
SCHIFF *n.* boat, ship, vessel.
    zu Schiff on board, by boat.
schiffbar navigable.
Schiffbruch *m.* shipwreck.
Schiffchen *n.* small boat, shuttle.
schiffen to ship, sail.
Schiffer *m.* sailor.
Schiffsbesatzung *f.* crew.
Schiffskörper *m.* hull.
Schiffsladung *f.* cargo.
Schiffswerft *m.* wharf, dock.
Schild *m.* shield, coat of arms, sign.
    im Schilde führen to have something up one's sleeve.
schildern to relate, describe.
Schilderung *f.* description.
Schimmel *m.* mold, mildew.
schimmelig moldy.
Schimmer *m.* glitter.
schimmern to glitter, gleam.
Schimpf *m.* disgrace, insult.
schimpfen to kick, gripe, scold.
    schimpfen mit to scold.
schimpflich disgraceful.
Schimpfwort *n.* invective.
SCHINKEN *m.* ham.
    Eier mit Schinken ham and eggs.
Schirm *m.* umbrella, shelter, lampshade.
Schlacht *f.* combat, battle.
schlachten to slaughter, kill, butcher.
Schlächter *m.* butcher.
Schlachtfeld *n.* battlefield.
Schlachthaus *n.* slaughterhouse.
Schlachtschiff *n.* battleship.
SCHLAF *m.* sleep.
    im Schlaf liegen to be asleep.
Schlafanzug *m.* pajamas.
Schläfchen *n.* nap.
SCHLAFEN to sleep.
    schlafen gehen to go to bed.
Schlafenszeit *m.* bedtime.
schlaff slack, loose, relaxed.
Schlaffheit *f.* laxity.
Schlafkrankheit *f.* sleeping sickness.
schlaflos sleepless.
Schlaflosigkeit *f.* insomnia.
Schlafmittel *n.* narcotic.
schläfrig sleepy.
Schlafsaal *m.* dormitory.
Schlafwagen *m.* sleeping-car.
Schlafwandler *m.* sleepwalker.

Schlafzimmer *n.* bedroom.
SCHLAG *m.* blow, stroke, striking (clock).
  zwei Fliegen auf einen Schlag treffen to
  kill two birds with one stone.
Schlagader *f.* artery.
Schlaganfall *m.* stroke, fit.
SCHLAGEN to beat, knock, hit, strike, throb.
  sich schlagen to fight.
  sich geschlagen geben to give up.
  schlagen nach to take after.
  eine geschlagene Stunde a whole hour.
schlagfertig quick at repartee.
Schlagfertigkeit *f.* quickness at repartee.
Schlagsahne *f.* whipped cream.
Schlagwort *n.* slogan.
Schlagzeile *f.* headline.
Schlagzeug *n.* percussion instrument.
Schlamm *m.* mud, ooze.
schlammig muddy, oozy.
Schlange *f.* snake.
  Schlange stehen to make a line.
Schlangernbiss *m.* snake bite.
schlank slim, slender.
Schlankheit *f.* slimness, slenderness.
schlapp weak, tired, limp, flabby.
  schlapp machen to collapse.
schlau sly, cunning.
Schlauberger *m.* sly fox.
Schlauch *m.* hose, tube.
Schlauheit *f.* slyness, cunning.
Schlaukopf *m.* sly fox.
SCHLECHT bad, poor, inferior, ill, wicked.
  mir ist schlecht I feel sick.
  schlecht machen to run down.
  schlecht und recht somehow.
  schlecht werden to spoil (food).
schlechtgelaunt in a bad temper.
Schlechtigkeit *f.* badness, wickedness.
schleichen to creep, drag, sneak.
  sich davon schleichen to steal away.
  wie die Katze um den heissen Brei
  schleichen to beat around the bush
  ("to creep like the cat around the hot roast").

schlicht simple, plain, even.
schlichten to make simple, smooth.
Schlichtheit *f.* simplicity.
Schliesse *f.* clasp, fastening.
SCHLIESSEN to close, lock, shut, break up.
  in die Arme schliessen to embrace.
  geschlossen enclosed.
Schliessfach *n.* locker.
schliesslich final, finally, after all.
Schliessung *f.* closing.
schlimm bad, sore.
  schlimmstenfalls if the worst comes to the
  worst.
Schlinge *f.* knot, loop.
  sich aus der Schlinge ziehen to get out of a
  difficulty.
Schlips *m.* necktie (coll.).
Schlitten *m.* sled, sleigh.
Schlittenfahrt *f.* sleigh driving.
Schlittschuh *m.* skate.

Schlittschuh laufen to skate.
Schlittschuhläufer *m.* skater.
SCHLOSS *n.* castle, lock.
Schlosser *m.* locksmith.
Schluck *m.* gulp, draught.
Schluckauf *m.* hiccup.
schlucken to gulp, swallow.
Schlucker *m.* hiccup.
  armer Schlucker poor wretch.
Schlummer *m.* slumber.
schlummern to slumber.
Schlüpfer *m.* panties.
SCHLUSS *m.* closing, shutting, conclusion.
Schlüssel *m.* key, code.
Schlüsselbund *m.* bunch of keys.
Schlüsselloch *m.* keyhole.
Schlusslicht *n.* tail light.
Schlusswort *n.* summary, last word.
Schmach *f.* disgrace, dishonor, humiliation.
schmachten to languish.
schmachvoll disgraceful, humiliating.
schmackhaff tasty, savory.
schmähen to abuse.
schmählich disgraceful.
SCHMAL narrow, thin, slender, poor.
  Hier ist Schmalhans Küchenmeister. We are
  on short rations here.
schmälern to diminish, lessen.
Schmalz *n.* drippings.
SCHMECKEN to taste, try.
  Es schmeckt gut. It tastes good.
  Es schmeckt mir nicht. I don't like it.
  schmecken nach to taste of.
  Wie schmeckt's? How do you like it?
Schmeichelei *f.* flattery.
schmeichelhaft flattering.
Schmeichelkatze *f.* wheedler.
schmeicheln to flatter.
Schmeichler *m.* flatterer.
schmeichlerisch flattering.
schmelzen to melt.
SCHMERZ *m.* pain, ache, hurt, sorrow.
SCHMERZEN to hurt, pain, grieve.
Schmerzensgeld *n.* smart money, compensation.
schmerzerfüllt deeply affected.
schmerzhaft painful.
schmerzlich grievous, sad.
schmerzlos painless.
schmerzstillend soothing.
Schmetterling *m.* butterfly.
Schmied *m.* blacksmith.
Schmiede *f.* forge.
schmieden to forge, hammer.
schmiegen to bend.
schmiegsam flexible, supple.
Schmiegsamkeit *f.* flexibility.
schmieren to spread, grease, smear.
Schminke *f.* rouge, paint, make up.
schminken to make up, paint the face.
Schmöker *m.* bad novel, trashy book.
schmollen to sulk.
Schmorbraten *m.* stewed steak.
SCHMUCK *m.* jewelry, ornament, decoration.
schmücken to decorate, adorn.

Schmuckstück *n.* piece of jewelry.
Schmuggel *m.* smuggling.
schmuggeln to smuggle.
schmunzeln to grin.
Schmutz *m.* dirt, mud.
schmutzen to dirty.
Schmutzfleck *m.* stain, spot.
schmutzig dirty.
Schnabel *m.* beak, bill.
schnarchen to snore.
schnaufen to breathe heavily, pant.
Schnecke *f.* snail.
   wie eine Schnecke kriechen to go at a
   snail's pace.
SCHNEE *m.* snow.
Schneeball *m.* snowball.
Schneefall *m.* snowfall.
Schneeflocke *f.* snowflake.
Schneeglöckchen *n.* snowdrop.
Schneekette *f.* non-skid chain (automobile).
Schneeschuh *m.* ski.
Schneetreiben *n.* blizzard.
schneeweiss snow-white.
SCHNEIDEN to cut, carve.
   sich schneiden to cut oneself.
schneidend sharp, bitter.
Schneider *m.* tailor.
schneien to snow.
SCHNELL quick, fast, swift, prompt, speedy.
Schnelligkeit *f.* rapidity, velocity.
Schnellzug *m.* express train.
Schnippchen *n.* snap of the fingers.
   ein Schnippchen schlagen to play a trick.
Schnitt *m.* cut, cutting, incision.
   der goldene Schnitt A medial section.
Schnittblumen *pl.* cut flowers.
Schnittmuster *n.* cut pattern.
Schnittwunde *f.* cut.
schnitzen to carve, cut.
Schnupfen *m.* (head) cold.
schnupfen to take snuff.
Schnur *f.* string, cord.
   über die Schnur hauen to kick over the traces.
Schnurrbart *m.* moustache.
schnurren to hum, buzz, purr.
schnurstracks immediately.
Schock *m.* shock.
Schokolade *f.* chocolate.
SCHON already, all right, very, yet, even,
   indeed, certainly.
   Schon gut! All right!
   Wenn schon! So what!
SCHÖN beautiful, handsome, fine, nice, fair, noble.

Danke schön (Schönen Dank).	Thanks.
Das wäre noch schöner!	That's all we need!
die Schönen Künste	the fine arts.
schön tun	to flatter.
Schönen Gruss an Ihre Frau.	Best regards to your wife.
Schönsten Dank.	Many thanks.
sich schön machen.	to smarten oneself.

schonen to spare, save, look after.
schonend careful, considerate.
Schöngeist *m.* wit; esthete.
schöngeistig esthetical.
Schönheit *f.* beauty.
Schönheitsmittel *n.* cosmetic.
Schönheitspflege *f.* beauty treatment.
Schonung *f.* indulgence.
schonungslos pitiless.
schöpfen to draw, create.
Schöpferkraft *f.* creative, power.
Schöpflöffel *m.* strainer.
Schornstein *m.* chimney, funnel.
Schoss *m.* lap.
Schotte *m.* Scotsman.
schottisch Scottish.
schräg diagonally.
Schräge *f.* slant, slope.
Schramme *f.* scratch, scar.
schrammen to scratch.
Schrank *m.* wardrobe.
Schranke *f.* fencing, enclosure, gate.
   sich in Schranken halten to keep within bounds.
schrankenlos boundless, without limits.
Schrankkoffer *m.* wardrobe trunk.
Schraube *f.* screw, propeller, bolt.
schrauben to screw, turn, wheel.
Schraubenschlüssel *m.* wrench.
Schraubenzieher *m.* screwdriver.
SCHRECK (EN) *m.* scare, fright, fear, dread, horror.
   in Schrecken setzen to terrify.
schrecken to frighten.
Schreckgespenst *n.* terrible vision.
schreckhaft timid, easily frightened.
schrecklich terrible, awful.
Schreckschuss *m.* false alarm.
Schrei *m.* scream, cry.
SCHREIBEN to write, spell.
   auf der Maschine schreiben to type.
   sage und schreibe precisely.
Schreiberei *f.* writing, correspondence.
Schreibfehler *m.* slip of the pen.
Schreibmappe *f.* writing case, portfolio, blotter.
Schreibmaschine *f.* typewriter.
Schreibpapier *n.* note paper.
Schreibstube *f.* office.
Schreibwaren *pl.* stationery.
Schreibwarengeschäft *n.* stationery store.
Schreibwarenhändler *m.* stationer.
Schreibwarenhandlung *f.* stationery store.
SCHREIEN to scream, shout, yell.
schreiend loud, gaudy.
Schreier *m.* shouter, bawler.
Schreiner *m.* carpenter, cabinetmaker.
Schreinerei *f.* cabinetmaker's.
SCHRIFT *f.* writing, handwriting, script.
schriftlich in writing, written.
Schriftführer *m.* secretary (association or politics).
Schriftsteller *m.* writer (author).
SCHRITT *m.* step, stride.
   auf Schritt und Tritt everywhere, all the time.
   Schritt fahren! Drive slowly!

Schritt für Schritt step by step.
Schritt halten to keep pace with.
schrubben to scrub.
Schrubber *m.* scrubber.
schrumpfen to shrink, contract.
Schrumpfung *f.* shrinking, contraction.
Schubfach *n.* drawer.
Schublade *f.* drawer.
schüchtern bashful, timid.
Schüchternheit *f.* bashfulness, timidity.
Schuft *m.* scoundrel.
SCHUH *m.* shoe.
einem etwas in die Schuhe schieben to put the blame on someone.

Schuhanzieher *m.* shoehorn.
Schuhkrem *f.* shoe-polish.
Schuhmacher *m.* shoemaker.
Schuhputzer *m.* bootblack.
Schuhriemen *m.* shoelace.
Schuhsohle *f.* sole of a shoe.
Schuhwichse *f.* boot polish.
Schularbeit *f.* lesson, homework.
Schulbesuch *m.* attendance at school.
Schulbildung *f.* schooling, education.
SCHULD *f.* obligation, debt, cause, blame.
in jemandes Schuld stehen to have an obligation.
Schuld sein to be guilty of.
Schulden machen to make debts.
Schuld geben to accuse.
schuldbewusst guilt-conscious.
Schuldbrief *m.* bond.
schulden to owe.
Schuldenmacher *m.* contractor of debts.
schuldig owing, due, obliged, guilty.
Dank Schuldig sein to be indebted.
Geld schuldig sein to owe money.
keine Antwort schuldig bleiben never to be at a loss for an answer.
Schuldigkeit *f.* duty, obligation.
schuldlos innocent.
Schuldner *m.* debtor.
Schuldschein *m.* bond, promissory note.
SCHULE *f.* school, academy, courses.
die Schule schwänzen to cut classes.
Schule machen to find followers.
schulen to school, train, teach.
Schüler *m.* student, pupil.
Schulferien *pl. m.* (**-in** *f.*) school holidays.
schulfrei having a holiday.
Schulfreund *m.* school friend.
Schulgeld *n.* school fees.
Schulmappe *f.* schoolbag, satchel.
Schulmeister *m.* schoolmaster, teacher.
schulmeistern to teach school, censure.
Schulstunde *f.* school lesson.
Schulter *f.* shoulder.
Schulung *f.* school training.
Schulzeugnis *n.* school certificates.
Schuppe *f.* scale (fish).
Schürze *f.* apron.

Schuss *m.* shot, report, round.
schussbereit ready to shoot.
Schusswaffe *f.* firearm.
Schussweite *f.* range.
Schusswunde *f.* bullet wound.
schütteln to shake.
schütten to pour in.
SCHUTZ *m.* shelter, protection, refuge.
im Schutz der Nacht under cover of the night.
in Schutz nehmen to defend.
Schutz suchen to take shelter.
Schütze *m.* rifleman, private soldier.
schützen to protect.
sich schützen to protect oneself.
Schutzengel *m.* guardian angel.
Schutzhaft *f.* protective custody.
Schutzimpfung *f.* vaccination.
schutzlos defenseless, unprotected.
Schutzmann *m.* policeman.
Schutzpockenimpfung *f.* vaccination against smallpox.
Schutztruppe *f.* colonial force, occupation forces.
SCHWACH weak, frail, faint, feeble.
Schwäche *f.* weakness, debility.
schwächen to weaken.
Schwächheit *f.* weakness, feebleness.
schwächlich weak, delicate.
Schwächlichkeit *f.* delicacy, infirmity.
Schwachsinn *m.* imbecility.
Schwachsinnig imbecile.
Schwager *m.* brother-in-law.
Schwägerin *f.* sister-in-law.
Schwalbe *f.* swallow.
Schwamm *m.* sponge, mushroom.
Schwan *m.* swan.
schwanger pregnant.
Schwank *m.* prank, short anecdote, farce.
schwanken to rock, toss, sway.
Schwankung *f.* variation.
Schwanz *m.* tail, end.
Schwarm *m.* crowd, multitude.
schwärmen to swarm, riot.
Schwärmer *m.* enthusiast, fanatic.
Schwärmerei *f.* enthusiasm.
schwärmerisch enthusiastic, fanatic.
Schwarte *f.* rind, skin.
SCHWARZ black, dark, dirty, gloomy.
ins Schwarze treffen to hit the bull's eye.
schwarz auf weiss in black and white.
Sie sieht immer alles schwarz. She always sees the dark side of things.
Schwarzbrot *n.* black bread.
Schwarze *m.* Negro.
Schwarzhandel *m.* black market.
Schwarzwald *m.* Black Forest.
Schwatz *m.* chat, talk.
Schwatzbase *f.* chatterbox.
schwatzen to chatter, gossip.
Schwätzer *m.* (**-in** *f.*) gossip.
schwatzhaft talkative.
Schwatzhaftigkeit *f.* loquacity.
Schwebe *f.* suspense.
in der Schwebe sein to be undecided.

Schwebebahn *f.* suspension railway.
schweben to be suspended, pending.
    auf der Zunge schweben to have on the tip
    of the tongue.
    in Gefahr schweben to be in danger.
Schwede *m.* Swede.
schwedisch Swedish.
Schwefel *m.* sulphur.
Schweigen *n.* silence.
schweigsam silent, taciturn.
Schweigsamkeit *f.* taciturnity.
Schwein *n.* pig, hog.
Schweinebraten *m.* roast pork.
Schweinefleisch *n.* pork.
Schweiss *m.* sweat, perspiration.
Schweisstropfen *m.* bead of perspiration.
Schweizer *m.* Swiss.
schweizerisch Swiss.
schwelgen to feast, celebrate.
Schwelle *f.* threshold.
schwellen to swell, rise, grow.
Schwellung *f.* swelling, tumor, growth.
SCHWER heavy, hard, difficult, serious, strong;
    heavily, seriously, strongly.
    etwas schwer nehmen to take something
    to heart.
    schwer fallen (halten) to be difficult.
schwerblütig melancholy.
schwerfällig heavy, clumsy.
Schwerfälligkeit *f.* heaviness, clumsiness.
Schwergewicht *n.* heavyweight.
schwerhörig hard of hearing.
Schwerhörigkeit *f.* deafness.
Schwerkraft *f.* force of gravity.
Schwerkriegsbeschädigte *m.* disabled soldier.
schwerlich hardly, scarcely, with difficulty.
Schwermut *f.* melancholy, sadness.
schwermütig melancholy, sad.
Schwerpunkt *m.* center of gravity.
Schwert *n.* sword.
Schwerverbrecher *m.* criminal, gangster.
schwerwiegend serious, grave.
SCHWESTER *f.* sister, hospital nurse.
schwesterlich sisterly.
Schwiegereltern *pl.* parents-in-law.
Schwiegermutter *f.* mother-in-law.
Schwiegersohn *m.* son-in-law.
Schwiegertochter *f.* daughter-in-law.
Schwiegervater *m.* father-in-law.
schwierig difficult.
Schwierigkeit *f.* difficulty.
Schwimmanstalt *f.* swimming-pool.
SCHWIMMEN to swim, float, sail.
Schwimmhose *f.* swimming shorts.
Schwimmweste *f.* life jacket.
Schwindel *m.* swindle; dizziness.
Schwindelanfall *m.* fit of dizziness.
schwindeln to swindle, cheat; be dizzy.
    Mir schwindelt. I feel dizzy.
Schwindler *m.* swindler.
schwindlig dizzy.
schwingen to swing, sway, oscillate, vibrate.

Schwingung *f.* oscilliation.
Schwips *m.* Smack! Slap!
    einen Schwips haben to be tipsy.
schwören to swear, take an oath.
schwül sulty, muggy.
Schwung *f.* swing (push), vault.
    in Schwung bringen to set going.
schwungvoll energetic.
Schwur *m.* oath.
    Schwur leisten to take an oath.
SECHS six.
SECHSTE sixth.
SECHZEHN sixteen.
SECHZEHNTE sixteenth.
SECHZIG sixty.
SECHZIGSTE sixtieth.
See *m.* lake.
SEE *f.* sea, seaside.
    an die See gehen to go to the seaside.
    in See stechen to put to sea.
Seebad *n.* seaside resort.
seefest seaworthy.
    Seefest sein to be a good sailor.
Seegang *m.* heavy sea, swell.
Seehund *m.* seal.
seekrank seasick.
    seekrank sein to be seasick.
Seekrankheit *f.* seasickness.
SEELE *f.* soul, mind, spirt.
    jemandem aus der Seele sprechen to express
    a person's thoughts.
    Sie sind mit Leib und Seele dabei. They are
    in it with heart and soul.
seelisch spiritual, mental, emotional.
Seemann *m.* sailor.
Seemeile *f.* nautical mile (1.852 kilometers).
Seenot *f.* distress (at sea).
Seewasser *n.* sea-water.
Segel *n.* sail, canvas.
Segelboot *n.* sailboat.
Segelflugzeug *n.* glider.
segeln to sail.
Segelschiff *n.* sailboat.
Segen *m.* blessing.
segnen to bless.
SEHEN to see, look, behold, contemplate.
    darauf sehen to watch carefully.
    gut sehen to have good eyesight.
    Ich kenne sie nur vom Sehen. I know her only
    by sight.
    schlecht sehen to have poor eyesight.
    sehen nach to look after.
sehenswert worth seeing, remarkable.
Sehenswürdigkeit *f.* point of interest.
Sehkraft *f.* eyesight.
Sehne *f.* sinew, ligament.
SEHNEN to long, yearn for.
sehnlich ardent, longing.
Sehnsucht *f.* longing, yearning.
sehnsüchtig longing, yearning.
SEHR very; very much.
    Bitte sehr. You are quite welcome.

seicht shallow.
SEIDE *f.* silk.
Seidenpapier *n.* tissue paper.
Seidenraupe *f.* silkworm.
seidig silky.
Seife *f.* soap.
Seifenflocken *pl.* soapflakes.
Seifenpulver *n.* soap powder.
Seil *n.* rope, line.
Seilbahn *f.* cable.
Sein *n.* being.
SEIN to be, exist.
    es sei denn, dass unless.
SEIN *poss. adj.* his, her, its.
SEIN(ER, -E, -ES) *poss. pron.* his, hers.
    die Seinen one's own people.
seinetwegen because of him, for his sake.
SEIT *prep. (with dat.)* since, for.
    Ich warte seit einer Stunde. I have been
    waiting for an hour.
    seit kurzer Zeit lately.
    seit meiner Ankunft since my return.
    Seit Wann? Since when?
seitdem *conj.* since, since that time.
SEITE *f.* side, page, party, member.
    auf die Seite aside, away.
    auf die Seite gehen to step aside.
    Schwache Seite weakness.
    Seite an Seite side by side.
    zur Seite stehen to stand by, help.
Seitenflügel *m.* side aisle, wing.
Seitenstrasse *f.* side street.
Seitenzahl *f.* number of pages.
seither since then.
seitlich lateral, collateral.
seitwärts sideways, aside.
Seke *m.* champagne.
Sekretär *m.* (**-in** *f.*) secretary.
SEKUNDE *f.* second (time, music, fencing).
Sekundenzeiger *m.* second hand (on clocks).
selbe (der, die, das) same.
selber self.
    ich selber myself.
SELBST 1. *adj. or pron.* self.
    Ich habe es selbst getan. I did it myself.
    Das versteht sich von selbst. That goes
    without saying.
    2. *adv.* even.
    Ich habe alles zu Hause gelassen, selbst
    mein Geld. I left everything at home, even
    my money.
selbständig independent.
Selbstbeherrschung *f.* self-control.
selbstbewusst self-assured.
Selbstbewusstsein *n.* self-assurance.
Selbsterhaltung *f.* self-preservation.
Selbsterkenntnis *f.* self-knowledge.
selbstgefällig self-satisfied, complacent.
Selbstgefühl *n.* self-respect.
Selbstgespräch *m.* monologue, soliloquy.
selbstherrlich autocratic.
Selbstkostenpreis *m.* cost price.

selbstlos unselfish, disinterested.
Selbstlosigkeit *f.* unselfishness.
Selbstmörder *m.* suicide.
selbstredend self-evident, obvious.
Selbstsucht *f.* selfishness, egoism.
selbstsüchtig selfish, egoistic.
SELBSTVERSTÄNDLICH evident.
Selbstvertrauen *n.* self-confidence.
selbstzufrieden self-satisfied.
selig blessed.
Seligkeit *f.* happiness, bliss.
Sellerie *f.* celery.
SELTEN rare, unusual.
Seltenheit *f.* rarity, scarcity.
SELTSAM strange, unusual, odd.
Selterwasser *n.* soda-water.
Semester *n.* term, session.
Seminar *n.* training college.
Senat *m.* senate.
senden to send, broadcast, transmit.
Sender *m.* transmitter.
Senderaum *m.* studio.
Sendung *f.* mission, transmission.
Senf *m.* mustard.
Senkel *m.* lace (shoe).
senken to lower, dip, sink.
    sich senken to settle.
sensationell sensational.
Sensationslust *f.* desire to cause a sensation.
Sentimentalität *f.* sentimentality.
SEPTEMBER *m.* September.
Serie *f.* series, issue.
Service *n.* service set.
Servierbrett *n.* tray.
servieren to serve, wait at a table.
Serviette *f.* table napkin.
Sessel *m.* armchair.
sesshaft settled, established.
SETZEN to put, set, place, fix, erect, put up,
    sit down.
    alles daran setzen to risk everything.
    gesetzt den Fall, dass suppose that.
    in Freiheit setzen to set free.
    Setzen Sie sich! Sit down!
    sich etwas in den Kopf setzen to get an idea
    into one's head.
    sich in Verbindung setzen mit to get in
    touch with.
    unter Druck setzen to put pressure on.
Seuche *f.* epidemic.
seufzen to sigh.
sezieren to dissect.
SICH oneself, himself, herself, itself, yourself,
    yourselves, themselves, each other, one
    another.
    sich selbst itself, oneself, etc.
SICHER secure, safe, certain, positive, surely.
    aus sicherer Hand on good authority.
    seiner Sache sicher sein to be certain of a
    thing.
    sicher gehen to be on the safe side.
    sicher stellen to put in safe keeping.
    sicher wissen to know for certain.

Sicherheit *f.* safety, security.
　in Sicherheit bringen to secure.
　Sicherheit leisten to give security.
sicherheitshalber for safety's sake.
Sicherheitsnadel *f.* safety-pin.
Sicherheitsschloss *n.* safety-lock.
sicherlich surely, certainly.
sichern to protect.
Sicherung *f.* protection.
SICHT *f.* sight, visibility.
　sichtbar visible, apparent.
sichten to sight; to sift, sort.
SIE (sie) *pers. pron. 3rd pers. sing. (fem., nom. &*
　acc.); 3rd pers. pl. (m., f., n., nom. & acc.)
　she, her, it; they, them.
SIE (Sie) *pers. pron. 2nd pers., polite form (nom. &*
　acc.) you.
Sieb *n.* collander, strainer.
sieben to sift, strain.
SIEBEN seven.
SIEBENTE seventh.
SIEBZEHNTE seventeenth.
SIEBZIG seventy.
siebzigst seventieth.
siech sickly, ailing, infirm.
siedeln to settle, colonize.
SIEG *m.* victory, triumph.
Siegel *n.* seal.
Sieger *m.* victor, winner.
siegesgewiss certain or confident of
　victory.
siegreich victorious.
Signal *n.* signal.
Signalhupe *f.* siren.
signalisieren to signal.
Signatur *f.* mark, sign, characteristic.
Silbe *f.* syllable.
Silber *n.* silver.
Silberpapier *n.* silver paper.
Silversterabend *m.* New Year's Eve.
SINGEN to sing.
Singstimme *f.* singing voice, vocal part.
sinken to sink, drop, fall.
SINN *m.* sense, faculty, mind, understanding,
　intellect.
　anderen Sinnes werden to change one's mind.
　in gewissem Sinn in a way, in a sense.
　im Sinn haben to intend.
　sich etwas aus dem Sinn schlagen to dismiss
　a thing from one's mind.
Sinnbild *n.* symbol, emblem, allegory.
sinnbildlich symbolic.
sinnen to think, reflect, meditate.
sinnlich sensual, sensuous, material.
sinnlos senseless, absurd.
Sinnlosigkeit *f.* senselessness, foolishness.
sinnreich sensible, clever.
Sippschaft *f.* kinship, relatives.
Sirene *f.* siren.
Sitte *f.* custom, habit.
Sittengesetz *n.* moral law, moral code.

Sittenlehre *f.* moral, philosophy, ethics.
sittenlos immoral, dissolute.
sittlich moral.
sittsam modest.
Sittsamkeit *f.* modesty.
SITZ *m.* seat, residence.
SITZEN to sit, fit, adhere.
　etwas auf sich sitzen lassen to put up with.
　sitzen bleiben to remain seated.
　sitzen lassen to leave.
Sitzgelegenheit *f.* seating accommodation.
Sitzplatz *m.* seat.
Skandal *m.* scandal.
Skelett *n.* skeleton.
skeptisch sceptical.
Ski *m.* ski.
　skilaufen to ski.
Skiläufer *m.* skier.
Skispringen *n.* ski-jumping.
Skizze *f.* sketch.
skizzieren to sketch.
Sklave *m.* slave.
sklavisch slavish, servile.
Skrupel *m.* scruple.
SO so, thus, in this way, like that, anyhow.
　Ach so! Oh, I see!
　So? Is that so? Indeed? Really?
　so...auch however.
　so bald als as soon as.
　so ... doch yet, nevertheless.
　so ein such a.
　so etwas a thing like that.
　so gut wie as if, practically.
　so oder so this way or that way.
　so...so though...yet.
　so wie as, the way.
Sock *f.* sock.
Sockenhalter *m.* garter (man's).
sodann then.
sodass so that.
soeben just, just now.
sofern so far as.
sofort immediately, at once.
sogar even.
sogenannt so-called.
sogleich at once, immediately.
Sohle *f.* sole.
sohlen to resole.
SOHN *m.* son.
solange so, as long as.
SOLCH such, the same.
　solch ein such a.
Soldat *m.* soldier.
Solist *m.* soloist.
SOLLEN ought, shall, to have to, must, be
　supposed to, be said to.
　Du sollst nicht töten. Thou shalt not kill.
　Di Schüler sollen fleissig sein. Students
　must be industrious.
　Er soll ein Millionär sein. They say he is a
　millionaire.

'Sollte er nicht zu Hause sein? Is it possible that he is not at home?

'Sollte er telefonieren? 'Should he telephone?

Was soll das heissen? What is the meaning of that?

Was soll es bedeuten? What does that mean?

somit consequently.

SOMMER *m.* summer.

'Sommernachtstraum *m.* Midsummer Night's Dream.

Sommerfrische *f.* health-resort.

Sommersprosse *f.* freckle.

Sonderausgabe *f.* special edition.

SONDERBAR strange, peculiar.

sonderbarerweise strange to say.

sondergleichen unequaled, unique.

Sonderling *m.* strange character.

Sondermeldung *f.* special announcement.

SONDERN but (in a negative sentence).

Ich wollte nicht ausgehen, sondern zu Hause bleiben. I did not want to go out but to stay home.

nicht nur....sondern auch   not only....but also.

Sie war nicht nur schön, sondern auch gut. She was not only beautiful but kind as well.

SONNABEND *m.* 'Saturday.

SONNE *f.* sun.

Sonnenaufgang *m.* sunrise.

Sonnenblume *f.* sunflower.

Sonnenbrand *m.* sunburn.

Sonnenbrille *f.* sunglasses.

Sonnenstrahl *m.* sunbeam.

Sonnenuntergang *m.* sunset.

sonnig sunny.

SONNTAG *m.* 'Sunday.

sonntags on 'Sunday.

SONST else, moreover, besides, otherwise, formerly.

Sonst noch etwas? Anything else?

sonst jemand anybody else.

sonst nichts nothing else.

sonst niemand? No one else?

sonst und jetzt formerly and now.

Was konnte ich sonst tun? What else could I do?

Wenn es sonst nichts wäre!

If that were all it was!

wie sonst as usual.

sonstwie in some other way.

sonstwo elsewhere.

Sopran *m.* soprano.

SORGE *f.* grief, sorrow, anxiety, worry, trouble, care.

einem Sorgen machen to worry someone.

sich Sorgen machen to worry.

Sorge tragen   to see about something.

SORGEN to care for, look after, take care of, provide.

sich sorgen um to be concerned about.

sorgen für to look after.

Sorgenkind *n.* delicate child.

sorgenvoll worried.

Sorgfalt *f.* carefulness, care, accuracy.

sorgfältig careful, painstaking.

sorglich thoughtful.

sorglos carefree, careless.

Sorglosigkeit *f.* light-heartedness.

SORTE *f.* kind, sort, brand, grade.'

sortieren to sort, arrange.

Souffleur *m.* prompter.

SOVIEL as much as, so far as.

soweit as far as.

sowenig as little as.

sowie as soon as.

sowieso anyway, anyhow.

sozial social.

Sozialismus *m.* Socialism.

Sozialist *m.* Socialist.

sozialistisch socialistic.

Sozialwissenschaft *f.* sociology.

Sozius *m.* partner.

spähen to be on the look out, patrol.

Spalier bilden to line.

Spalt *m.* crack, slot, gap.

spalten to split, divide.

sich spalten to split.

Spaltholz *n.* firewood sticks.

Spange *f.* buckle, brooch.

Spanier *m.* (**–in** *f.*) Spaniard.

spanisch Spanish.

Spanische *n.* Spanish (language).

Spanne *f.* short space of time, margin.

SPANNEN to put up, stretch, pull, tighten.

gespannt sein to be anxious, curious.

Ich bin auf die Antwort gespannt. I am curious to know the answer.

spannend fascinating, absorbing, thrilling.

Spannung *f.* tension, strain, suspense, voltage.

Sparbüchse *f.* money-box (piggy bank).

Spareinlage *f.* savings deposit.

Spargel *m.* asparagus.

Sparkasse *f.* savings bank.

spärlich scarce, frugal, thin.

Spärlichkeit *f.* scarcity.

SPARSAM economical, thrifty.

Sparsamkeit *f.* economy, thrift.

Spass *m.* joke, fun.

spassen to joke.

Spassmacher *m.* joker.

SPÄT late, belated, backward.

Besser spät als nie. Better late than never.

zu spät kommen   to be late.

Wie spät ist es? What time is it?

Spaten *m.* spade.

später later, afterwards.

späterhin later on.

spätestens at the latest.

Spatz *m.* sparrow.

SPAZIEREN to walk about, stroll.

spazieren gehen to go for a walk.

Spazierfahrt *f.* drive.

Spaziergang *m.* walk.

Spaziergänger m. walker, stroller.
Speck m. bacon.
Speckschwarte f. rind of bacon.
Spediteur m. mover, shipper, forwarding agent.
Speicher m. storage room.
speichern to store.
SPEISE f. food, meal.
Speiseeis n. ice cream.
Speisekarte f. menu.
Speisenfolge f. menu.
Speisesaal m. dining room.
Speisewagen m. dining car.
Spekulant m. speculator.
spekulieren to speculate.
Spende f. gift, present, donation.
spenden to dispense, bestow, administer.
Spender m. giver, donor, benefactor.
spendieren to pay for.
Sperre f. gate, closing, barrier.
sperren to close, shut, block, barricade.
   ins Gefängnis sperren to put in prison.
Sperrguthaben n. blocked account.
Sperrholz n. plywood.
Spesen f. pl. charges, expenses.
Spezialarzt n. specialist.
spezialisieren to specialize.
speziell special, particular.
spezifisch specific.
spezifizieren to specify.
Spiegel m. mirror.
Spiegelbild n. reflected image.
spiegelglatt smooth as a mirror.
spiegeln to shine, glitter.
   sich spiegeln to be reflected.
SPIEL n. game, deck of cards, playing, play,
   sport, touch (music).
   auf dem Spiel stehen to be at stake.
   aufs Spiel setzen to risk.
   Lassen Sie mich aus dem Spiel. Leave me
   out of this.
   leichtes Spiel haben to have no difficulties.
   seine Hand im Spiel haben to have a finger in
   the pie.
   sein Spiel treiben mit to make game of.
Spieldose f. musical box.
SPIELEN to play, act, perform, gamble, pretend.
   Was spielt man heute abend? What's
   playing tonight?
Spielerei f. trifle.
Spielplan m. program, repertory.
Spielsachen pl. toys.
Spielverderber m. kill-joy.
Spielzeug n. toy.
Spiess m. lance, spear, pike.
Spiessbürger m. bourgeois.
Spinat m. spinach.
Spinne f. spider.
spinnen to spin.
Spinngewebe n. cobweb.
Spinnrad n. spinning wheel.
Spion m. spy.

Spionage f. spying, espionage.
Spionageabwehr f. counterespionage.
spionieren to spy.
Spiritus m. spirits, alcohol.
SPITZ pointed, sharp, acute, caustic.
Spitze f. point, tip (tongue), top, head, lace,
   sarcasm.
   etwas auf die Spitze treiben to carry to
   extremes.
SPITZEN to sharpen, point.
   seine Ohren spitzen to prick one's ears.
Spitzenleistung f. record, maximum.
Spitzenlohn m. maximum pay.
Spitzentanz m. toe-dance.
spitzfindig pointed, sharp, sarcastic, subtle.
Spitzfindigkeit f. subtlety.
spitzig pointed, sharp, sarcastic.
Spitzname m. nickname.
Splitter m. splinter, chip.
splittern to splinter, split.
spontan spontaneous.
Sporn m. spur.
Sport m. sport.
   Sport treiben to go in for sports.
Sportfunk m. radio sports news.
Sportler m. sportsman.
sportlich sporting, athletic.
Sportname m. nickname.
Spott m. mockery, ridicule.
Spöttelei f. chaff, raillery.
spötteln to laugh, sneer at.
spotten to mock, make fun, defy.
spöttisch mocking, scoffing, sarcastic.
SPRACHE f. language, speech, talk.
   mit der Sprache herausrücken to come out
   something.
   zur Sprache bringen to bring up a subject.
   zur Sprache kommen to be mentioned.
Sprachfertigkeit f. fluency.
sprachgewandt fluent.
sprachkundig proficient in languages.
Sprachlehre f. grammar.
sprachlich linguistic.
sprachlos speechless.
Sprachschatz m. vocabulary.
Sprachschnitzer m. blunder, mistake.
Sprachstörung f. speech defect.
SPRECHEN to speak, talk, say, converse, discuss.
   Der herr Doktor ist nicht zu sprechen. The
   doctor is busy.
   gut zu sprechen sein auf to be kindly disposed
   to.
   Ich bin für niemanden zu sprechen. I am in to
   no one.
   sich herumsprechen to be whispered about town.
   Sie sprechen nicht miteinander. They are not
   on speaking terms.
   Sprechen Sie Deutsch? Do you speak German?
   Sprechen Sie langsam, bitte. Please speak
   slowly.
   Wen wünschen Sie zu sprechen? Whom do you
   want to see?

Sprecher *m.* speaker.
Sprechstunde *f.* office hours, office (doctor).
Sprechstundenhilfe *f.* doctor's receptionist.
Sprechweise *f.* diction.
Sprechzimmer *n.* consulting room.
sprengen to burst, blow up, blast, spray.
Sprengung *f.* blowing up.
Sprichwort *n.* proverb.
Springbrunnen *m.* fountain.
SPRINGEN to jump, skip, spring, play.
   Das ist der springende Punkt. That is the crucial point.
   in die Augen springen to be obvious.
spritzen to spray, splash, sprinkle.
spröde reserved, shy.
Sprosse *f.* rung (ladder).
Sprössling *m.* sprout, shoot, offshoot.
Spruch *m.* aphorism, saying.
spruchreif ripe for decision.
sprudeln to bubble up.
sprühen to spark.
Sprühregen *m.* drizzle, drizzling rain.
SPRUNG *m.* leap, jump, crack.
   Es ist nur ein Sprung von meinem Haus. It is only a stone's throw from my house.
   Ich war auf dem Sprung auszugehen. I was just going to leave.
Sprungschanze *f.* ski-jump.
spucken to spit.
   Spucken Verboten! No spitting!
Spuk *m.* ghost.
Spülbecken *n.* washtub.
spülen to rinse.
Spülwasser *n.* dishwater.
Spund *m.* plug, stopper.
SPUR *f.* trace, trail, track, footprint.
   einem auf die Spur kommen to be on a person's tracks.
   Keine Spur! Not in the least!
spüren to feel perceive, experience.
   spüren nach to track, follow.
spurlos trackless.
Spürsinn *m.* shrewdness.
   Spürsinn haben to have a flair.
STAAT *m.* state, government, pomp, parade, show.
   in vollem Staat in full dress.
   Staat machen to show off.
staatlich public, political.
Staatsaktion *f.* political event.
Staatsangehörige *m. & f.* subject, national.
Staatsangehörigkeit *f.* nationality, citizenship.
Staatsanwalt *m.* public prosecutor.
Staatsdienst *m.* civil service.
Staatsmann *m.* statesman, politician.
staatsmännisch statesmanlike.
Stab *m.* stick, rod, bar, staff.
   den Stab brechen über to condemn.
stabil stable.
stabilisieren to stabilize.
Stachel *m.* thorn, prickle, sting, spur.
Stachelbeere *f.* gooseberry.

Stacheldraht *m.* barbed wire.
Stadion *n.* stadium, arena.
Stadium *n.* phase, stage.
STADT *f.* town, city.
Stadtbahn *f.* city railway.
stadtbekannt known all over town.
Städter *m.* townsman.
Stadtgespräch *n.* talk of the town.
städtisch municipal, urban.
Stadtteil *m.* quarter (of a town).
Stahl *m.* steel.
stählern steely.
Stahlguss *m.* steel.
Stall *m.* stable.
Stamm *m.* stem, root, trunk.
Stammbaum *m.* genealogical tree.
stammeln to stammer.
stammen to spring from, come from.
Stammgast *m.* regular customer.
Stammhalter *m.* eldest son.
stämmig sturdy, strong, vigorous.
stampfen to stamp, mash, crush.
Stand *m.* standing position.
   einen schweren Stand haben to have a tough job.
   guten Stand haben to be in good condition.
Standbild *n.* statue.
Ständchen *n.* serenade.
Standesamt *n.* registrar's office.
Standesbeamte *m.* registrar.
Standesehe *f.* marriage for position or rank.
standesgemäss in accordance with one's rank.
Standesgericht *n.* court martial.
Standesunterschied *m.* difference of class.
standhaft steady, constant.
standhalten to hold firm.
ständig permanent.
Standort *m.* station, position.
Standpunkt *m.* point of view.
Standuhr *f.* grandfather's clock.
Stange *f.* pole, bar, perch.
   eine Stange Gold a bar of gold.
   von der Stange ready-made.
Stanze *f.* stanza.
stanzen to stamp.
STARK strong, stout, considerable, hard.
   Das ist denn doch zu stark! That is too much!
   stark auftragen to exaggerate, boast.
Stärke *f.* strength, force, vigor, intensity, energy, violence.
stärken to strengthen, fortify, starch, confirm.
Starkstrom *m.* power current.
Starkstromleitung *f.* power-circuit.
starr stiff, hard, paralyzed.
   starren vor Staunen to be dumbfounded.
starren to stare, be numb.
starrköpfig stubborn.
Starrsinn *m.* obstinacy.
Start *m.* start.
Startbahn *f.* runway.

starten to start.
startklar ready for the take off.
Station *f.* station, stop, ward.
    freie Station free board and lodging.
Stationsarzt *m.* resident physician.
Stationsvorsteher *m.* station master.
Statistik *f.* statistics.
statistisch statistical.
STATT *f.* place.
    an Kindesstatt annehmen to adopt a child.
STATT (anstatt) *prep. (gen.)* instead of.
stattfinden to take place.
stattgeben to permit, allow.
statthaft admissible, legal.
stattlich stately, magnificent, imposing.
Stattlichkeit *f.* dignity, magnificence.
Statue *f.* statue.
Staub *m.* dust, powder.
    in den Staub ziehen to depreciate.
    Staub wischen to dust.
stauben to be dusty.
staubig dusty.
Staublappen *m.* duster.
Staubsauger *m.* vacuum-cleaner.
staunen to be surprised.
STECHEN to stick, bite, sting.
    sich stechen to prick oneself.
    in die Augen stechen to take one's fancy.
Stechfliege *f.* horse-fly.
Steckdose *f.* wall-plug, socket.
STECKEN to stick, pin up, fasten, fix, plant, stuff.
    Dahinter steckt etwas. There is something behind this.
    in Brand stecken to set fire.
steckenbleiben to be stuck.
Steckenpferd *n.* hobby, pet project.
Stecker *m.* plug.
Stecknadel *f.* pin.
STEHEN to stand, stop, be, suit, become.
    gut stehen to be becoming. (Rot steht ihr. Red is becoming to her.)
    gut stehen mit to be on good terms with
    geschrieben stehen to be written.
stehenbleiben to stop, remain standing.
stehend standing, stationary, permanent.
    stehenden Fusses at once.
stehenlassen to leave (standing).
Stehlampe *f.* floor lamp.
STEHLEN to steal, rob, take away.
steif stiff.
Steig *m.* path.
STEIGEN to climb, go up, ascend, rise, increase.
    zu Kopf steigen to go to one's head.
steigend growing, increasing.
steigern to raise, increase, intensify.
    sich steigern in to intensify, work up.
Steigerung *f.* raising, increase, gradation, climax.
steil steep, precipitous.
Steilhang *m.* steep slope.
STEIN *m.* stone, rock, jewel.

Das hat den Stein ins Rollen gebracht. That started the ball rolling.
    Das ist nur ein Tropfen auf den heissen Stein. That's only a drop in the bucket.
    einen Stein im Brett haben bei to be in favor with.
    Mir fällt ein Stein vom Herzen! I feel so relieved!
    Stein des Anstosses stumbling block.
    Stein und Bein schwören to swear by all the gods.
Steinbruch *m.* quarry.
steinern of stone.
steinhart as hard as stone.
steinig stony, rocky.
Steinobst *n.* stone-fruit.
steinreich very wealthy.
Steinzeit *f.* Stone Age.
STELLE *f.* spot, place, position, situation, passage.
    auf der Stelle on the spot.
    offene Stelle vacancy.
    von der Stelle kommen to make progress.
    zur Stelle sein to be present.
    an Stelle von instead of.
STELLEN to put, place, set, arrange, regulate, provide, furnish.
    auf den Kopf stellen to turn upside down.
    auf sich selbst gestellt sein to be dependent on oneself.
    eine Bedingung stellen to make a condition.
    eine Frage stellen to ask a question.
    Er ist sehr gut gestellt. He is very well off.
    sich stellen to stand.
    kalt stellen to put in a cool place.
    sich gut stellen mit to be on good terms with.
    sich stellen zu to behave toward.
    zur Verfügung stellen to place at one's disposal.
Stellengesuch *n.* application for a position.
stellenlos unemployed.
Stellennachweis *m.* employment reference.
Stellenvermittlung *f.* employment agency.
STELLUNG *f.* position, situation, stand, job.
    Stellung nehmen zu to express one's opinion.
Stellungnahme *f.* opinion, comment.
Stellungsgesuch *n.* application for a position.
stellungslos unemployed.
Stellungswechsel *m.* change of position.
Stellvertreter *m.* representative.
Stempel *m.* stamp, postmark.
Stempelkissen *n.* ink-pad.
stempeln to stamp, mark.
stenografieren to write in shorthand.
stenografisch stenographic.
Stenogramm *n.* shorthand.
    Stenogramm aufnehmen to take down in shorthand.
Stenotypist *m.* (**–istin,** *f.*) stenotypist.
Steppdecke *f.* quilt.
Sterbebett *n.* deathbed.
Sterben *n.* death.

im Sterben liegen to be dying.
STERBEN to die.
sterblich mortal.
  sterblich verliebt madly in love.
Sterblichkeit *f.* death rate.
steril sterile.
sterilisieren to sterilize.
Stern *m.* star.
Sternbild *n.* constellation.
Sterndeuter *m.* astrologer.
Sternschnuppe *f.* shooting-star.
stets always, forever.
Steuer *n.* rudder, helm, steering wheel.
Steuer *f.* tax.
steuerfrei tax-free.
steuern to steer, pilot, drive.
steuerpflichtig subject to taxation.
Steuerrad *n.* steering wheel.
Steuerzahler *m.* taxpayer.
Stich *m.* sting, prick, stitch.
  im Stich lassen to forsake.
Stichtag *m.* fixed day.
Stichwort *n.* catchword, cue.
Stiefbruder *m.* stepbrother.
Stiefmutter *f.* stepmother.
Stiefmütterchen *n.* pansy.
Stiefschwester *f.* stepsister.
Stiefsohn *m.* stepson.
Stieftochter *f.* stepdaughter.
Stiefvater *m.* stepfather.
Stiel *m.* handle, stick, stem.
Stier *m.* bull.
Stierkämpfer *m.* bullfighter.
Stift *m.* pencil, crayon.
stiften to donate; to found, establish.
Stifter *m.* founder; donor.
Stiftung *f.* foundation.
Stil *m.* style, manner.
stilgerecht in good style, taste.
STILL still, quiet, silent, secret.
  Seien Sie still! Be quiet!
STILLE *f.* silence, calm, quietude, peace.
  im Stillen secretly.
  in aller Stille privately, secretly.
stillen to quiet, appease, satisfy, quench, nurse.
stillhalten to keep still.
Stillleben *n.* still life (art).
stilllegen to shut down, close, discontinue.
stillschweigen to be silent.
stillschweigend silent.
Stillstand *m.* standstill, stop.
stillstehen to stand still, stop.
  Still gestanden! Attention!
stilvoll in good style, taste.
Stimmabgabe *f.* vote, voting.
stimmberechtigt entitled to vote.
STIMME *f.* voice, part, comment, vote.
  Stimme abgeben to vote.
STIMMEN to tune, vote, be correct, impress
  someone, influence someone's mood.
  Das stimmt! That is correct!
  Werden Sie für oder dagegen stimmen? Are

you going to vote for or against?
Stimmrecht *n.* right to vote.
STIMMUNG *f.* tuning, pitch, key, mood, humor,
  impression, atmosphere.
  Stimmung machen für to create a mood for, to
  make propaganda for.
Stimmungsmensch *m.* moody person.
stimmungsvoll impressive.
Stimmzettel *m.* ballot.
Stirn *f.* forehead, front, impudence.
  die Stirn runzeln to frown.
  einem die Stirne bieten to show a bold front.
Stock *m.* stick, rod, cane, floor (story).
  über Stock und Stein up hill and down dale.
  Welcher Stock? What floor?
stockdumm utterly stupid.
stocken to stop, stand still.
  ins Stocken geraten to get tied up.
stockfinster pitch-dark.
Stockfisch *m.* dried cod.
Stockwerk *n.* story, floor.
Stoff *m.* matter, substance.
stöhnen to groan.
stolpern to stumble, trip over.
stolz proud.
stopfen to darn, fill, stuff.
Stopfgarn *n.* darning thread.
Stopfnadel *f.* darning needle.
stoppen to stop.
Stoppuhr *f.* stop-watch.
Stöpsel *m.* stopper, cork.
stöpseln to cork.
Storch *m.* stork.
STÖREN to disturb, trouble, inconvenience.
  Nicht stören! Do not disturb!
störrisch stubborn.
Störung *f.* disturbance, upset.
  geistige Störung mental disorder.
Stoss *m.* push, poke, pile, jerk, shock.
stossen to push, shove, hit, kick, knock.
  stossen auf to run into.
Stosseufzer *m.* deep sigh, groan.
Stosstange *f.* bumper.
stottern to shutter, stammer.
Strafanstalt *f.* penitentiary.
strafbar liable to punishment.
Strafe *f.* punishment, penalty, fine.
  bei Strafe von on pain of.
strafen to punish.
Straferlass *m.* amnesty.
straff stretched, tense, tight, strict.
straffällig punishable.
straffen to tighten.
sträflich criminal, punishable.
straffrei exempt from punishment, unpunished.
Strafgefangene *m.* convict.
Strafgericht *n.* criminal court.
Strafporto *n.* extra postage, surcharge.
Strafpredigt *f.* reprimand.
Strafprozess *m.* criminal case.
strafwürdig punishable.
STRAHL *m.* ray, beam, stream.
strahlen to radiate, beam, shine.

stramm tight, close.
    stramm stehen to stand at attention.
STRAND m. seashore, beach, strand.
Strandbad n. seaside, resort.
stranden to run around or ashore.
Strandschuhe pl. beach shoes.
STRANG m. rope, cord, track.
    am gleichen Strang ziehen to act in concert.
    über die Stränge schlagen to kick over the traces.
    wenn alle Stränge reissen if the worst comes to the worst.
    zum Strang verurteilen to condemn to the gallows.
Strapaze f. fatigue.
strapazieren to tire, enervate.
STRASSE f. street, highway, road.
    an der Strasse by the wayside.
    auf der Strasse in the street.
Strassenarbeiter m. roadman.
Strassenbahn f. tramway.
Strassenfeger m. street cleaner.
sträuben to ruffle up, bristle.
Strauch m. shrub, bush.
streben to endeavor, aspire, aim at.
Streber m. climber, careerist.
Strecke f. distance, way, route, tract.
    auf freier Strecke on the road.
strecken to stretch, extend, stretch out.
    die Waffen strecken to lay down arms.
    sich strecken to stretch.
Streich m. stroke, blow.
    einem einen Streich spielen to play a trick on a person.
streichen to spread, rub, strike, erase, cancel, paint, wander, stroll, migrate.
    Frisch gestrichen! Wet paint!
Streichholz n. match.
Streichmusik f. string music.
Streichquartett n. string quartet.
Streife f. patrol, raid.
streifen to touch lightly, stripe, brush, wander.
Streik m. strike.
    in den Streik treten to go on strike.
streiken to strike.
STREIT m. fight, quarrel, dispute.
streitbar valiant.
streiten to fight, quarrel.
Streitfall m. quarrel, controversy.
Streitfrage f. matter in dispute.
    einem etwas streitig machen to contest a person's right to a thing.
STRENG strict, stern, severe.
    streng genommen strictly speaking.
Strenge f. severity, strictness.
strenggläubig orthodox.
streuen to strew, scatter, spread.
Strich m. dash, stroke, line, compass point.
    Machen wir einen Strich darunter. Let's put an end to that.
    nach Strich und Faden thoroughly.
Strichpunkt m. semicolon.

Strick m. cord, rope.
    wenn alle Stricke reissen if everything else fails.
stricken to knit.
Stroh n. straw.
Strohhalm m. straw (for drinking).
STROM m. large river, stream, current.
    Es regnet in Strömen. It's pouring.
stromabwärts downstream.
stromaufwärts upstream.
strömen to stream, flow, pour.
Strömung f. current, stream.
Stromzähler electric meter.
Strudel m. whirlpool.
Strumpf m. stocking, sock.
Strumpfband n. garter.
Strumpfhalter m. garter (woman's)
struppig bristly, unkempt.
STUBE f. room, chamber, living room.
Stubenhocker m. stay-at-home.
stubenrein house-broken.
STÜCK n. piece, play, extract, morsel.
    aus einem Stück all of a piece.
    aus freien Stücken of one's own free will.
    ein starkes Stück a bit stiff.
    ein Stück Arbeit a stiff job.
    ein Stück mitnehmen to give a lift.
    Er hält grosse Stücke auf ihn. He thinks a lot of him.
    in allen Stücken in every respect.
stückweise piece by piece, by the piece.
Student m. (–in, f.) student.
Studie f. study, sketch (art).
studieren to study.
Studium n. study, university education.
Stufe f. step, stair, level.
    auf gleicher Stufe mit on a level with.
stufenweise by degrees, gradually.
STUHL m. chair, seat.
stumm dumb, silent, mute.
Stummheit f. dumbness.
stumpf blunt, obtuse, dull.
    mit Stumpf und Stiehl root and branch.
Stumpfsinn m. stupidity.
stumpfsinnig stupid, dull.
STUNDE f. hour; lesson, period.
stundenlang for hours.
Stundenplan m. timetable.
Stundenzeiger m. hour-hand.
stündlich hourly.
Stundung f. delay of payment.
STURM m. storm, gale.
stürmen to take by storm.
stürmisch stormy, impetuous.
Sturz m. fall, crash, tumble, overthrow, collapse.
    zum Sturz bringen to overthrow.
stürzen to overthrow, throw down, fall down, plunge into, crash.
    Nicht stürzen! Handle with care!
Stütze f. stay, support, help.
stutzen to trim, cut short, stop short.
stützen to support, base, prop up.

Stutzer *m.* dandy.
Stützpfeiler *m.* pillar, support.
Stützpunkt *m.* base, strong point.
Subjekt *n.* subject.
Substantiv *n.* substantive, noun.
Substanz *f.* substance.
substrahieren to subtract.
Suche *f.* search, quest.
    auf die Suche gehen to go in search of.
    auf der Suche nach in search of.
SUCHEN to look for, try, seek.
    das Weite suchen to run away.
    nach Worten suchen to be at a loss for words.
    Sie hat hier nichts zu suchen. She has no
    business here.
Sucht *f.* passion, rage.
Süden *m.* south.
Südfrüchte *pl.* tropical fruits.
südlich southern, (to the) south.
Südpol *m.* south pole.
Sühne *f.* expiation.
sühnen to expiate.
Summe *f.* sum, amount.
summieren to add up.
Sumpf *m.* swamp.
Sünde *f.* sin.
Sünder *m.* (**-in** *f.*) sinner.
sündhaft sinful.
sündigen to sin.
Suppe *f.* soup, broth.
suspendieren to suspend.
SÜSS sweet, fresh, lovely.
Süsse *f.* sweetness.
süsslich sweetish, mawkish.
Symbol *n.* symbol.
symbolisch symbolical.
Sympathie *f.* sympathy.
sympathisch nice, likable, congenial.
Symphonie *f.* symphony.
Symptom *n.* symptom.
Synagoge *f.* synagogue.
System *n.* system.
Szene *f.* scene.
Szenerie *f.* scenery, settings.

T

Tabak *m.* tobacco.
Tabelle *f.* table, index, schedule.
Tablett *n.* tray.
Tablette *f.* tablet.
Tadel *m.* reprimand, blame.
tadellos excellent, perfect.
tadeln to blame, find fault.
TAFEL *f.* board, blackboard, bar, plate, table.
    die Tafel aufheben to rise from table.
TAG *m.* day, daylight; life (one's days).
    alle acht Tage every week.
    alle Tage every day.
    am Tag during the day, in the daytime.
    an den Tag bringen to bring to light.

    auf ein paar Tage for a few days.
    auf seine alten Tage in his old age.
    bei Tage in the daytime.
    den ganzen Tag all day long.
    dieser Tage one of these days.
    einen um den andern Tag every other day.
    eines Tages some day.
    Er lebt in den Tag hinein. He lives from hand
    to mouth.
    Guten Tag! Good morning!
    in acht Tagen in a week.
    Tag aus, Tag ein, day in, day out.
    Tag für Tag day by day.
    unter Tage arbeiten to work underground.
    vierzehn Tage two weeks.
    vor acht Tagen a week ago.
Tagebuch *n.* diary.
tagelang for days.
Tagesgespräch *n.* topic of the day.
Tageszeitung *f.* daily paper.
Tagewerk *n.* day's work.
taghell as light as day.
täglich daily.
tagsüber during the day.
Tagung *f.* conference, meeting.
Taille *f.* waist.
Takt *m.* time measure (music).
Taktgefühl *n.* tact.
Taktik *f.* tactics.
taktisch tactical.
taktlos tactless.
Taktlosigkeit *f.* tactlessness, indiscretion.
Taktstock *m.* baton.
taktvoll tactful, discreet.
Tal *n.* valley.
Talent *n.* talent, ability.
talentiert talented.
talentvoll talented.
Talk *m.* talcum powder.
Talsperre *f.* river dam.
talwärts downhill.
Tank *m.* tank (car).
tanken to fill up (car).
Tanne *f.* fir tree.
Tannenadeln *pl.* fir needles.
Tannenbaum *m.* fir tree.
Tannenzapfen *m.* fir cone.
Tante *f.* aunt.
Tanz *m.* dance, ball.
    Darf ich um den nächsten Tanz bitten?
    May I have the next dance?
TANZEN to dance.
Tänzer *m.* (**-in** *f.*) dance partner.
Tapete *f.* wallpaper.
Tapezier *m.* paperhanger, upholsterer.
tapezieren to paper.
tapfer brave, gallant.
Tapferkeit *f.* bravery, gallantry.
Tarif *m.* rate, tariff.
tarifmässig in accordance with the tariff.
tarnen to camouflage, disguise.
Tarnung *f.* camouflage.

TASCHE *f.* pocket, bag, purse.
   jemandem auf der Tasche liegen
   to be a financial drain to a person.
Taschenbuch *n.* pocketbook.
Taschendieb *m.* pickpocket.
Taschenlampe *f.* flashlight.
Taschenmesser *n.* pocket knife.
Taschentuch *n.* handkerchief.
Taschenuhr *f.* pocket-watch.
TASSE *f.* cup.
   eine Tasse Kaffee a cup of coffee.
Taste *f.* key (music and typewriter).
tasten to touch, feel.
TAT *f.* deed, act, fact, achievement, feat.
   auf frischer Tat in the very act.
   in der Tat indeed, as a matter of fact.
tatenlos inactive, idle.
Täter *m.* perpetrator.
tätig active.
   tätig sein to be active.
Tätigkeit *f.* activity, job.
tatkräftig energetic.
Tatsache *f.* fact.
tatsächlich real, actual.
Tau *m.* dew.
Tau *n.* rope.
taub deaf, empty, hollow.
Taube *f.* pigeon.
Taubheit *f.* deafness.
taubstumm deaf and dumb.
Taubstumme *m.* deaf-mute.
tauchen to dive, dip, plunge.
Taucher *m.* diver.
tauen to thaw.
Taufe *f.* baptism, christening.
   aus der Taufe heben to be godfather (or
   godmother).
taufen to baptize.
taugen to be of use.
Taugenichts *m.* good-for-nothing.
Tauglichkeit *f.* fitness, suitability.
Tausch *m.* exchange.
tauschen to exchange, swap.
täuschen to delude, deceive, disappoint.
   Mich können Sie nicht täuschen.
   You can't fool me.
   sich täuschen to be mistaken, fool oneself.
   sich täuschen lassen to let oneself be fooled.
Täuschung *f.* deception.
TAUSEND thousand.
tausendmal a thousand times.
Tauwetter *n.* thaw.
Taxe *f.* tax, rate, duty.
Taxi *n.* taxi.
   ein Taxi holen to call a cab.
taxieren to appraise, value.
Technik *f.* technology.
technisch technical.
Tee *m.* tea.
Teelöffel *m.* teaspoon.
Teer *n.* tar.

Teich *m.* pond.
Teig *m.* dough.
TEIL *m.* & *n.* part, share, portion.
   ich für mein Teil as for me.
   sich sein Teil denken to have one's own ideas.
   zum Teil partly.
   zum grössten Teil for the most part.
teilbar divisible.
Teilchen *n.* particle.
TEILEN to divide, share, distribute, deal out.
   geteilte Gefühle mixed feelings.
   geteilter Meinung sein to be of a different
   opinion.
   sich teilen in to divide, split.
Teilhaber *m.* partner, participant.
Teilhaberschaft *f.* partnership.
Teilnahme *f.* participation, condolences.
   Meine aufrichtige Teilnahme my sincere
   condolences.
teilnahmslos indifferent.
teilnahmsvoll sympathetic.
teilnehmen to take part in.
Teilnehmer *m.* participant, subscriber.
teilweise partial.
Teilzahlung *f.* part-payment, installment.
TELEFON *n.* telephone.
Telefonanruf *m.* telephone call.
Telefonbuch *n.* telephone directory.
TELEFONIEREN to telephone.
telefonisch telephonic, by telephone.
Telefonist *m.* (–in, *f.*) telephone operator.
Telefonnummer *f.* telephone number.
Telefonzelle *f.* telephone booth.
Telefonzentrale *f.* telephone exchange.
Telegrafie *f.* telegraphy.
TELEGRAFIEREN to telegraph.
telegrafisch by telegram.
TELEGRAMM *n.* telegram.
Telegrammformular *n.* telegraph form.
Teller *m.* plate.
Temperament *n.* temperament, character, disposition.
Temperatur *f.* temperature.
Temperaturschwankungen *pl.* variations in
   temperature.
Tempo *n.* time, measure, speed.
Tendenz *f.* tendency, inclination.
Tennis *n.* tennis.
Tennisplatz *m.* tennis court.
Tennisschläger *m.* tennis racket.
Tenor *m.* tenor.
Teppich *m.* carpet.
Termin *m.* deadline.
Terrasse *f.* terrace.
Territorium *n.* territory.
Testament *n.* testament.
TEUER expensive, high, costly.
Teuerung *f.* dearness, scarcity, high cost of living.
Teufel *m.* devil.
   Den Teufel an die Wand malen. Speak of the
   devil and there he is.
teuflisch devilish, diabolical.

Text *m.* text, libretto.
   aus dem Text kommen to lose the thread.
Textbuch *n.* words, libretto.
Textilien *pl.* textiles.
Textilwaren *pl.* textiles.
THEATER *n.* theater, stage.
Theaterbesuch *m.* playgoing.
Theaterbesucher *m.* playgoer.
Theaterdirektor *m.* manager of a theater.
Theaterkasse *f.* box office.
theatralisch theatrical.
Theke *f.* counter, bar.
Thema *n.* theme, subject.
Theologe *m.* theologian.
Theoretiker *m.* theoretician.
Thermometer *n.* thermometer.
Thermometerstand *m.* thermometer reading.
Thron *m.* throne.
Thronbesteigung *f.* accession to the throne.
TIEF deep, low, deeply, far.
   Das lässt tief blicken. That tells a tale.
   in tiefer Nacht late at night.
Tiefe *f.* depth, profundity.
tiefgründig deep, profound.
tiefliegend sunken.
Tiefsee *f.* deep sea.
tiefsinnig profound, pensive, melancholy.
Tiefstand *m.* lowness, low level.
TIER *n.* animal, beast.
Tierarzt *m.* veterinary.
Tiergarten *m.* zoo.
Tiger *m.* tiger.
Tinte *f.* ink.
   in der Tinte sitzen to be in a mess.
Tintenfass *n.* inkwell.
Tintenfleck *m.* blot, ink spot.
TISCH *m.* table.
   bei Tisch during the meal.
   Bitte, zu Tisch! Dinner is ready!
   Er ist gerade zu Tisch gegangen.
   He has just gone out to lunch.
   reinen Tisch machen to make a clean sweep.
   unter den Tisch fallen to be ignored.
Tischdecke *f.* tablecloth.
Tischler *m.* cabinet-maker.
Tischplatte *f.* table top.
Tischrede *f.* after-dinner talk.
Tischtennis *n.* table tennis, ping-pong.
Tischtuch *n.* tablecloth.
Tischzeit *f.* dinner-time.
Titel *m.* title, claim.
Titelbild *n.* frontispiece.
Titelblatt *n.* title page.
Titelhalter *m.* title-holder.
Toast *m.* toast.
toasten to drink toasts.
toben to rage, rave.
Tobsucht *f.* raving madness.
tobsüchtig raving mad.
TOCHTER *f.* daughter.
TOD *m.* death, decease.
   des Todes sein to be doomed.

Todesanzeige *f.* death notice.
Todeskampf *m.* death agony.
Todesstrafe *f.* capital punishment, death penalty.
Todestag *m.* death anniversary.
todkrank very ill.
tödlich fatal, deadly, mortal.
todmüde dead tired.
Toilette *f.* toilet, dress, dressing table, lavatory.
   Toilette machen to dress, get dressed.
tolerant tolerant.
toll mad, insane, raving, awful.
tölpisch clumsy.
Ton *m.* sound, note, stress, accent.
tönen to sound, resound.
Tonfall *m.* musical intonation.
Tonfilm *m.* sound film.
Tonkunst *f.* music, musical art.
Tonleiter *f.* scale.
tonlos soundless, voiceless.
Tonne *f.* barrel, ton.
Tönung *f.* shading.
Topf *m.* pot.
Tor *n.* gate.
Tor *m.* fool.
Torheit *f.* foolishness, folly.
töricht foolish, silly.
Torte *f.* layer cake.
tosen to rage, roar.
TOT dead, dull.
   tote Zeit dead season.
   toter Punkt deadlock.
totarbeiten (sich) to kill oneself with work.
Tote *m.* dead person, deceased.
TÖTEN to kill.
   sich töten to commit suicide.
   sich totlachen to die laughing.
Totenbett *n.* deathbed.
totenbleich deadly pale.
totenstill still as death.
Tötung *f.* killing, slaying.
Tour *f.* tour, excursion.
   in einer Tour without stopping.
Tournee *f.* tour (theater).
Trab *m.* trot.
   im Trab quickly.
Tracht *f.* dress, costume.
trachten to strive, seek after.
   einem nach dem Leben trachten
   to make an attempt on a person's life.
traditionell traditional.
Trage *f.* barrow, litter.
TRAGEN to carry, bear, wear, take, endure, suffer,
   produce.
   die Schuld tragen an to carry the blame for.
   Sie trägt Trauer. She is in mourning.
TRÄGER *m.* porter.
Tragfähigkeit *f.* capacity.
Tragfläche *f.* wing of aircraft.
Tragflügel *m.* wing of aircraft.
Tragik *f.* tragic (art).
tragisch tragic.
Tragödie *f.* tragedy.

trainieren to train.

Träne *f.* tear.

Trank *m.* drink.

tränken to water, soak.

transpirieren to perspire.

Transport *m.* transport.

Traube *f.* grape, bunch of grapes.

Traubenlese *f.* grape harvest.

Traubenmost *m.* grape juice.

trauen to marry, give in marriage, join, trust, rely.
> Ich traue ihm alles zu. I believe him capable of everything.
> sich trauen lassen   to get married.

Trauer *f.* sorrow, grief, affliction.

Traueranzeige *f.* announcement of a death.

Trauermarsch *m.* funeral march.

trauern to mourn, grieve.

Trauerspiel *n.* tragedy.

Traufe *f.* gutter.
> vom Regen in die Traufe   out of the frying pan into the fire.

träufeln to drop.

traulich intimate, cosy.

TRAUM *m.* dream, fancy, illusion.
> Träume sind Schäume.   All dreams are lies.

träumen to dream.

Träumer *m.* dreamer.

träumerisch dreamy.

traumhaft dreamlike.

TRAURIG sad, sorrowful, mournful.

Traurigkeit *f.* sadness.

Trauschein *m.* marriage certificate.

Trauung *f.* marriage ceremony.

Trauzeuge *m.* witness to a marriage.

TREFFEN to meet, hit, strike, affect, touch, fall upon.
> Alle nötigen Vorbereitungen sind getroffen worden. All the necessary arrangements have been made.
> sich getroffen fühlen   to feel hurt.
> sich gut treffen   to be lucky.
> sich treffen   to meet.
> Vorsichtsmassregeln treffen   to take all the necessary precautions.

treffend to the point.

Treffer *m.* target, luck, winning ticket, prize.

trefflich excellent, admirable.

Trefflichkeit *f.* excellence.

treiben to drive, set in motion, float, drift.
> Wintersport treiben   to practice winter sports.

Treibhaus *n.* conservatory.

trennbar sparable, divisible.

TRENNEN to separate, divide, dissolve.
> getrennt leben   to live separately.
> sich trennen   to part.
> sich trennen von   to part from.

Trennung *f.* separation.

Treppe *f.* stairway, stairs.

Treppenabsatz *m.* landing.

Treppengeländer *n.* banisters, railing.

Tresor *m.* treasury.

TRETEN to step, tread, walk, go.
> in jemandes Fusstapfen treten   to follow one's footsteps.
> in Kraft treten   to go into effect.
> in Verbindung treten   to get in touch.
> mit Füssen treten   to trample under foot.
> zu nahe treten   to hurt one's feelings.

TREU faithful, true, loyal.

treubrüchig faithless, perfidious.

Treue *f.* fidelity, faithfulness, loyalty.

treuherzig frank, naive.

treulich faithfully.

treulos unfaithful.

Treulosigkeit *f.* faithlessness.

Tribüne *f.* tribune.

Trieb *m.* sprout, shoot, motive power.

trinkbar drinkable.

TRINKEN to drink, absorb.

Trinker *m.* drunkard.

Trinkgeld *n.* tip.

Trinkspruch *m.* toast.

Tritt *m.* step, footstep.

Trittbrett *n.* running board.

Triumph *m.* triumph, victory.

triumphieren to triumph.

trocken dry, arid, dull.
> im Trockenen sein   to be under cover.

Trockenmilch *f.* dry milk.

trocknen to dry up.

Trommel *f.* drum.

trommeln to beat the drum.

Trompete *f.* trumpet.

Trompeter *m.* trumpeter.

Tropen *pl.* tropics.

tropfen to drop, drip.

tropfenweise by drops, drop by drop.

TROST *m.* comfort.

trostbedürftig in need of consolation.

trösten to comfort, console, cheer up.
> sich trösten   to cheer up.

tröstlich consoling, comforting.

trostlos discouraged.

Trostlosigkeit *f.* despair, hopelessness.

trostreich comforting, consoling.

Trottoir *m.* pavement.

TROTZ *prep. (gen.)* in spite of.
> Trotz der Kälte ging ich jeden Tag spazieren. In spite of the cold, I took a walk every day.

Trotz *m.* obstinacy, stubbornness, defiance.
> jemandem zum Trotz   in defiance of someone.
> Trotz bieten   to defy.

trotzdem nevertheless, anyway, although.
> Trotzdem es sehr kalt ist, werde ich spazieren gehen. Although it is very cold, I shall take a walk.

trotzen to defy, be obstinate.

trotzig defiant.

trüb dark, sad, gloomy.

trüben to dim, trouble, spoil.
> Der Himmel trübt sich. The sky is clouding over.

Trübsal *f.* affliction.

trübselig sad, gloomy, dreary.

trübsinnig melancholy.

trügen to deceive.

trügerisch deceitful.

Truhe *f.* chest, trunk.

Trümmer *f.* ruins, debris.

   in Trümmer gehen to be shattered.

Trumpf *m.* trump.

trumpfen to trump.

Trunk *m.* drink.

Trunkenheit *f.* drunkenness.

Truppe *f.* troop, company.

Truthahn *m.* turkey.

Tube *f.* tube.

tuberkulös tuberculous.

TUCH *n.* cloth, fabric, shawl.

tüchtig good, able, fit, qualified, competent, efficient.

Tüchtigkeit *f.* fitness, ability, efficiency.

Tücke *f.* malice, spite.

tückisch malicious, spiteful.

TUGEND *f.* virtue.

tugendhaft virtuous.

tugendsam virtuous.

Tulpe *f.* tulip.

Tumult *m.* tumult, commotion.

TUN to do, make, act, perform, execute.

   Das tut nichts. That does not matter.

   des Guten zu viel tun to overdo something.

   Er tut nur so. He is only pretending.

   Es tut mir leid. I am sorry.

   es zu tun bekommen mit to have trouble with.

   Haben Sie sich weh getan? Did you hurt yourself?

   Mir ist darum zu tun. It is very important for me.

   tun als ob to pretend.

   Tun Sie als ob Sie zu Hause wären. Make yourself at home.

   Wir haben viel zu tun. We are very busy.

tunlich feasible, practicable.

Tunnel *m.* tunnel.

tupfen to dot, touch lightly, dab.

TÜR *f.* door, doorway,

   vor der Tür stehen to be imminent.

Türgriff *m.* doorknob.

Türklinke *f.* latch (handle).

Turm *m.* tower, steeple.

Turmuhr *f.* church clock.

Turnen *n.* gymnastics.

turnen to do gymnastics.

Turnhalle *f.* gymnasium.

Turnier *n.* tournament.

Tusche *f.* India ink.

Tüte *f.* paper bag.

typisch typical.

Tyrann *m.* tyrant.

tyrannisieren to tyrannize.

U

Übel *n.* evil, ailment, misfortune, inconvenience.

ÜBEL evil, wrong, bad, ill.

   Das ist nicht übel. That is not bad.

   Mir ist übel. I feel sick.

   übel daran sein to be in a bad way.

übelgelaunt cross, grumpy.

übelgesinnt evil-minded.

Übelkeit *f.* nausea.

übelnehmen to mind.

übelnehmerisch touchy, susceptible.

Übelstand *m.* inconvenience, drawback.

Übeltäter *m.* evil-doer, criminal.

üben to exercise, practise.

ÜBER 1. *prep.* (*dat.* when answering question, Wo?; *acc.* when answering question, Wohin?, and depending on the idiom) higher, while, concerning, via.

   den Winter über the whole winter long.

   Er schwamm über den See. He swam across the lake.

   Er zog sich die Decke über den Kopf. He pulled the blanket over his head.

   Ich wundere mich über ihre Einstellung. I am surprised at her attitude.

   Sie sprach über ihre Sorgen. She spoke about her sorrows.

   über Bord overboard.

   Über der Erde ziehen Wolken. Clouds are floating above the earth.

   über kurz oder lang sooner or later.

   über und über over and over.

   Seine Liebe geht ihr über alles. She places his love above everything.

   überall all over.

   von Berlin über Strassburg nach Paris from Berlin to Paris via Strassburg.

   2. *adv.* wholly, completely, in excess.

   3. *prefix.*

   a) *separable (when meaning* above).

   Das Flugzeug fliegt über dem Ozean. The airplane flies above the ocean.

   b) *inseparable (in all uses where it does not mean* above.)

   Er übersetzt ein Gedicht von Schiller. He translates a poem by Schiller.

überaltert too old.

überanstrengen to overwork, overstrain.

überarbeiten to review, go over.

   sich überarbeiten to overwork oneself.

überbelichten to overexpose (photo).

überbieten to excel, surpass.

Überblick *m.* perspective, summary, survey.

überblicken to survey, sum up.

überdachen to roof.

überdauern to outlast.

überdies besides, moreover.

Überdruss *m.* boredom, satiety, disgust.

   zum Überdruss werden to become a bore.

überdrüssig tired of, sick of, bored with.
Übereifer m. excess zeal.
übereignen to transfer, assign, convey.
übereilen to rush, hurry, precipitate.
   sich übereilen to be in a great hurry.
   Übereilen Sie sich nicht! Don't rush!
Übereilung f. hastiness, rush.
übereinkommen to agree.
Übereinkunft f. agreement, arrangement.
übereinstimmen to agree, coincide.
Übereinstimmung f. agreement, conformity.
überessen to overeat.
überfahren to overrun (signal) run over.
Überfahrt f. crossing.
Überfall m. holdup.
überfallen to hold up.
überfällig overdue.
Überfallkommando n. flying squad (police).
überfliegen to fly over, skim through.
überfliessen to overflow, run over.
überflügeln to surpass, outstrip.
Überfluss m. abundance, profusion.
   im Überfluss abundantly.
   zum Überfluss unnecessarily.
überflüssig superfluous, unnecessary.
überfordern to overcharge.
Überfracht f. excess freight, overweight.
überführen to convey, transport.
Überführung f. conveying, transfer.
überfüllen to overload, crowd.
Überfüllung f. overloading.
Übergabe f. delivery, surrender.
Übergang m. passage, crossing.
übergeben to hand over, deliver.
übergehen (*separable prefix*) to cross, pass over.
übergehen (*inseparable prefix*) to pass by, omit.
   Das Geschäft ist in andere Hände
   übergegangen. This store has changed hands.
Übergewicht n. overweight, excess weight.
   das Übergewicht bekommen to lose one's
   balance.
übergiessen to spill.
Überhandnahme f. increase.
überhandnehmen to increase, spread.
Überhang m. curtain, hangings.
überhangen to hang over.
ÜBERHAUPT in general, altogether.
   überhaupt nicht not at all.
überheben to save, spare, exempt.
überheblich presumptuous.
Überhelichkeit f. presumption, arrogance.
überholen to pass (car), surpass, overhaul.
überholt outdated.
überhören to miss, ignore.
Überkleid n. overdress, overall.
überkochen to boil over.
überladen to overload.
überlassen to leave, give up, cede.
überlasten to overload.
überlaufen to run over, boil over, desert.
Überläufer m. deserter.

überleben to survive, outlive.
   sich überlebt haben to be outdated.
Überlebende m. survivor.
überlegen to reflect, consider.
   sich überlegen to think over, consider.
überlegen adj. superior.
   Ich habe es mir anders überlegt. I've changed
   my mind.
   überlegen sein to be better than.
Überlegenheit f. superiority.
überliefern to deliver, transmit.
Überlieferung f. delivery, tradition, surrender.
überlisten to outwit.
ÜBERMACHT f. superiority, predominance.
Übermass n. excess.
   im Übermass to excess, excessive.
übermässig excessive, immoderate.
Übermensch m. superman,
übermenschlich superhuman.
übermitteln to transmit.
Übermittlung f. transmission.
ÜBERMORGEN the day after tomorrow.
übermüden to overtire.
Übermüdung f. over-fatigue.
Übermut m. high spirits.
übermütig to be in high spirits.
übernachten to stay overnight, spend the night.
Übernahme f. taking over.
übernatürlich supernatural.
übernehmen to take over, seize.
   sich übernehmen to overstrain oneself.
überordnen to set over.
überraschen to surprise.
Überraschung f. surprise.
überreden to persuade.
überreichen to hand over, present.
überreif overripe.
Überrest m. remainder.
überrumpeln to surprise, take by surprise.
Überrumpelung f. surprise, sudden attack.
überschätzen to overrate, overestimate.
überschauen to overlook, survey.
Überschlag m. estimate.
überschlagen to estimate; to skip.
überschneiden to intersect, overlap.
überschreiten to cross, exceed, overstep.
Überschreitung f. crossing, excess,
   transgression.
Überschrift f. heading, title.
Überschuh m. overshoe, galosh.
Überschuss m. surplus, excess.
überschüssig in excess.
überschwemmen to inundate.
Überschwemmung f. inundation, flood.
Übersee f. overseas.
übersehen to survey, overlook.
übersenden to send, transmit.
Übersender m. sender.
Übersendung f. transmission.
übersetzen to pass across.
ÜBERSETZEN to translate.

Übersetzer *m.* translator.
Übersetzung *f.* translation.
Übersicht *f.* view, review, summary.
übersichtlich clear, visible.
Übersichtlichkeit *f.* clearness, lucidity.
übersinnlich transcendental.
überspannen to stretch over, span.
überspannt eccentric.
Überspanntheit *f.* eccentricity.
überspitzt too subtle.
überspringen to jump across.
überstehen to endure, come through.
überstrahlen to shine upon, outshine.
überströmen to overflow.
Überstunden *pl.* overtime.
    Überstunden machen to work overtime.
ÜBERSTURZEN to rush, hurry, act hastily.
    Überstürzen Sie sich nicht! Don't rush
    yourself!
übertragbar transferable.
übertragen to transfer, give up, entrust with,
    transmit, broadcast.
Übertragung *f.* transfer, transcription, transmission.
übertreffen to excell, surpass.
übertreiben to exaggerate.
Übertreibung *f.* exaggeration.
übertreten to go over, change over, violate.
Übertretung *f.* violation, transgression.
übertrumpfen to outdo.
übervölkert overpopulated.
übervorteilen to take advantage.
überwachen to watch over, supervise.
Überwachung *f.* observation, surprise.
überwältigen to overwhelm.
Überwältigung *f.* overwhelming.
überweisen to transfer, remit.
    telegraphisch überweisen to send a cable.
Überweisung *f.* transfer, remittance.
überwiegen to outweigh.
überwiegend preponderant, predominant.
überwinden to overcome.
Überwindung *f.* overcoming, conquest.
Überzahl *f.* numerical superiority, majority.
überzählig surplus.
überzeugen to convince.
Überzeugung *f.* conviction, belief.
    der Überzeugung sein to be convinced.
überziehen to cover, re-cover; to overdraw (bank
    account).
    das Bett überziehen to change the sheets.
üblich usual, customary.
U-Boot *n.* submarine.
ÜBRIG left over, remaining, other.
    das Übrige the rest.
    ein übriges tun to do more than necessary.
    Haben Sie ein paar Minuten für uns übrig?
    Can you spare us a few minutes?
    im übrigen otherwise.
    nichts übrig haben für to care little for.
    übrig bleiben to be left over.
    übrig lassen to leave.

    zu wünschen übrig lassen to leave much to
    be desired.
ÜBRIGENS besides, by the way.
ÜBUNG *f.* exercise, practice, drill.
UFER *n.* shore, bank (river).
UHR *f.* hour, clock, watch.
    nach der Uhr sehen to look at the time.
    um halb fünf at half past five.
    Um wieviel Uhr? At what time?
    Wieviel Uhr ist es? What time is it?
Uhrmacher *m.* watchmaker.
Uhrzeiger *m.* clock hand.
UM 1. *prep. (acc.).* at, about, around, because of,
    Der Zug verlässt Düsseldorf um drei Uhr. The
    train leaves Düsseldorf at three o'clock.
    einer um den anderen one after the other.
    Ihre Zeit ist um. Your time is up.
    Tag um Tag every day, day after day.
    Wir ängstigen uns um sie. We worry about her.
    Wir sitzen um den Tisch. We sit around the
    table.
    Um Himmels willen! For God's sake!
    um jeden Preis at any cost.
    um keinen Preis not at any price.
    um so besser all the better.
    um zwei Jahre älter two years older.
    2. *Adv.* around.
    um und um around.
    um herum all around.
    3. *Conj.* (um...zu). in order to.
    Um den Frieden zu erhalten, dankt der Prinz
    ab. The prince abdicates in order to preserve
    peace.
    4. *Prefix.* a) *inseparable (implies the meaning
    of around).*
    Gärten umgeben das Schloss. The castle is
    surrounded by gardens.
    b) *separable. (implies the meaning of to upset,
    to transform).*
    Er warf den Stuhl um. He overturned the chair.
umadressieren to redirect a letter.
umändern to change, alter.
Umänderung *f.* change, alteration.
umarbeiten to remodel.
Umarbeitung *f.* remodeling.
umarmen to embrace, hug.
Umarmung *f.* embrace ,hug.
Umbau *m.* rebuilding, reconstruction.
umbinden to tie round, put on.
umblättern to turn over.
umblicken to look about.
umdrehen to turn, turn round.
Umdrehung *f.* turning round.
umfahren to drive around.
Umfahrt *f.* circular tour.
umfallen to topple over.
Umfang *m.* circumference, extent, size.
umfangreich comprehensive, extensive.
umfassen to clasp, embrace, enclose.
umfassend comprehensive, extensive, complete,
    full.

umformen to transform, remodel.
Umfrage *f.* inquiry.
Umgang *m.* association, relations.
umgänglich sociable.
Umgangsformen *pl.* manners.
Umgangssprache *f.* colloquial speech.
umgeben to surround.
Umgebung *f.* surroundings, environs.
Umgegend *f.* neighborhood, vicinity.
UMGEHEN to go around, circulate, haunt, evade.
　　umgehend antworten to answer by return.
umgekehrt opposite, reverse, contrary.
umgestalten to alter, transform, reform.
umgraben to dig up.
umgruppieren to regroup.
Umhang *m.* cape, shawl.
UMHER around, about, here and there.
umherblicken to glance around, look around.
umhin about.
　　Ich kann nicht umhin. I can't help (refrain from).
umhüllen to wrap, cover, veil.
Umkehr *f.* return, change.
UMKEHREN to turn back, turn around, turn upside down, invert, reverse.
Umkehrung *f.* inversion, reversal.
umkleiden to change clothes.
Umkreis *m.* circle, circuit.
umkreisen to revolve, circle around.
Umkreisung *f.* encirclement.
Umlauf *m.* rotation, revolution, circulation.
　　in Umlauf setzen to circulate.
umleiten to divert (traffic).
Umleitung *f.* detour.
　　Strassenbau! Umleitung! Road under repair! Detour!
umliegend surrounding, neighboring.
umpflanzen to transplant.
umreissen to outline, sketch.
Umriss *m.* sketch, outline, contour.
Umsatz *m.* sale, turnover.
umschalten to switch over.
Umschalter *m.* switch, commutator.
UMSCHLAG *m.* envelope, cover, wrapper, hem, compress, change.
umschlagen to fell, knock down, put on, change.
umschliessen to enclose.
umschwärmen to swarm around.
Umschwung *m.* change, revolution.
umsehen to look back, round.
　　Sie sehen sich nach einer neuen Wohnung um. They are looking for a new apartment.
Umsicht *f.* circumspection, prudence, caution.
umsichtig cautious, prudent.
umsonst gratis, for nothing; in vain.
UMSTAND, *m.* circumstances, fact.
　　ohne Umstände without ceremony.
　　mildernde Umstände extenuating circumstances.
　　sich Umstände machen to put oneself out.
　　Sie ist in anderen Umständen. She is ex-

pecting a baby.
　　Umstände machen to make a fuss.
　　unter allen Umständen in any case, by all means.
　　unter keinen Umständen on no account.
　　unter gewissen Umständen in certain circumstances.
umständlich laborious.
Umsteige fahrschein *m.* transfer-ticket.
　　einen Umsteige fahrschein verlangen to ask for a transfer.
umsteigen to change trains.
umstimmen to tune to another pitch.
umstritten disputed, controversial.
Umsturz *m.* downfall, revolution.
umstürzen to throw down, overturn.
Umtausch *m,* exchange.
umtauschen to change for.
umtun to drape around.
umwechseln to exchange, change (money).
Umweg *m.* detour.
Umwelt *f.* surroundings, environment.
umwenden to turn, turn over.
umwerben to court.
umwickeln to wrap up.
umziehen to change clothes.
Umzug *m.* procession.
unabhängig independent.
Unabhängigkeit *f.* independence.
unabkömmlich indispensable.
unablässig incessant.
unabsehbar incalculable.
unabsichtlich unintentional.
unabwendbar inevitable.
unachtsam careless.
unangebracht out of place.
unangefochten undisputed.
unangemessen inadequate, improper.
unangenehm unpleasant, disagreeable.
unannehmbar unacceptable.
Unannehmlichkeit *f.* inconvenience, trouble.
Unansehnlichkeit *f.* plainness.
unanständig improper, indecent.
unappetitlich unappetizing, uninviting.
Unart *f.* bad behavior, rudeness.
unartig naughty.
unauffindbar undiscoverable.
unaufgefordert unasked.
unaufhaltsam inevitable, impetuous.
unaufhörlich incessant, incessantly.
unaufmerksam inattentive.
unaufrichtig insincere.
unausbleiblich unfailing, certain.
unausführbar impracticable, not feasible.
unaussprechlich inexpressible.
unausstehlich intolerable, unbearable.
unbarmherzig unmerciful, pitiless, brutally.
Unbarmherzigkeit *f.* mercilessness.
unbeabsichtigt unintentional, undesigned.
unbeachtet unnoticed.
unbeanstandet not objected to, unopposed.
unbeantwortet unanswered.

unbedachtsam inconsiderate, thoughtless.
unbedenklich harmless.
unbedeutend insignificant, trifling.
unbedingt unconditional, absolute.
    Sie müssen unbedingt dabei sein. You must
    be there whatever may happen.
unbeeinflusst unprejudiced.
unbefangen impartial, unprejudiced.
Unbefangenheit *f.* impartiality; facility.
unbefriedigend unsatisfactory, unsatisfactorily.
unbefriedigt unsatisfied.
unbefugt incompetent.
unbegabt not gifted, not clever.
unbegreiflich inconceivable.
unbegrenzt unbounded, unlimited.
unbegründet unfounded, groundless.
Unbehagen *n.* discomfort.
unbehaglich uncomfortable.
unbehelligt undisturbed.
unbehilflich helpless.
unbehindert unrestrained.
unbeholfen clumsy.
UNBEKANNT unknown.
    Er ist hier unbekannt. He is a stranger
    here.
unbekümmert unconcerned.
unbeliebt unpopular.
unbemerkt unnoticed.
UNBEQUEM uncomfortable, inconvenient.
Unbequemlichkeit *f.* discomfort.
unberechenbar incalculable.
unberechtigt unauthorized, unjustified.
unberührt untouched, intact, innocent.
unbeschädigt undamaged, uninjured.
unbescheiden immodest, insolent.
unbeschreiblich indescribable.
unbeschwert light.
unbesehen without inspection, hesitation.
unbesiegbar invincible.
Unbesonnenheit *f.* indiscretion, imprudence.
unbesorgt unconcerned.
    Seien Sie unbesorgt. Don't worry.
unbeständig unstable, unsteady.
unbestechlich incorruptible.
unbestimmt undetermined, undefined, indefinite.
unbestreitbar indisputable.
unbeträchtlich inconsiderable.
unbeugsam inflexible, stubborn.
unbewandert inexperienced.
unbeweglich motionless.
unbewohnt uninhabited.
unbewusst unconscious.
unbezahlbar priceless.
unbezwingbar invincible.
unbrauchbar useless, of no use.
UND and.
    und so weiter and so forth.
Undank *m.* ingratitude.
undankbar ungrateful.
Undankbarkeit *f.* ingratitude.
undenkbar unconceivable.
undeutlich indistinct, vague.

undicht leaky.
Unding *n.* absurdity, impossibility.
unduldsam intolerant.
undurchdringlich impenetrable.
uneben uneven, rough.
unebenbürtig inferior.
unecht not genuine, false, improper, artificial.
unehelich illegitimate.
unehrbar indecent, immodest.
unehrenhaft dishonorable.
unehrlich dishonest.
uneigennützig unselfish.
uneinig disunited.
Uneinigkeit *f.* discord, disagreement.
uneins divided.
    uneins sein to disagree.
unempfindlich insensible.
UNENDLICH infinite, endless, infinitely.
    unendlich lang endless.
unentbehrlich indispensable.
unentgeltlich free of charge.
unentschieden undecided.
unentschlossen irresolute.
unentschuldbar inexcusable.
unerbittlich inexorable.
unerfahren inexperienced.
unerforschlich impenetrable.
unerfreulich unpleasant, unsatisfactory.
unerfüllbar unrealizable.
unerhört unheard of, insolent.
unerklärlich inexplicable.
unerlaubt illicit, unlawful.
unermesslich boundless, infinite.
unermüdlich untiring.
unerreichbar inaccessible.
unerreicht unequaled.
unerschrocken fearless.
unerschütterlich imperturbable.
unersetzlich irreplaceable.
unerträglich unbearable, intolerable.
unerwartet unexpected.
unerwünscht undesired, unwelcome.
unerzogen uneducated, ill-bred.
UNFÄHIG incapable, unable.
Unfähigkeit *f.* inefficiency.
Unfall *m.* accident.
Unfallversicherung *f.* insurance against accidents.
unfehlbar certainly, surely.
unfreiwillig involuntary.
unfreundlich unfriendly, unpleasant.
unfruchtbar unproductive, sterile.
Unfug *m.* wrong, mischief, nonsense.
ungebildet uneducated.
ungebührlich indecent, improper.
ungebunden unbound, unrestrained.
ungedeckt uncovered (also for a check).
ungeduldig impatient, impatiently.
ungeeignet unsuitable, unfit.
UNGEFÄHR approximately, about, nearly.
    von ungefähr by chance.
ungefährlich harmless.
ungehalten angry.

Ungeheuer *n.* monster.
ungeheuer huge, enormous, vast, monstrous.
ungehorsam disobedient.
ungerünstelt unaffected, simple.
ungelegen inconvenient.
ungelernt unskilled.
ungemütlich uncomfortable.
ungeniert free and easy.
ungeniessbar inedible, unbearable.
ungenügend insufficient.
ungepflegt neglected, untidy.
UNGERECHT unjust.
ungerechtfertigt unjustified.
Ungerechtigkeit *f.* injustice.
UNGERN unwillingly, reluctant.
ungeschehen undone.
Ungeschick *n.* misfortune.
Ungeschicklichkeit *f.* awkwardness.
ungeschickt awkward, clumsy.
ungesetzlich illegal.
ungestört undisturbed.
ungestüm impetuous.
ungesund unhealthy.
ungetreu faithless.
ungewiss uncertain.
Ungewissheit *f.* uncertainty.
ungewöhnlich unusual, strange.
ungewohnt unaccustomed, unfamiliar.
ungezogen ill-bred, naughty.
Unglaube *m.* disbelief.
ungläubig incredulous.
unglaublich incredible.
ungleich unequal, unlike.
UNGLÜCK *n.* misfortune, bad luck, accident.
unglücklich unfortunate, unlucky.
unglücklicherweise unfortunately.
Unglücksvogel *m.* unlucky person.
Ungnade *f.* disgrace, displeasure
   in Ungnade fallen bei to displease someone.
ungültig void, invalid.
   für ungültig erkären to annul.
ungut
   Nichts für ungut. No harm meant.
Unheil *n.* mischief, harm, disaster.
unheilbar incurable, irreparable.
unheilvoll disastrous.
unheimlich sinister.
unhöflich impolite, rude.
Uniform *f.* uniform.
UNIVERSITÄT *f.* university, college.
unkenntlich unrecognizable.
Unkenntnis *f.* ignorance.
unklar not clear.
unklug imprudent, unwise.
Unkosten *pl.* expenses.
Unkraut *n.* weeds.
unleserlich illegible.
unliebenswürdig unamiable, unkind.
unlogisch illogical.
unmässig immoderate, disproportionate.
unmenschlich inhuman.
Unmenschlichkeit *f.* inhumanity, cruelty.

unmerklich imperceptible.
unmittelbar immediate.
UNMÖBLIERT unfurnished.
unmodern old-fashioned, antiquated.
UNMÖGLICH impossible.
Unmöglichkeit *f.* impossibility.
unmoralisch immoral.
unmündig minor
   unmündig sein to be a minor.
unnachsichtig strict, severe.
unnahbar unapproachable, inaccessible.
unnatürlich unnatural, affected.
UNNÖTIG unnecessary, needless.
unordentlich disorderly, untidy.
UNORDNUNG *f.* disorder.
   in Unordnung bringen to mess up.
unparteiisch impartial.
unpassend inappropriate.
unpässlich indisposed, ailing.
unpersönlich impersonal.
unpraktisch impractical.
unpünktlich unpunctual.
Unrecht *n.* injustice.
   im Unrecht in the wrong.
   Unrecht haben to be wrong.
   zu Unrecht unlawfully, unjustly
UNRECHT wrong, unjust, unfair.
unredlich dishonest.
unregelmässig irregular.
unreif unripe.
unrein unclean.
   ins Unreine schreiben to make a rough copy.
Unruhe *f.* uneasiness.
Unruhen *pl.* riots.
unruhig restless, uneasy.
Unruhstifter *m.* agitator.
UNS *acc. and dat. of the pers. pron. wir; reflexive
   and reciprocal pron.:* us, to us, ourselves,
   each other.
unsachlich subjective, personal.
unsagbar unspeakable.
unsauber dirty, filthy.
Unsauberkeit *f.* dirt, filth.
unschädlich harmless.
   unschädlich machen to render harmless,
   neutralize, disarm.
unschätzbar invaluable.
unscheinbar insignificant, plain homely.
unschlüssig wavering, irresolute.
UNSCHULDIG innocent.
unselbständig helpless, dependent.
UNSER *Poss. adj.* our.
UNSER (er-e -es) *Poss. pron.* ours.
unsereins people like us.
unsererseits as for us, for our part.
unseresgleichen people like us.
unserethalben for our sakes, on our behalf.
unseretwegen for our sakes.
unseretwillen for our sakes.
UNSICHER unsafe, uncertain, unsteady.
Unsicherheit *f.* insecurity, uncertainty.

Unsinn *m.* nonsense.
Unsitte *f.* bad habit, abuse.
unsterblich immortal.
unstet changeable, unsteady.
unsympathisch unpleasant.
untätig inactive.
untauglich useless; unfit (sports, army).
UNTEN below, beneath, underneath.
    von oben bis unten from top to bottom, from
    head to foot.
UNTER 1. *Prep. (dat. when answering question,*
    Wo?; acc. when answering question, Wohin?,
    and depending on the idiom): under underneath,
    below, beneath, among, during, by.
    Ich habe meine Schuhe unter das Bett gestellt.
    I put my shoes under the bed.
    Ich sass unter den Zuschauern.
    I sat among the spectators.
    Unter anderem hat sie mir gesagt ...
    Among other things, she told me ...
    unter freiem Himmel in the open air.
    unter uns gesagt between us.
    unter vier Augen privately ("under four eyes").
    2. *Prefix.*
    a) separable (when meaning under).
    Die Sonne geht im Westen unter.
    The sun sets in the West.
    b) inseparable when not meaning under.
    Wir unterhielten uns über die Ferien.
    We talked about the holidays.
unterbauen to lay a foundation.
unterbelichten to underexpose (photo).
Unterbewusstsein *n.* sub-conscious.
unterbieten to undersell.
UNTERBRECHEN to interrupt, disconnect, cut off.
    Fräulein, wir sind unterbrochen worden.
    Operator, we have been cut off.
Unterbrechung *f.* interruption.
unterbringen to put up, accommodate, place.
unterdessen meanwhile, in the meantime.
unterdrücken to oppress, suppress.
Unterdrückung *f.* repression, oppression.
untereinander among ourselves, reciprocally.
Unterernährung *f.* malnutrition.
Unterführung *f.* underpass.
Untergang *m.* setting, going down, destruction,
    fall; decline.
    der Sonnenuntergang the sunset.
Untergebene *m. & f.* subordinate.
UNTERGEHEN to go down, set, sink.
Untergrundbahn *f.* subway.
unterhalb below.
Unterhalt *m.* maintenance, living.
UNTERHALTEN to support, maintain, keep up.
    sich gut unterhalten to have a good time.
    sich unterhalten to converse, talk.
unterhandeln to negotiate.
Unterhemd *n.* vest.
Unterhosen *pl.* shorts, drawers.
unterirdisch underground.
Unterkleidung *f.* underwear.

unterkommen to find accommodations, find a situation.
Unterkunft *f.* accommodation.
Unterlage *f.* foundation, support, evidence, pad.
Unterlass *m.* stopping
    ohne Unterlass incessantly.
unterlassen to omit, neglect, fail to.
unterlegen to lay under, put under.
unterliegen to be defeated.
Unterlippe *f.* lower lip.
Untermieter *m.* subtenant.
UNTERNEHMEN to undertake, attempt.
unternehmend enterprising.
Unternehmer *m.* contractor.
Unternehmung *f.* enterprise, undertaking.
unterordnen to subordinate, submit.
Unterordnung *f.* subordination.
unterreden to converse, confer with.
Unterredung *f.* talk, conference.
UNTERRICHT *m.* instruction, teaching, education,
    lesson.
unterrichten to teach, instruct.
Unterrock *m.* slip, petticoat.
unterschätzen to underestimate, underrate.
unterscheiden to distinguish, differentiate,
    discriminate.
    sich unterscheiden to differ
Unterscheidung *f.* distinction, discrimination.
UNTERSCHIED *m.* difference.
    ohne Unterschied alike.
unterschiedlich different, distinct.
unterschiedslos indiscriminately.
unterschlagen to embezzle.
Unterschlagung *f.* embezzlement.
unterschreiben to sign.
Unterschrift *f.* signature.
Unterseeboot *n.* submarine.
unterstehen to stand under, be subordinate.
    sich unterstehen to dare.
unterstützen to support, aid, assist.
Unterstützung *f.* support, aid, relief.
untersuchen to examine, investigate.
Untersuchung *f.* examination, investigation.
Untertasse *f.* saucer.
Untertitel *m.* subtitle (movie).
Unterwäsche *f.* underwear.
unterwegs on the way.
unterweisen to instruct.
Unterweisung *f.* instruction.
Unterwelt *f.* underworld.
unterwerfen to subjugate.
unterwürfig submissive.
unterzeichnen to sign, ratify.
Unterzeichner *m.* signatory.
Unterzeichnung *f.* signature, ratification.
untragbar not transferable, not negotiable; unbearable.
untrennbar inseparable.
UNTREU untrue, unfaithful.
untröstlich disconsolate.
Untugend *f.* vice, bad habit.
unübersehbar immense, vast.
unübertrefflich unequaled.

ununterbrochen continuously.
unverantwortlich irresponsible.
unverbesserlich incorrigible.
unverbindlich not obligatory, without obligation.
unverdient undeserved.
unverdorben unspoilt, pure.
unvergänglich imperishable, immortal.
unvergleichlich imcomparable.
unverheiratet unmarried.
unverhofft unexpected.
unverkennbar unmistakable.
unverletzt unhurt, uninjured.
unvermeidlich inevitable.
Unvermögen *n.* inability, incapacity.
unvermutet unexpected.
unvernünftig unreasonable.
unverrichtet unperformed.
    unverrichteter Sache unsuccessfully.
unverschämt impudent, fresh.
unversehens unexpectedly.
unversehrt intact, safe.
unverständlich unintelligible, incomprehensible.
unverwüstlich indestructible, inexhaustible.
unverzeihlich unpardonable.
unverzollt duty unpaid.
unverzüglich immediate.
unvollkommen imperfect.
unvollständig incomplete, defective.
unvorhergesehen unforeseen.
UNVORSICHTIG careless.
unvorteilhaft unprofitable, unbecoming.
unweiblich unwomanly.
unweit not far off, near.
Unwesen *n.* mischief, abuse.
    sein Unwesen treiben to be up to one's tricks.
unwesentlich unessential, immaterial.
    Das ist ganz unwesentlich. That does not matter.
Unwetter *n.* storm, hurricane.
unwiderruflich irrevocable
unwiderstehlich irrestible.
Unwille *m* indignation.
unwillkommen unwelcome.
unwillkürlich instinctively, involuntarily.
unwirksam ineffective, inefficient.
unwirtlich inhospitable, dreary.
unwirtschaftlich uneconomic.
unwissend ignorant.
UNWOHL not well, indisposed.
Unwohlsein *n.* indisposition.
unwürdig unworthy.
Unzahl *f.* endless number.
unzählig countless.
unzeitgemäss inopportune, out of season.
unzerbrechlich unbreakable.
unzivilisiert uncivilized, barbarian.
unzufrieden dissatisfied.
unzulänglich inadequate.
unzulässig forbidden.
unzureichend insufficient.
unzuverlässig unreliable.

unzweideutig unequivocal, unambiguous.
unzweifelhaft undoubted, indubitable.
üppig luxuriant, abundant, voluptuous.
Üppigkeit *f.* luxury.
uralt very old, ancient.
Uraufführung *f.* first performance, opening night.
Ureinwohner *m.* original inhabitant.
Urgrosseltern *pl.* great-grandparents.
Urkunde *f.* deed, document, record.
Urkundenfälscher *m.* forger of documents.
urkundlich documentary, authentic.
Urlaub *m.* leave, furlough, vacation.
    der bezahlte Urlaub the paid vacation.
URSACHE *f.* cause, reason.
    Keine Ursache! Don't mention it!
Ursprung *m.* source, origin.
ursprünglich original, primitive.
URTEIL *n.* judgment, decision, sentence, opinion.
urteilen to judge, pass a sentence, give an opinion.
urteilsfähig competent to judge.
urteilslos without judgment.
Urteilsspruch *m.* sentence, verdict.

V

Vagabund *m.* vagabond.
Vanille *f.* vanilla.
Variante *f.* variant.
Variation *f.* variation.
Varieté *n.* music-hall.
variieren to vary.
Vase *f.* vase.
Vaselin *n.* vaseline.
VATER *m.* father.
Vaterhaus *n.* home.
Vaterland *n.* native land, fatherland.
vaterländisch national, patriotic.
vaterlandsliebend patriotic.
väterlicherseits on the father's side.
vaterlos fatherless.
Vaterstadt *f.* native town.
vegetarisch vegetarian.
Veilchen *n.* violet.
Vene *f.* vein.
Ventil *n.* valve.
verabreden to agree upon, make an agreement.
    verabredet sein to have a date or appointment.
Verabredung *f.* agreement, engagement; appointment.
verabreichen to give, dispense.
verabscheuen to detest.
verabschieden to dismiss, discharge.
    sich verabschieden to say good-bye.
verachten to despise, scorn, disdain.
verächtlich contemptuous, disdainful.
Verachtung *f.* contempt, scorn, disdain.
verallgemeinern to generalize.
veraltet old, obsolete.
veränderlich variable, unstable.
VERÄNDERN to change, alter, vary.
Veränderung *f.* change, alteration, variation.
verängstigt intimidated.
veranlagt inclined.
    gut veranlagt sein to be talented.

Veranlagung *f.* talent.
veranlassen to cause.
Veranlassung *f.* reason, suggestion.
veranschlagen to estimate.
    zu hoch veranschlagen to overrate.
veranstalten to arrange, organize, set up.
Veranstaltung *f.* arrangement, organization.
verantworten to answer for, account for.
verantwortlich responsible.
VERANTWORTUNG *f.* responsibility.
    auf seine Verantwortung at his own risk.
    zur Verantwortung ziehen to call to account.
verantwortungslos irresponsible.
verarbeiten to use, work up, manufacture.
Verarbeitung *f.* manufacturing.
Verband *m.* bandage, association.
verbannen to banish, exile.
Verbannung *f.* banishment, exile.
VERBESSERN to improve, correct.
Verbesserung *f.* improvement, correction.
verbeugen to bow.
Verbeugung *f.* bow.
verbiegen to bend, twist.
verbieten to forbid.
    Rauchen verboten! No smoking!
    Strengstens verboten! Strictly forbidden!
verbinden to tie, bind, bandage, connect,
    combine, join.
    Fräulein, Sie haben mich falsch verbunden!
    Operator, you gave me the wrong number!
    sich verbinden to unite.
    sich zu Dank verbunden fühlen to feel
    indebted to.
verbindlich obligatory, courteous.
Verbindlichkeit *f.* obligation.
VERBINDUNG *f.* union, combination.
    sich in Verbindung setzen mit to get in
    touch with.
verblüffen to disconcert.
verblüffend amazing.
Verblüffung *f.* stupefaction, amazement.
verbluten to bleed to death.
verborgen hidden, concealed, secret.
Verborgenheit *f.* concealment, retirement,
    seclusion.
Verbot *n.* prohibition, ban.
verboten prohibited, forbidden.
Verbrauch *m.* consumption.
verbrauchen to consume, use.
Verbraucher *m.* consumer.
Verbrechen *n.* crime.
    ein Verbrechen vergehen to commit a crime.
Verbrecher *m.* criminal.
verbrecherisch criminal.
verbreiten to spread, diffuse.
verbrennen to burn, cremate.
    sich verbrennen to burn oneself.
Verbrennung *f.* burning, combustion.
verbringen to spend, pass time.
verbunden obliged.
verbürgen to guarantee.

Verdacht *m.* suspicion.
verdächtig suspicious.
verdächtigen to distrust.
Verdächtigung *f.* insinuation, false charge.
verdammen to condemn.
verdammenswert damnable.
Verdammnis *f.* damnation.
Verdammung *f.* condemnation.
verdanken to owe something.
Verderb *m.* ruin.
Verderben *n.* ruin, destruction.
    jemanden ins Verderben stürzen to ruin a
    person.
VERDERBEN to spoil, ruin.
    Ich möchte es mir nicht mit ihm verderben. I
    don't want to displease him.
    sich den Magen verderben to upset one's
    stomach.
Verderber *m.* corrupter.
verderblich pernicious.
verdienen to earn, gain, deserve, merit.
Verdienst *m.* gain, profit.
Verdienst *n.* merit.
verdienstlich deserving.
verdienstvoll deserving.
verdient deserving.
    sich verdient machen um to deserve well of.
Verdikt *n.* verdict.
verdingen (sich) to take a situation.
verdolmetschen to interpret.
verdoppeln to double.
verdorben spoilt.
verdrängen to displace, push aside.
verdrehen to twist, sprain.
    einem den Kopf verdrehen to turn one's head.
verdummen to grow stupid.
verdünnen to thin, dilute.
Verdünnung *f.* attenuation, rarefaction, dilution.
verdunsten to evaporate.
Verdunstung *f.* evaporation.
verdursten to die of thirst.
veredeln to ennoble, improve, refine, finish.
verehren to respect, worship, adore.
Verehrer *m.* worshipper.
Verehrung *f.* respect.
vereidigen to swear in, put on oath.
Vereidigung *f.* swearing in, taking of an oath.
Verein *m.* union, association.
vereinbar compatible, consistent.
Vereinbarung *f.* agreement.
vereinfachen to simplify.
vereinigen to join, unite, reconcile.
    die Vereinigten Staaten von Amerika. The
    United States of America.
vereisen to turn to ice.
vereiteln to frustrate, thwart.
verelenden to sink into poverty.
vererben to bequeath, transmit, hand down.
verewigen to perpetuate, immortalize.
Verfall *m.* decay, ruin.
    im Verfall geraten to go to ruin, decay.

verfallen to decline, go to ruin, grow weaker, expire.
  einem verfallen to become dependent on a person.
  verfallen lassen to let go to waste.
  verfallene Züge sunken features.
verfassen to compose, write.
Verfasser *m.* author, writer.
Verfassung *f.* state, condition.
verfechten to stand up for.
verfliegen to fly away, disappear, vanish.
verfolgen to follow, pursue, prosecute.
  heimlich verfolgen to shadow.
  gerichtlich verfolgen to prosecute.
Verfolgung *f.* pursuit, prosecution.
verfügbar available.
verfügen to arrange, decree, obtain.
  verfügen über to dispose of, have at one's disposal.
  zur Verfügung stellen to place at one's disposal.
verführen to induce, prevail upon, seduce.
Verführer *m.* tempter, seducer.
verführerisch tempting, seductive.
Verführung *f.* temptation.
Vergangenheit *f.* past; past tense (grammar).
vergänglich transitory, perishable.
Vergaser *m.* carburetor.
vergeben to give away, dispose of, confer, forgive.
vergebens in vain, vainly.
Vergebung *f.* pardon, forgiveness.
vergelten to pay back, repay, retaliate.
Vergeltung *f.* return, recompense.
VERGESSEN to forget, neglect.
vergesslich forgetful.
Vergesslichkeit *f.* forgetfulness.
vergiften to poison.
Vergiftung *f.* poisoning.
Vergleich *m.* comparison, agreement, arrangement.
VERGLEICHEN to compare, check, settle.
VERGNÜGEN *n.* pleasure, joy, fun.
vergnügen (sich) to amuse, enjoy oneself.
VERGNÜGT pleased, glad.
  Ich komme mit Vergnügen. I'll be delighted to come.
  Viel Vergnügen! Have a good time!
  Vergnügungsreise, *f.* pleasure trip.
vergnügungssüchtig pleasure-seeking.
vergraben to bury, hide in the ground.
vergrössern to enlarge, magnify.
Vergrösserung *f.* enlargement.
Vergünstigung *f.* privilege.
Verhältnis *n.* relation, ratio, love-affair.
verhältnismässig relative, proportional.
verhasst hated, hateful, odious.
verheimlichen to conceal, keep secret.
verheiraten to marry off.
verherrlichen to glorify.
Verherrlichung *f.* glorification.
verhindern to hinder, prevent.

Verhinderung *f.* hindrance, draw-back.
Verhör *n.* examination.
verhören to examine, interrogate.
verhungern to die of hunger.
verirren to lose one's way, go astray.
VERKAUF *m.* sale.
VERKAUFEN to sell.
  billiger verkaufen to undersell.
  zu verkaufen for sale.
VERKÄUFER *m.* (—in. *f.*) sales person.
verkäuflich for sale.
VERKEHR *m.* traffic, circulation, communication, trade.
verkehren to associate, transform, convert, change, run (buses).
  verkehren mit to associate with, see a good deal of.
Verkehrsampel *f.* signal light.
Verkehrsschutzmann *m.* traffic policeman.
Verkehrsunfall *m.* traffic-accident.
verkehrt wrong, backwards, upside down, absurd.
  verkehrt gehen to go the wrong way.
verkennen to fail to recognize, mistake, misunderstand, undervalue.
verkleiden to disguise, camouflage.
Verkleidung *f.* disguise, camouflage.
verkommen to be ruined, become bad, degenerate.
Verkommenheit *f.* depravity, degeneracy.
verkörpern to personify, incarnate, embody.
Verlag *m.* publication, publishing firm.
verlangen to demand, desire, require.
  auf Verlangen by request, on demand.
  verlangen nach to long for.
verlängern to extend, prolong.
Verlängerung *f.* extension, prolonging.
Verlass *m.* trustworthiness.
  Auf ihn ist kein Verlass. He cannot be relied on.
VERLASSEN to leave, abandon, desert.
verlegen embarrassed, self-conscious, confused.
  um etwas verlegen sein to be at a loss for.
  um Geld verlegen sein to be short of money.
Verlegenheit *f.* embarrassment, difficulty.
Verleger *m.* publisher.
verleihen to lend out, confer, bestow, grant.
verletzbar vulnerable, susceptible.
verletzen to hurt, injure, offend.
Verletzung *f.* injury, offense, violation.
verleugnen to deny, injure, offend.
Verleugnung *f.* denial, denunciation.
verleumden to calumniate, slander.
Verleumder *m.* slanderer.
verleumderisch slanderous.
Verleumdung *f.* slander, defamation, libel.
VERLIEBEN (sich) to fall in love.
verliebt in love.
  Sie ist verliebt bis über die Ohren. She is head over heels in love.
VERLIEREN to lose, waste, disappear.
  An ihm ist nicht viel verloren. He's no great loss.

Ich habe keinen einzigen Augenblick zu verlieren. I don't have a single moment to lose.

verloben (sich) to get engaged.

Verlobte *m. & f.* fiancé(e).

Verlobung *f.* engagement.

Verlust *m.* loss, waste, escape.

vermehren to increase.

Vermehrung *f.* increase.

vermieten to rent, let, hire out.

Vermieter *m.* landlord.

vermissen to miss.

vermuten to suppose, presume, suspect.

vermutlich presumable, probable.

vernachlässigen to neglect.

Vernachlässigung *f.* neglect.

verneigen to bow.

Verneigung *f.* bow.

vernichten to annihilate, destroy.

Vernichtung *f.* annihilation, destruction.

VERNUNFT *f.* reason, understanding, intelligence, good sense, judgment.

Vernunft annehmen to listen to reason.

zur Vernunft bringen to bring to one's senses.

veröffentlichen to publish.

Veröffentlichung *f.* publication.

verordnen to order, decree.

Verordnung *f.* order, decree, prescription.

verpacken to pack up, wrap up.

Verpackung *f.* packing up, wrapping up.

verpfänden to pawn, mortgage.

verpflegen to feed, board.

Verpflegung *f.* feeding, board, food.

Zimmer mit Verpflegung. Room and board.

verpflichten to oblige, bind, engage.

sich verpflichten to commit (bind) oneself.

verpflichtet sein to be under obligation.

Verpflichtung *f.* obligation, duty, engagement.

Verrat *m.* treason, betrayal.

verraten to betray, disclose, reveal.

Verräter *m.* traitor.

verräterisch treacherous.

verrechnen to reckon up, charge, account; miscalculate.

Verrechnung *f.* settling of an account, reckoning.

verreisen to go away.

verreist sein to be away.

verrichten to execute, perform, accomplish.

die Hausarbeit verrichten to do the housework.

Verrichtung *f.* execution, performance, function, work.

VERRÜCKT crazy, mad.

Vers *m.* verse, stanza.

versagen to deny, refuse; fail, miss.

VERSAMMELN to assemble, bring together, gather.

sich versammeln to gather.

versäumen to neglect, omit, miss.

Versäumnis *f. n.* neglect, omission.

verschenken to give away.

verschicken to send away, dispatch, evacuate.

Verschickung *f.* dispatch, transportation, evacuation.

VERSCHIEDEN different from, distinct, various.

verschlafen to oversleep, sleepy.

verschlimmern to aggravate.

Verschlimmerung *f.* deterioration.

verschlissen worn out, threadbare.

verschlucken to swallow the wrong way.

Verschluss *m.* lock, fastener, clasp, seal, plug, zipper.

verschmachten to languish.

verschonen to spare, exempt from.

verschönern to beautify, embellish, adorn.

Verschönerung *f.* embellishment.

verschreiben to prescribe, order in writing, write for.

sich verschreiben to make a mistake in writing.

verschwägert related by marriage.

verschwenden to waste, lavish.

Verschwender *m.* spendthrift, extravagant person.

verschwenderisch wasteful, extravagant.

verschwiegen discreet, close.

Verschwiegenheit *f.* secrecy, discretion.

verschwistert like brothers and sisters, closely united.

Versehen *n.* mistake, oversight.

VERSEHEN to provide, furnish, supply with; to overlook.

ehe man sich's versieht unexpectedly, suddenly.

sich versehen to make a mistake.

versehentlich by mistake.

VERSETZEN to displace, transfer, pledge, pawn.

den Verstand verlieren to go out of one's mind.

Just put yourself in my place.

Versetzung *f.* transfer, moving up.

VERSICHERN to insure, affirm.

Versicherung *f.* insurance.

versöhnen to reconcile, conciliate.

Versöhnung *f.* reconciliation.

versorgen to provide, supply.

Versorger *m.* support, breadwinner.

Versorgung *f.* supply.

verspätet late.

Verspätung *f.* delay, lateness.

Verspätung haben to be late.

verspielen to lose, gamble away.

VERSPRECHEN to promise.

Ich habe mich nur versprochen.

It was only a slip of the tongue.

sich etwas versprechen von to expect much of.

Versprechung *f.* promise.

VERSTAND *m.* mind, sense, brain, intellect.

den Verstand verlieren to go out of one's mind.

zu Verstand kommen to arrive at the age of discretion.

verständig intelligent, sensible, wise.

verständigen to inform, notify.

sich verständigen to come to an understanding with.

verständlich understandable, clear, comprehensible.

sich verständlich machen to make oneself understood.

Verständlichkeit *f.* intelligibility, clearness.

Verständnis comprehension, understanding.

Verständnis haben für to appreciate.
verständnislos unappreciative, stupid.
verständnisvoll understanding, appreciative.
Versteck *n.* hiding place.
verstecken to hide, conceal.
versteckt hidden, concealed.
versteckte Absichten ulterior motives.
VERSTEHEN to understand, comprehend, know.
falsch verstehen to misunderstand.
Ich verstehe nicht! I don't understand!
sich verstehen to understand each other.
sich von selbst verstehen to go without saying.
Was verstehen Sie darunter? What do you understand by that?
zu verstehen geben to give to understand.
versteifen to stiffen.
sich versteifen auf to insist on.
versteigern to sell at auction.
Versteigerung *f.* auction.
verstellbar adjustable.
verstellen to change order or position, block, disguise.
sich verstellen to put on an act.
Verstellung *f.* dissimulation, disguise, hypocrisy.
versteuern to pay duty on.
verstimmen to annoy, upset.
Verstimmung *f.* ill humor, bad temper.
Versuch *m.* experiment, trial.
VERSUCHEN to try, attempt, taste, sample.
es versuchen mit to give a trial to, put to the test.
Versuchung *f.* temptation.
vertagen to adjourn.
vertauschen to exchange.
verteidigen to defend.
Verteidiger *m.* defender, advocate, attorney.
Verteidigung *f.* defense.
verteilen to distribute, dispense, assign.
Verteilung *f.* distribution.
Vertrag *m.* contract, treaty, agreement.
VERTRAGEN to carry away, bear, stand, endure, tolerate, digest.
ich kann diese Speise nicht vertragen. This food does not agree with me.
sich vertragen to get along.
sich wieder vertragen to settle one's differences.
Vertrauen *n.* confidence.
vertrauen to trust.
vertrauensvoll confident.
vertrauenwürdig trustworthy.
vertraulich confidential.
vertraut familiar.
im Vertrauen in confidence, confidentially.
im Vertrauen auf relying on, trusting to.
sich vertraut machen to become familiar.
Vertraute *m. f.* intimate friend.
vertreten to represent, substitute for; to sprain.
Vertreter *m.* representative, substitute.
VERTRETUNG *f.* representation, replacement.

eine Vertretung übernehmen to take the place of, represent.
vertrösten to put off, console.
verunglücken to have an accident.
verurteilen to sentence, condemn.
Verurteilung *f.* sentence, condemnation.
vervielfältigen to multiply, duplicate, reproduce.
verwahren to keep, put away.
verwaisen to become an orphan.
verwaist orphaned, deserted.
verwandt related, similar, allied.
Verwandte *m. f.* relation, relative.
Verwandtschaft *f.* relationship, relations.
verwechseln to take for, mistake for.
Verwechslung *f.* mistake, confusion.
verweigern to deny, refuse.
Verweigerung *f.* denial, refusal.
Verweis *m.* reproof, reprimand, reference.
Verweisung *f.* exile, banishment.
VERWENDEN to use, utilize, employ, expend.
sich verwenden für to put in a good word for.
verwenden auf to put in on, spend on.
Verwendung *f.* use, utilization, application.
verwirklichen to realize, materialize.
Verwirklichung *f.* realization, materialization.
Verwöhnung *f.* spoiling, pampering.
verwunderlich astonishing, surprising.
verwundern to surprise.
Verwunderung *f.* surprise, astonishment.
verzagen to lose heart, despair.
VERZEIHEN to pardon, forgive, excuse.
Verzeihen Sie! Excuse me!
verzeihlich excusable.
VERZEIHUNG *f.* pardon, excuse.
Ich bitte Sie um Verzeihung! Please excuse me!
Verzicht *m.* resignation, renunciation.
verzichten to renounce, resign, give up.
verzinsen to pay interest on.
verzögern to delay.
verzollen to pay duty on.
Haben Sie etwas zu verzollen? Have you anything to declare?
Verzollung *f.* payment of duty, clearance.
verzweifeln to despair.
verzweifelt desperate, despairing.
Verzweiflung *f.* despair, desperation.
zur Verzweiflung bringen to drive one mad.
Veto *n.* veto
Veto einlegen to veto a thing.
VETTER *m.* cousin.
Vieh *n.* cattle.
Viehhändler *m.* cattle dealer.
VIEL much, a great deal, a lot of.
ein bisschen viel a little too much.
in vielem in many respects.
noch einmal so viel as much again.
viele many.
sehr viele many (people).
Viel Glück! Lots of luck!
Viel Vergnügen! Have a good time!

vielerlei many kind of.

VIELLEICHT perhaps.

vielseitig many-sided, versatile.

VIER four.

    zu vieren, zu viert four of us.

Viereck *n.* square.

viereckig square, quadrangular.

VIERTE fourth.

VIERTEL *n.* quarter, fourth.

    Es ist viertel vor zwei. It is a quarter to two.

vierteljährlich quarterly.

Viertelstunde *f.* a quarter of an hour.

viertelstündlich every quarter of an hour.

VIERZEHN fourteen

    vierzehn Tage two weeks.

VIERZEHNTE fourteenth.

VIERZIG forty.

VIERZIGSTE fortieth.

Viola *f.* viola.

Violine *f.* violin.

virtuos masterly.

Virtuose *m.* virtuoso.

Virtuosität *f.* virtuosity.

Vision *f.* vision.

Visite *f.* visit.

Visitenkarte *f.* visiting-card.

Vitrine *f.* show-case.

VOGEL *m.* bird.

    den Vogel abschiessen to carry off the prize.

Vogelscheuche *f.* scarecrow.

Vokabel *f.* word.

Vokabelschatz *m.* vocabulary (range).

VOLK *n.* people, nation, crowd.

    das arbeitende Volk the working classes.

    das gemeine Volk the mob.

    der Mann aus dem Volk the man in the street.

Volksabstimmung *f.* plebiscite.

Volkslied *n.* folk song.

Volksschule *f.* elementary or primary school.

volkstümlich national, popular.

    volkstümliche Preise popular prices.

Volksversammlung *f.* public meeting.

Volkswagen *m.* people's car.

VOLL 1. *adj. & adv.* full, filled, complete, whole, entire; fully, completely.

    aus vollem Herzen from the bottom of the heart.

    aus voller Kehle at the top of one's voice.

    den Mund voll nehmen to boast.

    Die Rechnung ist voll bezahlt. The bill is paid in full.

    in voller Fahrt at full speed.

    Man kann ihn nicht für voll nehmen.

    One cannot take him too seriously.

    2. Prefix.

    a) separable (meaning to fill)

    Sie giesst die Gläser voll. She fills up the glasse

    b) inseparable (meaning to accomplish, finish).

    Er vollführte eine gute Leistung.

    He executed a good performance.

Vollbart *m.* beard.

vollblütig full-blooded.

vollbringen to finish, accomplish, complete.

Volldampf *m.* full steam.

völlig complete, entire, quite.

volljährig of age.

Volljährigkeit *f.* majority (of age).

VOLLKOMMEN perfect, complete.

Vollkommenheit *f.* perfection.

Vollkraft *f.* full vigor.

Vollmacht *f.* full power, power of attorney.

Vollmilch *f.* unskimmed milk.

Vollmond *m.* full moon.

vollständig complete.

vollzählig complete. full, completely, absolutely.

VON 1. *prep. (dat.).* from, by, with, of, on, upon, about.

    Amerika wurde von Kolumbus entdeckt.

    America was discovered by Columbus.

    Der Platz war voll von Menschen.

    The place was full of people.

    ein Gedicht von Heine a poem by Heine.

    eine Feder von Gold a gold pen.

    von heute ab from today on.

    Von meinem Fenster sehe ich auf den Garten.

    From my window I see the garden.

    2. *adv.*: apart, separate.

    von einander apart.

    von klein auf from childhood (on).

    von mir aus as far as I am concerned.

    von selbst by itself, automatically.

    von Nutzen sein to be needful, necessary.

VOR 1. *prep. (dat. when answering question, Wo?; acc. when answering question, Wohin?, and depending on the idiom).* before, in front of, ahead of, for, with, against, from.

    Das Bild ist vor mir. The picture is in front of me.

    Es ist ein viertel vor elf. It is a quarter to eleven.

    Ich werde sie vor ihm warnen. I will warn her against him.

    nach wie vor as usual.

    nicht vor not until.

    vor acht Tagen a week ago.

    vor allem above all, first of all.

    vor der Klasse before class.

    vor Hunger sterben to die of hunger.

    Vor ihm müssen Sie sich in Acht nehmen.

    With him, you must be on your guard.

    vorzeiten formerly

    vorab above all.

    2. *separable prefix (implies movement forward, presentation, demonstration).*

    Der Lehrer las ein Gedicht vor. The teacher read a poem aloud.

    Die Soldaten rückten vor. The soldiers moved forward.

    Wir bereiten uns auf die Prüfung vor.

    We prepare ourselves for the examination.

vorahnen to have a presentiment.

Vorahnung *f.* presentiment.

voran ahead, before.

vorangehen to precede.

mit gutem Beispiel vorangehen
to set a good example.
Voranschlag *m.* estimate.
Voranzeige *f.* preliminary advertisement.
Vorarbeit *f.* preliminary work.
Vorarbeiter *m.* foreman.
VORAUS in front of, ahead of.
etwas voraus haben vor to have an advantage
over a person.
im Voraus in advance.
weit voraus way ahead.
vorausgehen to lead the way, precede.
voraussetzen to presuppose, assume.
Voraussetzung *f.* supposition, assumption.
voraussichtlich presumable, probable.
Vorbehalt *m.* reservation, proviso.
ohne Vorbehalt unconditionally
unter Vorbehalt aller Rechte all rights reserved.
vorbehalten to keep in reserve, withhold.
sich vorbehalten to reserve to oneself.
vorbehaltlos unconditional.
vorbei by, along, past, over, gone.
vorbeireden (aneinander) to be at cross-purposes.
vorbereiten to prepare, make ready.
Vorbereitung *f.* preparation.
vorbeugen to hinder, prevent.
Vorbeugungsmassregel *f.* preventive measure.
Vorbild *n.* model, pattern, standard.
vorbildlich model, ideal.
Vorbildung *f.* preparatory training, education.
vorder fore, forward, anterior.
Vordergrund *m.* foreground.
Vorderhaus *n.* front part of the house.
vordringlich urgent.
voreilig hasty.
Voreiligkeit *f.* precipitation, rashness.
voreingenommen prejudiced.
Voreingenommenheit *f.* prejudice.
vorenthalten to keep back, withhold.
Vorfall *m.* occurrence, event.
vorfallen to occur, happen, take place.
Vorfreude *f.* joy of anticipation.
vorführen to demonstrate, produce.
Vorführung *f.* demonstration.
Vorgang *m.* occurrence.
Vorgänger *m.* predecessor.
VORGEHEN to go on, go forward, go first, lead,
take place, occur, act, be of special importance.
Gehen Sie schon vor! Go right ahead!
Vorgeschichte *f.* previous history.
Vorgeschmack *m.* foretaste.
Vorgesetzte *m. & f.* chief, boss.
VORGESTERN the day before yesterday.
vorhaben to have on, wear, to intend, plan.
Haben Sie morgen etwas vor?
Do you have any plans for tomorrow?
Vorhang *m.* curtain.
vorher before, beforehand, in advance, previously.
vorherrschen to predominate, prevail.
vorherrschend predominant, prevailing.
Vorjahr *n.* preceding year.

Vorkenntnis *f.* previous knowledge.
vorkommen to come forward, occur, happen.
Es kommt Ihnen nur so vor.
You are just imagining that.
Vorkommnis *n.* occurrence, event.
Vorlage *f.* model, pattern, copy.
vorlassen to give precedence to.
vorläufig preliminary.
Vorleger *m.* mat, rug.
vorlesen to read aloud.
Vorlesung *f.* lecture, recital.
vorletzt one before the last.
Vorliebe *f.* predilection, preference.
vormachen to put, place before, impose on someone,
fool.
vormerken to make a note of, put down.
sich vormerken lassen to book.
Vormittag *m.* morning ("before noon").
Vormund *m.* guardian.
Vormundschaft *f.* guardianship.
VORN in front, in front of.
nach vorn forward.
nach vorne heraus wohnen to live in the
front part of a house.
von vorn from the front.
von vorn anfangen to start afresh.
von vorn herein from the first.
Vorname *m.* Christian name.
vornehm of high rank, noble, distinguished.
Vornehmheit *f.* distinction, high rank.
vornehmlich principally, chiefly, especially.
Vorort *m.* suburb.
Vorplatz *m.* court, hall, vestibule.
Vorrang *m.* precedence, priority.
Vorrat *m.* store, stock, provision.
vorrätig in stock, on hand.
nicht mehr vorrätig out of stock.
Vorratskammer *f.* storeroom, panty.
vorsagen to dictate, say, prompt.
Vorsatz *m.* purpose.
Vorschlag *m.* proposal, proposition.
vorschlagen to propose, offer.
vorschreiben to set a copy.
Vorschrift *f.* copy, direction.
vorschriftmässig according to instructions.
vorsehen to provide for, consider, take care.
Vorsehung *f.* providence.
VORSICHT *f.* foresight, caution, prudence.
Vorsicht! Take care! Beware!
Vorsicht Stufe! Mind the step!
vorsichtig cautious, prudent.
vorsichtshalber as a precaution.
Vorsichtsmassregel *f.* precaution, measure.
Vorsitz *m.* presidency, chairman.
den Vorsitz führen to provide in the chair.
Vorspeise *f.* hors d'oeuvre, relish.
vorsprechen to pronounce, recite.
vorsprechen bei to call on.
Vorsprung *m.* projection, projecting part.
Vorstadt *f.* suburb.
Vorstand *m.* board of directors.

vorstellen to place before, put in front of, demonstrate, introduce, represent, act.
    sich etwas vorstellen to imagine something.
    sich vorstellen to introduce oneself.
vorstellig *adj.*
    vorstellig werden to present a case, petition.
VORSTELLUNG *f.* introduction, presentation, performance, picture.
    Wann fängt die Vorstellung an? When does the performance start?
Vorstellungsvermögen *n.* imagination.
Vorteil *m.* advantage, profit.
VORTEILHAFT advantageous, favorable.
    vorteilhaft aussehen to look one's best.
Vortrag *m.* reciting, delivery, execution, lecture.
vortragen to carry forward, recite, declaim, execute, perform.
vortrefflich excellent, admirable, splendid.
Vortrefflichkeit *f.* excellence.
vorüber past, over, by, along.
vorübergehen to go by, pass.
Vorurteil *n.* prejudice.
vorurteilslos unprejudiced.
Vorverkauf *m.* booking in advance (theater); advance sale.
vorvorgestern three days ago.
Vorwand *m.* pretext, pretense, excuse.
VORWÄRTS forward, onward, on.
    Vorwärts! Go on! Go ahead!
vorwärtsgehen to go on, advance, progress.
vorwärtskommen to get on, advance, prosper.
vorwärtskommend predominant.
Vorwurf *m.* reproach.
    Vorwürfe machen to blame.
vorwurfsvoll reproachful.
vorzeigen to show, produce, exhibit, display.
vorzeitig premature, precocious.
vorziehen to draw forward, prefer.
Vorzimmer *n.* antechamber.
Vorzug *m.* preference, superiority.
vorzüglich excellent, superior, first-choice.
Vorzüglichkeit *f.* excellency, superiority.
Vorzugspreis *m.* special price.

W

WAAGE (Woge) *f.* balance, scales.
    einem die Waage halten to be a match for.
    sich die Waage halten to counterbalance each other.
    wagerecht horizontal level.
WACH awake, alive, brisk.
Wachdienst *m.* guard duty.
Wache *f.* guard, watch, sentry.
WACHEN to be awake, remain awake.
    wachen über to watch over.
Wachs *n.* wax.
wachsam vigilant, watchful.
Wachsamkeit *f.* vigilance.
WACHSEN to grow, increase, extend.
    ans Herz wachsen to grow fond of.
    einem gewachsen sein to be a match for one.

    einer Sache gewachsen sein to be equal to a task.
Wachstum *n.* growth, increase.
Wacht *f.* guard, watch.
Wächter *m.* watchman, guard.
Waffe *f.* weapon, arm.
Waffel *f.* wafer, waffle.
Waffeleisen *n.* waffle-iron.
Waffenschein *m.* gun-license.
Waffenstillstand *m.* armistice.
WAGEN *m.* car, automobile, railroad car, cab, wagon.
wagen tọ venture, risk, dare.
    gewagt daring, risky, perilous.
Wagnis *n.* risk.
WAHL *f.* choice, selection, election.
    in engere Wahl kommen to be on the short list.
    seine Wahl treffen to make one's choice.
    vor die Wahl stellen to let one choose.
wahlberechtigt entitled to vote.
WÄHLEN to choose, select, pick out, elect, dial.
Wähler *m.* elector, selector.
wählerisch particular, fastidious.
Wahlkampf *m.* election, contest.
wahllos indiscriminately.
Wahlstimme *f.* vote.
Wahn *m.* delusion, illusion.
Wahnsinn *m.* insanity, madness, craziness.
wahnsinnig insane, mad.
WAHR true, sincere, genuine, real, proper, veritable.
    etwas nicht wahr haben wollen not to admit a thing.
    Nicht wahr? Isn't it? Don't you think so?
    so wahr ich lebe as sure as I live.
    wahr werden to come true.
WÄHREND 1. *prep. (gen.):* during, for, in the course of.
    Während des Winters verleben wir unsere Ferien in den Bergen. During the winter we spend our vacations in the mountains.
    2. *conj.* while.
    Sie kam während Sie weg waren. She came while you were out.
WAHRHEIT *f.* truth.
    Ich habe ihm gehörig die Wahrheit gesagt. I really gave him a piece of my mind.
wahrheitsgetreu truthful, true.
wahrheitslebend truthful.
wahrnehmbar perceptible, noticeable.
wahrsagen to tell fortunes, prophesy.
Wahrsagerin *f.* fortune teller.
WAHRSCHEINLICH probable, likely.
Wahrscheinlichkeit *f.* probability.
Währung *f.* standard, currency.
Waise *f. & m.* orphan.
Waisenhaus *m.* orphanage.
Wal *m.* whale.
WALD *m.* forest, woodland.

waldig woody.

Waldung *f.* woodland, wood.

Wall *m.* rampart, dike.

Walnuss *f.* walnut.

Walze *f.* roller, barrel.

walzen to walz.

Walzer *m.* waltz.

WAND *f.* wall, partition.

Wandel *m.* change, alteration.

    Handel und Wandel trade, commerce.

wandelbar perishable; changeable, fickle.

wandern to wander.

Wanderschaft *f.* trip, tour, travels.

Wanderung *f.* excursion, trip, hike, migration.

Wandgemälde *n.* mural painting, fresco.

Wandschrank *m.* cupboard.

Wankelmut *m.* inconsistency, fickleness.

WANN when.

    wann immer whenever.

    dann und wann now and then.

Wanne *f.* tub, bath.

Wannenbad *n.* tub bath.

WARE *f.* article, goods, merchandise.

Warenhaus *n.* department store.

Warenprobe *f.* sample.

WARM warm.

    Ist es Ihnen warm genug? Are you warm enough?

    warm stellen to keep hot.

Wärme *f.* heat, warmth.

WÄRMEN to warm, heat.

Wärmflasche *f.* hot-water bottle.

warnen to warn, caution.

Warnung *f.* warning.

Warnungssignal *n.* danger signal.

WARTEN to wait, attend to, nurse.

    warten auf to wait for.

    warten lassen to keep waiting.

Wärter *m.* attendant.

Wartesaal *m.* waiting-room.

Wartezimmer *n.* doctor's waiting room.

WARUM why, for what reason.

WAS what, whatever, that which, which, that.

    Ach was! Nonsense!

    Nein so was! Well, I never!

    was ... auch immer no matter what, whatever.

    was für ein what sort of, what a.

Waschbecken *n.* wash basin.

WÄSCHE *f.* wash; linen, underclothing.

    in die Wäsche geben to send to the laundry.

    grosse Wäsche haben to have washing day.

    schmutzige Wäsche soiled linen, dirty clothes.

waschecht fast color.

Wäschegeschäft *n.* haberdashery, lingerie store.

Wäscheklammer *f.* clothespin.

Wäscheleine *f.* clothesline.

waschen to wash.

Wäscherei *f.* laundry.

WASSER *n.* water.

fliessendes Wasser running water.

ins Wasser fallen to end in smoke.

mit allen Wassern gewaschen sein to be cunning.

sich über Wasser halten to keep one's head above water.

zu Wasser und zu Lande by land and sea.

Wasserball *m.* water polo.

Wasserbehälter *m.* reservoir, tank.

wasserdicht waterproof.

Wasserfall *m.* waterfall.

Wasserfarbe *f.* water-color.

Wasserflugzeug *n.* sea plane.

Wasserglas *n.* glass, tumbler.

wasserhältig containing water.

wässerig watery.

    einem den Mund wässerig machen to make a person's mouth water.

Wasserkanne *f.* watering-can.

Wasserleitung *f.* water supply, water pipes, faucet, sink.

Wasserspiegel *m.* water-surface.

Wasserstiefel *pl.* rubber boots.

Wasserstrahl *m.* jet of water.

Watte *f.* wadding, cotton-wool.

weben to weave.

Weber *m.* weaver.

Wechsel *m.* change, alteration, succession, turn.

    gezogener Wechsel draft.

Wechselgeld *n.* change (money).

    Bitte, zählen Sie ihr Wechselgeld nach. Please count your change.

Wechselkurs *m.* rate of exchange.

WECHSELN to change, exchange, alternate, shift.

    seinen Wohnort wechseln to move away.

    den Besitzer wechseln to change ownership.

wechselseitig reciprocal, mutual, alternate.

WECKEN to wake, awaken.

Wecker *m.* alarm-clock.

weder neither.

    weder...noch neither...nor.

WEG *m.* way, path, road, street, walk.

    am Weg by the roadside.

    auf gütlichem Weg in a friendly way.

    auf halbem Weg halfway.

    aus dem Weg gehen to make way for, stand aside.

    in die Wege leiten to prepare for.

    seiner Wege gehen to go one's way.

    sich auf den Weg machen to set out.

WEG 1. *adv.* away, off, gone, lost, disappeared.

    Hände weg! Hands off!

    Ich muss weg. I must go.

    2. *separable prefix (implies a motion away from the speaker).*

    Er warf das alte Buch weg. He threw the old book away.

    Geh weg! Go away!

wegbleiben to stay away, be omitted.

wegbringen to take away, remove.

WEGEN *prep. (gen.):* because of, for the sake of, owing to.
    Wegen des Krieges konnte ich nicht von Europa zurückkommen. Because of the war, I could not come back from Europe.

wegfahren to drive off, away.

weggehen to go away, depart, leave.

weglegen to put away.

wegnehmen to take away, carry off, confiscate, occupy.

Wegweiser *m.* signpost.

wegwerfen to throw away.

wegwerfend disparaging, contemptuous.

WEH sore, aching, painful.
    weh tun to ache, to hurt.

wehleidig plaintive.

Wehmut *f.* sadness, melancholy.

wehmütig sad, melancholy.

Wehrdienst *m.* military service.

wehren to hinder, forbid, arrest, defend.
    sich seiner Haut wehren to defend one's life.

wehrfähig able-bodied.

wehrlos unarmed, defenseless, weak.

Wehrmacht *f.* armed forces.

Wehrpflicht *f.* conscription.

wehrpflichtig liable to military service.

Weib *n.* woman.

weibisch effeminate.

weiblich female, feminine, womanly.

Weiblichkeit *f.* womanhood, femininity.

WEICH soft, mold, mellow, tender, smooth.
    weiches Ei soft-boiled egg.

weichen to retreat, give in, yield; soften, soak.

weichherzig soft-hearted.

weichlich soft, flabby, weak.

weigern to refuse.

Weigerung *f.* refusal.

Weihe *f.* consecration, initiation, inauguration.

weihen to consecrate, dedicate, devote.

WEIHNACHTEN *pl.* Christmas.

weihnachtlich of Christmas.

Weihnachtsabend *m.* Christmas Eve.

Weihnachtsbaum *m.* Christmas tree.

Weihnachtslied *n.* Christmas carol.

WEIL because, since.

WEILE *f.* while, space of time.
    Damit hat es gute Weile. There is no hurry.
    Eile mit Weile. Haste makes waste.

WEIN *m.* wine, vine.

Weinberg *m.* vineyard.

WEINEN to weep, cry.

Weinessig *m.* wine vinegar.

Weinfass *n.* wine cask.

Weinkarte *f.* winelist.

Weinlese *f.* vintage.

Weinprobe *f.* wine-tasting.

Weinrebe *f.* vine.

Weinstock *m.* vine.

Weintraube *f.* grape, bunch of grapes.

WEISE *f.* manner, way, tune.
    auf diese Weise in this way.

    in der Weise, dass in such a way that, so that.

WEISEN to show, refer, direct, point out, point at.

Weisheit *f.* wisdom, prudence.

weismachen to make one believe, hoax.

WEISS white, blank, clean.
    Weisser Sonntag Sunday after Easter.

weissagen to predict, prophesy.

Weissager *m. (−in, f.)* prophet.

WEIT distant, far, vast, loose, wide, big.
    bei weitem by far, by much.
    bei weitem nicht by no means.
    es weit bringen to get on well, be successful.
    nicht weither sein not to be worth much.
    von weitem from a distance.
    weit gefehlt quite wrong.
    weit und breit far and wide.
    weit voraus way ahead.
    weit weg far away.
    wenn alles so weit ist when everything is ready.

weitab far away.

weitaus by far.

Weitblick *m.* foresight.

Weite *f.* width, size, extent, distance, length.

WEITER further, farther, more, else, additional.
    bis auf weiteres until further notice.
    des weiteren furthermore.
    nichts weiter nothing more.
    niemand weiter no one else.
    Nur weiter! Go on!
    ohne weiteres immediately.
    und so weiter and so on.
    was weiter what else.
    wenn's weiter nichts ist if that's all there is to it.

Weitere *n.* rest, remaining part.

weiterführen to continue, carry on.

weitergeben to pass on to.

Weiterreise *f.* continuation of a trip.

weitgehend far-reaching, full, much.

weither from afar.

weitläufig distant, wide, extensive, roomy.

weitschweifig detailed, tedious.

weitsichtig far-sighted.

Weizen *m.* wheat, corn.

WELCH (ein) what (a)
    Welch ein Zufall! What a coincidence!

WELCH(-ER, -E, -ES) 1. *inter. pron. & adj.* what, who, whom, which.
    2. *rel. pron.* what, which, that, who, whom.

Welle *f.* wave, surge.
    Wellen schlagen to rise in waves.

Wellenlinie *f.* wavy line.

Wellenreiter *m.* surf-rider.

WELT *f.* world, universe, people.
    alle Welt everybody, everyone in the world.
    auf der Welt on earth.
    auf die Welt kommen to come into the world, be born.
    aus der Welt schaffen to put out of the way.

in der ganzen Welt on earth.
in die Welt setzen (zur Welt bringen) to give
birth to.
Weltall *n.* universe.
Weltanschauung *f.* world outlook.
weltbekannt world-famous.
weltfremd secluded, solitary.
Weltmann *m.* man of the world.
Weltmeister *m.* world champion.
Weltraum *m.* space, universe.
Weltuntergang *m.* end of the world.
WEM *dat. of wer.* to whom.
WEN *acc. of wer.* whom.
Wende *f.* turn, turning point.
wenden to turn, turn around.
Bitte wenden! Please turn over!
Wendepunkt *m.* turning point.
WENIG little, few, a few.
ein wenig a little, a bit.
WENIGER less, fewer, minus.
immer weniger less and less.
nichts weniger als anything but.
vier weniger eins four minus one.
wenigst (er,-e,-es) least.
wenigstens at least.
WENN if, in case of, when.
auch wenn even if.
immer wenn whenever.
Rufen Sie mich an wenn Sie kommen wollen.
Call me when you want to come.
selbst wenn even if, supposing that.
wenn auch (wenn gleich, wenn schon) although.
Wenn das nur wahr wäre! If it were only true!
wenn nur provided that.
Wenn schon! What of it!
wenn Sie kommen könnten If you could come.
WER *inter. pron.* who, what.
wer anders who else.
wer auch immer whoever.
Wer da? Who is it?
werben to recruit; to court, propose (marriage).
WERDEN 1. to become, turn out, prove, happen.
Was soll aus ihr werden? What's to become
of her?
2. *aux. verb to form future and passive.*
shall, will, is, are.
werfen to throw, cast, toss.
WERK *n.* work, labor, production, performance, deed.
ans Werk! Go to it!
ins Werk setzen to set going.
zu Werk gehen to begin.
Werkstatt *f.* workshop.
Werktag *m.* working day.
werktags on weekdays.
werktätig active
die werktätige Bevölkerung working classes.
Werkzeug *m.* utensil.
WERT worth, valuable, worthy, honored, esteemed.
im Werte von at a price of.
nichts wert sein to be no good.
Wertangabe *f.* declaration of value.

Wertgegenstände *pl.* valuables.
wertlos worthless.
Wertpapier *n.* security, bond.
Wertsachen *pl.* valuables.
wertvoll valuable, precious.
Wesen *n.* creature, soul, personality.
wesentlich essential, substantial.
WESSEN *gen. of wer.* whose? whose.
Weste *f.* waistcoat, vest.
Westen *m.* the West, Occident.
nach Westen west (direction).
westlich western, occidental.
westwärts westwards.
Wette *f.* bet, wager.
eine Wette eingehen to make a bet.
um die Wette laufen to race someone.
wetteifern to emulate; to vie.
wetten to bet, wager.
WETTER *n.* weather.
Alle Wetter! My word!
Heute ist das Wetter wunderschön!
The weather is wonderful today!
Wetterbericht *m.* meteorological report.
Wetterlage *f.* weather conditions.
Wettkampf *m.* match, contest, prize fighting.
Wettstreit *m.* competition, match.
WICHTIG important.
sich wichtig machen to act important.
WIDER 1. *prep. (acc.).* against, contrary to, versus.
Wider meinen Willen against my will.
2. *inseparable prefix.* (con-,re-, anti-, contra-)
widerhallen to echo, resound.
widerlegen to refute.
Widerlegung *f.* refutation.
widerlich repulsive, disgusting.
Widerrede *f.* contradiction.
widerrufen to revoke, withdraw, retract, cancel.
Widersacher *m.* adversary.
widersetzen (sich) to oppose, resist.
widerspiegeln to reflect, mirror.
Widerstand *m.* resistance, opposition.
Widerwille *m.* repugnance, disgust.
widerwillig reluctant, unwilling.
widmen to dedicate.
Widmung *f.* dedication.
WIE how, as, such, like.
so ... wie as ... as.
wie auch immer however.
Wie bitte? What did you say?
wie dem auch sei be that as it may.
Wie geht es Ihnen? How are you?
wie gesagt as has been said.
WIEDER 1. *adv.* again, anew, back, in return for.
hin und wieder now and then.
immer wieder again and again.
2. *prefix.*
a) *inseparable.* In verb wiederholen (to repeat).
b) *separable (implies the idea of repetition or
opposition).*
wiederbekommen to get back, recover.
wiederbeleben to revive, reanimate.

Wiederbelebungsversuch *m.* attempt at resuscitation.
wiederfinden to find, recover.
wiedererkennen to recognize.
wiedererlangen to get back.
wiedererobern to reconquer.
Wiedergabe *f.* return; reproduction, recital (work of art).
wiedergeben to give back, return.
Wiedergutmachung *f.* reparation.
WIEDERHOLEN to repeat, renew, reiterate, fetch, bring back.
Wiederholung *f.* repetition, reiteration.
    im Wiederholungsfalle if it should happen again.
wiederhören to hear again.
    auf Wiederhören! Good-bye! (radio, tel.).
WIEDERSEHEN to see again, meet again.
    auf Wiedersehen! Good-bye! So long!
Wiege *f.* cradle.
wiegen to rock, move to, shake, sway.
Wiese *f.* meadow.
wieso why.
WIEVIEL how much.
    Der wievielte ist heute? What date is today?
wieviele how many.
WILD wild, rough, angry, furious, savage, untidy.
Wild *n.* game (hunting).
Wildbraten *m.* venison.
Wilddieb *m.* poacher.
Wildente *f.* wild duck.
Wildleder *n.* deerskin, suede.
Wildnis *f.* wilderness, desert.
WILLE *m.* will, way, determination, purpose.
    aus freiem Willen voluntarily.
    guter Wille kind intention.
    letzter Wille last will.
willenlos lacking will power, irresolute.
Willenlosigkeit *f.* lack of will power.
Willenskraft *f.* will power.
willfahren to gratify, grant, please.
Willkommen *n.* welcome, reception.
Willkür *f.* discretion, arbitrariness.
willkürlich arbitrary, despotic.
WIND *m.* wind, breeze.
    bei Wind und Wetter in storm and rain.
    guter Wind fair wind.
    in den Wind reden to talk in vain.
    in den Wind schlagen to disregard.
    vor dem Wind segeln to run before the rain.
Windel *f.* baby's diaper.
Windelkind *n.* infant.
windeln to swaddle.
winden to wind.
windig windy, breezy.
Windstille *f.* calm.
Wink *m.* sign, nod, wink.
Winkel *m.* corner, angle, secret spot.
winken to wave, nod, wink.
WINTER *m.* winter.
    im Winter in winter.
Winterfrische *f.* winter resort.
Winterschlaf *m.* hibernation.
Wintersport *m.* winter sports.

winzig tiny, diminutive.
Winzigkeit *f.* tininess.
Wirbel *m.* whirlpool, eddy.
Wirbelknochen *m.* vertebra.
wirbeln to whirl.
Wirbelsäule *f.* spine.
Wirbelsturm *m.* tornado, hurricane.
wirken to act, do, work, produce.
WIRKLICH real, actual, true, genuine.
Wirklichkeit *f.* reality, actuality.
wirksam active, effective.
Wirkung *f.* action, working, operation.
wirkungslos ineffectual, inefficient.
wirkungsvoll effective, striking.
Wirt *m.* host, proprietor, landlord.
wirtlich hospitable.
Wirtschaft *f.* housekeeping, economy, tavern, public house.
    die Wirtschaft führen to keep house.
wirtschaften to manage.
Wirtschaftsgeld *n.* housekeeping money.
Wirtschaftslage *f.* economic situation.
Wirtschaftsprüfer *m.* general adviser, accountant.
Wirtshaus *n.* inn, public house.
WISSEN *n.* knowledge, learning.
    meines Wissens as far as I know.
    nach bestem Wissen und Gewissen most conscientiously.
    wider besseres Wissen against one's better judgment.
WISSEN to know, be aware of, understand, be acquainted with.
    Ich weiss nicht. I don't know.
    nicht dass ich wüsste not that I am aware of.
Wissenschaft *f.* science, knowledge.
Wissenschaftler *m.* scientist, scholar.
wissenwert worth knowing, interesting.
Witwe *f.* widow.
Witwer *m.* widower.
Witz *m.* wittiness, witticism, wit, joke, pun.
witzig witty.
WO where, in which; when.
    wo auch immer wherever.
woanders elsewhere.
wobei whereat, whereby, in which, upon which.
WOCHE *f.* week.
    diese Woche this week.
    heute in einer Woche a week from today.
Wochenende *n.* weekend.
wochenlang for weeks.
wochentags on weekdays.
Wochenschau newsreel; weekly publication.
wöchentlich weekly.
wodurch by which, whereby, how.
wofür for which, for what.
WOHER from where, from what place?
    Woher wissen Sie das? How do you know that?
WOHIN to where, to what place?
WOHL *n.* welfare, prosperity, good health.
    sich wohl fühlen to feel well.
WOHL well, all right, probably, presumably, very

likely, indeed.
Ich verstehe wohl. I can well understand.
Leben Sie wohl! Good-bye!
wohl oder übel willy nilly.
Zum Wohl! To you! (a toast)
Wohlbehagen *n.* comfort, ease.
wohlbekannt well-known, familiar.
Wohlfahrt *f.* welfare.
Wohlgeruch *m.* fragrance, sweet, perfume.
wohlhabend wealthy, well-off.
Wohlklang *m.* harmony, melody.
wohlschmeckend tasty, palatable.
Wohlstand *m.* well-being, wealth, fortune.
wohltuend comforting, pleasant.
wohlverdient well-deserved, merited.
WOHNEN to live, dwell, reside, stay.
zur Miete wohnen to live as a tenant,
rent-payer.
wohnhaft living, dwelling.
wohnlich comfortable, cozy.
WOHNUNG *f.* house, dwelling, residence, flat.
Wohnviertel *n.* residential district.
Wohnzimmer *n.* sitting-room.
Wolf *m.* wolf.
Wolke *f.* cloud.
aus allen Wolken fallen to be thunderstruck.
Wolkenbruch *m.* cloudburst.
Wolkenkratzer *m.* skyscraper.
WOLLE *f.* wool.
WOLLEN to want, wish, will, desire, like, mean.
Das will etwas heissen. That means something.
Das will was heissen. That's really something.
Er mag wollen oder nicht. Whether he likes it
or not.
Wie Sie wollen. As you like.
WOMIT with what, by which, with which.
Womit kann ich dienen? What can I do for you?
womöglich if possible.
WORAN whereon, by what.
woran liegt es? how is it that?
WORAUF on what, upon which.
WORAUS of what, out of which.
WORIN in which, in what.
WORT *n.* word, expression, saying, promise.
aufs Wort gehorchen to obey implicitly.
das grosse Wort führen to brag.
das Wort ergreifen to begin to speak.
das Wort führen to be spokesman.
einen beim Wort nehmen to take one at
one's word.
Er hat sein Wort gebrochen. He broke
his promise.
Ich habe kein Wort davon gewusst.
I did not know a thing about it.
ins Wort fallen to interrupt, cut short.
mit anderen Worten in other words.
Sie macht viele Worte. She talks too much.
ums Wort bitten to ask for the floor.
zu Wort kommen lassen to let one speak.
Wörterbuch *n.* dictionary.
Wortschatz *m.* vocabulary.

wortwörtlich word for word.
WORÜBER of what, about which, whereof.
WORUNTER among what, which.
WOVON about what, which.
WOVOR of what, for what, before what, which.
WOZU before what, of what, for what, which.
wund sore, wounded.
Wunde *f.* wound.
Wunder *n.* wonder, miracle.
sein blaues Wunder erleben to be amazed.
WUNDERBAR wonderful, marvelous.
Wunderbar! Wonderful! Splendid!
wunderbarerweise strange to say.
Wunderkind *n.* child prodigy.
wunderlich strange, odd.
WUNDERN to astonish, surprise.
sich wundern to be surprised, wonder.
wunderschön beautiful, lovely, exquisite.
WUNSCH *m.* wish, desire, request.
auf Wunsch by request, if desired.
Haben Sie noch eine Wunsch?
Is there anything else you'd like?
nach Wunsch as one desires.
WÜNSCHEN to wish, desire, long for.
Glück wünschen to congratulate (wish luck).
Was wünschen Sie? May I help you?
Würde *f.* dignity, honor, title, rank.
in Amt und Würden holding a high office.
würdelos undignified.
würdevoll dignified.
würdig worthy, deserving of, respectable.
würdigen to value, appreciate.
nicht eines Wortes würdigen not to say a word.
Würfel *m.* die, cube.
Der Würfel ist gefallen. The die is cast.
würfeln to play dice.
Würfelspiel *n.* dice game.
Würfelzucker *m.* lump of sugar.
würgen to choke, strangle.
Wurm *m.* worm.
Wurst *f.* sausage.
Würze *f.* seasoning, spice, flavor.
Wurzel *f.* root.
würzen to season.
würzig spicy.
wüst waste, deserted, desolate, wild, dissolute.
Wüste *f.* desert.
Wüstling *m.* libertine, dissolute person.
WUT *f.* rage, fury.
in Wut geraten to fly into a rage.
wüten to rage, be furious.
wütend enraged, furious.

X

xmal ever so often, any number of times.

Y

Y the twenty-fifth letter of the alphabet.

Z

zagen to be afraid, hesitate.

zähe tough, tenacious, stubborn.
ZAHL *f.* figure, number, numeral.
zahlbar payable, due.
zahlen to pay.
ZÄHLEN to count, number, calculate.
   gezählt numbered.
Zahlkarte *f.* money-order form.
zahllos countless, innumerable.
zahlreich numerous.
Zahltag *m.* pay-day.
Zahlung *f.* payment.
zahlungsfähig solvent.
zahm tame, domestic.
zähmen to tame, break in.
ZAHN *m.* tooth.
   ein schlechter Zahn a bad tooth.
   die Zähne putzen to brush the teeth.
   einem auf den Zahn fühlen to sound a person.
   künstliche Zähne artificial teeth.
Zahnarzt *m.* dentist.
Zahnbürste *f.* toothbrush.
Zahnfleisch *n.* gum.
Zahnfüllung *f.* filling.
zahnlos toothless.
Zahnpasta *f.* toothpaste.
Zahnschmerzen *pl.* toothache.
Zahnstein *m.* tartar.
Zahnstocher *m.* toothpick.
Zahnweh *n.* toothache.
Zange *f.* pincers.
Zank *m.* quarrel.
zanken to quarrel.
zänkisch quarrelsome.
zanksüchtig quarrelsome.
ZART tender, soft, delicate, fragile, frail.
zartfühlend tactful, sensitive.
Zartgefühl *n.* delicacy of feeling.
Zartheit *f.* tenderness, delicacy.
Zauber *m.* magic, charm, spell.
Zauberei *f.* magic, witchcraft.
Zauberflöte *f.* magic flute.
zauberhaft magical, enchanting.
zaubern to practice magic, conjure.
zaudern to hesitate, delay.
Zaun *m.* hedge, fence.
   Streit von Zaune brechen to pick a quarrel.
Zebra *n.* zebra.
Zehe *f.* toe.
Zehenspitze *f.* point of the toe.
   auf Zehenspitzen gehen to tiptoe.
ZEHN ten.
zehnfach tenfold.
ZEHNTE tenth.
Zeichen *n.* sign, signal, token, brand.
   zum Zeichen dass as a proof that.
Zeichensetzung *f.* punctuation.
Zeichensprache *f.* sign language.
ZEICHNEN to draw, design, mark.
ZEICHNUNG *f.* drawing, sketch, design.
Zeigefinger *m.* forefinger, index.
ZEIGEN to show, point at, point out, exhibit,
   display.

Zeiger *m.* hand of the clock, pointer.
ZEIT *f.* time, duration, period, epoch, season.
   Damit hat es Zeit. There is no hurry.
   die freie Zeit leisure, spare time.
   Es ist an der Zeit. It is high time.
   höchste Zeit high time.
   in der letzten Zeit lately.
   in jüngster Zeit quite recently.
   Lassen Sie sich Zeit! Take your time!
   mit der Zeit gradually.
   Zeit seines Lebens during life.
   zu gleicher Zeit at the same time.
   zur rechten Zeit in the nick of time.
   zur Zeit at present.
   Zeit ist Geld. Time is money.
Zeitalter *n.* age, generation.
zeitgemäss timely, seasonable.
Zeitgenosse *m.* contemporary.
zeitgenössisch contemporary.
ZEITIG early, timely, mature, ripe.
zeitlebens for life.
Zeitpunkt *m.* time, moment.
Zeitschrift *f.* journal, periodical, magazine.
ZEITUNG *f.* newspaper, paper.
Zeitungsausschnitt *m.* press cutting.
Zeitungskiosk *m.* newsstand.
Zeitungsnotiz *f.* notice, item, paragraph.
Zeitungsstand *m.* newsstand.
Zeitungsverkäufer *m.* news vendor.
Zeitvertreib *m.* pastime, amusement.
Zeitwort *n.* verb.
Zelle *f.* cell, booth.
Zelt *n.* tent, canopy.
Zement *m.* cement.
Zentimeter *m. & n.* centimeter (.3937 inch).
Zentrale *f.* central office, station, telephone
   exchange.
Zentralheizung *f.* central heating.
ZENTRUM *n.* center.
zerbrechen to break, smash.
   sich den Kopf zerbrechen to rack one's
   brains.
zerbrechlich fragile.
Zerbrechlichkeit *f.* fragility, brittleness.
Zeremonie *f.* ceremony.
zerreissbar tearable.
zerreissen to tear, lacerate.
zerren to drag, pull.
zerschmettern to crush, destroy.
zerstören to destroy, demolish, devastate, ruin.
Zerstörer *m.* destroyer, devastator.
Zerstörung *f.* devastation, demolition, destruction.
zerstreuen to disperse, scatter, dissipate, divert.
zerstreut absent-minded.
Zerstreuung *f.* dispersion, distraction, amusement.
Zerwürfnis *n.* disagreement, quarrel.
Zettel *m.* slip, note, label, ticket, poster, bill.
Zeug *n.* stuff, material, cloth, fabric, utensils,
   things.
   sich ins Zeug legen to set to work.
Zeuge *m.* witness.
zeugen to testify, bear witness, give evidence.

Zeugenaussage *f.* evidence, deposition.
Zeugenvernehmung *f.* hearing of witnesses.
Ziege *f.* goat.
Ziegel *m.* brick, tile.
Ziegelstein *m.* brick.
ZIEHEN to pull, draw, haul, tug, tow, extract, move, migrate, weigh.
   den Kürzeren ziehen to get the worst of it.
   nach sich ziehen to have consequences.
   Er zieht den Hut. He tips his hat.
   zur Rechenschaft ziehen to call to account.
Ziehung *f.* drawing of lottery.
Ziel *n.* goal.
   sich ein Ziel setzen to aim at.
zielbewusst systematic, methodical.
zielen to aim.
ziellos aimless.
Zielscheibe *f.* target.
   Zielscheibe des Spottes sein to be a laughing stock.
ziemen to become, be suitable.
ZIEMLICH rather, pretty, fairly, quite, considerable.
   so ziemlich about, pretty much.
   ziemlich viele quite a few.
Zierde *f.* ornament, decoration.
zieren to decorate, adorn, embellish.
zierlich elegant, graceful, delicate.
Ziffer *f.* figure, cipher.
Zifferblatt *n.* dial, face.
ZIGARETTE *f.* cigarette.
Zigarettenetui *n.* cigarette-case.
Zigarettenspitze *f.* cigarette-holder.
Zigarre *f.* cigar.
Zigarrenkiste *f.* cigar-box.
Zigeuner *m.* gypsy.
ZIMMER *n.* room, apartment, chamber.
Zimmerdecke *f.* ceiling.
Zimmermädchen *n.* chambermaid.
Zimmermann *m.* carpenter.
zimperlich supersensitive, prudish, affected.
Zimt *m.* cinnamon.
Zinn *n.* tin, pewter.
Zins *m.* tax, duty, rent; interest.
   auf Zinsen ausleihen to lend money at interest.
   mit Zins und Zinseszins in full measure.
Zinseszins *m.* compound interest.
Zinsfuss *m.* rate of interest.
Zirkel *m.* circle, compasses.
Zirkus *m.* circus.
Zitat *n.* quotation.
Zitrone *f.* lemon.
Zitronenlimonade *f.* lemonade.
Zitronenpresse *f.* lemon-press.
Zitronensaft *m.* lemon juice.
zittern to tremble, shake, quiver, shiver.
zivil civil, reasonable, moderate.
   in Zivil in plain clothes.
Zivilbevölkerung *f.* civilian population.
Zivilisation *f.* civilization.
zivilisieren to civilize.

Zivilist *m.* civilian.
zögern to hesitate, delay, linger.
ZOLL *m.* duty, toll, tariff, customs.
Zoll *m.* inch.
Zollabfertigung *f.* customs inspection.
ZOLLAMT *n.* customhouse.
Zollbeamte *m.* customhouse officer.
zollfrei free of duty.
Zollgebühr *f.* duty.
Zöllner *m.* customs collector.
zollpflichtig subject to customs.
Zollschranke *f.* customs barrier.
Zollstock *m.* yardstick.
Zollverschluss *m.* customs seal.
Zone *f.* zone.
Zopf *m.* braid, pigtail.
Zorn *m.* anger, rage, wrath.
zornig angry.
ZU 1. *prep. (dat.).* to, at, by, near, beside, for, with, in front of, on.
   Die Deutschen essen immer Kartoffeln zum Fleisch. Germans always eat potatoes with meat.
   Er war nicht zu Hause. He was not at home.
   Ich gehe zu meiner Tante. I am going to my aunt's.
   Setzen Sie sich zu mir. Sit down by me.
   Wenn es friert, wird das Wasser zu Eis. When it freezes, water turns to ice.
   Wir essen Eier zum Frühstück. We eat eggs for breakfast.
   zu Fuss, zu Pferd on foot, on horseback.
   zu meinem Erstaunen to my surprise.
   zum König gekrönt werden to become a king.
   zum Teil partly.
   zum "Weisses Rössl" at the "White Horse" (inn).
   2. *adv.* too (more than enough), toward.
   zu viel to much.
   3. *before infinitive* to.
   Sie wussten nicht was zu tun. They did not know what to do.
   4. *Separable prefix (implies direction toward the speaker, increase, continuation, closing, confession).*
   Sie liefen dem Walde zu. They ran toward the forest.
   Der Verbrecher gab es zu. The criminal confessed.
   Ich darf nicht mehr zunehmen. I must not gain more weight.
   Mach die Tür zu! Close the door!
   Nur zu! Come on!
Zubehör *m. & n.* accessories, trimmings, belongings.
zubereiten to prepare, cook, mix.
Zubereitung *f.* preparation.
Zucht *f.* breeding, training, education; breed, race, stock.
züchten to breed, grow, cultivate, train.
züchtig chaste, modest.
züchtigen to punish, correct, chastise.

zucken to flash.
    mit den Achseln zucken to shrug one's shoulders.
ZUCKER *m.* sugar.
Zuckerguss *m.* icing.
zuckerhältig containing sugar.
zuckerkrank diabetic.
zuckern to sugar, sweeten.
Zuckerwerk *n.* confectionery, sweets.
zudem besides, moreover.
zudrücken to shut, close.
    ein Auge zudrücken to be indulgent.
zuerst at first, in the first place.
Zufahrt *f.* Drive.
Zufall *m.* chance, accident, occurrence.
    durch Zufall by accident.
zufällig casual, by accident, by chance.
    zufällig tun to happen to do.
zufälligerweise by chance.
Zuflucht *f.* refuge, shelter.
    seine Zuflucht nehmen zu to take refuge with.
ZUFRIEDEN satisfied, content.
    sich zufrieden geben to rest content with.
    zufrieden lassen to let alone, leave in peace.
Zufriedenheit *f.* contentment, satisfaction.
zufriedenstellen to content, satisfy.
zufriedenstellend satisfactory.
ZUG *m.* train; drawing, draft; procession, march, impulse; feature, characteristic.
    Er liegt in den letzten Zügen. He is breathing his last.
    Zug um Zug without delay, uninterruptedly.
    Wann kommt der Schnellzug aus Berlin an? When does the express train from Berlin arrive?
Zugabe *f.* extra, addition, encore.
Zugang *m.* entrance, door, access.
zugänglich accessible, open to.
zugeben to add, allow, permit.
Zügel *m.* bridle, rein.
zügellos unbridled, unrestrained.
Zugeständnis *n.* concession, admission.
Zugluft *f.* draught, current of air.
zugunsten in favor of, for the benefit of.
zugute (halten) to allow for, take into consideration, give credit for.
    zugute kommen to come in handy, be an advantage to.
Zuhilfenahme *f.* (unter Zuhilfenahme von) with the help of.
zuhören to listen to.
Zuhörer *m.* hearer, listener.
Zuhörerschaft *f.* audience.
ZUKUNFT *f.* future.
zukünftig future.
zulächeln to smile at.
Zulage *f.* addition, raise.
zulangen to hand, give.
zulässig admissible, permissible.
Zulassung *f.* admission, permission.
ZULETZT finally, ultimately.
    zuletzt kommen to arrive last.
zuliebe (tun) to do for someone's sake.

einem zuliebe tun to please someone.
zumachen to close, shut, fasten; to hurry.
zumal especially, particularly.
zumindest at least.
zumuten to expect of.
    sich zu viel zumuten to attempt too much.
Zumutung *f.* unreasonable demand, imputation.
zunächst first, first of all, above all.
zünden to catch fire, inflame, arouse enthusiasm.
zunehmen to grow, increase, get fuller.
zuneigen to lean forward, incline.
Zuneigung *f.* liking, affection, sympathy, inclination.
ZUNGE *f.* tongue.
    Das Wort liegt mir auf der Zunge. I have the word on the tip of my tongue.
    eine belegte Zunge a fuzzy tongue.
    eine feine Zunge haben to be a gourmet.
zurechnungsfähig responsible, of sound mind.
Zurechnungsfähigkeit *f.* responsibility.
zurecht right, in order, in time.
zurechtfinden to find one's way about.
zurechtsetzen (einem den Kopf zurechtsetzen) to bring one to reason.
Zurechtweisung *f.* reprimand, reproach.
ZURÜCK 1. *adv.* back, backwards, late, behind. 2. *separable prefix* (implies the idea of a return motion; back).
    Wir kamen erst um elf Uhr zurück. We only came back at eleven.
zurückbeben to start back, recoil.
zurückbehalten to keep back, retain.
zurückbekommen to get back, recover.
zurückbleiben to stay behind.
zurückbringen to bring back.
zurückfahren to drive back, return.
zurückfordern to reclaim.
zurückgehen to go back, return, retreat, decrease, decline.
zurückgezogen retired, secluded, lonely.
Zurückgezogenheit *f.* retirement.
zurückhalten to hold back, delay, detain.
zurückhaltend reserved.
zurückkehren to return, go back, come back.
zurücklassen to leave behind.
zurücknehmen to take back, withdraw.
zurücksetzen to put back, replace, reduce, neglect.
Zurücksetzung *f.* neglect.
zurückstellen to put back, replace, reserve, put aside.
zurücktreten to step back, withdraw, resign.
zurückversetzen to put back, restore.
    sich in eine Zeit zurückversetzen to go back (in imagination) to a time.
zurückweisen to send away, send back, repulse.
zurückzahlen to pay back, repay.
Zurückzahlung *f.* repayment.
zurückziehen to draw back, take back.
Zuruf *m.* acclamation, shout, call.
zurufen to call to, shout to.
Zusage *f.* acceptance, promise.
ZUSAGEN to promise, please, appeal.

einem etwas auf den Kopf zusagen to tell a person plainly.

ZUSAMMEN together, altogether.

zusammenfassen to sum up, summarize.

zusammenfassend comprehensive.

zusammengehören to belong together, match, be correlated.

Zusammenhalt *m.* holding together.

Zusammenhang *m.* connection.

zusammenhangslos disconnected.

Zusammenkunft *f.* meeting, reunion, assembly.

Zusammenspiel *n.* playing together, teamwork.

Zusammenstoss *m.* collision, clash.

zusammenstossen to smash, collide.

zusammentreffen to meet each other, coincide.

zusammenzählen to count up, add up.

zusätzlich additional.

ZUSCHAUER *m.* spectator.

Zuschauerraum *m.* theater auditorium.

Zuschlag *m.* addition, increase in price.

zuschlagpflichtig liable to additional payment.

zuschliessen to lock, lock up.

Zuschrift *f.* letter, communication.

zuschulden *adv.*

sich etwas zuschulden kommen lassen to be guilty of doing something.

zusehen to look on, watch for, wait.

zusehends visibly, noticeably.

zusichern to assure of, promise.

Zusicherung *f.* insurance.

zuspitzen to point, sharpen.

zusprechen to encourage.

Trost zusprechen to comfort, console.

Zuspruch *m.* consolation, encouragement.

ZUSTAND *m.* state, condition, position, situation.

zustande bringen to do, get done.

zuständig belonging to, responsible, authorized, competent.

Zuständigkeit *f.* competence.

zustimmen to consent, agree.

Zustimmung *f.* consent.

Zustrom *m.* influx, crowd, multitude.

zutrauen to believe (one) capable of.

zutraulich confiding, trusting.

zutreffend correct.

ZUTRITT *m.* admission, entrance.

Zutritt verboten! No admittance!

zuverlässig reliable, trustworthy.

Zuversicht *f.* confidence, trust.

zuversichtlich confident.

ZUVIEL too much.

zuvor before, previously, formerly.

zuvorkommen to come first.

zuvorkommend obliging.

Zuvorkommenheit *f.* politeness, kindness.

ZUWEILEN sometimes, now and then, occasionally.

zuwider offensive, repugnant.

zuwider (sein) to be repugnant.

Das ist mir zuwider. I hate it.

zuzahlen to pay extra.

zuziehen to draw together, call, invite, consult.

zuzüglich including, plus.

Zwang *m.* compulsion, constraint, pressure.

sich Zwang antun to restrain oneself.

sich keinen Zwang antun to be quite free and easy.

zwanglos free and easy.

Zwanglosigkeit *f.* freedom, ease.

Zwangslage *f.* condition of constraint.

sich in einer Zwangslage befinden to be under compulsion.

zwangsläufig necessarily, inevitably.

ZWANZIG twenty.

Zwanziger *m.* figure 20, a 20-year old.

in den Zwanzigern sein to be in one's twenties.

ZWANZIGSTE twentieth.

ZWAR indeed, although.

und zwar in fact, namely.

ZWECK *m.* purpose, design, aim, object, end, goal.

keinen Zweck haben to be of no use.

Zu welchem Zweck? Why? What for?

zwecklos useless.

Zwecklosigkeit *f.* uselessness, aimlessness.

zweckmässig expedient.

ZWEI two.

zu zweien by pairs, two by two.

zweideutig ambiguous.

zweierlei of two kinds, different.

zweifach twofold, double.

ZWEIFEL *m.* doubt, suspicion.

zweifelhaft doubtful.

zweifellos doubtless, indubitable.

zweifeln to doubt, question, suspect.

Zweifelsfall *m.* im Zweifelsfall in case of a doubt.

zweifelsohne without doubt, doubtless.

Zweig *m.* branch.

Zweigstelle *f.* branch office.

Zweikampf *m.* duel.

zweimal twice.

zweireihig double-breasted.

zweischneidig two-edged, ambiguous.

Zweisitzer two-seater.

ZWEITE second, next.

zu zweit two by two.

zweitens secondly, in the second place.

Zwerg *m.* dwarf.

Zwieback *m.* rusk, biscuit.

Zwiebel *f.* onion, bulb (plant).

Zwielicht *n.* twilight, dusk.

Zwietracht *f.* discord.

Zwilling *m.* twin.

zwingen to compel, force, get through, finish.

zwingend forcible.

zwinkern to blink.

Zwirn *m.* thread, sewing-cotton.

ZWISCHEN *prep. (dat. when answering question, Wo?; acc. when answering question, Wohin?, and depending on the idiom).* among, between Zwischen den Städten Duisburg und Köln lieg Düsseldorf. Between the cities of Duisburg

and Cologne lies Düsseldorf.
zwischen drei und vier between three and four
Zwischenbemerkung *f.* digression.
Zwischendeck *n.* lower deck.
zwischendurch through, in the midst of.
Zwischenfall *m.* incident, episode.
Zwischenlandung *f.* intermediate landing or stop (flight).
Zwischenpause *f.* interval, break.
Zwischenraum *m.* space, gap, interval.

Zwischenzeit *f.* interval.
in der Zwischenzeit in the meantime.
zwitschern to twitter.
ZWÖLF twelve.
ZWÖLFTE twelfth.
Zyklus *m.* cycle, course, series.
Zylinder *m.* cylinder.
Zyniker *m.* cynic.
zynisch cynical.
Zynismus *m.* cynicism.

GLOSSARY OF PROPER NAMES.

Albrecht Albert.
Alfred Alfred.
Andreas Andrew.
Anne Ann.
Anton Anthony.
August August.
Barbara Barbara.
Bernhard Bernard.
Bertha Bertha.
Eduard Edward.
Elisabeth (Else) Elizabeth.
Emilie Emily.
Emma Emma.
Erich Eric.
Ernst Ernest.
Eugen Eugene.
Franz Frank.
Franziska Frances.
Friedrich Frederick.

Fritz Fred.
Genoveva. Genevieve.
Georg George.
Gertrud (Trudchen) Gertrude.
Gretchen Margaret.
Gustav Gustave.
Heinrich Henry.
Helene Helen.
Ilse Elsie.
Jakob James.
Johann John.
Johanna Jane, Joan.
Josef Joseph.
Karl Charles.
Katharina (Kätchen) (Käthe) Katherine (Kate).
Klaus Nicholas.
Lotte Charlotte.
Ludwig Lewis.
Luise Louise.

Maria Mary.
Martha Martha.
Michael Michael.
Minna Wilhelmina.
Moritz Maurice.
Otto Otto.
Paul Paul.
Paula Paula.
Peter Peter.
Richard Richard.
Robert Robert.
Rosa Rose.
Rüdiger Roger.
Rudolph Ralph.
Susanne Susan.
Theodor Theodore.
Therese Theresa.
Thomas Thomas.
Wilhelm William.

GLOSSARY OF GEOGRAPHICAL NAMES

Aachen *n.* Aix-la-Chapelle.

Afrika *n.* Africa.

Agypten *n.* Egypt.

Alpen *pl.* Alps.

Amerika *n.* America.

die Vereinigten Staaten *pl.* the United States.

Nord Amerika *n.* North America.

Süd Amerika *n.* South America.

Mittel-Amerika *n.* Central America

Antwerpen *n.* Antwerp.

Asien *n.* Asia.

Atlantik *m.* (der Atlantische Ozean) Atlantic (the Atlantic Ocean).

Australien *n.* Australia.

Belgien *n.* Belgium.

Berlin *n.* Berlin.

Bonn *n.* Bonn.

Brasilien *n.* Brazil.

Brüssel *n.* Brussels.

Dänemark *n.* Denmark.

Deutschland *n.* Germany.

Europa *n.* Europe.

Frankfurt *n.* Frankfort.

Frankreich *n.* France.

Griechenland *n.* Greece.

Haag (der) The Hague.

Hamburg *n.* Hamburg.

Holland *n.* Holland.

Indien *n.* India.

Irland *n.* Ireland.

Italien *n.* Italy.

Japan *n.* Japan.

Jugoslavien *n.* Yugoslavia.

Kanada *n.* Canada.

London *n.* London.

Mexico *n.* Mexico.

Moskau *n.* Moscow.

München *n.* Munich.

Norwegen *n.* Norway.

Nürnberg *n.* Nuremberg.

Österreich *n.* Austria.

Polen *n.* Poland.

Portugal *n.* Portugal.

Preussen *n.* Prussia.

Rhein *m.* Rhine.

Rheinland *n.* Rhineland.

Rumänien *n.* Rumania.

Russland *n.* Russia.

Saar *f.* Saar.

Sachsen *n.* Saxony.

Schlesien *n.* Silesia.

Schottland *n.* Scotland.

Schweden *n.* Sweden.

Schweiz *f.* Switzerland.

Stille Ozean (der) Pacific Ocean.

Tschechoslovakei *f.* Czechoslovakia.

Türkei *f.* Turkey

Ungarn *n.* Hungary.

Wien *n.* Vienna.

English-German

A

a (an) ein, eine.
abandon (to) verlassen.
abbreviate (to) abkürzen.
abbreviation abkürzung, f.
ability Fähigkeit, f.
able fähig.
able (to be) können.
abolish (to) abschaffen.
about ungefähr; um (acc.) (around).
above über.
abroad im Ausland.
absence Abwesenheit, f.
absent abwesend.
absolute unbedingt.
absorb (to) aufsaugen
abstain (to) sich enthalten.
abstract abstrakt.
absurd unvernünftig.
abundant reichlich.
abuse Missbrauch, m.
academy Akademie, f.
accent Akzent, m.
accent (to) betonen.
accept (to) annehmen.
acceptance Annahme, f.
accident Unfall, m.; Zufall, m. (chance).
accidental zufällig.
accidentally nebenbei.
accommodate (to) unterbringen.
accommodation Unterkunft, f.
accompany (to) begleiten.
accomplish (to) vollführen.
accord Übereinstimmung, f.
according to zu (dat.); zufolge dem.
account Rechnung, f.; Konto, n. (balance).
　　on no account auf keinen Fall.
　　to pay the account die Rechnung bezahlen.
accuracy Genauigkeit, f.
accurate genau, richtig, akkurat.
accuse (to) anklagen, beschuldigen.
accustom (to) gewöhnen.
ace Ass, n.
ache Schmerz, m.
ache (to) schmerzen.
achieve (to) vollbringen.
achievement Vollbringung, f.; Leistung (result).
acid sauer
acknowledge (to) anerkennen.
acknowledgment Anerkennung, f.
acquaintance Bekannte, m. & f.
acquire (to) erwerben.
across gegenüber.
act Handlung, f.; Akt, m. (of a play); Gesetz, n. (law).
active tätig.
activity Tätigkeit, f.
actor Schauspieler, m.
actress Schauspielerin, f.

actual wirklich.
acute akut.
adapt (to) anpassen.
add (to) zufügen.
addition Zusatz, m.; Addition, f. (math.).
　　in addition to Zusätlich zu (dat.).
address Adresse, f.; Anschrift, f.; Ansprache, f.;
　　Anrede, f. (speech).
address (to) adressieren; anreden, ansprechen,
　　sich wenden an (speech).
adequate angemessen.
adjective Eigenschaftswort, n.
adjoining angrenzend.
administer (to) verwalten.
admiral Admiral, m.
admiration Bewunderung, f.
admire (to) bewundern.
admission Eintritt, m.
admit (to) einlassen; zugeben (concede).
admittance Zutritt, m.
　　no admittance Zutritt verboten.
adopt (to) adoptieren (child); annehmen (idea).
adult Erwachsene(r) noun, m. & f.; erwachsen (adj.).
advance (to) vorangehen (lead); steigen (price).
　　in advance im Voraus.
advantage Vorteil, m.
adventure Abenteuer, n.
adverb Adverb, n.
advertise (to) anzeigen; Reklame machen.
advertisement Anzeige, f.; Reklame, f.
advice Rat, m.
advise (to) raten.
affair Geschäft, n. (business); Sache, f. (thing).
affect (to) betreffen.
affected geziert, affektiert (pretentious); gerührt
　　(moved).
affection Zuneigung, f.
affectionate herzlich, zärtlich, liebevoll.
affirm (to) bestätigen, bekräftigen.
affirmation Bestätigung, f.; Bekräftigung, f.
afloat schwimmend.
afraid ängstlich.
after nach (dat.).
afternoon Nachmittag, m.
afterward nachher.
again wieder.
against gegen (acc.); wider (acc.).
age Alter, n. (also old age); Epoche, f. (history).
agency Vertretung, f.
agent Agent, m.
aggravate (to) verschlimmern; ärgern (annoy).
ago vor (dat.).
　　three days ago vor drei Tagen.
agree (to) übereinstimmen.
agreeable angenehm.
agreed abgemacht.
agreement Übereinstimmung, f.; Vertrag,
　　m. (contract).
agricultural landwirtschaftlich.
agriculture Landwirtschaft, f.

ahead voran, voraus.
aid Hilfe, *f.*
    first aid Erste Hilfe.
aid (to) helfen.
aim Ziel, *n.;* Zweck, *m.*
aim (to) erreichen; zielen (shooting).
air Luft, *f.*
air force Luftwaffe, *f.*
air mail Luftpost, *f.*
airfield Flugplatz, *m.*
airplane Flugzeug, *n.*
airport Flughafen, *m.*
aisle Seitenschiff, *n.*
alarm Alarm, *m.*
alarm clock Wecker, *m.*
alcohol Alkohol, *m.*
alike gleich, ähnlich.
all ganz, alles.
    all right in Ordnung, bestimmt.
    not at all keineswegs.
alliance Verbindung *f.;* Allianz, *f.* (pact).
allow (to) erlauben, gestatten.
allowed gestattet.
ally Verbündete, *m.*
almost fast, beinahe.
alone allein.
along entlang.
already schon, bereits.
also auch.
altar Altar, *m.*
alter (to) ändern, verwandeln.
alternate abwechselnd.
alternate (to) abwechseln.
although obwohl, obgleich.
altitude Höhe, *f.*
altogether zusammen; gänzlich (wholly).
always immer
amaze (to) erstaunen.
amazement Verwunderung, *f.*
ambassador Botschafter, *m.*
ambassadress Botschafterin, *f.*
ambitious ehrgeizig.
amend (to) berichtigen.
American Amerikaner (noun, *m.*); amerikanisch
    (adj.).
among mitten; unter (dat. or acc.).
amount Betrag, *m.*
ample geräumig.
amuse (to) amüsieren.
amusement Unterhaltung, *f.*
amusing amüsant.
analyze (to) analysieren.
ancestors Vorfahren, *pl.*
anchor Anker, *m.*
ancient alt.
and und.
anecdote Anekdote, *f.*
angel Engel, *m.*
anger Ärger, *m.*
angry ärgerlich, bös.
animal Tier, *n.*
animate (to) beleben.

annex Nebengebäude, *n.*
annihilate (to) vernichten.
anniversary Hochzeitstag, *m.*
announce (to) ansagen.
announcement Anzeige, *f.*
annoy (to) ärgern.
annual jährlich.
annul (to) annulieren; ungültig machen.
anonymous anonym.
another ein anderer.
answer Antwort, *f.*
answer (to) antworten.
anterior vorhergehend.
anticipate (to) vorhersehen (foresee); erwarten
    (expect).
antique altertümlich, antik.
anxiety Unruhe, *f.*
anxious unruhig.
any etwas (some); irgend ein (whatever).
anybody irgendjemand.
anyhow sowieso.
    anyway irgendwie.
anything irgendetwas.
anywhere irgendwo.
apart abseits.
apartment Wohnung, *f.*
apiece jeder; jedes Stück.
apologize (to) sich entschuldigen.
apparent scheinbar.
appeal (to) gefallen.
appear (to) erscheinen.
appearance Erscheinung, *f.*
appease (to) besänftigen.
appendix Anhang, *m.*
appetite Appetit, *m.*
applaud (to) applaudieren; klatschen.
applause Applaus, *m.*
apple Apfel, *m.*
application Antrag, *m.* (request); Gewissenhaftig-
    keit, *f.* (diligence).
apply (to) sich bewerben (for a job); auftragen (use).
appoint (to) ernennen.
appointment Verabredung, *f.*
appreciate (to) schätzen.
appreciation Anerkennung, *f.*
appropriate angemessen.
approve (to) genehmigen.
April April, *m.*
apron Schürze, *f.*
arbitrary eigenwillig.
arcade Arkade, *f.*
architect Architekt, *m.;* Baumeister, *m.*
architecture Architektur, *f.*
ardent feurig, glühend.
area Gebiet, *n.*
argue (to) verhandeln, diskutieren.
argument Wortwechsel, *m.*
arise (to) aufsteigen; aufstehen (get up).
arm Arm, *m.*
    firearms Waffen, *pl.*
arm (to) bewaffnen.
army Heer, *n.;* Armee, *f.*

around herum, um (acc.).
arouse (to) erregen (revolt); erwecken (suspicion); aufwecken (wake up).
arrange (to) ordnen.
arrangement Ordnung, f.(order); Anordnung, f. (preparation).
arrest Verhaftung, f.
arrest (to) verhaften.
arrival Ankunft, f.
arrive (to) ankommen.
art Kunst, f.
article Artikel, m.
artificial künstlich.
artist Künstler, m.
artistic künstlerisch.
as als (when); so (as much); da (because).

as .... as	so .... wie.
as long as	so lange wie.
as soon as	sobald.
as to	mit Bezug auf (business); was...anbetrifft.
as well	sowohl, auch.
as yet	bis jetzt.

ascertain (to) feststellen.
ash Asche, f.
ashamed beschämt; verschämt (shy).
aside beiseite, abseits.
ask (to) fragen.
asleep schlafend.
aspire (to) sich sehnen.
aspirin Aspirin, n.
assault Angriff, m.
assemble (to) versammeln.
assembly Versammlung, f. (congress); Gesellschaft, f.
assign (to) zuteilen.
assist (to) beistehen.
assistant Gehilfe, m.
associate (to) vereinigen.
assume (to) annehmen.
assurance Versicherung, f.
assure (to) versichern.
astonish (to) erstaunen.
astound (to) verblüffen.
asylum Asyl, n.
at an, in (dat. or acc.); bei, zu (dat.).

at home	zu Hause.
at first	zuerst.
at last	endlich.
at once	sofort.
at times	zuweillen.

athlete Athlet, m.
athletics, Gymnastik, f.
atmosphere Atmosphäre, f.
attach (to) anhängen.
attain (to) erreichen.
attempt (to) versuchen.
attend (to) beiwohnen.
attendant Gehilfe, m.
attention Aufmerksamkeit, f.
attic Dachkammer, f.
attitude Haltung, f.; Einstellung, f. (mental).

attorney Anwalt, m.
attract (to) anziehen.
attraction Anziehung, f.
attractive schön, anziehend.
audience Zuhörer, pl.
August August, m.
aunt Tante, f.
author Autor, m.
authority Autorität, f.
authorize (to) ermächtigen.
automatic automatisch.
automobile Auto, n.
autumn Herbst, m.
available verügbar.
average Durchschnitt, m.
avoid (to) vermeiden.
awake wach.
awake (to) wecken; erwachen (oneself).
award Belohnung, f.
award (to) zuerkennen.
aware gewahr.
away fort, weg.
    to go away   weggehen.
awful furchtbar.
awkward ungeschickt.

B

baby Kind, n.
back Rücken (noun, m.) (body); zurück (adv.).
background Hintergrund, m.
backwards rückwärts.
bacon Speck, m.
bad schlecht.
badge Marke, f.
bag Beutel, m.
baggage Gepäck, n.
baker Bäcker, m.
bakery Bäckerei, f.
balance Gleichgewicht, n.
balcony Balkon, m.
ball Ball, m.
balloon Ballon, m.
banana Banane, f.
band Band, n.; Musikkapelle, f.
bandage Verband, m.
banister Treppengeländer, n.
bank Bank, f.
bank note Banknote, f.
bankruptcy Bankrott, m.
banquet Bankett, n.
bar Barre, f. (metal); Bar, f. (for drinks).
barber Frisör, m.
bare bloss, bar.
barefoot barfuss.
barge Barke, f. Lastschiff, n.
barn Scheune, f.
barrel Fass, n.
barren unfruchtbar.
basin Becken, n.
basis Grundlage, f.

basket Korb, *m.*
bath Bad, *n.*
bathroom Badezimmer, *n.*
bathe (to) baden.
battle Schlacht, *f.*
bay Bucht, *f.*
be (to) sein.
    to be hungry hungrig sein.
    to be right Recht haben.
    to be thirsty Durst haben.
    to be tired müde sein.
    to be wrong Unrecht haben.
beach Strand, *m.*
bean Bohne, *f.*
bear (to) aushalten.
beard Bart, *m.*
beat (to) schlagen.
beautiful schön, wunderschön.
beauty Schönheit, *f.*
beauty parlor Schönheitssalon, *m.*
because weil.
become (to) werden.
becoming passend, vorteilhaft.
bed Bett, *n.*
beef Rindfleisch, *n.*
beer Bier, *n.*
beet Rübe, *f.*
before vor (dat. or acc.); bevor (conj.).
beg (to) betteln.
beggar Bettler, *m.*
begin (to) beginnen, anfangen.
beginning Anfang, *m.*
behave (to) sich betragen, sich benehmen.
behavior Verhalten, *n.*
behind hinter (dat. or acc.).
belief Glaube, *m.*
believe (to) glauben.
bell Glocke, *f.*
belong (to) gehören.
below unter (dat. or acc.).
belt Gürtel, *m.*
bench Bank, *f.*
bend (to) biegen.
beneath unten; unter (dat. or acc.).
benefit Vorteil, *m.*
beside neben (dat. or acc.).
besides ausserdem.
best beste (der, die, das) (adj.); am besten (adv.).
bet Wette, *f.*
bet (to) wetten.
betray (to) verraten.
better besser.
between zwischen (dat. or acc.).
beware (to) sich hüten.
    Beware! Achtung!
beyond jenseits (gen.).
bicycle Fahrrad, *n.*
bid (to) bieten; befehlen (order).
big gross.
bill Rechnung, *f.*
    bill of fare Speisekarte, *f.*
billion Billion, *f.*

bind (to) binden.
bird Vogel, *m.*
birth Geburt, *f.*
birthday Geburtstag, *m.*
biscuit Zwieback, *m.*
bishop Bischof, *m.*
bit Stück, *n.;* Gebiss, *n.* (horse).
bite Biss, *m.*
bite (to) beissen.
bitter bitter.
bitterness Bitterkeit, *f.*
black schwarz.
blade Klinge, *f.* (razor); Blatt, *n.* (grass).
blame Schuld, *f.;* Tadel, *m.*
blame (to) tadeln.
blank unbeschrieben (page); verwundert (expression).
blanket Decke, *f.*
bleed (to) bluten.
bless (to) segnen.
blessing Segnung, *f.;* Segen, *m.*
blind blind.
block Block, *m.*
block (to) versperren.
blood Blut, *n.*
blotter Loschpapier, *n.*
blouse Bluse, *f.*
blow Schlag, *m.*
blow (to) blasen; putzen (nose).
blue blau.
blush (to) erröten.
board Brett, *n.* (plank); Verpflegung, *f.* (food).
boarding house Pension, *f.*
boast (to) prahlen.
boat Boot, *n.*
body Körper, *m.*
boil (to) kochen, sieden.
boiler Kessel, *m.*
bold kühn.
bomb Bombe, *f.*
    atom bomb. Atombombe, *f.*
bond Aktie, *f.* (stock).
bone Knochen, *m.*
book Buch, *n.*
bookseller Buchhändler, *m.*
bookstore Buchhandlung, *f.*
border Grenze, *f.*
boring langweilig.
born geboren.
borrow (to) borgen, leihen.
both beide.
bother (to) ärgern, plagen, bemühen.
    Don't bother! Bemühen Sie sich nicht!
bottle Flasche, *f.*
bottle opener Flaschenöffner, *m.*
bottom Boden, *m.*
bounce (to) aufspringen.
bowl Schale, *f.*
box Schachtel, *f.*
boy Junge, *m.;* Knabe, *m.*
bracelet Armband, *n.*
braid Borte, *f.;* Zopf, *m.* (hair).
brain Gehirn, *n.*

brake Bremse, *f.*
branch Ast, *m.* (tree); Filiale, *f.* (business).
brave tapfer.
brassiere Büstenhalter, *m.*
bread Brot, *n.*
break (to) brechen; lösen (engagement).
breakfast Frühstück, *n.*
   have breakfast frühstücken.
breath Atem, *m.*
breathe (to) atmen.
breeze Wind, *m.;* Brise, *f.*
bribe (to) bestechen.
brick Backstein, *m.*
bride Braut, *f.*
   bridegroom Bräutigam, *m.*
bridge Brücke, *f.*
brief kurz.
bright hell, klar.
brighten (to) erheitern; sich aufklären (weather).
brilliant glänzend.
bring (to) bringen.
bring up (to) erziehen.
British britisch.
broad weit, breit.
broil (to) braten.
broken zerbrochen.
brook Bach, *m.*
broom Besen, *m.*
brother Bruder, *m.*
brother-in-law Schwager, *m.*
brown braun.
bruise (to) quetschen.
brush Bürste, *f.*
bubble Blase, *f.*
buckle Schnalle, *f.*
bud Knospe, *f.*
budget Budget, *n.*
build (to) bauen.
building Gebäude, *n.*
bulletin Bulletin, *n.*
bundle Bündel, *n.*
burn (to) brennen.
burst (to) bersten.
bus Autobus, *m.* Omnibus, *m.*
bush Busch, *m.*
business Geschäft, *n.*
businessman Geschäftsmann, *m.*
busy beschäftigt.
but aber; sondern (neg.).
butcher Metzger, *m.*
butcher shop Metzgerei, *f.*
butter Butter, *f.*
button Knopf, *m.*
buy (to) kaufen.
buyer Käufer, *m.*
by von (dat.); durch (acc.); neben (dat. & acc.)
   (close to); um (acc.) (time).

C

cab Taxi, *n.*
cabbage Kohl, *m.;* Kraut, *n.*
cable Kabel, *n.*

cage Käfig, *m.*
cake Kuchen, *m.*
calendar Kalender, *m.*
calf Kalb, *n.*
call Ruf, *m.*
call (to) rufen; anrufen; telefonieren (telephone);
   heissen (name).
calm ruhig.
camera Kamera, *f.*
camp Lager, *n.*
camp (to) lagern.
can Büchse, *f.;* Dose, *f.*
can (to be able) können.
can opener Büchsenöffner, *m.*
cancel (to) rückgängig machen, annulieren.
candidate Kandidat, *m.*
candle Kerze, *f.*
candy Bonbons, *pl.*
cap Mütze, *f.*
capital Hauptstadt, *f.* (city); Kapital, *n.* (finance).
capricious launisch; eigensinning (temperamental).
captain Hauptmann, *m.* (army); Kapitän, *m.* (navy).
captive Gefangene, *m.*
capture (to) fangen; einnehmen.
car Wagen, *m.*
carbon paper Durchschlagpapier, *n.*
card Karte, *f.*
care Sorge, *f.* (anxiety); Sorgfalt, *f.* (caution).
   care of bei
   take care of pflegen
care (to) sich sorgen.
   care about sich kümmern.
   care for (to like) gern haben.
   I don't care. Das ist mir gleich.
career Laufbahn, *f.*
careful vorsichtig, sorgfältig.
careless nachlässig, sorglos.
caress Liebkosung, *f.*
carpenter Zimmermann, *m.*
carpet Teppich, *m.*
carry (to) tragen.
carve (to) schnitzen.
case Fall, *m.;* Aktentasche, *f.* (container).
   in case im Falle.
cash Bargeld, *n.*
   to pay cash bar zahlen.
cash (to) einlösen, kassieren.
cashier Kassierer, *m.*
castle Schloss, *n.*
cat Katze, *f.*
catch (to) fangen.
category Kategorie, *f.*
cathedral Dom, *m.*
Catholic katholisch.
cattle Vieh, *n.*
cause Grund, *m.;* Ursache, *f.*
cause (to) verursachen.
cavalry Reiterei, *f.*
cease (to) aufhören.
ceiling Decke, *f.*
celebrate (to) feiern.
cellar Keller, *m.*
cement Zement, *m.*

cemetery Kirchhof, *m.*; Friedhof, *m.*
center Zentrum, *n.*
central zentral.
central heating Zentralheizung, *f.*
century Jahrhundert, *n.*
cereal Getreide,*n.* (grain); Mehlspeise, *f.* (prepared).
ceremony Zeremonie, *f.*
certain gewiss.
certainty Gewissheit, *f.*; Sicherheit, *f.*
certificate Zeugnis, *n.*
chain Kette, *f.*
chair Stuhl, *m.*
chairman Vorsitzende, *m.*; Präsident, *m.*
chalk Kreide, *f.*
challenge Herausforderung, *f.*
challenge (to) herausfordern.
champion Meister, *m.*
   world champion Weltmeister, *m.*
chance Zufall, *m.*
change Veränderung, *f.*; Kleingeld, *n.* (money).
change (to) ändern; wechseln (money).
chapel Kapelle, *f.*
chapter Kapitel, *n.*
character Charakter, *m.*
characteristic charakteristisch.
charge (to) beladen; berechnen (price).
charitable wohltätig.
charity Wohltätigkeit, *f.*
charming reizend.
chase (to) jagen.
chat (to) plaudern.
cheap billig.
cheat (to) betrügen.
check Scheck, *m.*; Rechnung, *f.* (in a restaurant).
check (to) kontrollieren; aufgeben (baggage).
cheek Wange, *f.*
cheer (to) aufheitern.
cheerful heiter, freudig, fröhlich.
cheese Käse, *m.*
chemical chemisch.
cherish (to) schätzen.
cherry Kirsche, *f.*
chest Brust, *f.*; Kiste, *f.* (box).
   chest of drawers Kommode, *f.*
chestnut Kastanie, *f.*
chew (to) kauen.
chicken Huhn, *n.*; Hühnchen, *n.*
chief Leiter, *m.*
chief (adj.) haupt—.
chime Glockenspiel, *n.*
chimney Schornstein, *m.*
chin Kinn, *n.*
china Porzellan, *n.*
chip Span, *m.*; Splitter, *m.*
chocolate Schokolade, *f.*
choice Wahl, *f.*
choir Chor, *m.*
choke (to) ersticken.
choose (to) auswählen.
chop Kotelett, *n.*
Christian Christ (noun, *m.*); christlich (adj.).
Christmas Weihnachten, *f.*

church Kirche, *f.*
cigar Zigarre, f.
cigarette Zigarette, *f.*
circle Kreis, *m.*
circular rund.
circulate (to) kreisen.
circumstances Umstände, *pl.*
citizen Bürger, *m.*
city Stadt, *f.*
city hall Rathaus, *n.*
civil zivil.
civilization Zivilisation, *f.*
civilize (to) zivilisieren.
claim Forderung, *f.*
claim (to) fordern.
clamor Geschrei, *n.*
clap (to) klatschen.
class Klasse, *f.*
classify (to) klassifizieren.
clause Klausel, *f.*
clean rein, sauber.
clean (to) reinigen.
cleaners Reinigungsanstalt, *f.*
cleanliness Reinlichkeit, *f.*
clear klar.
clerk Angestellte, *m.*
clever klug, schlau.
climate Klima, *n.*
climb (to) klimmen, steigen (stairway); besteigen
   (mountain).
clip Klammer, *f.*
clip (to) beschneiden (cut); zusammenfügen
   (attach).
clock Uhr, *f.*
close nahe.
close (to) zumachen, schliessen.
closed geschlossen.
closet Schrank, *m.*
cloth Tuch, *n.*
clothes Kleider, *pl.*
cloud Wolke, *f.*
cloudy bewölkt.
clover Klee, *m.*
club Klub, *m.*; Keule, *f.* (cards).
coal Kohle, *f.*
coarse roh.
coast Küste, *f.*
coat Mantel, *m.* (overcoat); Anzug, *m.* (suit).
code Gesetzbuch, *n.* (law); Code, *m.*
coffee Kaffee, *m.*
coffin Sarg, *m.*
coin Münze, *f.*
cold kalt.
coldness Kälte, *f.*
collaborate (to) zusammenarbeiten.
collar Kragen, *m.*; Halsband, *n.* (dog).
collect (to) sammeln.
collection Sammlung, *f.*
collective gesamt.
college Universität, *f.*
colonial kolonial.
colony Kolonie, *f.*

color Farbe, f.

color (to) färben.

column Spalte, f.; Kollonne, f. (military);
Säule, f. (arch).

comb Kamm, m.

comb (to) kämmen.

combination Verbindung, f.

combine (to) verbinden.

come (to) kommen.
come back zurückkommen.

comedy Komödie, f.

comet Komet, m.

comfort Behaglichkeit, f.; Trost, m. (moral).

comfort (to) trösten.

comfortable bequem.

comma Komma, n.

command Befehl, m.

command (to) befehlen.

commander Befehlshaber, m.

commercial geschäftsmässig.

commission Kommission, f.; Offizierspatent, m.

commit (to) begehen.

common gemein, gewöhnlich.

communicate (to) mitteilen.

communication Mitteilung, f.

community Gemeinde, f.

companion Genosse, m.

company Gesellschaft, f. (social);
Kompanie, f. (military).

compare (to) vergleichen.

comparison Vergleich, m.

compete (to) konkurrieren.

competition Konkurrenz, f.; Tournier, n. (sports).

complain (to) sich beklagen.

complaint Klage, f.

complete vollenden.

complex Komplex, (noun, m.); verwickelt (adj.).

complexion Gesichtsfarbe, f.

complicate (to) verwickeln, komplizieren.

complicated verwickelt, kompliziert.

compliment Kompliment, n.

compose (to) komponieren.

composer Komponist, m.

composition Komposition, f.

compromise Kompromiss, m.; Vergleich, m.

compromise (to) einen Kompromiss machen,
kompromittieren.

conceit Einbildung, f.

conceited eingebildet.

conceive (to) ersinnen.

concentrate (to) konzentrieren.

concern Angelegenheit, f. (matter); Sorge, f.
(anxiety); Geschäft, n. (business).

concern (to) betreffen.

concert Konzert, n.

concrete konkret.

condemn (to) verurteilen, verdammen.

condense (to) kondensieren.

condition Zustand, m.

conduct Benehmen, n.

conduct (to) führen; dirigieren (music).

conductor Führer, m. (guide); Schaffner, m. (vehicle);

Dirigent, m. (music).

confess (to) gestehen; beichten (church).

confession Geständnis, n.; Beichte, f. (church).

confidence Vertrauen, n.

confident vertrauend, vertrauensvoll.

confidential vertraulich.

confirm (to) bestätigen.

confirmation Bestätigung, f.

congratulate (to) gratulieren.

congratulations Glückwunsch, m.

connect (to) verbinden.

connection Verbindung, f.

conquer (to) erobern, besiegen.

conquest Eroberung, f.; Sieg, m.

conscience Gewissen, n.

conscientious gewissenhaft.

conscious bewusst.

consent Einwilligung, f.

conservative konservativ.

consider (to) betrachten (look); bedenken (think).

considerable beträchtlich.

consideration Betrachtung, f.

consist of (to) bestehen (aus – dat.).

consistent übereinstimmend.

constant beständig.

constitution Verfassung, f.; Gesundheit, f. (health).

constitutional verfassungsmässig.

consul Konsul, m.

contagious ansteckend.

contain (to) enthalten.

container Behälter, m.

contemporary Zeitgenosse, (noun, m.);
zeitgenössisch (adj.).

content zufrieden.

content (to) befriedigen.

contents Inhalt, m.; Gehalt, m.

continent Kontinent, m.

continual fortwährend.

continue (to) fortfahren.

contract Vertrag, m.

contractor Unternehmer, m.

contradict (to) widersprechen.

contradiction Widerspruch, m.

contradictory widersprechend.

contrary Gegenteil (noun, n.); entgegengesetzt (adj.).
on the contrary im Gegenteil.

contrast Gegensatz, m.

contrast (to) abstechen.

contribute (to) beitragen.

contribution Beitrag, m.

control Kontrolle, f.

control (to) kontrollieren.

controversy Meinungsverschiedenheit, f.

convenience Bequemlichkeit, f.

convenient passend; bequem (practical).

convent Kloster, n.

convention Versammlung, f.

conversation Gespräch, n.; Unterhaltung, f.

converse (to) sich unterhalten.

convert (to) verwandeln.

convict (to) verurteilen.

conviction Verurteilung, f.

convince (to) überzeugen.
cook Koch, *m.*; Köchin, *f.*
cook (to) kochen.
cool kühl.
cool (to) kühlen.
copy Kopie, *f.*
cork Kork, *m.*
corkscrew Korkenzieher, *m.*
corn Mais, *m.*
corner Ecke, *f.*
corporation Körperschaft, *f.*
correct richtig.
correct (to) berichtigen, korrigieren.
correction Berichtigung, *f.*
correspond (to) korrespondieren.
correspondence Briefwechsel, *m.*
correspondent Korrespondent, *m.*
corresponding entsprechend.
corrupt (to) verderben.
corruption Verdorbenheit, *f.*
cost Kosten, *f.*
costume Kostüm, *n.*
cottage Häuschen, *n.*
cotton Baumwolle, *f.;* Watte, *f.* (pharmacy).
couch Sofa, *n.*
cough Husten, *m.*
count Graf, *m.* (nobility); Zählung, *f.*
count (to) zählen.
counter Ladentisch, *m.*
countess Gräfin, *f.*
countless zahllos.
country Land, *n.;* Vaterland, *n.* (fatherland).
countryman Landsmann, *m.*
couple Paar, *n.*
courage Mut, *m.*
course Lauf, *m.* (direction); Kursus, *m.* (studies).
court Gericht, *n.*
courteous zuvorkommend.
courtesy Höflichkeit, *f.*
courtyard Hof, ·*m.*
cousin Vetter, *m.;* Cousine, *f.*
cover Decke, *f.*
cow Kuh, *f.*
crack Riss, *m.*
crack (to) knacken.
cradle Wiege, *f.*
crash Zusammenbruch, *m.*
crazy verrückt.
cream Sahne, *f.*
create (to) schaffen.
creature Geschöpf, *n.;* Wesen, *n.*
credit Kredit, *m.*
creditor Gläubiger, *m.*
crime Verbrechen, *n.*
crisis Krise, *f.*
crisp knusperig.
critic Kritiker, *m.*
critical kritisch.
criticize (to) kritisieren.
crooked krumm.
crop Ernte, *f.*
cross Kreuz, *n.*

crossing Übergang, *m.*
crossroads Strassenkreuzung, *f.*
crouch (to) sich ducken.
crow Krähe, *f.*
crowd Menge, *f.*
crowd (to) überfüllen.
crowded überfüllt.
crown Krone, *f.*
crown (to) krönen.
cruel grausam.
cruelty Grausamkeit, *f.*
crumb Krume, *f.*
crumble (to) zerbröckeln.
crust Kruste, *f.*
crutch Krücke, *f.*
cry Ruf, *m.;* Geschrei, *n.*
cry (to) weinen (weep); schreien (shout).
cuff Manschette, *f.*
cunning gerissen.
cup Tasse, *f.*
cure Heilung, *f.*
curiosity Neugier, *f.*
curious neugierig.
curl Locke, *f.*
current Strom (noun, *m.*); laufend (adj.).
curtain Vorhang, *m.*
curve Kurve, *f.*
cushion Kissen, *n.*
custom Sitte, *f.*
customary gebräuchlich.
customer Kunde, *m.*
customhouse Zollamt, *m.*
customs official Zollbeamter, *m.*
cut Schnitt, *m.*
cut (to) schneiden.

D

dagger Dolch, *m.*
daily täglich.
dainty zierlich.
dairy Milchgeschäft, *n.*
dam Damm, *m.*
damage Schaden, *m.*
damage (to) beschädigen.
damp feucht.
dance Tanz, *m.*
dance (to) tanzen.
danger Gefahr, *f.*
dangerous gefährlich.
dark dunkel.
darkness Dunkelheit, *f.*
dash (to) sich beeilen.
date Datum, *n.;* Verabredung, *f.* (meeting).
daughter Tochter, *f.*
dawn Morgendämmerung, *f.*
day Tag, *m.*
  day after tomorrow übermorgen.
  day before yesterday vorgestern.
  yesterday gestern.
dazzle (to) blenden.
dead tot.

deaf taub.

deal Teil, *m.;* Geschäft, *n.* (business).

deal (to) ausgeben (cards).

dealer Händler, *m.;* Geber, *m.* (cards).

dear lieb; teuer (*also* expensive).

death Tod, *m.*

debate Debatte, *f.*

debt Schuld, *f.*

debtor Schuldner, *m.*

decanter Karaffe, *f.*

decay Verfall, *m.* (ruin); Fäulnis, *f.* (rot).

decay (to) verfallen, verfaulen.

deceased verstorben.

deceit Falschheit, *f.*

deceive (to) betrügen.

December Dezember, *m.*

decent anständig.

decide (to) entscheiden.

decided entschieden.

decision Entscheidung, *f.;* Entschluss, *m.*

decisive entscheidend.

deck Deck, *n.*

declare (to) erklären.

decline Abnahme, *f.;* Fall, *m.*

decline (to) verfallen, abweisen; deklinieren (grammar).

decrease Abnahme, *f.;* Verminderung, *f.*

decrease (to) abnehmen, vermindern.

decree Verordnung, *f.*

dedicate (to) widmen.

deed Tat, *f.*

deep tief.

deer Hirsch, *m.*

defeat Niederlage, *f.*

defeat (to) besiegen.

defect Fehler, *m.*

defend (to) verteidigen.

defense Verteidigung, *f.*

defiance Trotz, *m.*

define (to) definieren.

definite bestimmt.

defy (to) trotzen.

degree Grad, *m.*

delay Verzögerung, *f.*

delay (to) aufhalten.

delegate Delegierter, *m.*

delegate (to) delegieren.

deliberate (to) erwägen.

deliberately absichtlich.

delicacy Delikatesse, *f.*

delicate zart.

delicious köstlich.

delight Freude, *f.*

delighted erfreut.

deliver (to) liefern.

deliverance Befreiung, *f.*

delivery Ablieferung, *f.*

demand Forderung, *f.;* Nachfrage, *f.* (business).

demand (to) fordern.

democracy Demokratie, *f.*

demonstrate (to) demonstrieren.

demonstration Kundgebung, *f.;* Demonstration, *f.*

denial Verleugnung, *f.*

denounce (to) denunzieren.

dense dicht.

density Dichte, *f.*

dentist Zahnarzt, *m.*

deny (to) ableugnen, verleugnen.

departure Abreise, *f.*

department Abteilung, *f.*

depend (to) abhängen.

dependent abhängig.

deplore (to) beweinen.

deposit Anzahlung, *f.*

depress (to) niederdrücken.

depression Depression, *f.*

deprive (to) berauben, entziehen.

depth Tiefe, *f.*

deride (to) verlachen, verhöhnen.

derive (to) ableiten.

descend (to) abstammen.

descendant Nachkomme, *m.*

descent Abstieg, *m.;* Abstammung, *f.* (family).

describe (to) beschreiben.

description Beschreibung, *f.*

desert Wüste, *f.*

desert (to) verlassen.

deserve (to) verdienen.

design Zeichnung, *f.* (drawing); Absicht, *f.* (intention).

designer Zeichner, *m.*

desirable wünschenswert.

desire (to) wünschen.

desire Wunsch, *m.*

desirous begierig.

desk Pult, *n.*

desolate trostlos.

despair Verzweiflung, *f.*

despair (to) verzweifeln.

desperate verzweifelt.

despise (to) verachten.

despite trotz (gen.).

dessert Nachtisch, *m.*

destiny Schicksal, *n.*

destroy (to) zerstören.

destruction Zerstörung, *f.*

detach (to) lösen.

detail Einzelheit, *f.*

detain (to) aufhalten.

detect (to) entdecken.

detective Detektiv, *m.*

detective story Kriminalgeschichte, *f.;* Detektivroman, *m.*

determination Entschlossenheit, *f.*

determine (to) bestimmen.

detest (to) verabscheuen.

detour Umweg, *m.*

detract (to) abziehen.

detrimental schädlich.

develop (to) entwickeln.

development Entwicklung, *f.*

device Kunstgriff, *m.*

devil Teufel, *m.*

devise (to) ersinnen.

devoid bar (gen.); ohne (acc.)
devote (to) widmen.
devour (to) verschlingen.
dew Tau, *m.*
dial Zifferblatt, *n.* (clock).
dial (to) wählen.
dialect Dialekt, *m.*
dialogue Dialog, *m.*
diameter Durchmesser, *m.*
diamond Diamant, *m.*
diary Tagebuch, *n.*
dictate (to) diktieren.
dictation Diktat, *n.*
dictionary Wörterbuch, *n.*
die (to) sterben.
diet Diät, *f.*
differ (to) sich unterscheiden.
difference Unterschied, *m.*
different verschieden.
difficult schwierig.
difficulty Schwierigkeit, *f.*
dig (to) graben.
digest (to) verdauen.
dignity Würde, *f.*
dim trübe.
dimension Dimension, *f.; Mass, *n.*
diminish (to) vermindern.
dining room Speisesaal, *m.*
dinner Abendessen, *n.*
dine (to) essen, speisen.
dip (to) senken, (ein)tauchen.
diplomacy Diplomatie, *f.*
diplomat Diplomat, *m.*
direct direkt.
direct (to) den Weg zeigen (show the way).
direction Richtung, *f.*
director Direktor, *m.*
directory Adressbuch, *n.*
dirt Schmutz, *m.*
dirty schmutzig.
disability Unfähigkeit, *f.*
disabled unfähig.
disadvantage Nachteil, *m.*
disagree (to) uneinig sein.
disagreeable unangenehm.
disagreement Meinungsverschiedenheit, *f.*
disappear (to) verschwinden.
disappearance Verschwinden, *n.*
disappoint (to) enttäuschen.
disapprove (to) missbilligen, ablehnen.
disaster Unglück, *n.; Katastrophe, *f.*
disastrous unheilvoll.
discharge Entlassung, *f.* (dismissal); Abfeuern, *n.* (gun).
discharge (to) entlassen (person); abfeuern (firearm).
discipline Zucht, *f.*
disclaim (to) bestreiten.
disclose (to) enthüllen.
disclosure Enthüllung, *f.*
discomfort Unbehaglichkeit, *f.*
disconnect (to) trennen.

discontent unzufrieden.
discontinue (to) aufhören.
discord Zwietracht, *f.*
discount Skonto, *m.* (financial); Rabatt, *m.*
discourage (to) entmutigen.
discouragement Entmutigung, *f.*
discover (to) entdecken.
discovery Entdeckung. *f.*
discreet diskret, vorsichtig.
discretion Klugheit, *f.; Urteil, *n.*
discuss (to) besprechen, erörtern.
discussion Erörterung, *f.; Diskussion, *f.*
disdain Verachtung, *f.*
disdain (to) verschmähen, verachten.
disease Krankheit, *f.*
disgrace Schande, *f.* (shame); Ungnade, *f.*
disguise Verkleidung, *f.*
disguise (to) verkleiden.
disgust Ekel, *m.*
disgust (to) (an)ekeln.
disgusted ekelhaft, angeekelt.
dish Speise, *f.* (food); Schüssel, *f.* (plate).
dishonest unehrlich.
disk Scheibe, *f.*
dislike Widerwille, *m.*
dislike (to) nicht mögen.
dismiss (to) entlassen.
dismissal Entlassung, *f.*
disobey (to) nicht gehorchen.
disorder Unordnung, *f.*
dispense (to) verteilen.
display Entfaltung *f.* (unfold); Schau, *f.* (exposition).
displease (to) missfallen.
displeasure Missfallen, *n.*
disposal Verfügung, *f.*
dispose (to) anordnen, verfügen.
dispute Streit, *m.*
dispute (to) streiten.
dissolve (to) auflösen.
distance Entfernung, *f.*
distant entfernt.
distinct deutlich.
distinction Auszeichnung, *f.; Unterschied, *m.* (difference).
distinguish (to) unterscheiden.
distort (to) verdrehen.
distract (to) verwirren.
distress Not, *f.*
distress (to) betrüben.
distribute (to) verteilen.
district Distrikt, *m.*
distrust Misstrauen, *n.*
distrust (to) misstrauen.
disturb (to) stören.
disturbance Störung, *f.*
ditch Graben, *m.*
dive (to) tauchen.
divide (to) verteilen.
divine göttlich.
division Teilung, *f.*
divorce (to) scheiden.

divorced geschieden.
dizziness Schwindel, *m.*
dizzy schwindlig.
do (to) tun, machen.
dock Dock, *n.*
doctor Arzt, *m.*
doctrine Lehre, *f.*
document Urkunde, *f.* Dokument, *n.*
dog Hund, *m.*
doll Puppe, *f.*
dome Kuppel, *f.*
domestic Häuslich; einheimisch (native).
domestic animal Haustier, *n.*
dominate (to) beherrschen.
door Tür, *f.*
dose Dosis, *f.*
dot Punkt, *m.*
double doppelt.
doubt Zweifel, *m.*
doubt (to) zweifeln.
doubtful zweifelhaft.
doubtless ohne Zweifel.
dough Teig, *m.*
down unter (dat. or acc.); hinunter, herunter.
dozen Dutzend, *n.*
draft Wechsel, *m.* (money); Zeichnung, *f.* (drawing).
drag (to) schleppen.
drain (to) entwässern.
drama Drama, *n.*
draught Zug, *m.*
draw (to) zeichnen.
draw back (to) schleppen.
drawer Schublade, *f.*

drawing-room Gesellschaftszimmer, *n.;* Salon, *m.;*
  Wohnzimmer, *n.*
dread Furcht, *f.*
dread (to) fürchten.
dreadful furchtbar, schrecklich.
dream Traum, *m.*
dream (to) träumen.
dreamer Träumer, *m.*
dress Kleid, *n.*
dress (to) sich anziehen.
dressmaker Schneiderin, *f.*
drink Getränk, *n.*
drink (to) trinken.
drip (to) tropfen.
drive (to) fahren.
driver Chauffeur, *m.*
drop Fall, *m.;* Tropfen, *m.* (liquid).
drown (to) ertrinken.
drug Droge, *f.*
drugstore Apotheke, *f.;* Drogerie, *f.*
drum Trommel, *f.*
drunk betrunken.
dry trocken.
dry (to) trocknen.
dryness Trockenheit, *f.*
duchess Herzogin, *f.*
duck Ente, *f.*
due Gebühr, *f.*

duke Herzog, *m.*
dull trüb (weather); matt (color); dumpf (sound).
dumb stumm; dumm (stupid).
  deaf and dumb taubstumm.
during während (gen.).
dust Staub, *m.*
dust (to) abstäuben.
dusty staubig.
Dutch holländisch.
duty Pflicht, *f.;* Dienst, *m.* (service); Zoll, *m.*
  (customs).
dwarf Zwerg, *m.*
dwell (to) wohnen.
dye Farbe, *f.*
dye (to) färben.

E

each jeder.
  each other einander.
  each time jedesmal.
eager eifrig.
eagle Adler, *m.*
ear Ohr, *n.*
early früh.
earn (to) verdienen.
earnest ernst.
earth Erde, *f.*
ease Bequemlichkeit, *f.* (comfort); Ruhe, *f.* (calm);
  Linderung, *f.* (relief); Leichtigkeit, *f.* (facility).
ease (to) lindern, erleichtern.
easily leicht.
east Osten, *m.*
Easter Ostern, *pl.*
eastern östlich.
easy leicht.
eat (to) essen.
echo Echo, *n.*
echo (to) widerhallen.
economical wirtschaftlich; sparsam.
economize (to) sparen.
edge Schneide, *f.* (blade); Rand, *m.* (rim).
edition Ausgabe, *f.;* Auflage, *f.*
editor Redakteur, *m.*
editorial Leitartikel (noun, *m.*); redaktionell (adj.).
education Bildung, *f.*
effect Wirkung, *f.*
effective wirkungsvoll.
efficiency Leistungsfähigkeit, *f.*
effort Anstrengung, *f.;* Bestreben, *n.* (endeavor).
egg Ei, *n.* (Eier, *pl.*)
egoism Egoismus, *m.;* Selbstsucht, *f.*
eight acht.
eighteen achtzehn.
eighteenth achtzehnte.
eighth achte.
eightieth achtzigste.
eighty achtzig.
either oder.
  either...or entweder...oder.
elastic elastisch.
elbow Ellbogen, *m.*
elder älter.

elderly älterer, ältlich.
eldest Älteste, *m. & f.*
elect (to) erwählen.
election Wahl, *f.*
elector Wähler, *m.*
electrical elektrisch.
electricity Elektrizität, *f.*
elegant elegant.
element Element, *n.*
elementary elementar.
elephant Elefant, *m.*
elevator Aufzug, *m.*
eleven elf.
eleventh elfte.
eliminate (to) ausscheiden.
eloquence Beredsamkeit, *f.*
eloquent beredt.
else ander, anders; sonst (otherwise).
  anyone else   irgend ein anderer.
  elsewhere   anderswo.
  everybody else jeder andere.
  nobody else   sonst niemand.
  someone else   ein anderer.
elude (to) ausweichen.
embark (to) (sich) einschiffen.
embarrass (to) in Verlegenheit bringen.
embarrassing unangenehm, beschämend.
embarrassment Verlegenheit, *f.*
embassy Botschaft, *f.*
embody verkörpern.
embrace (to) umarmen.
embroidery Stickerei, *f.*
emerge (to) herauskommen.
emergency Notfall, *m.*
eminent hervorragend.
emotion Aufregung, *f.*
emperor Kaiser, *m.*
emphasis Nachdruck, *m.*
emphasize (to) betonen.
emphatic nachdrücklich.
empire Reich, *n.*
employee Angestellte, *m. or f.*
employer Arbeitgeber, *m.*
employment Arbeit, *f.;* Beschäftigung, *f.*
empty leer.
enable (to) befähigen.
enamel Email, *n.*
enclose (to) einschliessen.
enclosure Anlage, *f.* (letter); Einzäunung, *f.* (fence).
encourage (to) ermutigen.
encouragement Ermutigung, *f.*
end Ende, *n.*
end (to) enden, aufhören.
endeavor Bestreben, *n.;* Bemühung, *f.*
endeavor (to) sich bemühen.
endorse (to) unterzeichnen.
endure (to) ertragen.
enemy Feind, *m.*
energy Energie, *f.*
enforce (to) durchsetzen.
engage (to) anstellen.
engaged beschäftigt (busy); verlobt (affianced).

engagement Verabredung, *f.* (appointment);
  Beschäftigung, *f.* (business); Verlobung, *f.*
  (marriage)
engine Maschine, *f.;* Lokomotive, *f.* (train).
engineer Ingenieur. *m.*
English englisch.
engrave (to) eingravieren.
enjoy (to) geniessen, amüsieren.
  enjoy oneself sich amüsieren.
enjoyment Vergnügen, *n.*
enlarge (to) vergrössern.
enlist (to) anwerben.
enormous ungeheuer.
enough genug.
enter (to) hineingehen.
  Enter! Herein!
entertain (to) unterhalten.
entertainment Unterhaltung, *f.,* Schau, *f.* (show).
enthusiasm Begeisterung, *f.*
enthusiastic begeistert.
entire ganz.
entitle (to) berechtigen.
entrance Eingang, *m.*
entrust (to) anvertrauen.
enumerate (to) aufzählen.
envelope Umschlag, *m.*
envious neidisch.
envy Neid, *m.*
envy (to) beneiden.
episode Episode, *f;* Begebenheit, *f.*
equal gleich.
equal (to) gleichen.
equality Gleichheit, *f.*
equator Äquator, *m.*
equilibrium Gleichgewicht, *n.*
equip (to) ausrüsten.
equipment Ausrüstung, *f.*
era Zeitalter, *n.*
erase (to) ausstreichen.
eraser Gummi, *m.*
erect (to) errichten.
err (to) sich irren.
errand Auftrag, *m.*
error Irrtum, *m.*
escalator Rolltreppe, *f.*
escape Flucht. *f.*
escape (to) entlaufen.
escort (to) begleiten, eskortieren.
especially besonders.
essay Aufsatz, *m.*
essence Essenz, *f.* (extract); Wesen, *n.*
essential wesentlich.
establish (to) errichten, gründen.
establishment Gründung, *f.*
estate Vermögen, *n.* (wealth); Gut, *n.* (land).
esteem Achtung, *f.*
esteem (to) schätzen.
estimate Kostenanschlag, *m.* (cost); Schätzung, *f.*
  (appraise).
estimate (to) veranschlagen.
eternal ewig.
eternity Ewigkeit, *f.*

European Europäer (noun, *m.*); europäisch. (adj.)
evade (to) entfliehen.
evasion Ausflucht, *f.*
eve Vorabend, *m.*
even eben (adj.); sogar. (adv.)
evening Abend, *m.*
   good evening! Guten Abend!
evening clothes Gesellschaftsanzug, *m.*
evening dress Abendkleid, *n.* (woman's).
event Ereignis, *n.*
ever je, jemals.
every jeder
   everybody jedermann.
   everything alles.
   everywhere überall.
evidence Beweis, *m.*
evident offenbar.
evil Übel (noun, *n.*); schlecht (adj.).
evoke (to) hervorrufen.
evolve (to) herausarbeiten, sich entwickeln.
exact genau.
exaggerate (to) übertreiben.
exaggeration Übertreibung, *f.*
exalt (to) erheben.
exaltation Erhebung, *f.*
examination Prüfung, *f.*
examine (to) prüfen.
example Beispiel, *n.*
exceed (to) überschreiten.
excel (to) übertreffen.
excellence Vortrefflichkeit, *f.*
excellent vortrefflich, ausgezeichnet
except ausgenommen; ausser (dat.).
except (to) ausnehmen.
exception Ausnahme, *f.*
exceptional aussergewöhnlich.
exceptionally ausnahmsweise.
excess Übermass, *n.*
excessive übermässig.
exchange Tausch, *m.*
exchange (to) wechseln.
excite (to) aufregen.
excitement Aufregung, *f.*
exclaim (to) ausrufen.
exclamation Ausruf, *m.*
exclude (to) ausschliessen.
exclusive auschliesslich.
excursion Ausflug, *m.*
excuse Verzeihung, *f.*
excuse (to) verzeihen, entschuldigen.
   Excuse me Verzeihung!(Entschuldigung!)
execute (to) ausführen (carry out); hinrichten (put
   to death).
execution Ausführung, *f.* (of plan or idea);
   Hindrichtung *f.* (of person).
exempt (to) befreien.
exercise Übung, *f.*
exercise (to) üben.
exert (to) sich anstrengen.
exertion Anstrengung, *f.*
exhaust (to) erschöpfen.
exhaustion Erschöpfung, *f.*

exhibit (to) ausstellen.
exhibition Ausstellung, *f.*
exile Verbannung, *f.*
exile (to) verbannen.
exist (to) existieren.
existence Existenz, *f.*
exit Ausgang, *m.*
expand (to) ausdehnen.
expansion Ausdehnung, *f.*
expensive teuer.
experience Erfahrung, *f.*
experience (to) erfahren.
experiment (to) experimentieren.
expert Fachmann, *m.*
expire (to) verscheiden, ablaufen.
explain (to) erklären.
explanation Erklärung, *f.*
explanatory erklärend.
explode (to) explodieren.
exploit Heldentat, *f.*
exploit (to) ausnützen.
explore (to) erforschen.
explosion Explosion, *f.*
export (to) ausführen, exportieren.
export Ausfuhr, *f.*; Export, *m.*
expose (to) aussetzen.
express Schnellzug, *m.*
express (to) ausdrücken.
expression Ausdruck, *m.*
expressive ausdrucksvoll.
expulsion Ausstossung, *f.*
exquisite vorzüglich.
extend (to) verlängern, ausdehnen.
extensive ausgedehnt.
extent Weite, *f.* (distance); Verlängerung, *f.* (time).
exterior Äussere (noun, *n.*); äusserlich (adj.).
exterminate (to) ausrotten.
external äusserlich, auswärtig.
extinction Erlöschen, *n.*
extinguish (to) erlöschen.
extra extra.
extraordinary aussergewöhnlich.
extravagant verschwenderisch.
extreme äusserst.
eye Auge, *n.*
eyebrow Augenbraue, *f.*
eyeglasses Brille, *f.*
eyelash Wimper, *f.*
eyelid Augenlid, *n.*
eyesight, Gesicht, *n.*; Sehkraft, *f.*

F

fable Fabel, *f.*
face Gesicht, *n.*
face (to) unter die Augen treten, gegenüberstehen
facilitate (to) erleichtern.
facility Leichtigkeit, *f.*
fact Tatsache, *f.*
   in fact in der Tat.
   as a matter of fact im übrigen.
factory Fabrik, *f.*

faculty Fähigkeit, *f.* (ability); Fakultät, *f.* (school).
fade (to) welken.
faded verschossen (color).
fail (to) fehlen; unterlassen (neglect); durchfallen (exam).
    without fail ganz gewiss.
failure Misserfolg, *m.*
faint (to) ohnmächtig werden.
fainting spell Ohnmacht, *f.*
fair schön (weather); hell (complexion); ehrlich (just).
    fair play ehrliches Spiel.
faith Glaube, *m.* (religion); Treue, *f.*
faithful treu.
fall Fall, *m;* Sturz, *m;* Herbst, *m.* (autumn).
fall (to) fallen, stürzen.
false falsch.
fame Ruhm, *m.*
familiar vertraut.
family Familie, *f.*
famine Hungersnot, *f.*
famous berühmt.
fan Fächer, *m.* Ventilator, *m.* (ventilator).
fancy Neigung, (noun, *f.*); bunt (adj.).
fantastic fantastisch.
far weit, fern.
farce Posse, *f.*
fare Fahrpreis, *m.*
farewell Abschied, *m.*
    Farewell! Lebe wohl!
farm Bauernhof, *m.*
farmer Landwirt, *m.*
farming Landwirtschaft, *f.*
farther weiter, ferner.
fashion Mode, *f.*
fashionable elegant, modisch, modern.
fast schnell.
fasten (to) befestigen.
fat Fett (noun, *n.*); fett, dick (adj.).
fatal tödlich, fatal.
fate Schicksal, *n.*
father Vater, *m.*
father-in-law Schwiegervater, *m.*
faucet Knopf; *m.;* Hahn, *m.*
fault Fehler, *m.*
favor Gunst, *f.*
    Do me a favor. Tun Sie mir einen Gefallen.
favor (to) begünstigen.
favorable günstig.
favorite Günstling, *m.;* Liebling, *m.;* lieblings (adj.)
fear Furcht, *f.*
fear (to) fürchten.
fearless furchtlos.
feather Feder, *f.*
feature (Gesichts)zug, *m.;* Merkmal, *n.;* Film, *m.* (movie).
February Februar, *m.*
federal Bundes.
federation Verband, *m.*
fee Gebühr, *f.*
feeble schwach.
feed (to) füttern.

feel (to) fühlen.
feeling Gefühl, *n.*
fellow Kamerad, *m.*
fellowship Kameradschaft, *f.;* Gemeinschaft, *f.*
female weiblich.
feminine fraulich.
fence Zaun, *m.*
fencing Fechten, *n.*
fender Kotflügel, *m.*
ferocious wild.
ferry Fähre, *f.*
fertile fruchtbar.
fertilize (to) befruchten.
fertilizer Düngemittel, *n.;* Dünger, *m.*
fervent inbrünstig.
fervor Inbrunst, *f.*
festival Fest, *n.*
fetch (to) holen.
fever Fieber, *n.*
few wenige.
    a few ein paar.
fiction Dichtung, *f.*
field Acker, *m.;* Feld, *n.*
fierce wild.
fiery feurig.
fifteen fünfzehn.
fifteenth fünfzehnte.
fifth fünfte.
fiftieth fünfzigste.
fifty fünfzig.
fig Feige, *f.*
fight Kampf, *m.*
fight (to) kämpfen.
figure Figur, *f.;* Ziffer (number).
file Feile, *f.* (tool); Ablage, *f.* (office).
fill (to) füllen.
filling (tooth) Füllung, *f.*
film Film, *m.*
filthy schmutzig.
final endgültig.
finance Finanz, *f.*
finance (to) finanzieren.
financial finanziell.
find (to) finden.
fine Geldstrafe (noun, *f.*); fein (adj.) (opp. of coarse); schön (adj.) (elegant).
finger Finger, *m.*
finish (to) beenden.
fire Feuer, *n.*
fireman Feuerwehrmann, *m.*
fireplace Kamin, *m.*
firm Firma, (noun, *f.*); fest, stark (adj.).
first erster.
    at first zuerst.
fish Fisch, *m.*
fish (to) fischen.
fisherman Fischer, *m.*
fishing Fischen, *n.*
fist Faust, *f.*
fit Anfall, (noun, *m.*); passend (adj.) (becoming); tauglich (adj.) (capable).
fitness Tauglichkeit, *f.*

five fünf.
fix (to) reparieren.
flag Fahne, f.
flame Flamme, f.
flank Seite, f.
flash Blitz, m. (lightning).
flashlight Blitzlicht, n.
flat flach.
flatter (to) schmeicheln.
flatterer Schmeichler, m.
flattery Schmeichelei, f.
flavor Aroma, n.
fleet Flotte, f.
flesh Fleisch, n.
flexibility Biegsamkeit, f.
flexible biegsam.
flight Flug, m.
fling (to) werfen.
flint Kieselstein, m.
float (to) treiben.
flood Überschwemmung, f.
flood (to) überschwemmen.
floor Boden, m.; Stock, m. (story).
flourish (to) blühen.
flourishing blühend.
flow (to) strömen.
flower Blume, f.
fluid flüssig.
fly Fliege, f.
fly (to) fliegen.
foam Schaum, m.
fog Nebel, m.
fold Falte, f.
fold (to) falten.
foliage Laubwerk, n.
follow (to) folgen.
following folgend.
fond zärtlich, liebevoll.
fondness Zärtlichkeit, f.
food Essen, n.
fool Narr, m.
foolish töricht, lächerlich.
foot Fuss, m.
football Fussball, m.
footstep Schritt, m.
for für (acc.); zu (dat.); wegen (gen.) (on account
    of); denn (because).
      as for me was mich betrifft.
      for a year während eines Jahres.
      for example zum Beispiel.
      word for word Wort für Wort.
forbid (to) verbieten.
force Kraft, f.
force (to) zwingen.
ford Furt, f.
foreground Vordergrund, m.
forehead Stirn, f.
foreign fremd, ausländisch.
foreigner Fremder, m; Ausländer, m.
forest Wald, m.
forget (to) vergessen.
forgetfulness Vergesslichkeit, f.

forget-me-not Vergissmeinnicht, n.
forgive (to) vergeben, verzeihen.
forgiveness Vergebung, f.
fork Gabel, f.
form Form, f.
formal offiziell, formell.
formation Bildung, f.
former früher; erster (as opposed to latter).
formerly vormals.
formula Formel, f.
forsake (to) verlassen.
fort Festung, f.
fortieth vierzigste.
fortunate glücklich.
fortunately glücklicherweise.
fortune Vermögen, n.; Glück, n. (luck).
forty vierzig.
forward vorwärts.
forward (to) absenden.
foster (to) pflegen.
foul faul.
found (to) gründen.
foundation Gründung, f.
founder Gründer, m.
fountain Brunnen, m.
fountain pen Füllfeder, f.
four vier.
fourteen vierzehn.
fourteenth vierzehnte.
fourth vierte.
fowl Geflügel, n.
fox Fuchs, m.
fragile zerbrechlich.
fragment Bruchstück, n.
fragrance Duft, m.
fragrant duftig.
frail zart.
frame Rahmen, m.
frame (to) rahmen.
frank aufrichtig, freimütig.
frankness Offenheit, f.
free frei.
freedom Freiheit, f.
freeze (to) frieren.
freight Fracht, f.
French französisch.
frequent häufig.
frequently oft, oftmals.
fresh frisch.
friction Reibung, f.; Friktion, f. (hair).
Friday Freitag, m.
fried gebraten.
friend Freund, m.
friendly freundlich.
friendship Freundschaft, f.
frighten (to) erschrecken.
frightening schrecklich. erschreckend.
fringe Rand, m.
frivolity Leichtsinn, f.
frog Frosch, m.
from von, aus (dat); nach (dat.) (according to).
    from morning till night von früh bis spät.

from time to time von Zeit zu Zeit.
from top to bottom von oben bis unten.
front Vorderseite, *f.; Front, f. (military).*
frozen gefroren.
fruit Frucht, sing. *f.;* Obst, coll., *n.*
fry (to) braten.
    fried eggs Spiegeleier, *pl.*
    fried potatoes Bratkartoffeln, *pl.*
frying pan Bratpfanne, *f.*
fuel Brennstoff, *m.*
fulfill (to) erfüllen.
full voll.
fully voll.
fun Scherz, *m;* Spass, *m.*
    to have fun sich amüsieren.
    to make fun sich lustig machen.
function Funktion, *f.*
function (to) funktionieren.
fund Fonds, *m.*
fundamental grundlegend; wesentlich.
funeral Begräbnis, *n.*
funny komisch.
fur Pelz, *m.*
furious wütend, rasend.
furnace Ofen, *m.*
furnish (to) möblieren.
furniture Möbel, *f.*
furrow Furche, *f.*
further weiter.
fury Wut, *f.*
future Zukunft (noun, *f.); zukünftig (adj.).*

G

gaiety Fröhlichkeit, *f.*
gain Gewinn, *m.*
gain (to) gewinnen.
gallant tapfer, ritterlich.
gallery Galerie, *f.*
gallop Galopp, *m.*
gamble (to) spielen.
game Spiel, *n.*
garage Garage, *f.*
garbage Abfälle, *pl.*
garden Garten, *m.*
gardener, Gärtner, *m.*
garlic Knoblauch, *n.*
gas Gas, *n.*
gasoline Benzin, *n.*
gate Tor, *n.*
gather (to) sammeln.
gay lustig.
gear Getriebe, *n.*
gem Edelstein, *m.*
general General, *m.* (military); allgemein (adj.).
generality Allgemeinheit, *f.*
generalize (to) verallgemeinern.
generation Geschlecht, *n.*
generosity Freigebigkeit, *f .;* Grossmut, *f.*
    (magnanimity).
generous grosszügig.
genius Genie, *n.*
genteel fein, vornehm.

gentle artig, vornehm, sanft.
gentleman Herr, *m.*
gentleness Sanftheit, *f.*
genuine echt.
geographical geographisch.
geography Geographie, *f.*
germ Keim, *m.*
German Deutscher (noun, *m.);* deutsch (adj.).
gesture Gebärde, *f.*
get (to) bekommen, erwerben, holen (fetch);
    werden (become);
        get down hinunterkommen.
        get off absteigen.
        get up aufstehen.
ghastly grässlich.
ghost geist, *m.*
giant Riese, *m.*
gift Geschenk, *n.*
gifted begabt.
girl Mädchen, *n.*
give (to) geben.
    to give back zurückgeben
glad froh.
gladly gern.
glance Blick, *m.*
glass Glas, *n.*
    looking glass Spiegel, *m.*
glasses Brille, *f.*
gleam Schein, *m.;* Schimmer, *m.*
gleam (to) scheinen.
glitter Glanz, *m;* Glitzen, *n.*
globe Kugel, *f.*
gloomy düster.
glorious glorreich.
glory Ruhm, *m.*
glove Handschuh, *m.*
glow Glut, *f.;* Glühen, *n.*
glue Leim, *m.*
go (to) gehen
    to go away weggehen.
    to go back zurückgehen.
    to go in hineingehen.
    to go out herausgehen, ausgehen.
    to go to bed zu Bett gehen.
God Gott, *m.*
godchild Patenkind, *n.*
godfather, Pate, *m.*
godmother Patin, *f.*
gold Gold, *n.*
golden golden.
golf Golf, *m.*
good gut.
    Good afternoon! Guten Tag!
    Good evening! Guten Abend!
    Good morning! Guten Morgen!
    Good night! Gute Nacht!
good-bye Auf Wiedersehen!
good-looking gut aussehend.
goodness Güte, *f.*
goods Waren, *pl.*
goodwill guter Wille, *m.*
goose Gans, *f.*

gossip Klatsch, *m.*
gossip (to) klatschen.
govern (to) regieren.
grace Gnade, *f.;* Anmut, *f.* (charm).
graceful anmutig.
grade Grad, *m.*
grain Korn, *n.*
grammar Grammatik, *f.*
grand grossartig.
grandchild Enkelkind, *n.*
granddaughter Enkelin, *f.*
grandfather Grossvater, *m.*
grandmother Grossmutter, *f.*
grandson Enkel, *m.*
grant Bewilligung, *f.;* Schenkung, *f.*
grant (to) bewilligen.
grape Weintraube, *f.*
grapefruit Pompelmuse, *f.*
grasp Griff, *m.*
grasp (to) greifen.
grass Gras, *n.*
grateful dankbar.
gratitude Dankbarkeit, *f.*
grave Grab, (noun, *n.*); ernst (adj.).
gravy Sauce, *f.*
gray grau.
grease Fett, *n.*
great gross.
greatness Grösse, *f.*
greedy gierig; gefrässig.
green grün.
greet (to) grüssen.
greeting Gruss, *m.*
grief Kummer, *m.*
grieve (to) sich grämen.
grin (to) grinsen.
grind (to) mahlen.
groan Stöhnen, *n.*
groan (to) stöhnen.
grocer Kolonialwarenhändler, *m.*
grocery store Kolonialwarenladen, *m.*
gross grob.
ground Boden, *m.*
group Gruppe, *f.*
group (to) gruppieren.
grow (to) wachsen; bauen (crops).
growth Gewächs, *n.*
grudge Groll, *m.*
guaranteed garantiert.
guess Vermutung, *f.*
guess (to) raten.
guide Führer, *m.*
gum Zahnfleisch, *n.* (teeth).
    chewing gum   Kaugummi, *n.*
gun Gewehr, *n.*
gush Erguss, *m.*
gush (to) hervorströmen.

H

habit Gewohnheit, *f.*
habitual gewöhnlich.

hail Hagel, *m.*
hair Haar, *n.*
hairdo Frisur, *f.*
hairdresser Frisör, *m.*
hairpin Haarnadel, *f.*
half halb.
hall Halle, *f.;* Saal, *m.* Diele, *f.*
ham Schinken, *m.*
hammer Hammer, *m.*
hand Hand, *f.*
hand (to) reichen.
handbag Handtasche, *f.*
handful Handvoll, *f.*
handkerchief Taschentuch, *n.*
handle Griff, *m.*
handle (to) tun.
handsome stattlich.
handy handlich.
hang (to) hängen.
happen (to) geschehen.
happiness Glück, *n.*
happy glücklich.
harbor Hafen, *m.*
hard hart.
harden (to) härten.
hardly kaum.
hardness Härte, *f.*
hardware Eisenwaren, *pl.*
hardware store Eisenwarengeschäft, *n.*
hardy abgehärtet.
hare Hase, *m.*
harm Schaden, *m.*
harm (to) schädigen.
harmful schädlich.
harmless harmlos.
harmonious harmonisch.
harmony Harmonie, *f.*
harsh barsch.
harvest Ernte, *f.*
haste Eile, *f.*
hasten (to) eilen.
hat Hut, *m.*
hate Hass, *m.*
hate (to) hassen.
hateful gehässig.
hatred Hass, *m.*
haughty stolz.
have (to) haben.
haven Hafen, *m.*
hay Heu, *n.*
he er.
head Kopf, *m.* (of a person); Chef, *m.* (of a firm);
    Haupt, *n.* (of a government).
headache Kopfschmerzen, *pl.*
heal (to) heilen.
health Gesundheit, *f.*
healthy gesund.
heap Haufen, *m.*
heap (to) (auf)häufen.
hear (to) hören.
hearing Gehör, *n.*
heart Herz, *n.*

heaven Himmel, *m.*
heavy schwer.
hedge Hecke, *f.;* Zaun, *m.*
heel Ferse, *f.* (of the foot); Absatz, *m.* (of a shoe).
height Höhe, *f.*
heir Erbe, *m.*
hell Hölle, *f.*
helm Ruder, *n.*
help Hilfe, *f.*
help (to) helfen.
helpful behilflich.
hem Saum, *m.*
hen Huhn, *n.;* Henne, *f.*
her ihr (pers. pr., dat.; poss. adj.);
    sie (pers. pr., acc.).
herb Kraut, *n.*
herd Herde, *f.*
here hier.
herewith hiermit.
hero Held, *m.*
heroic heldenhaft, heroisch.
heroine Heldin, *f.*
herring Hering, *m.*
hers ihr(er, -e, -es).
herself sie (ihr) selbst; sich.
hesitate (to) zögern.
hide (to) verstecken.
hideous scheusslich.
high hoch.
higher höher.
hill Hügel, *m.*
him ihn (acc.); ihm (dat.).
himself er (ihm, ihn) selbst; sich.
hinder (to) hindern.
hint Wink, *m.*
hint (to) andeuten.
hip Hüfte, *f.*
hire (to) mieten.
his sein (poss. adj.); sein(er, -e, -es) (pron.).
hiss (to) zischen.
historian Geschichtsschreiber, *m.*
historical historisch.
history Geschichte, *f.*
hoarse heiser.
hoe Hacke, *f.*
hold Halt, *m.*
hold (to) halten.
hole Loch, *n.*
holiday Feiertag, *m.*
holidays Ferien, *pl.*
holy heilig.
homage Huldigung, *f.*
home Heim, *n.*
honest ehrlich.
honesty Ehrlichkeit, *f.*
honey Honig, *m.*
honeymoon Flitterwochen, *pl.*
honor Ehre, *f.*
honor (to) ehren.
honorable ehrenvoll.
hood Kapuze, *f.;* Dach, *n.* (car).
hoof Huf, *m.*

hook Haken, *m.*
hope Hoffnung, *f.*
hope (to) hoffen.
hopeful hoffnungsvoll.
hopeless hoffnungslos.
horizon Horizont, *m.*
horizontal horizontal.
horn (auto) Hupe, *f.*
horrible schrecklich.
horse Pferd, *n.*
horseback (on) zu Pferde.
hosiery Strümpfe, *f.*
hospitable gastfrei.
hospital Krankenhaus, *n.*
host Gastgeber, *m.;* Wirt, *m.*
hostess Gastgeberin, *f.;* Wirtin, *f.*
hostile feindlich.
hot heiss.
hotel Hotel, *n.;* Gasthof, *m.*
hour Stunde, *f.*
house Haus, *n.*
household Haushalt, *m.*
housekeeper Haushälterin, *f.*
housemaid Hausmädchen, *n.*
how wie
    How are you?   Wie geht's?
however dennoch.
howl Heulen, *n.*
howl (to) heulen.
human menschlich.
humane human.
humanity Menschlichkeit, *f.*
humble demütig.
humid feucht.
humiliate erniedrigen, demütigen.
humility Demut, *f.*
humor Humor, *m.*
hundred hundert.
hundredth hundertste.
hunger Hunger, *m.*
hungry hungrig.
hunt Jagd, *f.*
hunter Jäger, *m.*
hurricane Orkan, *m.*
hurry Eile, *f.*
    Hurry up!   Beeilen Sie sich!
hurt (to) verwunden; verletzen.
husband Mann, *m.;* Gatte, *m.*
hush (to) schweigen.
hyphen Bindestrich, *m.*
hypocrite Heuchler, *m.*

I

I ich.
ice Eis, *n.*
ice cream Eis, *n.*
icy eisig.
idea Idee, *f.;* Einfall, *m.*
ideal Ideal, (noun, *n.);* ideal (adj.).
idealism Idealismus, *m.*
idealist Idealist, *m.*

identical identisch.
identity Identität, *f.*
idiot Idiot, *m.*
idle müssig.
idleness Müssigkeit, *f.*
if wenn, ob.
ignoble unedel.
ignorance Unwissenheit, *f.*
ignorant unwissend.
ignore (to) ignorieren.
ill krank.
illegal gesetzwidrig, ungesetzlich.
illness Krankheit, *f.*
illusion Täuschung, *f.*
illustrate (to) illustrieren.
illustration Abbildung, *f.*
image Einbildungskraft, *f.;* Ebenbild, *n.;* Bild, *n.*
imagination Fantasie, *f.*
imagine (to) sich einbilden.
imitate (to) nachahmen.
imitation Nachahmung, *f.*
immediate unmittelbar.
immediately sogleich, sofort.
immigrant Immigrant, *m.*
imminent bevorstehend.
immobility Unbeweglichkeit, *f.*
immoral unmoralisch.
immorality Unsittlichkeit, *f.*
immortal unsterblich.
immortality Unsterblichkeit, *f.*
impartial unparteiisch.
impassible gefühllos.
impatience Ungeduld, *f.*
imperfect Vergangenheit (noun, *f.*) (in grammar); unvollkommen (adj.).
impertinence Unverschämtheit, *f.*
impetuosity Ungestüm, *n.*
import Einfuhr, *f.;* Import, *m.*
import (to) einführen, importieren.
important wichtig.
imported importiert.
importer Importeur, *m.*
impossible unmöglich.
impress (to) Eindruck machen.
impression Eindruck, *m.*
imprison (to) einsperren.
improve (to) verbessern.
improvement Verbesserung, *f.*
improvise (to) improvisieren.
imprudence Unvorsichtigkeit, *f.*
imprudent unklug.
impulse Antrieb, *m.*
impure unrein.
in in (dat.).
inadequate unzulänglich.
inaugurate (to) eröffnen.
incapable unfähig.
incapacity Unfähigkeit, *f.*
inch Zoll, *m.*
incident Vorfall, *m.*
include (to) einschliessen.
included eingeschlossen.

income Einkommen, *n.*
income tax Einkommensteuer, *f.*
incomparable unvergleichlich.
incompatible unvereinbar.
incompetent untauglich; unzulänglich.
incomplete unvollständig.
inconvenient lästig, unbequem.
incorrect unrichtig.
increase Erhöhung, *f.*
increase (to) sich vermehren, erhöhen.
incredible unglaublich.
indebted verschuldet; verpflichtet.
indecision Unentschlossenheit, *f.*
indeed tatsächlich.
independence Unabhängigkeit, *f.*
independent unabhängig.
index Inhaltsverzeichnis, *n.*
index finger Zeigefinger, *m.*
indicate (to) zeigen.
indicative Indikativ (noun, *m.*) (in grammar); anzeigend (adj.).
indifference Gleichgültigkeit, *f.*
indifferent gleichgültig.
indigestion Verdauungsstörung, *f.*
indignant entrüstet.
indignation Entrüstung, *f.*
indirect indirekt.
indiscreet indiskret.
indiscretion Unbedachtsamkeit, *f.*
indispensable unentbehrlich.
individual einzeln.
indolent träge.
indoors im Hause.
induce (to) veranlassen.
indulge (to) sich hingeben.
indulgence Nachsichtigkeit, *f.*
indulgent nachsichtig.
industrial industriell.
industrious fleissig.
industry Industrie, *f.*
inefficient unfähig.
infancy Kindheit, *f.*
infant kleines Kind, *n.*
infantry Infanterie, *f.*
infection Infektion, *f.*
inferior minderwertig.
infernal höllisch.
infinite unendlich.
infinity Unendlichkeit, *f.*
influence Einfluss, *m.*
influence (to) beeinflussen.
inform (to) benachrichtigen.
information Auskunft, *f.;* Nachricht, *f.* (news).
ingenious geistig.
ingenuity Scharfsinn, *m.*
inhabit (to) bewohnen.
inhabitant Einwohner, *m.*
inherit (to) erben.
inheritance Erbgut, *n.*
inhuman unmenschlich.
initial Anfangsbuchstabe, *m.*
initiate (to) einweihen.

initiative Initiative, *f.*
injection Einspritzung, *f.*
injury Verletzung, *f.*
injustice Ungerechtigkeit, *f.*
ink Tinte, *f.*
inkwell Tintenfass, *n.*
inland Binnenland, *n.*
inn Gasthof, *m.*
innkeeper Gastwirt, *m.*
innocent unschuldig.
innocence Unschuld *f.*
inquire (to) sich erkundigen.
inquiry Erkundigung, *f.;* Auskunft, *f.*
insane geisteskrank.
inscription Inschrift, *f.*
insect Insekt, *n.*
insensible unempfindlich.
inseparable unzertrennlich.
inside drinnen.
insight Einsicht, *f.*
insignificant unbedeutend.
insincere unaufrichtig.
insinuate (to) andeuten.
insist (to) bestehen auf.
insistence Beharren, *n.*
inspect (to) besichtigen.
inspection Besichtigung, *f.*
inspiration Inspiration, *f.*
install (to) einstellen, installieren.
installment Rate, *f.;* Teilzahlung, *f.*
instance Beispiel, *n.;* Fall, *m.*
instant Augenblick, *m.*
instantly sofort.
instead of anstatt (gen.).
institute (to) herbeiführen.
institution Anstalt, *f.*
instruct (to) unterrichten.
instructor Lehrer, *m.*
instruction Anweisung, *f.;* Unterricht, *m.* (teaching).
instrument Instrument, *n.*
insufficient ungenügend.
insult Beleidigung, *f.*
insult (to) beleidigen.
insurance Versicherung, *f.*
insure (to) versichern.
intact unversehrt.
intellectual intellektuell.
intelligence Intelligenz, *f.*
intelligent intelligent.
intend (to) beabsichtigen.
intense intensiv.
intensity Heftigkeit, *f.*
intention Absicht, *f.*
interest Interesse, *n.*
interesting interessant.
interfere (to) sich einmischen.
interior Innere, *n.*
intermediate mittel.
intermission Pause, *f.*
international international.
interpret (to) interpretieren, ubersetzen;
    deuten (emotion).

interpreter Dolmetscher, *m.*
interrupt (to) unterbrechen.
interval Pause, *f.;* Zwischenzeit, *f.*
interview Interview, *n.*
intimacy Vertrautheit, *f.*
intimate vertraut.
into in (dat. or acc.).
intolerant unduldsam.
intonation Tonfall, *m.*
introduce (to) vorstellen.
introduction Vorstellung, *f.*
intuition Einfühlungsgabe, *f.*
invade (to) einfallen.
invent (to) erfinden.
invention Erfindung, *f.*
inventor Erfinder, *m.*
invert (to) umkehren, umdrehen.
invest (to) investieren; anlegen (money).
investment Kapitalanlage, *f.*
invisible unsichtbar.
invitation Einladung, *f.*
invite (to) einladen.
invoice Faktura, *f.*
invoke (to) anrufen.
involve (to) verwickeln.
iodine Jod, *n.*
Irish irländisch.
iron Eisen, *n.* (metal); Bügeleisen, *n.* (for ironing).
iron (to) bügeln.
irony Ironie, *f.*
irregular unregelmässig.
irresistible unwiderstehlich.
irritate (to) reizen, ärgern.
island Insel, *f.*
isolate (to) absondern, isolieren.
issue Ausgabe, *f.*
it es.
Italian Italiener (noun, *m.*); italienisch (adj.).
itch (to) jucken.
its sein (poss. adj.); sein(er, -e, -es), (poss. pron.).
itself es (ihm) selbst, sich.
ivory Elfenbein, *n.*
ivy Efeu, *n.*

J

jacket Jacke, *f.*
jail Gefängnis, *n.*
jam Marmelade, *f.*
January Januar, *m.*
Japanese Japaner (noun, *m.*); japanisch (adj.).
jar Krug, *m.*
jaw Kiefer, *m.*
jealous eifersüchtig.
jealousy Eifersucht, *f.*
jelly Gelee, *n.*
jewel Juwel, *m.*
jeweler Juwelier, *m.*
Jewish jüdisch.
job Arbeit, *f.*
join (to) binden.
joint Gelenk, *n.*

joke Witz, *m.*; Scherz, *m.*; Spass, *m.*
joke (to) scherzen.
jolly lustig.
journalist Journalist, *m.*
journey Reise, *f.*
joy Freude, *f.*
joyous freudig.
judge Richter, *m.*
judge (to) urteilen.
judgment Urteil, *n.*
judicial gerichtlich.
juice Saft, *m.*
July Juli, *m.*
jump Sprung, *m.*
jump (to) springen.
June Juni, *m.*
junior jünger.
jungle Dschungel, *m.*
just recht (fair); gerecht (justice); gerade (recent).
justice Gerechtigkeit, *f.*
justify (to) rechtfertigen.

K

keen scharf.
keep (to) halten (retain); hindern (hinder).
    keep off   abhalten.
    keep on   fortfahren.
    keep up   aufrechterhalten.
kernel Kern, *m.*
kettle Kessel, *m.*
key Schlüssel, *m.*
kick Fusstritt, *m.*
kick (to) ausschlagen.
kidneys Nieren, *pl.*
kill (to) töten.
kin Blutsverwandtschaft, *f.*
kind Art (noun, *f.*); gütig (adj.).
kindly freundlich.
kindness Güte, *f.*; Freundlichkeit, *f.*
king König, *m.*
kingdom Königreich, *n.*
kiss Kuss, *m.*
kiss (to) küssen.
kitchen Küche, *f.*
kite Drache, *m.*
knee Knie, *n.*
kneel (to) knieen.
knife Messer, *n.*
knight Ritter, *m.*
knit (to) stricken.
knock Schlag, *m.*; Hieb, *m.* (beating); Klopf, *m.*; Griff, *m.* (door).
knock (to) klopfen, schlagen, hauen, stossen; anklopfen (door).
knot Knoten, *m.*
know (to) wissen (have knowledge of); kennen (be acquainted with).
knowledge Kenntnis, *f.*

L

label Zettel, *m.*
labor Arbeit, *f.*
laboratory Laboratorium, *n.*
laborer Arbeiter, *m.*
lace Spitze, *f.* (ornamental); Senkel, *m.* (of a shoe).
lack Mangel, *m.*
lack (to) mangeln.
lady Dame, *f.*
lake See, *m.*
lamb Lamm, *n.*
lame lahm.
lamp Lampe, *f.*
land Land, *n.*
land (to) landen.
landscape Landschaft, *f.*
language Sprache, *f.*
languish (to) schmachten.
languor Schlaffheit, *f.*
lantern Laterne, *f.*
large gross
last letzt.
    last year   voriges Jahr.
last (to) dauern.
lasting dauernd.
latch Klinke, *f.* (knob); Drücker.
late spät.
lately kürzlich.
latter letzter.
laugh (to) lachen.
laughter Gelächter, *n.*
lavish freigebig.
lavish (to) überhäufen.
law Gesetz, *n.*; Recht, *n.* (code).
lawful rechtmässig.
lawn Rasenplatz, *m.*
lawyer Rechtsanwalt, *m.*
lay (to) legen.
layer Schicht, *f.*
lazy faul.
lead Blei, *n.*
lead (to) führen.
leader Führer, *m.*
leadership Führung, *f.*
leaf Blatt, *n.*
leak Leck, *n.*
lean (to) lehnen.
leap (to) springen.
leap Sprung, *m.*
learn (to) lernen.
learned gelehrt.
learning Gelehrsamkeit, *f.*
least wenigste.
    at least   mindestens.
leather Leder, *n.*
leave (to) verlassen (abandon); weggehen (on foot); wegfahren (by vehicle).
lecture Vortrag, *m.*

left linke.
to the left links.
leg Bein, *n.*
leg of lamb Hammelkeule, *f.*
legal gesetzmässig.
legend Sage, *f.*
legislation Gesetzgebung, *f.*
legislator Gesetzgeber, *m.*
legitimate legitim.
leisure Freizeit, *f.*
lemon Zitrone, *f.*
lemonade Limonade, *f.*
lend (to) leihen.
length Länge, *f.*
lengthen (to) verlängern.
less weniger.
lesson Stunde, *f.;* Lektion, *f.* (in book).
let (to) lassen; gestatten (allow); vermieten (rent).
letter Buchstabe, *m.* (alphabet); Brief, *m.* (correspondence).
level Niveau, *n.*
liable haftbar.
liar Lügner, *m.;* Lügnerin, *f.*
liberal liberal.
liberty Freiheit, *f.*
library Bibliothek, *f.*
license Erlaubnis, *f.*
lick (to) lecken.
lie Lüge, *f.*
lie (to) lügen (falsify); liegen (rest).
lieutenant Leutnant, *m.*
life Leben, *n.*
lift (to) heben.
light Licht (noun, *n.*); leicht (adj.).
light (to) anzünden.
to light up erleuchten.
lighten (to) erhellen (brightness); erleichtern (weight).
lighter Feuerzeug, *n.*
lighthouse Leuchtturm, *m.*
lighting Beleuchtung, *f.*
lightning Blitz, *m.*
like wie (as); ähnlich (similar).
like (to) gern haben, mögen, gefallen.
I'd like to ich möchte.
likely wahrscheinlich.
likeness Ähnlichkeit, *f.*
likewise gleichfalls.
liking Vorliebe, *f.*
limb, Glied, *n.*
limit Grenze, *f.*
limit (to) begrenzen.
limp hinken.
line Linie, *f.*
line up (to) sich anstellen.
linen Wäsche, *f.* (household); Leinwand, *f.* (fabric).
linger (to) weilen.
lingerie Damenwäsche, *f.*
lining Futter, *n.*
link Glied, *n.*
link (to) verbinden.

lion Löwe, *m.*
lip Lippe, *f.*
lipstick Lippenstift, *m.*
liquid Flüssigkeit (noun, *f.*); flüssig (adj.).
liquor Alkohol, *m.;* Likör, *m.* (liqueur).
list Liste, *f.*
literary literarisch.
literature Literatur, *f.*
little klein.
a little ein wenig.
live lebend.
live (to) leben.
lively lebhaft, lebendig.
liver Leber, *f.*
load Last, *f.* (burden); Ladung, *f.* (cargo).
load (to) laden.
loan (ver)leihen.
lobby Vorhalle, *f.*
local lokal.
locate (to) orientieren, finden.
location Platz, *m;* Gegend, *f.*
lock Schloss, *n.*
lock (to) zuschliessen.
locomotive Lokomotive, *f.*
log Klotz, *m.*
logic Logik, *f.*
logical logisch.
loneliness Einsamkeit, *f.*
lonely einsam.
long lang.
long ago vor langer Zeit; längst.
a long time lange.
long (to) sehnen.
longer länger.
longing Sehnsucht, *f.*
look Blick, *m.*
look (to) schauen; aussehen (appear).
Look! Sehen Sie her!
Look out! Passen Sie auf!
to look forward entgegensehen; sich freuen auf (rejoice).
loose lose.
loosen (to) lösen.
lose (to) verlieren.
loss Verlust, *m.;* Schaden, *m.*
lost verloren.
lot (a) viel (much).
loud laut.
love Liebe, *f.*
love (to) lieben.
lovely schön, reizend.
low niedrig.
lower (to) niederholen.
loyal treu.
loyalty Treue, *f.*
luck Glück, *n.*
lucky glücklich.
luggage Gepäck, *n.*
luminous leuchtend.
lump Klumpen, *m.*
lunch Mittagessen, *n.*
lung Lunge, *f.*

luxurious prächtig.
luxury Luxus, *m.*

M

machine Maschine, *f.*
mad verrückt.
madam gnädige Frau.
made gemacht.
madness Wahnsinn, *m.*
magazine Zeitschrift, *f.*
magistrate Magistrat, *m.*
magnificent prachtvoll.
maid Dienstmädchen, *n.* (servant).
mail Post, *f.*
main haupt—
　　the main thing　die Hauptsache.
maintain (to) erhalten; unterhalten (support).
maintenance Unterhalt, *m.*
majesty Majestät, *f.*
major Major, *m.*
majority Mehrheit, *f.*
make (to) machen.
man Mann, *m.;* Mensch, *m.* (human being).
manage (to) führen, verwalten.
management Leitung, *f.*
manager Leiter, *m.*
manicure Maniküre, *f.*
mankind Menschheit, *f.*
manner Art, *f.;* Weise, *f.*
manners Bildung, *f.*
manufacture Fabrikation, *f.*
manufactured hergestellt.
many viele.
map Karte, *f.*
marble Marmor, *m.*
March März, *m.*
march Marsch, *m.*
march (to) marschieren.
margin Rand, *m.*
marine Marine, *f.*
mark Kennzeichen, *n.*
mark (to) markieren.
market Markt, *m.*
marketplace Marktplatz, *m.*
marriage Heirat, *f.*
married verheiratet.
marry (to) heiraten, sich verheiraten; trauen
　　(perform the ceremony).
　　　to marry off　verheiraten.
marvel Wunder, *n.*
marvel (to) sich wundern.
marvelous wunderbar.
masculine männlich.
mask Maske, *f.*
mask (to) maskieren.
mason Maurer, *m.*
mass Masse, *f.;* Messe, *f.* (church).
massage Massage, *f.*
master Meister, *m.*
master (to) meistern.
masterpiece Meisterwerk, *n.;* Meisterstück, *n.*

match Streichholz, *n.* (incendiary); Gleiche, *n.*
　　(comparative).
match (to) zusammenpassen.
material Material, *n.*
maternal mütterlich.
mathematics Mathematik, *f.*
matter Angelegenheit, *f.* (affair); Stoff, *m.*
　　(substance).
　　　What's the matter?　Was ist los?
mattress Matratze, *f.*
mature erwachsen.
May Mai, *m.*
may dürfen (to be allowed); mögen (to be likely).
mayor Bürgermeister, *m.*
me mich (acc.); mir (dat.).
meadow Wiese, *f.*
meal Mahl, *n.*
mean übel (unkind).
mean (to) meinen (to be of the opinion); bedeuten
　　(to signify).
　　　What does it mean?　Was bedeutet das?
meaning Bedeutung, *f.* (significance).
means Mittel, *n.*
meanwhile inzwischen.
measure Mass, *n.*
measure (to) messen.
meat Fleisch, *n.*
mechanic Mechaniker, *m.*
mechanical mechanisch.
medal Medaille, *f.* (jewel); Orden, *m.*
medical ärztlich.
medicine Medizin, *f.* (science); Arznei, *f.*
　　(medication).
mediocre mittelmässig.
mediocrity Mittelmässigkeit, *f.*
meditate (to) grübeln, sinnen, nachdenken.
meditation Nachdenken, *n.*
medium mittel.
meet (to) treffen.
　　　Pleased to meet you　Sehr erfreut Sie
　　　　　　　　　　　　　kennenzulernen.
meeting Versammlung, *f.*
melon Melone, *f.*
melt (to) schmelzen.
member Mitglied, *n.*
memorize (to) auswendig lernen.
memory Gedächtnis, *n.*
mend (to) reparieren.
mental geistig.
mention (to) erwähnen.
menu Speisekarte, *f.*
merchandise Ware, *f.*
merchant Kaufmann, *m.*
merciful barmherzig.
merciless unbarmherzig.
mercury Quecksilber, *n.*
mercy Barmherzigkeit, *f.*
merit Verdienst, *n.*
merit (to) verdienen.
merry fröhlich, heiter, lustig.
message Nachricht, *f.*
messenger Bote, *m.*

metal Metall, *n.*
metallic metallisch.
method Methode, *f.*
Mexican Mexicaner (noun, *m.*); mexikanisch (adj.).
microphone Mikrofon, *n.*
middle Mitte, *f.*
middle age mittleres Alter, *n.*
Middle Ages Mittelalter, *n.*
midnight Mitternacht, *f.*
midway halbwegs.
might Macht, *f.*
mighty mächtig.
mild leicht, mild, sanft.
mildness Milde, *f.*
mile Meile, *f.*
military militärisch.
milk Milch, *f.*
milkman Milchhändler, *m.*
milky way Milchstrasse, *f.*
mill Mühle, *f.*
miller Müller, *m.*; Müllerin, *f.*
milliner Modistin, *f.*
million Million, *f.*
millionaire Millionär, *m.*
mind Verstand, *m.*; Sinn, *m.*
mind (to) beachten (to pay heed); aufpassen (*also* to watch over).
mine Grube, *f.* (coal).
mine (poss. pr.) mein(er, -e, -es).
miner Bergmann, *m.*
mineral mineralisch.
mineral Mineral, *n.*
minister Minister (state), *m.*; Geistliche, *m.* (church).
ministry Ministerium, *n.* (state); Amt, *n.* (church).
mink Nerz, *m.*
minor jüngere.
minority Minderheit, *f.*
minute Minute, *f.*
> Just a minute!   Einen Augenblick!
> Wait a minute!   Warten Sie einen Augenblick!
> Any minute now!   Jeden Augenblick!

miracle Wunder, *n.*
mirror Spiegel, *m.*
miscellaneous gemischt, verschieden.
mischief Unfug, *m.*
mischievous boshaft.
miser Geizhals, *m.*
miserly geizig.
misfortune Unglück, *n.*
Miss Fräulein, *n.*
miss (to) versäumen.
mission Mission, *f.*
mist Nebel, *m.*
mistake Fehler, *m.*
mistaken irrtümlich.
> You are mistaken. Sie sind im Irrtum.

Mister Herr.
mistrust (to) misstrauen.
misunderstand (to) missverstehen.
misunderstanding Missverständnis, *n.*
misuse (to) missbrauchen.

mix (to) mischen.
mixture Mischung, *f.*
mob Pöbel, *m.*
mobile beweglich.
mobilization Mobilmachung, *f.*
mobilize (to) mobilisieren.
mock (to) verspotten.
mockery Gespött, *n.*
mode Mode, *f.*
model Modell, *n.*
moderate mässigen.
moderation Mässigkeit, *f.*
modern modern.
modest bescheiden.
modesty Bescheidenheit, *f.*
modification Veränderung, *f.*
modify (to) verändern.
moist feucht.
moisten anfeuchten.
moment Augenblick, *m.*; Moment, *m.*
> Just a moment   Einen Augenblick.

monarchy Monarchie, *f.*
monastery Kloster, *n.*
Monday Montag, *m.*
money Geld, *n.*
monk Mönch, *m.*
monkey Affe, *m.*
monologue Monolog, *m.*
monotonous eintönig.
monotony Eintönigkeit, *f.*
monster Ungeheuer, *n.*
monstrous ungeheuer.
month Monat, *m.*
monthly monatlich.
monument Denkmal, *n.*
monumental monumental.
mood Stimmung, *f.*; Laune, *f.* (temper).
moody launisch.
moon Mond, *m.*
moonlight Mondschein, *m.*
mop Mop, *m.*
moral Moral, *f.*
morality Sittlichkeit, *f.*
more mehr.
moreover darüber hinaus.
morning Morgen, *m.*
morsel Bissen, *m.*
mortal sterblich.
mortality Sterblichkeit, *f.*
mortgage Hypothek, *f.*
mortgage (to) verpfänden.
mosquito Mücke, *f.*
most am meisten.
> most of   die meisten.

mostly meistens.
moth Motte, *f.*
mother Mutter, *f.*
mother-in-law Schwiegermutter, *f.*
motion Bewegung, *f.*
motionless bewegungslos.
motivate (to) beweisen, begründen.
motor Motor, *m.*
mount Hügel, *m.*

mountain Berg, *m.*
mountainous bergig.
mourn (to) trauern.
mournful traurig.
mourning Trauer, *f.*
mouse Maus, *f.*
mouth Mund, *m.*
move (to) bewegen.
movement Bewegung, *f.*
movies Kino, *n.*
moving rührend.
much viel.
    How much? Wieviel?
mud Schlamm, *m.*
muddy schlammig.
mule Maultier, *n.*
multiply (to) multiplizieren.
multitude Menge, *f.*
mumble (to) murmeln.
municipal städtisch.
munition Munition, *f.*
murder Mord, *m.*
murder (to) ermorden.
murderer Mörder, *m.*
murmur (to) murren.
muscle Muskel, *m.*
museum Museum, *n.*
mushroom Pilz, *m.*
music Musik, *f.*
musical musikalisch.
musician Musiker, *m.*
must müssen.
mustache Schnurrbart, *m.*
mustard Senf, *m.*
mute stumm.
mutton Hammelfleisch, *n.*
my mein
myself ich (mich, mir) selbst.
mysterious geheimnisvoll.
mystery Geheimnis, *n.*

N

nail Nagel, *m.*
nail (to) nageln.
naive harmlos, naive.
naked nackt.
name Name, *m.*
    first name Vorname, *m.*
    last name Zuname, *m.*
    What is your name? Wie heissen Sie?
namely nähmlich.
nap Schläfchen, *n.*
napkin Serviette, *f.*
narrow eng.
nasty garstig.
nation Nation, *f.*
national national.
nationality Nationalität, *f.*
native Eingeborene, *m., f., n.*
    native country Heimat, *f.*
natural natürlich.

naturally natürlich.
nature Natur, *f.*
naughty unartig.
naval see-.
navy Flotte, *f.*
near nah.
nearly beinahe.
neat nett, ordentlich.
neatness Niedlichkeit, *f.*; Sauberkeit, *f.*
necessary notwendig.
necessity, Notwendigkeit, *f.*
neck Hals, *m.*
necklace Halsband, *n.*
necktie Krawatte, *f.*; Schlips, *m.* (colloquial).
need Not, *f.*; Bedürfnis, *f.*
need (to) brauchen.
needle Nadel, *f.*
needless unnötig.
needy dürftig, bedürftig.
negative Negativ, *m.*
neglect Vernachlässigung, *f.*
neglect (to) vernachlässigen.
negotiate (to) unterhandeln.
negotiation Unterhandlung, *f.*
Negro Neger, *m.*
neighbor Nachbar, *m.*
neighborhood Nachbarschaft, *f.*
neither kein(er,-e,-es).
    neither...nor weder...noch.
nephew Neffe, *m.*
nerve Nerv, *m.*
    What a nerve! So eine Frechheit!
nervous nervös.
nest Nest, *n.*
net Netz, *n.*
neuter Neutrum, *n.*
neutral neutral.
never niemals, nie.
    Never mind! Das macht nichts!
nevertheless trotzdem; auf alle Fälle.
new neu.
news Nachrichten, *pl.*
newspaper Zeitung, *f.*
next nächst.
nice nett.
nickname Spitzname, *m.*
niece Nichte, *f.*
night Nacht, *f.*
nightgown Nachthemd, *n.*
nightmare Alpdrücken, *n.*
nine neun.
nineteen neunzehn
ninety neunzig.
ninth neunte.
no nein; kein (adj).
    no longer nicht mehr.
    no matter ungeachtet (gen.)
nobility Adel, *m.*
noble adlig.
nobody niemand.
noise Geräusch, *n.*
noisy geräuschvoll.

nominate (to) ernennen.
nomination Ernennung, *f.*
none kein(e, -er, -es).
nonsense Unsinn, *m.*
noon Mittag, *m.*
nor noch.
normal normal.
north Norden, *m.*
northern nordisch, nördlich.
northeast Nordosten, *m.*
northwest Nordwesten, *m.*
nose Nase, *f.*
nostril Nasenloch, *n.*
not nicht.
note Note, *f.*
note (to) notieren.
notebook Notizbuch, *n.*
nothing nichts.
notice Benachrichtung, *f.*
notice (to) bemerken
notify (to) benachrichtigen.
notion Idee, *f.;* Begriff, *m.*
noun Name, *m.*
nourish (to) nähren.
nourishment Nahrung, *f.*
novel Roman, *m.*
novelty Neuheit, *f.*
November November, *m.*
now jetzt.
    now and then. dann und wann; manchmal.
nowadays heutzutage.
nowhere nirgendwo.
nude nackt, bloss.
nuisance Unfug, *m.*
null null.
    null and void null und nichtig.
numb gefühllos.
number Nummer, *f.*
numerous zahlreich.
nun Nonne, *f.*
nurse Krankenschwester, *f.* (for the sick);
    Kindermädchen (for children).
nursery Kinderstube, *f.* (children); Gärtnerei, *f.*
    (trees)
nursery rhyme Kinderlied, *n.*
nut Nuss, *f.*
nutcracker Nussknacker, *m.*

O

oak Eiche, *f.*
oar Ruder, *n.*
oat Hafer, *m.*
oath Eid, *m.*
obedience Gehorsam, *m.*
obedient gehorsam.
obey (to) gehorchen.
object (to) einwenden, dagegen sein.
objection Einwand, *m.*
objective objektiv.
objectively sachlich.

obligation Verpflichtung, *f.*
oblige (to) verpflichten.
obliging gefällig.
obscure verdunkelt; verworren (meaning).
obscurity Dunkelheit, *f.*
observation Beobachtung, *f.*
observatory Sternwarte, *f.*
observe (to) beobachten.
obstacle Hindernis, *n.*
obstinacy Eigensinn, *m.*
obstinate eigensinnig.
obvious klar.
obviously offenbar, deutlich.
occasion Gelegenheit, *f.*
occasional gelegentlich.
occasionally zuweilen.
occupation Beschäftigung, *f.*
occupy (to) besitzen; besetzen (military).
occur (to) vorkommen (an event); einfallen
    (a thought).
occurrence Vorfall, *m.*
ocean Ozean, *m.*
October Oktober, *m.*
odd ungerade (uneven); sonderbar (unusual).
odor Geruch, *m.*
of von (dat.); aus (dat.) (made of).
    of course natürlich.
off fort, weg.
    off and on ab und zu.
offend (to) beleidigen.
offense Beleidigung, *f.*
offensive beleidigend.
offer (to) anbieten.
offering Gabe, *f.*
office Büro, *n.*
official offiziell.
often oft, oftmals.
oil Öl, *n.*
old alt.
olive Olive, *f.*
olive oil Olivenöl, *n.*
on auf (dat. or acc.); an (dat. or acc.) (date).
once einmal; vormals, einst (formerly).
    at once   sofort.
    once in a while manchmal.
    once more   noch einmal.
one ein(er, -e, -es).
one (pr.) man.
oneself sich, sich selbst.
onion Zwiebel, *f.*
only nur.
open offen.
open (to) öffnen.
opener Öffner, *m.*
opening Öffnung, *f.*
opera Oper, *f.*
operate (to) operieren.
operation Operation, *f.*
opinion Meinung, *f.*
opponent Gegner, *m.*
opportune gelegen.
opportunity Gelegenheit, *f.*

oppose (to) sich widersetzen.
opposite gegenüber.
opposition Widerstand, *m.*
oppress (to) unterdrücken.
oppression Unterdrückung, *f.*
optician Optiker, *m.*
optimism Optimismus, *m.*
optimistic optimistisch.
or oder.
orange Apfelsine, *f.*
orange juice Apfelsinensaft, *m.*
orator Redner, *m.*
orchard Obstgarten, *m.*
orchestra Orchester, *n.*
ordeal Prüfung, *f.*
order Ordnung, *f.* (neatness); Bestellung, *f.*
    (commercial); Befehl, *m.* (command); Orden, *m.*
    (decoration).
    out of order   kaputt.
    to put in order   in Ordnung bringen.
order (to) ordnen (regulate); bestellen (commercial);
    befehlen (command).
ordinary gewöhnlich.
organ Orgel, *f.* (music); Organ, *n.* (anatomy).
organization Organisation, *f.*
organize (to) organisieren.
Orient Orient, *m.*
oriental orientalisch.
origin Ursprung, *m.* (source); Herkunft, *f.* (descent).
original original.
originality Originalität, *f.*
ornament Ornament, *n.*
orphan Waisenkind, *n.*
orthodox orthodox.
other anderer.
ought (to) sollen.
ounce Unze, *f.*
our unser.
ours unser(er, -e, -es).
out aus (dat.); hinaus.
    out of   ausser (dat.)
outcome Folge, *f.;* Ergebnis, *n.*
outdo (to) übertreffen.
outdoors im Freien.
outer äusser.
outlast überdauern.
outlaw Geächtete, *m.*
outlaw (to) ächten.
outlay Auslage, *f.*
outlet Auslass, *m.;* Absatz, *m.* (market)
outline Umriss, *m.*
outlook Aussicht, *f.*
output Produktion, *f.;* Leistung, *f.* (machine).
outrage Schandtat, *f.*
outrageous schändlich.
outside Aussenseite (noun, *f.*); draussen (outdoors);
    ausserhalb (besides).
oval oval.
oven Ofen, *m.*
over über (acc.); vorbei (finished).
    over and over   wieder und wieder.
overboard über Bord.

overcoat Mantel, *m.*
overcome (to) überwinden.
overflow (to) überfliessen.
overlook (to) übersehen.
overrun überrennen.
overseas übersee.
overthrow umstürzen.
overwhelm (to) überwältigen.
owe (to) schulden.
owl Eule, *f.*
own eigen.
own (to) besitzen (possess); bekennen (admit).
owner Eigentümer, *m.*
ox Ochse, *m.*
oxygen Sauerstoff, *m.*
oyster Auster, *f.*

P

pace Schritt, *m.*
pace (to) schreiten.
pacific friedlich.
pack Kartenspiel, *n.* (cards).
pack (to) einpacken.
package Paket, *n.*
page Seite, *f.*
pain Schmerz, *m.*
pain (to) schmerzen.
painful schmerzhaft.
painless schmerzlos.
paint Farbe, *f.*
paint (to) malen (art); anstreichen (a wall).
painter Maler, *m.* (artist); Anstreicher (workman).
painting Gemälde, *n.*
pair Paar, *n.*
pajamas Pyjama, *m.*
palace Palast, *m.*
pale blass.
palm Palme, *f.*
pamphlet Broschüre, *f.*
pan Pfanne, *f.*
pancake Pfannkuchen, *m.*
pane Scheibe, *f.*
panel Füllung, *f.;* Liste, *f.* (persons).
panic Panik, *f.*
panorama Panorama, *n.*
panties Schlüpfer, *m.*
pants Hose, *f.*
paper Papier, *n.*
parachute Fallschirm, *m.*
parade Parade, *f.*
paragraph Paragraph, *m;* Absatz, *m.*
parallel parallel.
paralysis Lähmung, *f.*
paralyzed gelähmt.
parcel Paket, *n.*
pardon Verzeihung, *f.*
pardon (to) vergeben.
parenthesis Klammer, *f.*
parents Eltern, *pl.*
Parisian Pariser, *m.*
park Park, *m.*
park (to) parken.

parliament Parlament, *n.*
parrot Papagei, *m.*
parsley Petersilie, *f.*
part Teil, *n.* (share); Ersatzteil (machinery).
part (to) teilen; sich trennen (separate);
    scheiteln (hair).
partial teilweise.
partiality Vorliebe, *f.*
particular besonder(er, -e, -es).
particularly besonders.
partner Partner, *m.*
party (political) Partei, *f.;* Gesellschaft, *f.*
    (society).
pass Ausweis, *m.*
pass (to) durchgehen, vorbeigehen; passen (cards);
    bestehen (exam).
passage Durchgang, *m.;* Überfahrt, *f.* (travel).
passenger Passagier, *m.*
passion Leidenschaft, *f.*
passionately leidenschaftlich.
passive Passiv, *n.*
passport Pass, *m.*
past Vergangenheit (noun, *f.*); vorbei, vorige
    (time); nach (on the clock).
        ten past six   zehn nach sechs.
paste Kleister, *m.*
paste (to) kleistern.
pastry Gebäck, *n.*
pastry shop Konditorei, *f.*
patch Flicken, *m.*
patch (to) flicken.
patent Patent, *n.*
paternal väterlich.
path Weg, *m.*
pathetic pathetisch.
patience Geduld, *f.*
patient Patient (noun, *m.*); geduldig (adj.).
patriot Patriot, *m.*
patriotic patriotisch.
patron Gönner, *m.*
patronage Gönnerschaft, *f.*
patronize (to) unterstützen.
pattern Muster, *n.*
pause Pause, *f.*
pave (to) pflastern.
pavement Pflaster, *n.*
paw Pfote, *f.*
pay Lohn, *m.;* Löhnung, *f.;* Sold, *m.* (military).
pay (to) zahlen.
payment Bezahlung, *f.*
pea Erbse, *f.*
peace Frieden, *m.*
peaceful friedlich.
peach Pfirsich, *m.*
peak Gipfel, *m.*
peanut Erdnuss, *f.*
pear Birne, *f.*
pearl Perle, *f.*
peasant Bauer, *m.*
pebble Kieselstein, *m.*
peculiar sonderbar.
pedal Pedal, *n.*

pedantic pedantisch.
pedestrian Fussgänger, *m.*
peel Rinde, *f.;* Schale, *f.*
peel (to) schälen.
pen Feder, *f.*
    fountain pen   Füllfeder, *f.*
penalty Strafe, *f.*
pencil Bleistift, *m.*
penetrate (to) durchdringen.
peninsula Halbinsel, *f.*
penitence Reue, *f.*
pension Pension, *f.*
people Leute, *pl.*
pepper Pfeffer, *m.*
peppermint Pfefferminz, *m.*
per pro.
perceive (to) wahrnehmen.
percentage Prozentsatz, *m.*
perfect vollkommen.
perfection Vollkommenheit, *f.*
perfectly gänzlich.
perform (to) verrichten; aufführen (theater or
    surgery).
performance Vorstellung, *f.*
perfume Parfüm, *n.*
perfume (to) parfümieren.
perhaps vielleicht.
period Periode, *f.*
periodical periodisch.
permanent ständig.
permission Erlaubnis, *f.*
permit Erlaubnisschein, *m.*
permit (to) erlauben.
peroxide Hyperoxyd, *n.*
perpetual immerwährend.
perplex verwirren.
persecute (to) verfolgen.
persecution Verfolgung, *f.*
perseverance Ausdauer, *f.*
persist (to) beharren.
person Person, *f.*
personal persönlich.
personality Persönlichkeit., *f.*
perspective Perspektive, *f.*
perspiration Schweiss, *m.*
persuade (to) überreden.
pertaining gehören (zu).
petrol Petroleum, *n.*
petticoat Unterrock, *m.*
petty kleinlich.
pharmacist Apotheker, *m.*
pharmacy Apotheke, *f.*
phenomenon Phänomen, *n.*
philosopher Philosoph, *m.*
philosophical philosophisch.
philosophy Philosophie, *f.*
phonograph Plattenspieler, *m.*
photograph Fotografie, *f.*
photograph (to) aufnehmen.
photographer Fotograf, *m.*
phototast Lichtpause, *f.*
phrase Frase, *f.*

physical körperlich.
physician Arzt, *m;* Doktor, *m.*
piano Klavier, *n.*
pick (to) pflücken.
pick up (to) aufheben.
picnic Piknik, *n.*
picture Bild, *n.*
picturesque malerisch.
pie Torte, *f.*
piece Stück, *n.*
pier Mole, *f.*
pig Schwein, *n.*
pigeon Taube, *f.*
pile Haufen, *m.*
pile (to) aufhäufen.
pilgrim Pilger, *m.*
pill Pille, *f.*
pillar Säule, *f.*
pillow Kissen, *n.*
pilot Pilot, *m.*
pin Stecknadel, *f.*
pinch (to) kneifen.
pink rosa.
pious fromm.
pipe Pfeife, *f.* (tobacco); Rohr, *n.* (plumbing).
pirate Seeräuber, *m.;* Pirat, *m.*
pistol Pistole, *f.*
pitiful mitleidig.
pity Mitleid, *n.*
place Platz, *m.;* Stelle, *f.* (spot, situation);
   Ort, *m.* (locality).
     take place   stattfinden.
place (to) stellen.
plain Ebene (noun, *f.*); einfach (adj.).
plan Plan, *m.* (project); Grundriss, *m.*
plan (to) ausdenken.
plane Flugzeug, *n.*
planet Planet, *m.*
plant Pflanze, *f.*
plant (to) pflanzen.
plaster Verputz, *m.*
plastic Kunststoff (noun, *m.*); plastisch (adj.).
plate Teller, *m.*
platform Bahnsteig, *m.* (station).
platter Platte, *f.*
play Spiel, *n.;* Stück, *n.* (theater).
play (to) spielen.
plea Gesuch, *n.*
plead (to) plädieren.
pleasant angenehm.
please bitte.
please (to) gefallen.
pleasure Vergnügen, *n.*
pledge Pfand, *n.*
plenty genug (enough); reichlich (abundance).
plot Verschwörung, *f.* (conspiracy); Handlung, *f.*
   (of a story).
plot (to) anstiften.
plow Pflug, *m.*
plow (to) pflügen.
plum Pflaume, *f.*
plumber Klempner, *m.*

pneumonia Lungenentzündung, *f.*
pocket Tasche, *f.*
poem Gedicht, *n.*
poet Poet, *m.*
poetic poetisch.
poetry Dichtung, *f.*
point Punkt, *m.;* Spitze, *f.*
point (to) spitzen.
pointed spitz.
poise Gleichgewicht, *n.*
poison Gift, *n.*
poison (to) vergiften.
poisonous giftig.
polar pol—.
pole Pol, *m.*
police Polizei, *f.*
policeman Schutzmann, *m.;* Polizist, *m.*
policy Politik, *f.;* Police, *f.* (insurance).
Polish polnisch.
polish Glanz, *m.*
polish (to) glänzend machen; polieren.
polite höflich.
politeness Höflichkeit, *f.*
political politisch.
pond Teich, *m.*
pool Pfuhl, *m.*
poor arm.
Pope Papst, *m.*
popular volkstümlich.; beliebt (liked).
population Bevölkerung, *f.*
pork Schweinefleisch, *n.*
port Hafen, *m.*
porter Träger, *m.*
portrait Bild, *n.*
Portuguese Portugiese (noun, *m.*); portugiesisch
   (adj.).
position Stellung, *f.* (job); Lage, *f.* (site).
positive bestimmt.
possibility möglicherweise.
possible möglich.
post Post, *f.;* Stelle, *f.* (job).
postage Porto, *n.*
postcard Postkarte, *f.*
poster Plakat, *n.*
posterity Nachwelt, *f.*
post office Postamt, *n.*
pot Topf, *m.*
potato Kartoffel, *f.*
pound Pfund, *n.*
pour (to) giessen.
poverty Armut, *f.*
powder Pulver, *n.;* Puder, *m.* (cosmetic).
powder (to) pudern.
power Macht, *f.*
powerful mächtig.
practical praktisch.
practice (to) üben.
praise Lob, *n.*
praise (to) loben.
prank Prank, *m.;* Streich, *m.*
pray (to) beten.
prayer Gebet, *n.*

preach (to) predigen.
preacher Prediger, *m.*
precaution Vorsicht, *f.*
precede (to) vorangehen.
preceding vorangehend.
precept Vorschrift, *f.;* Beispiel, *n.* (example).
precious kostbar.
precise genau; steif (formal).
precision Genauigkeit, *f.*
predecessor Vorgänger, *m.*
preface Vorwort, *n.*
prefer (to) vorziehen.
preference Vorzug, *m.*
pregnant schwanger.
prejudice Vorurteil, *n.*
preliminary einleitend.
preparation Vorbereitung, *f.*
prepare (to) vorbereiten.
prepay (to) vorauszahlen.
prescribe (to) verschreiben.
prescription Rezept, *n.*
presence Gegenwart, *f.;* Anwesenheit, *f.*
present Gegenwart, *f.* (grammar); Geschenk, *n.* (gift); anwesend (adj.).
preserve (to) erhalten; konservieren (food).
preserves Konserven, *f.;* Eingemachte, *n.*
preside (to) präsidieren.
president Präsident, *m.*
press Presse, *f.*
press (to) drücken; bügeln (clothes).
pressing dringend.
pressure Druck, *m.;* Andrang, *m.* (blood—).
prestige Prestige, *n.;* Ansehen, *n.*
presume (to) vermuten.
pretend (to) vorgeben.
pretext Vorwand, *m.*
pretty hübsch, nett.
prevail (to) vorherrschen.
prevent (to) verhindern.
prevention Verhinderung, *f.*
previous frühere.
prey Raub, *m.*
price Preis, *m.*
pride Stolz, *m.*
priest Priester, *m.*
prince Prinz, *m.*
principal haupt— (adj.).
principle Grundsatz, *m.*
print (to) drucken.
prison Gefängnis, *n.*
prisoner Gefangene, *m.*
private privat.
privilege Vorrecht, *n.*
prize Preis, *m.*
prize (to) schätzen.
probable wahrscheinlich.
problem Problem, *n.*
procedure Verfahren, *n.*
proceed (to) fortschreiten.
process Verfahren, *n;* Prozess, *m.*
procession Prozession, *f.*
proclaim (to) bekanntmachen.

produce (to) erzeugen.
product Erzeugnis, *n.*
production Erzeugung, *f.;* Produktion, *f.*
productive fruchtbar.
profession Beruf, *m.*
professional berufsmässig.
professor Professor, *m;* Lehrer, *m.* (school).
profile Profil, *n.*
profit Gewinn, *m.*
profit (to) gewinnen.
program Programm, *n.*
progress Fortschritt, *m.*
progress (to) vorwärtskommen.
progressive fortschrittlich.
prohibit (to) verbieten.
prohibition Verbot, *n.*
project Projekt, *n.*
project (to) hervorstehen.
promise (to) versprechen.
prompt schnell.
pronoun Fürwort, *n.*
pronounce (to) aussprechen.
pronunciation Aussprache, *f.*
proof Beweis, *m.*
propaganda Propaganda, *f.*
proper passend; anständig (decent).
property Eigentum, *n.*
proportion Verhältnis, *n.*
proposal Vorschlag, *m.*
propose (to) vorschlagen.
prose Prosa, *f.*
prospect (to) Aussicht, *f.*
prosper (to) gedeihen.
prosperity Wohlstand, *m.*
prosperous gedeihlich, blühend.
protect (to) schützen.
protection Schutz, *m.*
protector Beschützer, *m.*
protest Einspruch, *m.*
protest (to) protestieren.
Protestant Protestant, *m.*
proud stolz.
prove (to) probieren.
proverb Sprichwort, *n.*
provide (to) versorgen.
provided that vorausgesetzt dass.
province Provinz, *f.*
provincial provinziell.
provision Provision, *f.*
provoke (to) herausfordern, reizen.
proximity Nähe, *f.*
prudence Vorsicht, *f.*
prudent klug, vorsichtig.
prune Backpflaume, *f.*
psychological psychologisch.
psychology Psychologie, *f.*
public Publikum (noun, *n.*); öffentlich (adj.).
publication Herausgabe, *f.* (literary); Veröffent. lichung, *f.* (notification)
publish (to) herausgeben (book); veröffentlichen (announcement).
publishing house Verlag, *m.*

publisher Verleger, *m.*
pull (to) ziehen.
pump Pumpe, *f.*
punish (to) bestrafen.
punishment Strafe, *f.*
pupil Schüler, *m.;* Schülerin, *f.*
purchase (to) kaufen.
purchase Einkauf, *m.*
pure rein.
purity Reinheit, *f.*
purple Purpur, *m.*
purpose Absicht, *f.*
purse Geldtasche, *f.*
pursue (to) verfolgen.
push (to) stossen.
put (to) legen (lay); setzen (set); stellen (place).
    put down aufschreiben.
    put off aufschieben.
    put on anziehen.
    put up aufstellen.
puzzle Rätsel, *n.*
puzzle (to) verwirren.

Q

quaint seltsam.
qualify berechtigen.
quality Qualität, *f.*
quantity Quantität, *f.*
quarrel Streit, *m.*
quarter Viertel, *n.*
queen Königin, *f.*
queer seltsam.
quench (to) löschen.
question Frage, *f.*
question (to) fragen.
quick schnell
quiet ruhig.
quit (to) verlassen.
quite ganz.
quote (to) anführen.

R

rabbit Kaninchen, *n.*
race Rennen, *n.* (contest); Rasse, *f.* (species).
radiator Heizkörper, *m.*
radio Radio, *n.*
rag Fetzen, *m.*
rage Wut, *f.*
ragged zerlumpt.
rail Schiene, *f.*
railroad Eisenbahn, *f.*
railroad car Eisenbahnwagen, *m.*
rain Regen, *m.*
rain (to) regnen.
rainbow Regenbogen, *m.*
raincoat Regenmantel, *m.*
rainy regnerisch.
raise (to) erhöhen.
raisin Rosine, *f.*
rake Rechen, *m.*

rank Rang, *m.*
rapid schnell.
rapidly schnell.
rapture Entzücken, *n.*
rash Hautausschlag (noun, *m.*) (skin); hastig (adj.).
rat Ratte, *f.*
rate Kurs, *m.* (exchange); Verhältnis, *n.*
rate (to) schätzen.
rather ziemlich, lieber, eher.
ration Ration, *f.*
rational vernünftig.
rave (to) schwärmen.
raw roh.
ray Strahl, *m.*
razor Rasiermesser, *n.*
razor blade Razierklinge, *f.*
reach (to) erreichen.
reach Bereich, *m;* Reichweite, *f.*
react (to) rückwirken, reagieren.
read (to) lesen.
reading Lesen, *n.;* Lektüre *f.*
ready fertig.
real wirklich.
realization Verwirklichung, *f.*
realize (to) verwirklichen.
really wirklich.
rear Hintergrund (noun, *m.*); hinter (adj.).
rear (to) grossziehen.
reason Grund, *m.* (cause); Vernunft, *f.* (intelligence).
reason (to) besprechen.
reasonable vernünftig.
reasoning Schlussfolgerung, *f.*
reassure (to) beruhigen.
rebel Rebell, *m.*
rebel (to) sich auflehnen.
rebellion Empörung, *f.*
recall (to) sich erinnern (memory); zurückrufen (to summon back).
receipt Quittung, *f.*
receive (to) empfangen
receiver Empfänger, *m.*
recent neu.
recently neulich.
reception Empfang, *m.*
recess Nische, *f.*
reciprocal gegenseitig.
recite (to) aufsagen; rezitieren (drama).
recognize (to) erkennen.
recollect (to) sich erinnern.
recollection Erinnerung, *f.*
recommend (to) empfehlen.
recommendation Empfehlung, *f.*
reconcile (to) versöhnen. ,
record Ordner, *m.*
    phonograph record (Schall)platte, *f.*
recover (to) sich erholen.
recruit Rekrut, *m.*
recruit (to) reknutieren.
red rot.
Red Cross Rote Kreuz, *n.*
redeem (to) erlösen.
reduce (to) herabsetzen; abnehmen (weight).

reduction Nachlass, *m.*
reed Schilf, *m.*
reef Riff, *n.*
refer (to) sich beziehen.
reference Bezugnahme, *f.*
referring to bezugnehmen auf.
refine (to) verfeinern.
refinement Bildung, *f.*
reflect (to) zurückstrahlen
reflection Widerschein, *m.* (image); Überlegung, *f.*
    (thoughts).
reform Besserung, *f.*
reform (to) sich bessern.
refrain (to) sich enthalten.
refresh (to) erfrischen.
refreshment Erfrischung, *f.*
refrigerator Kühlschrank, *m.*
refuge Zufluchtsort, *m.*
    take refuge flüchten.
refugee Flüchtling, *m.*
refund Rückzahlung, *f.*
refund (to) zurückzahlen.
refusal Verweigerung, *f.*
refuse (to) ablehnen, verweigern.
refute (to) widerlegen.
regard Ansehen, *n.*
regardless unbeachtet.
regime Regime, *n.*
regiment Regiment, *n.*
register (to) eintragen (membership); einschreiben
    (letter).
regret Bedauern, *n.*
regret (to) bedauern.
regular regelmässig.
regulate regulieren.
regulation Vorschrift, *f.*
rehearsal Probe, *f.*
rehearse (to) Probe halten.
reign Regierung, *f.*
reign (to) regieren.
reinforce (to) verstärken.
reject (to) verwerfen.
rejoice (to) sich freuen.
relapse Rückfall, *m.*
relate (to) erzählen.
relation Verwandtschaft, *f.*
relationship verwandtschaftliche Beziehung, *f.*
relative Verwandte, *m.*
relax (to) entspannen.
relaxation Entspannung, *f.*
release Befreiung, *f.*
release (to) freilassen.
reliable zuverlässig.
relic Überbleibsel, *n.;* Relique, *f.;* (religious).
relief Erleichterung, *f.;* Linderung, *f.* (of pain).
relieve (to) erleichtern, lindern.
religion Religion, *f.*
religious religiös.
relinquish (to) aufgeben.
relish (to) munden.
relish Geschmack, *m.*
reluctance Widerwille, *n.*

reluctant widerwillig.
rely (to) sich verlassen.
remain (to) bleiben.
remainder Rest, *m.*
remark Bemerkung, *f.*
remark (to) bemerken.
remarkable bemerkenswert.
remedy Arznei, *f.* (medicine); Hilfsmittel, *n.*
    (cure).
remember (to) sich erinnern.
remembrance Erinnerung, *f.*
remind (to) mahnen.
remorse Reue, *f.*
remote entfernt (distance); rückständig (antiquated).
removal Beseitigung, *f.*
remove (to) entfernen.
renew (to) erneuern.
renewal Erneuerung, *f.*
rent Miete, *f.*
rent (to) mieten.
repair Reparatur, *f.*
repay (to) zurückzahlen.
repeat (to) wiederholen.
repent (to) bereuen.
repetition Wiederholung, *f.*
reply Antwort, *f.*
reply (to) antworten.
report Bericht, *m.;* Zeugnis, *n.*
report (to) berichten.
reporter Reporter, *m.*
represent (to) vertreten.
representation Vertretung, *f.*
representative Vertreter, *m.*
repress (to) unterdrücken.
repression Unterdrückung, *f.*
reprimand Verweis, *m.*
reprimand (to) tadeln.
reprisal Gegenmassregel, *f.*
reproach Vorwurf, *m.*
reproach (to) vorwerfen.
reproduce (to) reproduzieren.
reproduction Reproduktion, *f.*
republic Republik, *f.*
reputation Ruf, *m.;* Ansehen, *n*
request Bitte, *f.*
request (to) bitten.
require (to) benötigen.
requirement Bedarf, *m.*
rescue (to) retten.
research Forschung, *f.*
resent (to) verübeln.
resentful empfindlich.
resentment Verdruss, *m.*
reservation Reservation, *f.*
reserve (to) reservieren.
reservoir Behälter, *m.*
residence Wohnstätte, *f.*
resident Bewohner, *m.*
resign (to) aufgeben.
resignation Rücktritt, *m.*
resist (to) widerstehen.
resistance Widerstand, *m.*

resolute entschlossen.
resolution Beschluss, *m.*
resolve (to) sich entschliessen (decide); lösen (problem).
resort Kurort, *m.* (health); Luftkurort, *m.* (vacation); Zuflucht, *f.* (recourse).
resource Hilfsmittel, *n.*
respect Achtung, *f.*
respectful ehrfürchtig, achtungsvoll.
respective bezüglich.
responsibility Verantwortlichkeit, *f.*
responsible verantwortlich.
rest Ruhe, *f.*
rest (to) ruhen.
restaurant Restaurant, *n.*
restless unruhig.
restoration Wiederherstellung, *f.*
restore (to) wiederherstellen, restaurieren.
restrain (to) zurückhalten.
restraint Zurückhaltung, *f.*
restrict (to) beschränken.
restriction Einschränkung, *f.*
result Resultat, *n.*
result (to) folgen.
resume (to) wiederaufnehmen, wieder anfangen.
retail Einzelverkauf, *m.; * Kleinhandel, *m.*
retail (to) im Kleinhandel verkaufen.
retain (to) behalten.
retaliate (to) vergelten.
retaliation Vergeltung, *f.*
retire (to) sich zurückziehen.
retirement Zurückgezogenheit, *f.*
retract widerrufen; zurückziehen.
retreat Rückzug, *m.*
retreat (to) sich zurückziehen.
return Rückkehr, *f.*
return (to) zurückkehren.
reveal (to) offenbaren, enthüllen.
revelation Offenbarung, *f.*
revenge Rache, *f.*
revenge (to) rächen.
revenue Einkommen, *n.*
reverence Ehrerbietung, *f.*
reverend erwürdig.
reverse Rückseite, *f.*
reverse (to) umkehren.
review (to) betrachten; mustern (inspect); rezensieren (critical).
review Überblick, *m.* Parade, *f.* (army); Revue, *f.* (theater), Rezension, *f.*
revise (to) revidieren, (critique).
revive neubeleben.
revival Wiederbelebung, *f.*
revoke (to) widerrufen.
revolt Aufstand, *m.*
revolt (to) sich empören.
revolution Revolution, *f.*
revolve (to) sich drehen.
reward Belohnung, *f.*
reward (to) belohnen.
rhyme Reim, *m.*
rhyme (to) reimen.

rib Rippe, *f.*
ribbon Band, *n.*
rice Reis, *m.*
rich reich.
richness Reichtum, *m.*
rid (to get) loswerden.
riddle Rätsel, *n.*
ride Fahrt, *f.*
ridiculous lächerlich.
rifle Gewehr, *n.*
right richtig (correct); rechts (position). all right ganz gut.
righteous gerecht.
rigid steif, fest, starr.
rigor Strenge, *f.*
rigorous streng, scharf, hart.
ring Ring, *m.* wedding ring Ehering, *m.*
ring (to) ringen.
rinse (to) spülen, ausspülen.
riot Aufruhr, *f.; * Schwelgerei, *f.* (army).
ripe reif.
ripen (to) reifen.
rise Steigung, *f.*
rise (to) aufstehen (get up); steigen (increase, mount); aufgehen (sun).
risk Gefahr, *f.*
risk (to) riskieren.
rite Ritus, *m.*
ritual rituell.
rival Rivale, *m.*
rivalry Mitbewerbung, *f.; * Konkurrenz, *f.*
river Fluss, *m.*
roach Schabe, *f.*
road Weg, *m.*
roar (to) brüllen.
roast Braten, *m.*
roast (to) braten.
rob (to) rauben.
robber Räuber, *m.*
robbery Diebstahl, *m.*
robe Morgenrock, *m.*
robust stark, rüstig.
rock Felsen, *m.*
rock (to) wiegen.
rocky felsig.
rocket Rakete, *f.*
rod Rute, *f.*
roll Rolle, *f.* (cylinder); Brötchen, *n.* (bread).
roll (to) rollen.
Roman Römer (noun, *m.*); römisch (adj.).
romantic romantisch.
roof Dach, *n.*
room Zimmer, *n.* (of a house); Raum, *m.* (space). There is no room. Da ist kein Platz.
roomy geräumig.
root Wurzel, *f.*
rope Seil, *n.*
rose Rose, *f.*
rot (to) faulen; vermodern.
rough rauh (coarse); roh (crude); stürmisch (stormy).

round Runde (noun, *f.*); rund (adj.).
round um (acc.); herum.
rouse (to) aufwecken; erzürnen (anger).
routine Routine,*f.;* Erfahrung, *f.*
row Reihe, *f.*
row (to) rudern.
royal königlich.
rub (to) reiben.
rubber Gummi, *m.*
ruby Rubin, *m.*
rude grob.
ruffle (to) verwirren.
ruin Ruine, *f.*
ruin (to) ruinieren.
rule Regel, *f.*
rule (to) regieren, beherrschen.
ruler Lineal, *n.*
rum Rum, *m.*
rumor Gerücht, *n.*
run (to) rennen, laufen.
    run away weglaufen.
rural ländlich.
rush (to) Sturz, *m.;* Andrang, *m.* (crowd).
Russian Russe (noun, *m.*); russisch (adj.)
rust (to) verrosten.
rusty rostig.
rye Roggen, *m.*

S

sacred heilig.
sacrifice Opfer, *n.*
sacrifice (to) opfern.
sacrilege Entweihung, *f.*
sad traurig.
sadden (to) trauern.
saddle Sattel, *m.*
sadness Traurigkeit, *f.*
safe Schliessfach (noun, *n.*) (of a bank);
    wohlbehalten (adj.) (in safekeeping);
    sicher (adj.) (secure).
safety Sicherheit, *f.*
sail (to) segeln.
sail Segel, *n.*
sailor Matrose, *m.*
saint Heilige, *m. & f.*
    patron saint Schutzheilige, *m. & f.*
sake (for the – of) um (gen.) willen.
salad Salat, *m.*
salami Salami, *f.*
salary Gehalt, *n.*
sale Verkauf, *m.;* Ausverkauf, *m.* (bargain).
saleslady Verkäuferin, *f.*
salesman Verkäufer, *m.*
salmon Lachs, *m.*
salt Salz, *n.*
salute Gruss, *m.*
salute (to) grüssen.
salvation Rettung, *f.*
Salvation Army Heilsarmee, *f.*
same der (die-, das-). selbe.
    the same as derselbe wie.
    all the same es spielt keine Rolle.

sample Muster, *n.*
sanctuary Zufluchtsort, *m.*
sand Sand, *m.*
sandal Sandale, *f.*
sandwich Butterbrot, *n.*
sandy sandig.
sanitary hygienisch.
sap Saft, *m.*
sapphire Saphir, *m.*
sarcasm Sarkasmus, *m.*
sarcastic sarkastisch.
sardine Sardine, *f.*
satiate (to) sättigen.
satin Seidenatlas, *m.*
satisfaction Befriedung, *f.*
satisfactory zufriedenstellend.
satisfy (to) befriedigen.
saturate (to) durchtränken.
Saturday Samstag, *m.*
sauce Sauce, *f.*
saucer Untertasse, *f.*
sausage Wurst, *f.*
savage wild.
save (to) sparen (hoard); retten (rescue).
saving Ersparnis, *f.*
savior Erretter, *m.*
Savior Heiland, *m.*
say (to) sagen.
scale Schuppe, *f.;* Tonleiter, *f.* (music).
scales Massstab, *m.*; Waage, *f.*
scalp Skalp, *m.*
scan (to) überblicken.
scandal Skandal, *m.*
scanty knapp, dürftig.
scar Narbe, *f.*
scarce knapp.
scarcely kaum.
scare (to) erschrecken.
scarf Schal, *m.*
scarlet scharlachrot.
scattered verstreut.
schedule Stundenplan, *m.* (time).
scheme Schema, *n.;* Entwurf, *m.*
scholar Gelehrte, *m & f.*
school Schule, *f.*
schoolteacher Lehrer, *m.;* Lehrerin, *f.*
science Wissenschaft, *f.*
scientific wissenschaftlich.
scientist Wissenschaftler, *m.*
scissors Schere, *f.*
scold (to) schelten.
scorn Verachtung, *f.*
scorn (to) verachten.
scornful verächtlich.
Scottish schottisch.
scrape (to) kratzen; schaben (vegetables).
scraper Schaber, *m.*
scratch Schramme, *f.*
scratch (to) kratzen.
scream Schrei, *m.*
scream (to) schreien.
screen Schirm, *m.*
    movie screen Leinwand, *f.*

screw Schraube, *f.*
scribble (to) kritzeln.
scruple Skrupel, *m.*
scrupulous gewissenhaft.
scrutinize (to) prüfen.
sculptor Bildhauer, *m.*
sculpture Bildhauerei, *f.*
sea Meer, *n.*
seal Siegel, *n.;* Seehund, *m.* (animal).
seal (to) siegeln.
seam Naht, *f.*
search Suche, *f.;* Untersuchung, *f.* (customs).
search (to) suchen; untersuchen.
seashore Seeküste, *f.*
seasickness Seekrankheit, *f.*
season Jahreszeit, *f.;* Saison, *f.* (events).
seat Sitz, *m.*
seat (to) setzen; stellen.
second zweit(er, -e, -es).
secret Geheimnis, noun, *n.;* geheim (adj.).
secretary Sekretär, *m.;* Sekretärin, *f.*
sect Sekte, *f.*
section Teil, *m.*
secure sicher.
secure (to) sichern.
security Sicherheit, *f.*
see (to) sehen.
seed Samen, *m.*
seek (to) suchen.
seem (to) scheinen.
seize (to) ergreifen, fassen.
seldom selten, rar.
select (to) wählen.
selection Auswahl, *f.*
selfish selbstsüchtig.
selfishness Selbstsucht, *f.*
sell (to) verkaufen.
semicolon Semikolon, *n.*
senate Senat, *m.*
senator Senator, *m.*
send (to) senden.
senior Ältere.
sensation Gefühl, *n.* (feeling); Sensation, *f.* (excitement).
sense Sinn, *m.*
senseless sinnlos.
sensibility Vernünftigkeit, *f.*
sensible vernünftig.
sensitive empfindlich.
sensitivity Empfindlichkeit, *f.*
sensual wollüstig.
sensuality Wollust, *f.* Sinnlichkeit, *f.*
sentence Urteil, *n.* (legal); Satz, *m.* (grammar).
sentiment Gefühl, *n.*
sentimental sentimental.
sentimentality Sentimentalität, *f.*
separate einzeln.
separate (to) trennen.
separately besonders.
separation Trennung, *f.*
September September, *m.*
serene heiter.
sergeant Sergeant, *m.*

series Serie, *f.*
serious ernst.
seriousness Ernst, *m.*
servant Diener, *m.*
serve (to) dienen.
service Dienst, *m.;* Gottesdienst, *m.* (church).
session Sitzung, *f.*
set festgelegt.
set Sammlung, *f.* (collection); Untergang, *m.* (sun); Satz, *m.* (series); Service, *n.* (dishes).
set (to) setzen; stellen (clock).
settle (to) begleichen (accounts); erledigen (conclude).
settlement Begleichung, *f.;* Erledigung, *f.* Siedlung *f.* (houses).
seven sieben.
seventeen siebzehn.
seventeenth siebzehnte.
seventh siebte.
seventieth siebzigste.
seventy siebzig.
several mehrere.
 several times mehrmals.
severe streng (stern, rigorous); heftig (pain).
severity Strenge, *f.*
sew (to) nähen.
sewer Abzugskanal, *m.*
sex Geschlecht, *n.*
shabby schäbig.
shade Schatten, *m.*
shadow Schatten, *m.*
shady schattig.
shake (to) schütteln; zittern (tremble).
 handshake Händedruck, *m.*
shallow seicht.
shame Schande, *f.* (disgrace); Scham, *f.* (modesty).
shameful schändlich.
shameless schamlos.
shampoo Shampoo, *n.*
shape Form, *f.*
share Teil, *m.;* Anteil, *m.;* Aktie, *f.* (stock).
share (to) teilen.
shareholder Aktionär, *m.*
sharp scharf.
sharpen schärfen.
shave (to) sich rasieren.
she sie.
shed (to) vergiessen (spill); abwerfen (discard).
sheep Schaf, *n.*
sheer rein, lauter.
sheet (Bett)laken, *n.* (linens); Blatt, *n.* (paper).
shelf Brett, *n.*
shell Muschel, *f.;* Geschoss, *n.* (artillery).
shelter Unterkunft, *f.;* Luftschutzraum, *m.* (air raids).
shelter unterstellen (from exposure); schützen (from danger).
shepherd Schäfer, *m.;*
shield Schild, *n.*
shield (to) schützen.
shift Schicht, *f.* (workers).
shift (to) schieben.
shine (to) scheinen; putzen (shoes).

ship Schiff, *n.*	**simply** nur (only).
ship (to) senden, befördern.	**simulate** (to) erheucheln, vortäuschen.
shipment Verladung, *f.*; Verschiffung, *f.*;	**simultaneous** gleichzeitig.
Beförderung, *f.*	**sin** Sünde, *f.*
shirt Hemd, *n.*	**sin** (to) sündigen.
shiver Schauer, *m.*	**since** seit (dat.); da, weil (because).
shiver (to) (er)schauern.	**sincere** aufrichtig.
shock Schlag, *m.* (blow); Stoss, *m.*	**sincerity** Aufrichtigkeit, *f.*
shock (to) anstossen (scandalize); erschüttern.	**sing** (to) singen.
shoe Schuh, *m.*	**singer** Sänger, *m.*; Sängerin, *f.*
shoemaker Schuhmacher, *m.*	**single** einzeln; ledig (unmarried).
shoot (to) schiessen.	**singular** einzigartig; seltsam (strange).
shop Laden, *m.*; Geschäft, *n.*	**sinister** unheilvoll.
short kurz.	**sink** Gussstein, *m.*; Ausguss, *m.*
shorten (to) kürzen.	**sink** (to) sinken.
shorthand Kurzschrift, *f.*; Stenographie, *f.*	**sinner** Sünder, *m.*; Sünderin, *f.*
shorts Unterhosen, *pl.* (men's).	**sip** (to) nippen.
shot Schuss, *m.*	**sip** Schluck, *m.*
shoulder Schulter, *f.*	**sir** Herr, *m.*
shout Schrei, *m.*	**sister** Schwester, *f.*
shout (to) schreien.	**sister-in-law** Schwägerin, *f.*
shovel Schaufel, *f.*	**sit** (to) sitzen (be seated); sich setzen (sit down).
show Vorstellung, *f.* (play); Ausstellung, *f.*	**site** Lage, *f.*; Bauplatz, *m.*
(exhibition).	**situation** Lage, *f.*
show (to) zeigen.	**six** sechs.
shower Schauer, *m.* (rain); Dusche, *f.* (shower-bath).	**sixteen** sechzehn.
shrill schrill.	**sixteenth** sechzehnte.
shrimp Krabbe, *f.*	**sixth** sechste.
shrink (to) einlaufen.	**sixtieth** sechzigste.
shrub Strauch, *m.*	**sixty** sechzig.
shrubbery Gebüsch, *n.*	**size** Grösse, *f.*
shun (to) meiden.	**skate** Schlittschuh, *m.*
shut geschlossen.	**skate** (to) Schlittschuh laufen.
shut (to) schliessen.	**skeleton** Gerippe, *n.*
shy schüchtern.	**sketch** Skizze, *f.*
sick krank.	**sketch** (to) skizzieren.
sickness Krankheit, *f.*	**skill** Geschicklichkeit, *f.*
side Seite, *f.*	**skillful** geschickt, kundig.
sidewalk Bürgersteig, *m.*	**skin** Haut, *f.*
siege Belagerung, *f.*	**skirt** Rock, *m.*
sigh Seufzer, *m.*	**skull** Schädel, *m.*
sigh (to) seufzen.	**sky** Himmel, *m.*
sight Aussicht, *f.*; Anblick, *m.*	**skyscraper** Wolkenkratzer, *m.*
sign Zeichen, *n.*	**slander** (to) verleumden.
sign (to) zeichnen.	**slap** Klaps, *m.*
signal Signal, *n.*	**slate** Schiefer, *m.*
signal (to) signalisieren.	**slaughter** (to) schlachten.
signature Unterschrift, *f.*	**slave** Sklave, *m.*; Sklavin, *f.*
significance Bedeutung, *f.*	**slavery** Sklaverei, *f.*
significant bezeichnend.	**sleep** Schlaf, *m.*
signify (to) bezeichnen (indicate); bedeuten (mean).	**sleep** (to) schlafen.
silence Schweigen, *n.*	**sleeve** Ärmel, *m.*
silent still, schweigend.	**sleigh** Schlitten, *m.*
silk Seide, *f.*	**slender** schlank.
silken seiden.	**slice** Schnitte, *f.*
silly ausgelassen, dumm.	**slice** (to) in Scheiben schneiden.
silver Silber, *n.*	**slide** (to) schleifen, gleiten.
silvery silbern.	**slight** gering.
similar ähnlich.	**slip** entschlüpfen.
similarity Ähnlichkeit, *f.*	**slip** Fehler, *m.* (mistake); Unterrock, *m.* (lingerie).
simple einfach.	**slope** Abhang, *m.*
simplicity Einfachheit, *f.*	**slot** Einwurf, *m.*; Schlitz, *m.* (mail).

slow langsam.
slumber Schlummer, *m.*
slumber (to) schlummern.
sly schlau.
small klein.
smart elegant (clothes); gescheit (clever).
smash (to) zerschmettern.
smear (to) schmieren.
smell Geruch, *m.*
smell (to) riechen.
smile Lächeln, *n.*
smile (to) lächeln.
smoke Rauch, *m.*
smoke (to) rauchen.
smooth glatt.
smother (to) ersticken.
smuggle (to) schmuggeln.
snail Schnecke, *f.*
snake Schlange, *f.*
snapshot (Moment)aufnahme, *f.*
snatch (to) ergreifen.
sneer (to) (ver)hönnen.
sneeze (to) niessen.
snore (to) schnarchen.
snow Schnee, *m.*
snowstorm Schneesturm, *m.*
so so.
    and so on   und so weiter
soak (to) einweichen; durchnässen (drench).
soap Seife, *f.*
sob Schluchzen, *n.*
sob (to) schluchzen.
sober nüchtern.
social gesellschaftlich.
society Gesellschaft, *f.*
sock Sock, *m.*
soda Sodawasser, *n.*
soft weich.
soften (to) erweichen, aufweichen.
soil (to) beschmutzen.
soil Erde, *f.; Boden, m.*
soiled schmutzig.
soldier Soldat, *m.*
sole Sohle, *f.*
solemn feierlich.
solemnity Feierlichkeit, *f.*
solicit (to) bitten; nachsuchen.
solid fest.
solitary einsam (lonely); einzeln (one).
solitude Einsamkeit, *f.*
solution Lösung, *f.*
solve lösen.
some einige (a few); etwas (partial).
somebody jemand.
somehow irgendwie.
something etwas.
sometimes zuweilen.
somewhat etwas.
somewhere irgendwo.
son Sohn, *m.*
song Lied, *n.*
son-in-law Schwiegersohn, *m.*

soon bald.
soot Russ, *m.*
soothe (to) besänftigen; lindern (pain).
sore Geschwür (noun, *n.*); wund, schmerzhaft (adj.);
    empfindlich, verärgert (annoyed).
    sore throat   Halsschmerzen, *pl.*
sorrow Kummer, *m.*
sorry bekümmert.
    I am sorry.   Es tut mir leid.
sort Sorte, *f.*
sort (to) sortieren.
sound Laut, *m.*
sound (to) lauten.
soup Suppe, *f.*
sour sauer.
source Quelle, *f.* (spring); Ursprung, *m.* (origin).
south Süden, *m.*
southeast Südost, *m.;* Südosten, *m.*
southern Süd–; südlich.
southwest Südwest, *m.;* Südwesten, *m.*
sovereign Herrscher, *m.*
sow (to) säen.
space Raum, *m.;* Zwischenraum, *m.* (space between).
spacious (ge)räumig.
spade Spaten, *m.;* Pik, *n.* (cards).
Spanish spanisch.
spare spärlich.
spare (to) entbehren.
spark Funke, *m.*
sparkle (to) funkeln, glänzen.
sparrow Sperling, Spatz, *m.*
speak (to) sprechen.
special besonders, extra.
specialty Spezialität, *f.*
specific eigen, spezifisch, genau.
specify (to) spezifizieren.
spectacle Schauspiel, *n.*
spectator Zuschauer, *m.*
speculate (to) spekulieren.
speech Sprache, *f.;* Rede, *f.*
speed Geschwindigkeit, *f.*
speedy schnell.
spell Zauber, *m.* (charm).
spell (to) buchstabieren, schreiben.
spelling Buchstabieren *n.*
spend (to) ausgeben.
sphere Sphäre, *f.*
spice Gewürz, *n.*
spice (to) würzen.
spicy würzig.
spider Spinne, *f.*
spill (to) verschütten.
spin (to) spinnen.
spine Rückgrat, *n.*
spirit Geist, *m.*
spiritual geistig.
spit (to) spucken.
spite Bosheit, *f.*
    in spite of   trotz (gen.), trotzdem (gen. or dat.).
splash (to) (be)spritzen.
splendid prachtvoll.
    Splendid!   Wunderbar!

splendor Pracht, *f.*; Glanz, *m.*
split Spalt, *m.*
split (to) spalten.
spoil (to) verderben; verwöhnen (child).
sponge Schwamm, *m.*
spontaneous spontan.
spoon Löffel, *m.*
spoonful Löffelvoll, *m.*
sport Sport, *m.*
spot Fleck, *m.* (stain); Stelle, *f.* (place).
spread (to) verbreiten; bestreichen (on bread).
spring Frühling, *m.* (season); Sprung, *m.* (jump);
    Quelle, *f.* (source).
spring (to) springen.
sprinkle sprenkeln.
sprout Sprössling, *m.*
spur Sporn, *m.*
spur (to) anspornen.
spurn (to) verschmähen.
spy Spion, *m.*
spy (to) spionieren.
squadron Schwadron, *f.*
square Quadrat, *n.*
squeeze (to) (aus)drücken.
squirrel Eichhörnchen, *n.*
stabilize (to) stabilisieren.
stable fest (adj.); stabil.
stack Stoss, *m.* (wood).
stack (to) aufstapeln.
stadium Stadion, *n.*
staff Stab (military), *m.*; Personal, *n.* (business).
stage Bühne, *f.* (theater).
stain Fleck, *m.*
stain (to) (be)flecken.
stairs Treppe, *f.*
stammer (to) stottern.
stamp Briefmarke, *f.*; Stempel, *m.*
stand Stand, *m.*
    Stand still!   Stillgestanden!
star Stern, *m.*
starch Stärke, *f.*
stare (to) starren.
start Anfang, *m.*
start (to) beginnen, anfangen.
starve (to) (ver)hungern.
state Staat, *m.* (country); Zustand, *m.* (condition).
state (to) angeben.
stately stattlich.
statement Erklärung, *f.*; Aufstellung, *f.* (account).
stateroom Kabine, *f.*
station Bahnhof, *m.* (railroad); Stellung, *f.*
    (position).
statistics Statistik, *f.*
statue Statue, *f.*
stay Aufenthalt, *m.*
stay (to) bleiben.
steady fest.
steak Beefsteak, *n.*
steal (to) stehlen.
steam Dampf, *m.*
steamer Dampfer, *m.*
steel Stahl, *m.*

steep steil.
steer (to) steuern.
stem Stiel, *m.*
stenographer Stenotypistin, *f.*
stenography Kurzschrift, *f.*; Stenographie, *f.*
step Schritt, *m.*; Stufe, *f.* (stairs).
step (to) schreiten.
sterilized sterilisiert.
stern ernst.
stew Ragout, *n.*
stew (to) schmoren.
steward Steward, *m.*
stick Stock, *m.*
stick (to) stecken; ankleben (paste).
stiff steif.
stiffen (to) (ver)steifen; verstärken.
stiffness Steifheit, *f.*
still still, ruhig (adj.); jedoch, noch (adv.)
still (to) stillen.
stimulant Anregungsmittel, *n.*
stimulate (to) anregen.
sting Stich, *m.*
sting (to) stechen.
stinginess Geiz, *m.*
stingy geizig.
stir (to) rühren, bewegen.
stirrup Steigbügel, *m.*
stitch Stich, *m.*; Masche, *f.*
stitch (to) heften; nähen (sew).
stock Warenbestand, *m.*; Stamm, *m.*
stocking Strumpf, *m.*
stomach Magen, *m.*
stone Stein, *m.*
stool Schemel, *m.*
stop Haltestelle, *f.*
stop (to) halten.
    Stop!   Halt!
store Laden, *m.*; Warenhaus, *n.*
stork Storch, *m.*
storm Sturm, *m.*
story Geschichte, *f.*
stove Ofen, *m.*
straight gerade.
    straight on   gerade aus.
straighten gerade machen, aufrichten.
strain Anstrengung, *f.*
strange seltsam, sonderbar.
stranger Ausländer, *m*; Fremde, *m.*
strap Riemen, *m.*
straw Stroh, *n.*; Strohhalm, *m.* (for drinking).
strawberry Erdbeere, *f.*
stream Strom, *m.*
street Strasse, *f.*
streetcar Strassenbahn, *f.*
strength Kraft, *f.*
strengthen verstärken; kräftigen.
strenuous angestrengt.
stress Druck, *m*; Betonung, *f.* (accentuation).
stretch Strecke, *f.*
stretch (to) strecken.
strict streng.
stride Schritt, *m.*

string Bindfaden, *m.*
strip (to) streifen; entkleiden (of clothes).
stripe Streifen, *m.*
strive (to) streben.
stroke Schlag, *m.;* Zug, *m.* (pen).
stroll Spaziergang, *m.*
stroll (to) spazierengehen.
strong stark.
structure Bau, *m.*
struggle Kampf, *m.*
struggle (to) kämpfen.
stubborn hartnäckig.
student Schüler, *m.* · Schülerin, *f.;* Student, *m.* & *f.*
studio Studio, *n.*
studious lernbegierig, lerneifrig.
study Studium, *n.* -
study (to) studieren.
stuff Stoff, *m.*
stuff (to) stopfen.
stumble (to) stolpern.
stump Stumpf, *m.*
stun (to) betäuben.
stunt Sensation, *f.*
stupendous fantastisch.
stupid dumm.
stupidity Dummheit, *f.*
stupor Betäubung, *f.*
sturdy kräftig.
stutter (to) stottern.
style Stil, *m.*
subdue (to) unterwerfen.
subject Angelegenheit, *f.;* Fach, *n.* (school).
subjugate (to) beherrschen.
subjunctive Konjunktiv, *m.*
sublime erhaben.
submission Unterwerfung, *f.*
submissive unterwürfig.
submit (to) unterwerfen.
subordinate untergeordnet.
subordination Unterordnung, *f.*
subscribe (to) abonnieren.
subscription Abonnement, *n.*
subsist (to) bestehen.
substance Substanz, *f.*
substantial beträchtlich.
substitute (to) ersetzen.
substitution Ersatz, *m.*
subtle scharfsinnig, fein, spitzfindig.
subtract abziehen.
subtraction Abzug, *m.*
suburb Vorstadt, *f.*
subway Untergrundbahn, *f.*
succeed (to) nachfolgen; gelingen (achieve).
success Erfolg, *m.*
successful erfolgreich.
succession Nachfolge, *f.*
successor Nachfolger, *m.*
such solch.
  Such a scandal!   Solch ein Skandal!
sudden plötzlich.
sue (to) verklagen.
suffer (to) leiden.

suffering Leiden, *n.*
sufficient genügend.
sugar Zucker, *m.*
suggest (to) andeuten, vorschlagen.
suggestion Anregung, *f.*
suicide Selbstmord, *m.*
suit Anzug, *m.;* Kostum, *n.* (lady's).
suitable passend.
sulk (to) schmollen.
sullen mürrisch.
sum Summe, *f.*
summary Auszug, *m.*
summer Sommer, *m.*
summit Gipfel, *m.*
summon (to) vorladen; einberufen.
sumptuous prächtig, kostbar.
sum up (to) abkürzen, zusammenfassen.
sun Sonne, *f.*
sunbeam Sonnenstrahl, *m.*
Sunday Sonntag, *m.*
sunny sonnig.
sunrise Sonnenaufgang, *m.*
sunset Sonnenuntergang, *m.*
sunshine Sonnenschein, *m.*
superb herrlich.
superficial oberflächlich.
superfluous überflüssig.
superintendent Inspektor, *m.*
superior Vorgesetzte, *m.* & *f.*
superiority Überlegenheit, *f.*
superstition Aberglaube, *m.*
supervise (to) beaufsichtigen.
supper Abendessen, *n.*
supplement Nachtrag, *m.;* Beilage, *f.*
supplementary ergänzend.
supply (to) versorgen.
support Stütze, *f.;* Unterstützung, *f.*
support (to) (unter)stützen.
suppose (to) vermuten, annehmen.
suppress (to) unterdrücken.
supreme höchst, oberst.
sure gewiss, sicher.
surety Sicherheit, *f.*
surface Oberfläche, *f.*
surgeon Chirurg, *m.*
surgery Chirurgie, *f.*
surname Zuname, *m.;* Nachname, *m.*
surpass übertreffen.
surprise Überraschung, *f.*
surprise (to) überraschen.
surrender Übergabe, *f.*
surrender (to) aufgeben, übergeben.
surroundings Umgebung, *f.*
survey Übersicht, *f.;* Vermessung, *f.*
survey (to) besichtigen, vermessen.
survive (to) überleben.
susceptibility Empfänglichkeit, *f.*
susceptible empfänglich.
suspect (to) verdächtigen.
suspense Ungewissheit, *f.;* Spannung, *f.*
suspicion Verdacht, *m.*
suspicious verdächtig.

sustain (to) ernähren.
swallow Schluck, *m.* (gulp); Schwalbe, *f.* (bird).
swallow (to) verschlucken.
swamp Sumpf, *m.*
swan Schwan, *m.*
swear (to) schwören.
sweat Schweiss, *m.*
sweat (to) schwitzen.
sweep (to) kehren; fegen.
sweet süss.
sweetness Süsse, *f.*
swell (to) (an)schwellen.
swift schnell, rasch.
swim (to) schwimmen.
swindle (to) schwindeln.
swindler Schwindler, *m.*
swing (to) schwingen.
Swiss Schweizer (noun, *m.*); schweizerisch (adj.).
switch Schalter, *m.*
sword Schwert, *n.*
syllable Silbe, *f.*
symbol Symbol, *n.*
symbolic symbolisch.
symbolize symbolisieren.
symmetrical symmetrisch.
sympathetic mitfühlend.
sympathize (to) mitfühlen.
sympathy Sympathie, *f.;* Verständnis, *n.*
symptom Symptom, *n.*
syrup Sirup, *m.*
system System, *n.*
systematic systematisch.

T

table Tisch, *m.*
tablecloth Tischtuch, *n.*
tacit stillschweigend.
taciturn schweigsam.
tact Takt, *m.*
tactful taktvoll.
tactless taktlos.
tail Schwanz, *m.*
tailor Schneider, *m.*
take (to) nehmen.
tale Erzählung, *f.*
talent Talent, *n.;* Begabung, *f.*
talk Gespräch, *n.*
talk (to) reden, plaudern.
talkative gesprächig.
tall hoch; gross (people).
tame zahm.
tame (to) zähmen.
tangle (to) verwickeln.
tank Tank, *m.*
tapestry Wandteppich, *m.*
tar Teer, *m.*
tardy spät.
target (Ziel)scheibe, *f.*
tarnish (to) trüben.
task Aufgabe, *f.*
taste Geschmack, *m.*

taste (to) schmecken.
tax Steuer, *f.*
taxi Taxi, *n.*
tea Tee, *m.*
teach (to) unterrichten.
teacher Lehrer, *m.;* Lehrerin, *f.*
team Gruppe, *f.;* Mannschaft, *f.* (sports).
tear Träne, *f.* (teardrop); Riss, *m.* (rip).
tear (to) (zer)reissen
tease (to) necken.
teaspoon Teelöffel, *m.*
technical technisch.
technique Technik, *f.*
tedious langweilig, ermüdend.
telegram Telegramm, *n.*
telegraph (to) telegrafieren.
telephone Telefon, *n.*
   telephone operator Telefonistin, *f.*
telephone (to) telefonieren, anrufen.
tell (to) sagen.
temper Laune, *f.*
temperate gemässig, mässig.
temperature Temperatur, *f.*
tempest Sturm, *m.*
temple Tempel, *m.;* Schläfe, *f.* (head).
temporary vorübergehend.
tempt (to) versuchen, verlocken.
temptation Versuchung, *f.*
ten zehn.
tenacious zäh.
tenacity Zähigkeit, *f.*
tenant Mieter, *m.*
tend (to) sich neigen zu.
tendency Neigung, *f.*
tender zart, empfindlich.
tennis Tennis, *n.*
tense gespannt.
tense Zeitform, *f.* (grammar).
tension Spannung, *f.*
tent Zelt, *n.*
tenth Zehntel (noun, *n.*) (fraction); zehnt (adj.).
tepid lauwarm.
term Ausdruck, *m.*
terrace Terrasse, *f.*
terrible schrecklich.
territy (to) (er)schrecken.
territory Gebiet, *n.*
terror Schrecken, *m.*
test Prüfung, *f.*
test (to) prüfen.
testify (to) bezeugen.
testimony Zeugnis, *n.*
text Text, *m.*
textbook Lehrbuch, *n.*
than als.
thank (to) danken.
   Thank you! Danke schön!
thankful dankbar.
that das (demonstrative); der, die, das, welch(er, -e, -es)
   (relative); dass, damit (conjunction).
thaw Tauwetter, *n.*
thaw (to) tauen.
the der, die, das.

theater Theater, *n.*
their ihr.
theirs ihr(er, -e, -es).
them sie (acc.); ihnen (dat.).
theme Thema, *n.*
themselves sie (ihnen) selbst, sich.
then dann.
theory Theorie, *f.*
there dort.
there is, there are es gibt.
thereafter danach.
thereby dadurch.
therefore deshalb, daher.
thereupon darauf.
thermometer Fiebermesser, *n.*
these diese.
thesis These, *f.*
they sie.
thick dick.
thief Dieb, *m.*
thigh Schenkel, *m.*
thimble Fingerhut, *m.*
thin dünn.
thing Sache, *f.;* Ding, *n.*
think (to) denken.
third dritte.
thirst Durst, *m.*
thirteen dreizehn.
thirteenth dreizehnte.
thirtieth dreissigste.
thirty dreissig.
this dieser.
thorn Dorn, *m.*
thorough gründlich, gänzlich.
though zwar, obwohl, obgleich.
thought Gedanke, *m.*
thoughtful nachdenklich.
thoughtless rücksichtslos.
thousand tausend.
thrash (to) dreschen.
thread Faden, *m.*
threat Drohung, *f.*
threaten (to) drohen.
three drei.
threshold Schwelle, *f.*
thrift Sparsamkeit, *f.*
thrifty sparsam.
thrill Schauer, *m.;* Begeisterung, *f.*
thrill (to) schauern.
thrilling ergreifend, begeisternd.
thrive (to) gedeihen.
thriving ergreifend.
throat Kehle, *f.;* Hals, *m.*
throb (to) schlagen.
throne Tron, *m.*
throng Menge, *f.*
through durch (acc.); durchaus.
throughout durchaus.
throw (to) werfen.
thumb Daumen, *m.*
thunder Donner, *m.*
thunder (to) donnern.
Thursday Donnerstag, *m.*

thus so.
thwart (to) vereiteln.
ticket Karte, *f.;* Fahrkarte, *f.* (train).
ticket window Schalter, *m.*
tickle (to) kitzeln.
ticklish kitzlig.
tide Flut, *f.* (high); Ebbe, *f.* (low).
tidiness Ordentlichkeit, *f.*
tidy ordentlich.
tie Band, *n.;* (bond); Krawatte, *f.*
(necktie).
tie (to) binden.
tiger Tiger, *m.*
tight eng.
tile Ziegel, *m.* (roof); Kachel, *f.* (wall); Fliese, *f.*
(kitchen).
till bis.
till now bisher.
tilt (to) kippen.
timber Bauholz, *n.*
time Zeit, *f.*
from time to time von Zeit zu Zeit.
on time pünktlich.
to have a good time sich vergnügen,
sich amüsieren.
what time is it? Wie spät ist es?
timid zaghaft, furchtsam.
timidity Furchtsamkeit, *f.*
tin Zinn, *n.*
tinkle (to) klingeln.
tiny winzig.
tip Spitze, *f.* (end); Trinkgeld, *n.*
(money).
tip (to) Trinkgeld geben.
tire Reifen, *m.*
tire (to) ermüden.
tired müde.
tireless unermüdlich.
tiresome langweilig.
title Titel, *m.*
to zu (with infinitive); nach, zu (dat);
an (dat. or acc.).
toad Kröte, *f.*
toast Toast, *m.*
tobacco Tabak, *m.*
today heute.
toe Zehe, *f.*
together zusammen.
toil (to) schwer arbeiten.
toilet Toilette, *f.*
token Andenken, *n;* Münze, *f.* (coin).
tolerable erträglich.
tolerance Toleranz, *f.;* Duldung, *f.*
tolerant duldsam.
tolerate (to) dulden.
toll (to) läuten.
tomato Tomate, *f.*
tomb Grab, *n.*
tomorrow morgen.
ton Tonne, *f.*
tone Ton, *m.*
tongs Zange, *f.*
tongue Zunge, *f.*

tonight heute abend.	**transportation** Beförderung, *f.*
too auch (also); zu (excessive).	**trap** Falle, *f.*
tool Werkzeug, *n.*	**trap** (to) fangen, ertappen.
tooth Zahn, *m.*	**trash** Plunder, *m.*
toothbrush Zahnbürste, *f.*	**travel** Reise, *f.*
toothpaste Zahnpasta, *f.*	**travel** (to) reisen.
toothpick Zahnstocher, *m.*	**traveler** Reisende, *m. & f.*
toothpowder Zahnpulver, *n.*	**tray** Tablett, *n.*
top Gipfel, *m.;* Oberst, *n.*	**treacherous** treulos.
topic Gesprächsstoff, *m.;* Thema, *n.*	**treachery** Treulosigkeit, *f.*
torch Fackel, *f.*	**treason** Verrat, *m.*
torment Qual, *f.*	**treasure** Schatz, *m.*
torment (to) quälen	**treasurer** Schatzmeister, *m.*
torture Folter, *f.*	**treasury** Schatzamt, *n.*
torture (to) foltern.	**treat** Bewirtung, *f.*
toss (to) werfen.	**treat** (to) behandeln.
toss Wurf, *m.*	**treatment** Behandlung, *f.*
total Gesamtsumme, *f.;* gesamt (adj.).	**treaty** Vertrag, *m.*
totally gänzlich.	**tree** Baum, *m.*
touch (to) berühren.	**tremble** (to) zittern.
touching rührend.	**trembling** Zittern, *n.*
touchy empfindlich.	**tremendous** ungeheuer.
tough hart.	**trench** Graben, *m.;* Schützengraben, *m.* (military).
tour Reise, *f.;* Rundreise, *f.*	**trend** Neigung, *f.*
tour (to) herumreisen, bereisen.	**trial** Probe, *f.*
tourist Tourist, *m.*	**triangle** Dreieck, *n.*
tournament Turnier, *n.*	**tribe** Stamm, *m.*
toward zu, nach (dat.); gegen (acc.).	**tribunal** Tribunal, *n.*
towel Handtuch, *n.*	**tribune** Tribüne, *f.*
tower Turm, *m.*	**tribute** Abgabe, *f.*
town Stadt, *f.*	**trick** Kniff, *m.*
toy Spielzeug, *n.*	**trifle** Kleinigkeit, *f.*
trace Spur, *f.*	**trifling** kleinlich (petty); gering (minor).
trace (to) zeichnen (drawing); nachspüren.	**trim** (to) besetzen (sewing); stutzen (hair).
track Spur, *f.*	**trimming** Verzierung, *f.;* Besatz, *m.* (clothes).
trade Handel, *m.*	**trip** Fahrt, *f.*
tradition Überlieferung, *f.*	**trip** (to) stolpern.
traditional herkömmlich, überliefert.	**triple** dreifach.
traffic Verkehr, *m.*	**triumph** Triumph, *m.*
tragedy Tragödie, *f.*	**triumph** (to) siegen.
tragic tragisch.	**trivial** geringfügig.
trail Fährte, *f.*	**trolley car** Strassenbahnwagen, *m.*
train Zug, *m.*	**troop** Truppe, *f.*
train (to) erziehen.	**trot** Trab, *m.*
training Erziehung, *f.*	**trot** (to) traben.
traitor Verräter, *m.*	**trouble** Unannehmlichkeit, *f.*
trample (to) niedertreten.	**trousers** Hose, *f.*
tranquil ruhig.	**truck** Lastwagen, *m.*
tranquillity Ruhe, *f.*	**true** wahr.
transaction Verhandlung, *f.;* Transaktion, *f.*	**truly** wahrhaftig; aufrichtig.
transfer (to) übertragen.	**trump** Trumpf, *m.*
transit Durchgang, *m.*	**trump** (to) trumpfen.
transition Übergang, *m.*	**trumpet** Trompete, *f.*
transitory vergänglich.	**trunk** Koffer, *m.*
translate (to) übersetzen.	**trust** Vertrauen, *n.*
translation Übersetzung, *f.*	**trust** (to) trauen.
translator Übersetzer, *m.*	**trustworthy** zuverlässig.
transmission Übersendung, *f.*	**truth** Wahrheit, *f.*
transmit (to) übersenden.	**truthful** wahrhaft.
transparent durchsichtig.	**truthfully** aufrichtig.
transport Transport, *m.*	**truthfulness** Aufrichtigkeit, *f.*
transport (to) transportieren.	**try** (to) versuchen, probieren.

tube Rohr, n.
tumble (to) stürzen.
tumult Aufruhr, m.
tune Melodie, f.
tune (to) stimmen.
tunnel Tunnel, m.
turf Rasen, m.
turkey Truthahn, m.
turmoil Aufruhr, f.; Unruhe, f.
turn (to) drehen.
   turn back zurückkehren
   Turn left. Biegen Sie links ein.
turnip weisse Rübe, f.
twelfth zwölfte.
twelve zwölf.
twentieth zwanzigste.
twenty zwanzig.
twice zweimal.
twilight Zwielicht, n.
twin Zwilling (noun, m.); doppelt (adj.).
twist (to) drehen.
two zwei.
type Modell, n.
type (to) mit der Schreibmaschine schreiben.
typewriter Schreibmaschine, f.
tyranny Tyrannei, f.
tyrant Tyrann, m.

U

ugliness Hässlichkeit, f.
ugly hässlich.
ultimate letzt.
umbrella (Regen)schirm, m.
umpire Schiedsrichter, m.
unable to unfähig.
unanimity Einmütigkeit, f.
unanimous einstimmig.
unawares unversehens.
unbearable unerträglich.
unbelievable unglaublich.
unbutton (to) aufknöpfen.
uncertain unsicher.
uncertainty Unsicherheit, f.
unchangeable unveränderlich.
uncle Onkel, m.
uncomfortable unbequem.
uncommon ungewöhnlich.
unconscious bewusstlos.
unconsciousness Ohnmacht, f.
uncouth ungebildet.
uncover (to) aufdecken.
undecided unentschieden.
undefinable undefinierbar.
undeniable unleugbar.
under unter (dat. or acc.).
undergo (to) durchmachen; erleiden (suffer).
underground Untergrund (noun, n.);
   unterirdisch (adj.)
underline (to) unterstreichen.
underneath unten.
understand (to) verstehen.

understanding Verständnis, n.; Einverständnis, n.
undertake (to) unternehmen.
undertaker Leichenbestatter, m.
underwear Unterwäsche, f.
undesirable unerwünscht.
undignified würdelos.
undo (to) aufmachen; auflösen (untie).
undress (to) sich ausziehen.
uneasy beunruhigt.
uneasiness Beunruhigung, f.
unemployed arbeitslos.
unequal ungleich; unvergleichlich.
uneven uneben.
uneventful öde.
unexpected unerwartet.
unfair ungerecht.
unfaithful untreu.
unfavorable ungünstig.
unforgettable unvergesslich.
unfortunate unglücklich.
unfortunately unglücklicherweise.
ungrateful undankbar.
unhappily leider.
unhappy unglücklich.
unharmed unverletzt.
unhealthy ungesund.
unheard (of) unerhört.
uniform Uniform (noun, f.); gleichförmig (adj.).
uniformity Gleichförmigkeit, f.
uniformly gleichförmig.
unify (to) vereinigen.
unimportant unwichtig.
unintentional unabsichtlich.
union Vereinigung, f.; Verband, m.
universal universal.
universe Weltall, n.
university Universität, f.
unjust ungerecht.
unkind unfreundlich.
unknown unbekannt.
unlawful ungesetzlich.
unless es sei denn dass.
unlike unähnlich, anders als.
unlikely unwahrscheinlich.
unlimited unbeschränkt.
unload (to) abladen, ausladen.
unluckily unglücklicherweise.
unnecessary unnötig.
unoccupied unbesetzt; unbeschäftigt.
unpack (to) auspacken.
unpleasant unangenehm.
unpublished unveröffentlicht.
unquestionably fraglos.
unravel (to) lösen.
unreal unwirklich.
unreasonable unvernünftig.
unreliable unzuverlässig.
unrestrained ungezwungen.
unroll (to) abwickeln, entrollen.
unsafe unsicher.
unsatisfactory unbefriedigend.
unsatisfied unbefriedigt.

unscrupulous bedenkenlos, skrupellos.
unselfish selbstlos.
unsteady unbeständig.
unsuccessful erfolglos.
unsuitable unpassend.
untidy unordentlich.
untie (to) lösen; aufbinden.
until bis, an, zu (dat.).
    until now bisher.
untrue unwahr; untreu (faithless).
unusual ungewöhnlich.
unwell unwohl.
unwholesome ungesund.
unwilling widerwillig.
unwise unklug.
unworthy unwürdig.
up auf (dat. or acc.).; aufwärts; oben.
uphold (to) stützen.
upkeep Instandhaltung, f.
upon auf, über (dat. or acc.).
upper ober.
upright aufrecht.
uprising Aufstand, m.
upset beunruhigt.
upset (to) umkehren; aufregen (distress).
upside down drunter and drüber.
upstairs oben.
upward steigend, aufwärts.
urge (to) dringen, drängen.
urgent dringend.
us uns.
use Gebrauch, m.; Verwendung, f. (utility).
use (to) gebrauchen; verwenden.
used to (to be) gewöhnt sein
useful nützlich.
useless nutzlos.
usual gewöhnlich.
utensil Werkzeug, n.; Gerät, n.
utility Nützlichkeit, f.
utilize (to) nutzbar machen.
utmost äusserst.
    to the utmost aufs äusserste.
utter (to) äussern, aussprechen.
utterly durchaus.

V

vacant frei.
vacation Ferien, pl.
vaccination Impfung, f.
vaccination certificate Impfschein, m.
vaguely unbestimmt.
vain eitel.
    in vain vergebens, umsonst.
valiant tapfer.
valid gültig.
validity Gültigkeit, f.
valley Tal, n.
valuable wertvoll.
value Wert, m.
value (to) schätzen.
valued geschätzt.

valve Ventil, n.
vanilla Vanille, f.
vanish (to) verschwinden.
vanity Eitelkeit, f.
vanquish (to) besiegen.
vapor Dampf, m.
variable veränderlich.
variation Abweichung, f.; Variation, f.
varied verschieden.
variety Abwechslung, f.; Mannigfaltigkeit, f.
various verschieden.
varnish (to) lackieren.
vary (to) verschieden.
vase Vase, f.
vast ungeheuer.
vault Gewölbe, n.
veal Kalbfleisch, n.
vegetable Gemüse, n.
vehicle Fahrzeug, n.
veil Schleier, m.
veil (to) verschleiern.
vein Ader, f. (body and mineral); Laune, f. (luck).
velvet Samt, m.
venerable ehrwürdig.
venerate (to) verehren.
veneration Verehrung, f.
vengeance Rache, f.
ventilation Lüftung, f.
ventilator Ventilator, m.; Entlüftung, f.
venture (to) wagen.
verb Zeitwort, n.
verdict Urteil, n.
verge Rand, m.
    on the verge of am Rand (gen).
verification Bestätigung, f.
verify (to) bestätigen.
verse Vers, m.; Dichtung, f. (poetry).
version Version, f. (translation); Darstellung, f.
    (account).
very sehr.
vest Weste, f.
veterinarian Tierarzt, m.
vice Laster, n.
vice-president Vizepräsident, m.
vice versa umgekehrt.
vicinity Nähe, f.; Nachbarschaft, f.
victim Opfer, n.
victor Sieger, m.
victorious siegreich.
victory Sieg, m.
view Aussicht, f.; Ansicht, f. (opinion).
vigorous kräftig.
vile abscheulich.
village Dorf, n.
vine Weinstock, m.
vinegar Essig, m.
vineyard Weingarten, m.
violence Gewalttätigkeit, f.; Heftigkeit, f.
violent gewaltig, heftig.
violet Veilchen, n.
violet violett.

violin Geige, *f.*
violinist Geiger, *m.*
virtue Tugend, *f.*
virtuous tugendhaft.
visible sichtbar.
vision Sehen, *n.;* Erscheinung, *f.* (ghost).
visit Besuch, *m.*
visit (to) besuchen.
visitor Besucher, *m.*
visualize (to) sich vorstellen.
vital lebens-; vital.
vitality Lebenskraft, *f.*
vivacious lebhaft.
vivacity Lebhaftigkeit, *f.*
vivid lebendig.
vocabulary Wortschatz, *m.*
vocal stimmlich, stimmhaft.
vocation Beruf, *m.*
vogue, Mode, *f.*
voice Stimme, *f.*
void Leere (noun, *f.*); leer (empty); ungültig (invalid).
volcano Vulkan, *m.*
volume Umfang, *m.*
voluntary freiwillig.
vote (to) stimmen.
vote Stimme, *f.*
vow Gelübde, *n.*
vow (to) geloben.
vowel Vokal, *m.*
vulgar gemein, niedrig.
vulnerable verwundbar.

W

wager Wette, *f.*
wager (to) wetten.
wages Gehalt, *n.*
waist Taille, *f.*
wait (to) warten.
   waiting room Wartezimmer, *n.*
waiter Kellner, *m.;* Kellnerin, *f.*
wake (to) aufwecken.
wake up (to) erwachen.
walk Spaziergang, *m.*
walk (to) gehen.
   take a walk spazierengehen.
wall Wand, *f.*
wallet Brieftasche, *f.*
walnut Walnuss, *f.*
wander wandern.
wanderer Wanderer, *m.*
want Mangel, *m.;* Not, *f.* (poverty).
want (to) wollen.
war Krieg, *m.*
ward Saal, *m.* (hospital).
wardrobe Kleiderschrank, *m.*
ware Ware, *f.*
warehouse Warenhaus, *n.*
warm warm.
warm (to) wärmen.
warmth Wärme, *f.*

warn (to) warnen.
warning Warnung, *f.*
warrior Krieger, *m.*
wash (to) waschen.
washroom Waschraum, *m.*
washstand Waschbecken, *n.*
waste Verschwendung, *f.*
waste (to) verschwenden.
watch Uhr, *f.*
watch (to) wachen.
watchful wachsam.
water Wasser, *n.*
waterfall Wasserfall, *m.*
waterproof wasserdicht.
wave Welle, *f.*
wave (to) schwenken; winken; wellen (hair).
wax Wachs, *n.*
way Weg, *m.* (road); Weise, *f.* (manner).
we wir.
weak schwach.
weaken (to) schwächen.
weakness Schwachheit, *f.*
wealth Reichtum, *m.*
wealthy reich.
weapon Waffe, *f.*
wear (to) tragen.
weariness Müdigkeit, *f.;* Langweile, *f.*
weary müde.
weather Wetter, *n.*
weave (to) weben.
wedding Hochzeit, *f.*
Wednesday Mittwoch, *m.*
weed Unkraut, *n.*
week Woche, *f.*
weekend Wochenende, *n.*
weekly wöchentlich.
weep (to) weinen.
weigh (to) wiegen.
weight Gewicht, *n.*
welcome Empfang, *m.*
welfare Wohlfahrt, *f.*
well gut.
well Brunnen, *m.*
   oil well Ölquelle, *f.*
west west; Westen, *m.*
westwards westwärts.
wet nass, feucht.
whale Walfisch, *m.*
what was; welch(er, -e, -es) (which).
   what kind of was für ein.
whatever was auch.
wheat Weizen, *m.*
wheel Rad, *n.*
when wenn, als; wann (interrogative).
whenever so oft wie.
where wo; wohin (whereto).
whereas da, nun.
wherever überall wo.
whether ob.
which der (die, das); welch(-er, -e, -es).
   which one welch(-er, -e, -es).
while Weile (noun, *f.*) ; indem, während (conj.).

whim Laune, *f.;* Einfall, *m.*	wonderful wunderbar.
whip Peitsche, *f.*	wood Holz, *n.*
whisper (to) flüstern.	woods Wald, *m.*
whistle Pfeife, *f.*	woodwork Holzwerk, *n.*
whistle pfeifen.	wool Wolle, *f.*
white weiss.	word Wort, *n.*
who der (die, das), welch(er, -e, -es) (pron.); wer (inter. pron.).	word by word Wort für Wort.
	work Arbeit, *f.*
whoever wer auch immer.	work of art Kunstgegenstand, *m.*
whole Ganze (noun, *n.*); ganz (adj.).	work (to) arbeiten.
wholesale Grosshandel, *m.*	worker Arbeiter, *m.*
wholesome heilsam, gesund.	workshop Werkstatt, *f.*
whose dessen (deren); wessen (inter.).	world Welt, *f.*
why warum.	wordly weltlich.
wicked böse.	worried besorgt.
wide breit.	worry Sorge, *f.;* Plage, *f.*
widen (to) breiten, erweitern.	worry (to) besorgen; plagen
widow Witwe, *f.*	Don't worry Sorgen Sie sich nicht!
widower Witwer, *m.*	(Machen Sie sich keine Sorgen!)
width Weite, *f.* Breite, *f.*	worse schlechter.
wife Frau, *f.*	worship (to) anbeten.
wig Perücke, *f.*	worst schlechtest.
wild wild.	worth Wert, *m.*
wilderness Wildnis, *f.*	worthless wertlos.
will Wille, *m.;* Testament, *n.* (legal).	worthy würdig.
will(to) wollen.	wound Wunde, *f.*
willing gewillt.	wound (to) verwunden.
willingly gern.	wounded verwundet.
win (to) gewinnen.	wrap (to) einschlagen, (ein)wickeln.
wind Wind, *m.*	wrath Zorn, *m.*
wind (to) winden.	wreath Kranz, *m.*
window Fenster, *n.*	wreck Wrack, *n.* Schiffbruch, *m.*
windy windig.	wreck (to) zertrümmern, scheitern.
wine Wein, *m.*	wrestle (to) (aus)wringen.
wing Flügel, *m.*	wrestler Ringkämpfer, *m.*
wink Blinzeln, *n.;* Augenzwinkern, *n.*	wrestling Ringkampf, *m.*
wink (to) blinzeln, zwinkern.	wretched elend, erbärmlich.
winner Sieger, *m.*	wring (to) ringen.
winter Winter, *m.*	wrist Handgelenk, *n.*
wipe (to) wischen; ausrotten (wipe out).	write (to) schreiben.
wire Draht, *m.*	writer Schreiber, *m.;* Schriftsteller, *m.*
wire (to) kabeln.	writing Schreiben, *n.;* Schrift, *f.* (work).
wisdom Weisheit, *f.*	in writing in Schrift, schriftlich.
wise weise.	wrong unrecht, falsch.
wish Wunsch, *m.*	You are wrong. Sie haben Unrecht.
wish (to) wünschen.	
wit Witz, *m.;* Geist, *m.*	**X**
witch Hexe, *f.*	
with mit (dat.).	
withdraw (to) zurückziehen; abheben.	X-ray Röntgenstrahlen, *pl.*
wither (to) verwelken.	
within drinnen.	
without ohne (acc.).	**Y**
witness Zeuge, *m.*	
witness (to) bezeugen.	yacht Yacht, *f.*
witticism Witz, *m.*	yard Hof, *m.* (courtyard).
witty witzig, geistreich.	yarn Garn, *n.*
woe Weh, *n.*	yawn Gähnen, *n.*
wolf Wolf, *m.*	yawn (to) gähnen.
woman Frau, *f.*	year Jahr, *n.*
wonder Wunder, *n.*	yearly jährlich.
wonder (to) sich wundern, sich fragen.	yearn (to) sich sehnen.

yearning Sehnen, *n.;* Sehnsucht, *f.*
yeast Hefe, *f.*
yell (to) schreien.
yellow gelb.
yes ja, doch.
yesterday gestern.
yet noch (*also* besides); doch, dennoch (however).
yield (to) aufgeben (give up); erzeugen (produce).
yoke Joch, *n.*
yolk (Ei) Dotter, *n.* (of an egg).
you Sie, du (familiar sing.); ihr (familiar pl.);
Sie, dich, euch (acc.); Ihnen, dir, euch (dat.).
young jung.
young lady junge Dame, *f.;* Fräulein, *n.*
your Ihr, dein, ihr.

yours Ihr(-er, -e, -es); dein(-er, -e, -es).
yourself Sie (Ihnen) selbst; du (dich, dir) selbst;
ihr (euch)
youth Jungend, *f.*

Z

zeal Eifer, *m.*
zealous eifrig.
zebra Zebra, *n.*
zero Null, *f.*
zipper Reissverschluss, *m.*
zone Zone, *f.*
zoo Tierpark, *m.;* Zoo, *m.*
Zoology Zoologie, *f.*

GLOSSARY OF PROPER NAMES

Albert Albrecht.
Alfred Alfred.
Andrew Andreas.
Ann Anna.
Anthony Anton.
August August.
Barbara Barbara.
Bernard Bernhard.
Bertha Bertha.
Charles Carl.
Charlotte Lotte.
Edward Eduard.
Elisabeth Elisabeth, Else.
Elsie Ilse.
Emily Emilie.
Eric Erich.
Ernest Ernst.

Eugene Eugen.
Frances Franziska.
Frank Franz.
Frederick Friedrich.
Fred Fritz.
George Georg.
Gertrude Gertrud, Trudchen.
Gustave Gustav.
Helen Helene.
Henry Heinrich.
Jane Johanna.
John Johann, Hans.
Joseph Josef.
Katherine Katharina,
Käthchen, Käthe.
Lewis Ludwig.

Louise Luise.
Margaret Gretchen, Margareta.
Martha Martha.
Mary Maria.
Maurice Moritz.
Michael Michael.
Nicolas Nikolaus, Klaus.
Otto Otto.
Paul Paul.
Peter Peter.
Ralph Rudolf, Rolf.
Roger Rüdiger.
Susan Susanne.
Theodore Theodor.
Theresa Therese.
Thomas Thomas.
William Wilhelm.

GLOSSARY OF GEOGRAPHICAL NAMES

Africa Afrika, *n.*
Aix-la-Chapelle Aachen, *n.*
Alps Alpen, *pl.*
America Amerika, *n.*
   North America Nordamerika, *n.*
   Central AmericaZentralamerika,*n.*, Mittelamerika,*n.*
   South America Südamerika, *n.*
Antwerp Antwerpen, *n.*
Arabia Arabien, *n.*
Asia Asien, *n.*
Atlantic Atlantik, *m.*
Australia Australien, *n.*
Austria Österreich, *n.*
Belgium Belgien, *n.*
Berlin Berlin, *n.*
Bonn Bonn, *n.*
Brazil Brasilien, *n.*
Brussels Brüssel, *n,*
Canada Kanada, *n.*
China China, *n.*
Czechoslovakia Tschechoslovakei, *f.*
Denmark Dänemark, *n.*
Egypt Ägypten, *n.*
England England, *n.*
Europe Europa, *n.*
France Frankreich, *n.*
Frankfort Frankfurt, *n.*
Germany Deutschland, *n.*
Hamburg Hamburg, *n.*
Greece Griechenland, *n.*
Hague Haag, *m.*

Holland Holland, *n.*
Hungary Ungarn, *n.*
India Indien, *n.*
Ireland Irland, *n.*
Italy Italien, *n.*
Japan Japan, *n.*
Jugoslavia Jugoslawien, *n.*
London London, *n.*
Mexico Mexico, *n.*
Moscow Moskau, *n.*
Munich München, *n.*
Norway Norwegen, *n.*
Nüremberg Nürnberg, *n.*
Pacific Ocean Stille Ozean, *m.*
Poland Polen, *n.*
Portugal Portugal, *n.*
Prussia Preussen, *n.*
Rhine Rhein, *m.*
Rhineland Rheinland, *n.*
Russia Russland, *n.*
Saar Saar, *f.*
Saxony Sachsen, *n.*
Scotland Schottland, *n.*
Silesia Schlesien, *n.*
Spain Spanien, *n.*
Sweden Schweden,*n.*
Switzerland Schweiz, *f.*
Turkey Türkei,*f.*
United States die Vereinigten Staaten, *pl.*
Vienna Wien, *n.*